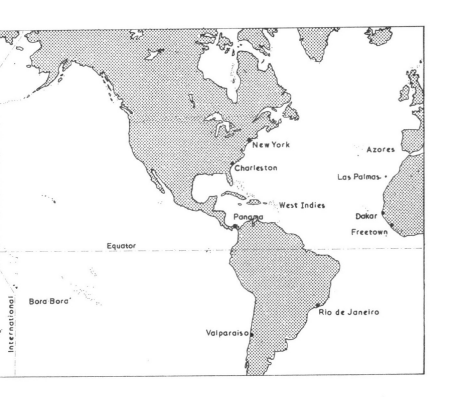

IN TIME OF WAR

IN TIME OF WAR

by

Alex. Aiken

1980

Published by
ALEX. AIKEN,
48 Merrycrest Avenue,
Giffnock, Glasgow,
Scotland

Printed by
HOLMES McDOUGALL LTD.. GLASGOW

To Jessie Russell Aiken
Died 24th July, 1979

"... the latest vessel is a typical example of the modern cargo liner of great capacity, admirable equipment and high speed ... several have attained over 19 knots on trials which have been carried out in light conditions, but which ensures that 17 knots will be maintained in service in loaded conditions. This great increase in speed compared with that common in pre-war cargo liners may prove to be of immense value in ensuring safe voyages in time of war."

Shipbuilding & Shipping Record
19th January 1939.

CONTENTS

ix

ILLUSTRATIONS (BOOK 1)

ILLUSTRATIONS (BOOK 2)

xi

MAPS AND DRAWINGS

THE END

Demolition of *m.v. Glenearn* commenced on 10th January, 1971.[298]* Whereas an American *Victory* class of ship would have required only about four weeks, the buyers estimated that it would take six to dispose of the Glen ship because of her much heavier build. The first week would be occupied simply in taking out all the papers, drapes, linen and soft furnishings; also the hard furnishings, wood panelling, parquet and lino floorings, refrigerated cargo space insulation and finally, cargo dunnage – to get rid of all the fire hazards before the acetylene burning of the ship into tiny fragments.

These fragments – weighing anything up to 5 tons – when burned off are either heaved down or hauled up, depending on their location, by a set of old derricks and masts off previously condemned vessels; loosely set up and wire-stayed alongside the berth. Power is provided by a couple of old Caterpillar tractor engines, somewhat insecurely bedded, through a fantastic system of belt drives. It would not be allowed by the British Department of Trade and Industry, but it was certainly very effective – in a Heath-Robinson sort of way – operating in Taiwan.

Alongside each berth is a plot of land about 100 yards wide; not enough to accommodate the length of an average ship. The plot is about 300 yards deep, and within this area the scrapped ship is laid out: good solid pieces of crank and propeller shafts are put into one heap, then side plating and bulkhead plating in another; deck house and superstructure plating – much thinner – go to yet another, and finally bits and pieces such as ventilators and air pipes form another separate pile. The number of piles increases. One of derrick and sampson-post columns, one of ropes and wires; galley oven equipment, blocks...

There is a common belief that when a ship is converted to

* See list of sources.

scrap the whole ends up in some crucible and eventually reappears as so much new metal, but this is far from being the case; a demolisher is in business to make a profit, and he must break up his purchase piecemeal and sell the bits as best he can. His method is to start aft, and as more and more weight is removed the propellers and shafts rise out of the water and can be taken away. By working forwards the whole ship is gradually demolished as it comes above the water, and as the work progresses the hulk is heaved astern to keep it within the length of the berth. Finally only No. 1 Double Bottom Tank is left floating; this is towed to the beach and burnt into pieces to be carried away from there.[59]

Demolition was completed on 28th February, 1971.[298]

BOOK ONE

CHAPTER 1

THE NOBLEST PROSPECT

Along its middle reaches the River Clyde today* is not very impressive. Its width is only about 120 yards, and along the water's edges lie miles of derelict works, acres of unused docks. Shipping on the river amounts to little more than a couple of stained carriers discharging ore, and a few minor naval vessels under construction. The onlooker recalls with nostalgia the forest of funnels and masts that spiked the warehouse skyline. What has become of the shipping and the shipbuilding industries? Are these the waters that so often divided to receive the world's greatest vessels? But, difficult though it may be to revive the memories of noise and excitement on this now quiet stretch of water, it requires even more effort to imagine its ancient course before it gave rise to Glasgow's commerce.[2]

At one time the river below Glasgow Bridge flowed in a channel which was both meandering and frequently shallow, but in the year 1768 the magistrates engaged the services of 1768 John Golborne, an eminent engineer of Chester, to advise them. He suggested that rubble jetties should be built out from the banks to concentrate the force of the waters into a narrow channel, which would be further deepened by ploughing and dredging.

By dint of such simple expedients there were in a few years depths of ten to twelve feet at spring tides the full thirteen miles from Glasgow to Dumbarton. Rennie, Telford and others followed; joining the ends of the jetties by parallel banks, widening and straightening the channel – and dredging, dredging, dredging. As a result of such continuing improvements, by 1827 ships of 17-foot draught could berth at Glasgow.[542]

Allan Carsewell Gow was born in Glasgow on 8th July 1823;[259] son of Leonard Gow a merchant from Arbroath,[361] 1823 and Mary Gow or Carsewell,[259] daughter of James Carsewell

*Written in 1976.

3

a builder in, and of, Glasgow.[361] Another boy – Leonard – was born on Christmas Day 1824,[349] and a daughter Mary on 3rd March 1827. When this youngest child was just six

1827 months old the father died,[622] and a few years later the younger brother at the age of seven was sent to live with an uncle, a farmer near Glamis.[552]

1840 Mary died shortly before her thirteenth birthday,[330] but Allan by his early twenties was employed by the ship-broking firm of Galbreath and Carsewell, whose premises were in Prince's Square off Buchanan Street. One of the principals, Alex. G. Carsewell, lived in Stirling's Road about 600 yards west of the Cathedral. All around this immediate area were other Carsewell business-men, and in among them at 10 Canning Place, Allan C. Gow[300] – presumably surrounded and possibly supported by his mother's family.[A] Canning Place was a short *cul de sac* of 4-storey tenements,[2] occupied in the main by merchants.

Whilst living there A. C. Gow set himself up in business as a ship and insurance agent,[300] with a little office on the west side of Union Street.[471] The 117-ton *Scotia* arrived from Limerick on the 21st February 1848 with 1,776 barrels of oats,[303] and during the next five weeks this vessel filled up with a mixed cargo ranging from cotton cloth to pig iron and coal, with a total value of close on £6,000.[304] With ships not leaving until their cargo spaces were more or less full, the date of sailing was a matter of uncertainty, while the date on which it would arrive at its destination was even more un-certain...[553] *Scotia* finally sailed for Gibraltar and Leghorn,[304] to be followed by the *Roberts* – 174 tons of Rothesay – on 5th April for Rio de Janeiro.[305] It would be August before the 96-ton *Inverness* loaded under his manage-ment,[306] but he had claims to work as a commission merchant too.[300]

Allan Carsewell Gow married Bridget Sword Nixon aged 24 of Edinburgh on 19th December 1849.[261] They set up home at 2 Chatham Place,[266] about 60 yards west of Canning Place,[2] and a daughter* was born there on 19th September

---

*Probably Anna. A son Leonard born 1st February 1852 died ten months later.[622]

1850.[331] In this year too he added to his responsibilities the post of Vice-Consul of Sicily and Naples – known as the Kingdom of the Two Sicilies – and in 1853 the agency for the Birkbeck Life Assurance Company.[300] Allan's young brother Leonard meanwhile had attended the parish schools of Kinettles and Glamis, before entering St. Andrews University in 1841.[552] There he spent three years as an Arts student before taking divinity for a further three.[295] In 1849 he was duly licensed as a probationer of the Church of Scotland; then his health broke down. Though for two years he conducted theological classes in King's College, Aberdeen,[552] he finally forced himself to give up the idea of becoming a minister.[349] At this juncture A. C. Gow and Company required assistance and so, almost by accident,[471] Leonard Gow entered the office of his elder brother.[349] From 1853 the outset he showed an aptitude for commerce and found resources equal to its demands[471] that belie any impression of a weakly younger brother.[A]

James McGregor was born on the 11th May 1826 at Tomintoul in the county of Banff;[260] a place later described as "the dirtiest, poorest village in the whole of the Highlands".[548] His father was a merchant. At the age of 29 the son was employed in Glasgow as a clerk and living at 12 Rose Street, Garnethill; on 13th December 1855 he married 1855 Henrietta Jemima Donaldson, aged 19, of the same address.[264] A daughter Jane was born 7th November 1856.[262] By the following year James McGregor was a senior employee of Allan C. Gow, and living at 193 Sauchiehall Street.[300] A son born 22nd November 1857 was named Allan Gow 1857 McGregor[263] – fifteen days before the arrival of Allan Carsewell Gow Jnr.[622] – and a few months later James was made a partner.[300]

Leonard married Jessie Macleod, and a son Leonard was born on the 14th January 1859,[622] four days after Allan C. 1859 Gow had died of typhus fever at his home at Kilcreggan. The illness had lasted 19 days; his life 35 years.[265] Leonard became head of the firm,[552] James McGregor moved from house to house: Lansdowne Crescent in 1858 to Holyrood

Crescent in 1864, then to Queen's Terrace in 1867. This last
flitting might be said to have brought him almost into line
with his superior, but for the fact that Leonard Gow had
moved from the nuptial home at 8 West Prince's Street to
Blair Cottage at "Campsie Junction".[300] This latter place was
six miles out of Glasgow on the railway line to Edinburgh,
and for a time had consisted of three cottages built as a
speculation by a Glasgow grocer. They could be neither let
nor sold, until the Edinburgh and Glasgow Railway
Company announced that anyone building a villa at a cost of
£500 or more would be entitled to free travel to and from
Glasgow for five years.[594] Blair Cottage was among the first
houses built.[X] The locality, from being not very attractive,
became extremely fashionable.[594] In due course, "Campsie
Junction" became "Lenzie", and "Blair Cottage" became
"Blair Villa".[300]

   A. C. Gow and Company went from strength to
strength.[471] The Vice-Consulship had ended,[300] it is true,
when the Sicilians overthrew the Bourbons and joined a
united Italy where Garibaldi had taken Naples in 1860,[R] but
the general leap forward of Clyde shipping commerce far
out-reached any loss in this anomalous direction.[A] A large
expansion of trade had already started when the American
Civil War encouraged the growth of cotton in India, with a
corresponding increase in Eastern trade, while the elegant
American clippers, which had forced British ships into second
place in the China tea trade, were driven from the seas by the
Confederate privateers.

   The Allan Line, with origins in the Saltcoats of 1815, had in
1854 started with steamers; the British India Steam
Navigation Company had begun in 1856 with only two
vessels. Two brothers, as a sideline, had started the "City
Line" by the purchase of a small colonial barque.[542] Now
A. C. Gow and Company took their first step into the world
of ship-owning with a share in an iron barque of 574 tons.[296]
Estrella de Chile was launched from the yard of Laurence Hill
& Co. on 1st October 1867, and was specially built for trading
with the west coast of South America. Other shareholders

1867

included her Master and a seed merchant[319] with premises in Argyle Street.[300] From Port Glasgow the new vessel was taken to the Broomielaw, arriving on the 12th.[307] There she loaded up with cotton and spirits before sailing* for Valparaiso with a crew of 18 and 2 passengers.[308]

Such a venture on the part of the firm could hardly have been more than an incidental speculation, or perhaps it whetted an appetite,[A] because early in April 1868[321] – long before the return of *Estrella de Chile*[309] – the keel of an iron ship was laid on the stocks at Dumbarton.[321] Archibald McMillan and Son built No. 146[294] in just four months;[321] launching her almost ready for the sea on the morning of 22nd June. *Glenavon* was so named by Miss Eliza Kirsop,[320] daughter of a neighbour of James McGregor.[300] The new ship had been designed with particular regard to speed,[320] ventilation of cargo and accommodation, and was intended for the East Indies trade. A few days after the launching she was towed to the Mersey before sailing for Calcutta.[321]

1868

Almost immediately, another keel was laid down, this time for a magnificent clipper ship[322] of 1,286 tons register.[296] As No. 148 duly left the ways,[294] she was named *Glenorchy* by a Miss Hutcheson[322] of Lansdowne Crescent.[300] Glenurchy or Glenorchy the original seat of the Clan Gregor;[572] Glen Avon to the west of Tomintoul[548] – one might conclude that James McGregor had a say in the choice of both names.[A]

At the end of December *Glenorchy* was towed down river from Glasgow to the Gareloch to adjust compasses before sailing for Bombay[323] with a cargo mainly of coals.[285] She headed down the North Channel into the Irish Sea.[X] There was a pilot on board, and it was still daylight when the ship struck the Kish Sandbank within eight miles of Kingstown, but it was the 1st of January 1869...

1869

Master and crew took to the boats, and their cries were heard by the captain of the mail steamer *Connaught*. Engines were reversed, blue lights burned and the ship waited 20 minutes, but as no boats appeared she was obliged to resume the journey to Holyhead. All three of *Glenorchy*'s boats

*14th November 1867.

reached safety eventually,[417] and four tugs went out and salvaged some materials, but within a few days the ship became a total wreck. However, over a period of months, divers recovered no less than 929 chairs and 12 cases of keys.[285]

In the days of unconditional insurance at owner's valuation, the loss of a heavily-insured ship could result in the repayment of the full amount of the original investment, and perhaps more.[432] So the loss of *Glenorchy* could have paid for the 661-ton barque *Glenaray* with something left over.[A] She was launched from McMillan's yard on 19th April intended for trade with the west coast of Africa.[324]

An event calculated to upset the cost factors of ship-operating took place on 17th November. The opening of the Suez Canal reduced the sailing distance of 11,600 nautical miles to Calcutta by 3,600, and to the Far East ports by almost the same amount.[R] If the Canal were a success it could be predicted that steam would entirely supersede sail in both the China and India trades;[325] no more sailing tonnage would be built, as cargo steamers with the new coal-economising engines would provide faster and cheaper transport. Shrewd business-men would be well-advised to invest in steam vessels;[426] A. C. Gow and Company ordered their first steamship.[291]

Up to 1830, there had been little or no shipbuilding in Glasgow, but it was found that beyond a certain size it was impossible to make wooden ships strong enough to hold the engines required to propel them; the development of the iron ship found Glasgow with its ironworks conveniently placed for a new industry. By the mid-sixties iron shipbuilding was virtually a monopoly of the United Kingdom, with the Clyde shipyards claiming the lion's share of the orders.[542]

The Clyde Engineering and Iron Shipbuilding Company Limited had been incorporated in April 1864, but within a few months the name had been changed to the London and Glasgow Engineering and Iron Ship Building Company Limited, with addresses in London at 1 East India Avenue and 4 Lime Street, E.C.1.[256] By the time A. C. Gow & Co.'s order came along it was firmly believed that there was no shipyard on the Clyde – or anywhere else – that could build such fine ships so quickly as on "the Limited's" slipway at Govan.[555]

Yard No. 145[296] was going to have three decks, to be 280 feet long, 33 feet across the beam and 24 feet 6 inches deep to the spar deck. The engines were nominally of under 200 horse power[380] according to Boulton and Watt's Rule, but because of the enormous increase of speeds and pressures this figure was meaningless;[285] in terms of the power expended by the steam in driving the piston the "indicated" horse power would be about 1,500.[A] These engines were designed on the compound principle and would incorporate all the latest improvements for turning the screw efficiently.[380] Both masts fully rigged for sails.[291] Gross register tonnage 1,600.[296] Handsome accommodation for First Class Passengers.[380] Messrs Gow's first steamship; built and completely equipped for a total outlay of £27,500.[291]

While she was building life went on. Spanish brigs,[332] iron **1870** barques and clipper ships arrived at Glasgow Harbour[333] and were despatched to Havana, Bangkok, Batavia, Colombo, Valparaiso and Madras.[334] On the domestic front James had taken the lease of Blairquhosh House, Strathblane;[300] a nine-roomed villa built for the Factor of Sir Archibald Edmonston, Bt.[41] James' seventh child was born there, although the family seems to have spent most of the time at their Glasgow address.[267]

On the afternoon of Saturday, 27th August 1870, the new ship took to the water.[380] *Glengyle* was named after a glen at the head of Loch Katrine, Perthshire.[547] Until the recent past it had been in the possession of one James MacGregor of Glengyle, chief of one of the principal houses of the Clan Gregor.[348]

September must have been a month of concealed eagerness and suppressed excitement for the partners.[A] To heighten the tension dense fog settled over the city on the 28th,[383] and held up most of the river traffic[381] for five days. As soon as it lifted the splendid new ship under its commander Hugh Auld[334] moved to Stobcross Quay and commenced loading general cargo. Shippers sent their goods down to the wharf,[335] and their bills of lading to the office at 87 Union Street. 1 o'clock on the 10th of October was the last moment for these and the Customs formalities,[336] and the same day *Glengyle* left for the Gareloch to adjust her compasses.[337] After speed trials[384] she sailed on the 11th from the Tail of the Bank for Liverpool.[338] Having filled up there, the new steamer left on 2nd November for Calcutta and Madras.[339]

While *Glengyle* was at sea carrying so many of the firm's hopes and so much of its capital,[A] headquarters were moved to premises at 19 Waterloo Street, Corn Exchange Place.[300] There the partners could consider the next phase of their mercantile adventure: China.[A] For years cargoes of tea had been carried in clipper ships which sailed round the Cape of Good Hope, racing each other with the first crop of the season and the merchants giving a prize of 10% on the price of the tea.[488] The first screw steamer to bring a cargo of tea direct from China had been the *Erl King* of 1865,[542] while two years later Alfred Holt's *Ajax* had reached London from Shanghai in 68 days.[378] Compared to *Sir Lancelot*'s 96 days of sailing for the same voyage,[379] this settled the argument of steam against sail in the China trade,[378] even before the Suez Canal further reduced the voyages home to between 50 and 60 days.[382] Leonard Gow was convinced that, with the opening of the Canal, steamers must be the ships of the future,[552] while James McGregor was impressed by the need for speed.[291]

1871   *Glengyle* arrived at London from Calcutta on 22nd July 1871[340] with a mixed cargo which included packets of linseed; saltpetre, india rubber, turmeric, rice, rapeseed and buffalo horn tips in bags; silk, hemp, hides, safflower and jute in bales; lacquer dye, and 85 chests of tea. The firm of John and Robert Grant were the London agents.[312] It had been a highly successful maiden voyage.[291] Steamship owners who did their own managing, and took all the financial risks, could expect a gross dividend on their investment of 25 to 30%;*

* Per voyage, presumably.

less 6% put aside annually for a depreciation fund and new boilers.[432]

Before *Glengyle* sailed on her second voyage – this time for China[341] – another steamer had been ordered from the London and Glasgow Company. This was a sister ship to the *Rydall Hall*, launched about the time of *Glengyle*'s arrival at London. The new Glen ship's turn came on 14th October, being named *Glenroy* by the daughter[385] of the principal of Messrs. Alex. Reid & Son, dyers.[300] *Glenlyon* followed a year later[386] and in 1873 *Glenfalloch*,[387] *Glenartney*[388] and *Glenearn* all went down the ways at Govan;[389] all bore place-names associated with incidents in the history of the MacGregors.[R]

1873

In the same year, London offices were opened at 1 East India Avenue,[291] and it may be supposed that James spent much of his time there, and in travelling between the two cities.[A] The "Glen" Line was becoming established.[390] *Glenaray* and *Glenavon* meanwhile had been sailing to India from various ports: the Clyde, London, Cardiff and Cork; the former vessel, however, was sold and *Glenavon* put on the run to Spain.

While *Estrella de Chile* steadily shuttled to and from South America[296] importing Peruvian guano,[319a,300] the steamers were all voyaging to China from both Glasgow and London.[296] All the tea sent from Hankow for Europe was transhipped at Shanghai, except for the new season's teas which were sent direct in the three or four deep-sea steamers which sailed up the Yang-tse River for the purpose.[544] Within five years of the opening of the Suez Canal fast steamships had completely taken over from the sailing clippers, but keen interest was still taken in the annual "race" to be first home. In 1874 *Glenartney* arrived first and made the fastest run; the time claimed from Woosung near the mouth of the River was only forty-four days, including all stoppages – a little more than a third of the time frequently taken by the sailing ships.

1874

Before this event the firm of McGregor, Gow and Company had been set up,[488] although A. C. Gow still owned all the ships;[296] nevertheless, the new firm took credit for eight

steamers,[488] of which one – *Gleneagles* – did not yet exist. She
would be the next "Glen" ship,[296] but shipbuilding costs had
reached £19 per ton,[434] while freight rates were declining.[542]
Glenartney carried the first teas from Hankow again in
1875 1875.[418]

With the departure of James McGregor to make his home
in Bermondsey[300] – thus returning his wife to within four
miles of her birthplace[266] – the "Glen" Line became centred
on London.[A] Back in Scotland Leonard Gow had also moved
house but a distance of only a mile and a half.[300] The Royal
Burgh of Kirkintilloch was as old as Lenzie was new; with
traces of inhabitants believed to be 90,000 years old it was
perhaps no wonder that the Antonine Wall* was known
familiarly as "Grahame's Dyke". Hayston House had been
built in 1865, complete with gatehouse and a road crossing the
Kelvin by a private bridge, thus avoiding road tolls on the
way to and from the busy pavements and fashionable shops of
Kirkintilloch.[156]

Busy offices in Glasgow also beckoned.[A] From small
beginnings in 1872 the State Line had grown in importance in
the Atlantic passenger trade. A reconstruction of the
Company had taken place in 1875, when the management had
been taken over by A. C. Gow and Company.[472] Sailings were
every Friday from Glasgow to New York via Larne (Belfast),
with saloon cabins advertised at 12 to 15 guineas, second-class
cabins – including all necessaries for the voyage – at 8 guineas,
steerage 5 guineas.[342] Although most of the passengers were
emigrants bound for the United States,[472] passages could be
booked through to China, India, New Zealand and Australia
via San Francisco.[347] From their own offices A. C. Gow and
Company were agents for ships owned by others; a
responsibility sometimes shared with Messrs. Thomas
Skinner & Co. of Gordon Street.[343]

Although the Suez Canal had finished off the tea
clippers,[521] it had become clear that the day of the iron sailing
ship was not yet over.[426] So the Scotia Shipping Company
Limited was incorporated in November 1877 to acquire an

* Built A.D. 140.

interest in three Glasgow ships: *Zamora, Corina* and *Saraca*. The major shareholders were Glasgow business-men; A. C. Gow & Co. were appointed general managers,[258] and the ships flew the Gow house flag.[545]

Meanwhile McGregor, Gow were not doing badly.[402] *Quang Se*, built in 1872 by the London and Glasgow Company,[300] and bought when other ship owners were having difficulty finding cargoes,[X] was by October 1876 sailing between the Far East and New York for the Glen Line[419] and would soon be renamed *Glenorchy*.[296] *Glenartney* had for the third successive year arrived first, making the passage from Woosung in 41 days 16 hours.[395] *Glenearn* was the second steamer from Hankow, while *Glenfinlas* was first from Foochow – also in 41 days. With the new *Gleneagles* expected to be ready for the season of 1877 the Glen Line seemed poised to sweep the board in the Ocean Tea Race.[392]

1876

When a rival appeared in the shape of *Loudon Castle*, built for Thomas Skinner and Company,[393] there was considerable excitement in nautical and mercantile circles,[394] and heavy bets were laid on the result of the forthcoming race. Both steamers passed Woosung at 5 p.m. on 25th May 1877. After eight days' steaming Singapore was reached with *Loudon Castle* 2 hours ahead; by the time Port Said had been left behind, the gap had widened to 20 hours, partly due to *Gleneagle*'s longer coaling spells. The *Loudon* docked at 6 a.m. on the 3rd of July and *Gleneagles* at the same time the following day.[346]

1877

Glenartney was not far behind the leaders, in spite of having been detained two days[344] in saving all but four of the passengers and crew of the French mail steamer *Meikong*,[397] wrecked on the 17th June four miles east of Cape Gardafui.[285] *Glenearn* was first home from Foochow.[344] Having reduced the passage between Woosung and Gravesend to an unprecedented 38 days 11 hours,[345] Skinner's vessel quietly faded from the ocean scene.[A]

Two years later the new *Glencoe** left Hankow on 19th May with four million pounds' weight of new season's congou

1879

---

* Launched 26.11.1878 by James McGregor's daughter Caroline.[400]

on board. Passing Woosung on the 27th,[420] she arrived at London late on 3rd July after the fastest passage on record:[421] 37 days 22 hours, including a detention of about 28 hours in the Canal.[477] The following day, several sales were made at 1s. 1½d. to 2s. 3d. per lb., making the value of her cargo about £400,000;[421] on which the freight was £10,700.[422] So, after ten years, by careful management and a willingness to meet the requirements of the times, the Company was in a most prosperous condition.[402] New season's teas carried by the Glen Line were on sale in every town in Scotland.[399]

About this time a major reshuffle of ownership took place. In 1879 the only ship actually owned by McGregor, Gow was the *Gleniffer*,[296] launched 6th November 1877 at Hull as the *Ladybird* for a London firm;[489] but by the following year all

1880   the "Glen" steamships had been transferred to McGregor, Gow, leaving only the sailing vessels – less *Glenavon*, sold early in 1880 – in the possession of the original Company.[296] One can imagine Leonard Gow's relief at having reduced his commitments to the minimum consistent with that of a majority shareholder, after so long double-harnessed in pursuit of sometimes debatable desiderata: speed at a price, cut-throat competition, expansion, progress, profits. With such goads gone, a good opportunity to build up a modest fleet flying the Gow flag along less pressing passages:[A] the Mediterranean, the Black Sea, the Atlantic. Such a new start was made with the *Waterloo*, of 1,398 tons.[490a] To perform the traditional naming ceremony,* not the child of some influential shipper present or potential,[A] but the daughter of the firm's founder; Miss Anna Gow, living quietly still at Kilcreggan.[401]

1881   The pioneer *Glengyle* was sold in 1881 to the Atlas Steamship Company to be renamed *Alvena*;[296] about the same time *Glenavon* was revived in a new steamer of that name,[402] but the most notable Glen ship of that year must be the two-funnelled *Glenogle*. *Glenogle*, in turn, cannot be separated from her rival, Thomas Skinner's *Stirling Castle*.

---

* 6th May 1879.[490]

Both ships were Clyde-built and designed for speed almost regardless of cost.[291] *Glenogle*'s engines were expected to develop at least 5,250 horse-power[492] for the sum of £90,000;[291] *Stirling Castle*'s indicated 8,237 horse-power[491] and she cost £180,000.[291] Skinner's ship was planned from the beginning as the largest that could ascend the River to Hankow, and proved on trials to be the fastest thing afloat.[493]

1882

Glenogle sailed from Glasgow on 28th March 1882[403] on her maiden voyage to Shanghai. On the return passage *Stirling Castle* was first away from Hankow and passed the lightship at the mouth of the Yang-tse at 3.45 a.m. on the 23rd of May,[424] with the Glen ship five days behind.[423] Skinner's vessel passed Gravesend at 2 a.m. on the 22nd June, having made the passage in just under 30 days*[424] at an average speed of $16\frac{1}{2}$ knots.[A] *Glenogle* did not make any sort of contest, arriving on 12th July[404] only hours ahead of *Glencoe*[405] which had left Woosung three days behind her.[423a]

Together with *Gleneagles* from Foochow the Glen Line the following day delivered four million pounds of tea to London.[425] Unfortunately, these hurried supplies from China, when added to the heavy stock still in the warehouses, had the effect of worsening the general trade depression, so that dealers were able to buy tea at cheaper rates than they had ever known; in some cases at below the cost of production.[427]

After a year of general trading[A] *Glenogle* passed Woosung on 22nd May 1883,[429] the same day as *Stirling Castle* left Hankow 600 miles up-river.[428] After a good run the Glen ship passed Gravesend on 26th June,[431] but her rival had already done so four days before.[430] *Glenogle*, designed for a service speed of 15 knots,[291] just could not match the 18 of *Stirling Castle* but the latter, designed to revolutionise the tea trade, was a failure financially on account of her huge fuel bills.[521] The amounts of coal both ships consumed were appalling; *Glenogle* was capable of burning 110 tons in a day.[288] Alfred Holt on the other hand had already reduced consumption to

1883

* If the 8-hour difference between local and Greenwich time is ignored, which it apparently invariably was.

less than 20 tons per day at an average speed of 9 knots. Nevertheless, between the fastest and the most economical, *Glenogle* was a successful ship.[291] *Stirling Castle*, after the Pyrrhic victory in the race of 1883, was sold to an Italian firm,[296] leaving the field to *Glenogle*. But although the tea races interested the public, the bulk of the trade with China was carried at reasonable speeds and normal rates which were quite good enough to please the shippers.[521]

While McGregor, Gow and Co. had assumed a leading position,[349] Allan C. Gow and Co. were not entirely trouble-free. The Scotia Shipping Company and the State Steamship Company were well-known all over the world,[471] but the latter enterprise was in difficulties. Although responsible for the carrying of tens of thousands of emigrants to the United States, the ships were not big enough to be economic, and after a few years in which the shareholders received no dividends[326] the management was taken over by a W. W. Wright in 1883[300] – but with no better results.[532]

That same year the great prosperity in the shipping industry came to an end,[542] and one of the periodic depressions set in. Back in 1879 the Glen Line, the Peninsular and Oriental, the Ocean Steamship Company, Thomas Skinner and others had entered into a combination or "Conference" to limit the numbers of vessels employed in the China tea trade in an attempt to maintain profits.[436] In 1884 the Mogul Steamship Company, whose vessels were mainly engaged in the Australian trade, decided to send ships to the Chinese ports to take advantage of the high freight rates during the tea season.[433] It was agreed that two of their ships could load cargoes, on condition that none were carried during the next two years.

In 1885 this agreement was honoured,[X] but the "ring" took the precaution of offering a 5% rebate to any shipper who dealt solely with Conference companies. The Mogul Company appealed to the Courts, claiming that the combination was illegal, and asked for an injunction restraining the defendants – who retorted that shareholders in the plaintiff Company were themselves members of the

1884

1885

"Conference" for the Australian ports, and that in order to keep up a regular and barely profitable service all the year round it was necessary to be sure of getting the only profitable freights, which were those obtaining during the tea season:[433] £3 10s. a ton for the first vessel and £3 for others.[436] The application was dismissed on 6th August 1885 with costs.[433] By the time Mogul's appeal had been heard and dismissed,*[435] a war of rates had broken out,[530] with one of the Conference vessels offering 25s. a ton, instead of sixty or seventy shillings, in anticipation of the arrival of Mogul's ships, *Pathan* and *Afghan*.[436] 1886

It is possible that this imbroglio,[A] rather than a disagreement over the economics of fast steamers, caused the rift between the two partners in the Glen Line.[55] Though shrewd, energetic and far-seeing in his business affairs, the keynote of Leonard Gow's character was his integrity and sense of honour;[349] his view could have been that every trader had a right to carry on his business as he thought fit, provided he took care not to interfere with the same right of others.[530] James McGregor may have taken[A] the more practical view that capitalists may combine and use the most forceful measures to drive out competitors.[530]

As a result of the initiative of James McGregor the Glen Line was in the front rank of the companies trading to the East. McGregor, Gow and Company had also been the originators of the first China and New York conference, in which trade Glen steamers carried first season's teas from China and Japan to New York via the Suez Canal. As trade grew the Company kept pace with it.[291] New ships followed each other down the slipways of the London and Glasgow Shipbuilding Co. at the rate of one a year;[296] in February 1887 *Glenshiel* was the sixteenth vessel launched for the Glen Line by the same builders.[529] Mild steel for ships' plates and scantlings had superseded iron;[542] sails had been abandoned and two pole masts were the standard rig for all new ships.[291] But times were hard; in the year to 30th June 1887 the "London and Glasgow" made a profit of only £1,048 11s. 1887

* 29th June 1886.[435]

11d.,[531] while the rate for freight was down to 20 shillings per ton.[542]

Apart from departing new vessels, the Clyde saw only the occasional Glen ship,[A] like *Glenogle* which sailed on 3rd December 1890 for Hong Kong and Shanghai with a cargo consisting mainly of scrap iron.[311] Two years before this, the old *Estrella de Chile* had been wrecked* off Cumberland,[285] and the sailing ships of the Scotia Shipping Company had gone; followed by the Company.[258] The State Line also disappeared about this time.[296]

On at least one occasion A. C. Gow had operated as joint agents with the firm of D. H. Dixon & Harrison, 16 Bothwell Street.[311] Following the death of Dixon, on 1st November 1895,[554] the three steamers of the Gow fleet joined the six belonging to the other firm under the designation Gow, Harrison & Company.[296] Leonard Gow, Junior, who had entered his father's firm in 1889[300] became a partner in the joint company,[554] and Leonard Gow, Senior, retired.[552] The older man had returned to the West End of Glasgow in 1884.[300] He retained his senior partnership of the London firm, although taking little part in the active management of it.[349]

Ever since the first cultivation of tea in Assam about 1840, and in Ceylon in 1876,[551] the cheaper Indian tea, although not at first of such good quality as the Chinese, had taken more and more of the market;[438] by 1890 the extinction of the Chinese tea trade was seen as only a matter of time.[437] Ocean tea races had become things of the past, and the need for expensive steamers was over. Owners of fast tonnage were faced with the problem of replacing such ships by vessels designed for new conditions.[477]

James McGregor had been diabetic for several years and had suffered from a malignant disease of the liver for a year before he died at his Hampstead home on 23rd January 1896 aged 69.[268] His Will, drawn up and signed five days beforehand, left one thousand pounds to his wife,† £9,000 in

1895

1896

---

* 24th November 1888.
† Not his first wife.[268]

trust for his daughter Jane, and about the same amount to each of his three surviving sons, Douglas, Allan and Bertram. Most of this money, however, was tied up either in the Glen Line[269] or the London and Glasgow Ship Building Company.[271] Some of the deceased's relatives were given small allowances by Leonard Gow, Senior, so things were not too happy.[55]

And in the fullness of time a long honourable career, as distinguished in commerce as in philanthropy,[406] sailed gracefully towards its home port loaded down[A] with directorships, chairmanships, governorships and board memberships ranging from the Cassel Gold Extracting Company Limited to the Scottish Imperial Insurance Company Limited, and from the Western Infirmary to the Canal Boatmen's Friendly Society.[552] On 25th November 1910, the lofty spirit of Leonard Gow,[349] honorary Doctor of Laws St. Andrews University,[295] Justice of the Peace in the County of Dunbarton and the County of the City of Glasgow,[552] elder of Park Parish Church,[350] weighed anchor; leaving a widow, four sons and three daughters,[349] a library of six thousand volumes,[552] and an estate valued at £144,103 10s. 8d.[352] The funeral of his earth-bound remains took place at the Necropolis and among the large number of mourners were representatives of the various public bodies and institutions he had supported; including some from the firm of McGregor, Gow and Company (Glen Line).[351]

1910

CHAPTER 2

THE ROAD TO DUNDEE

Since 1895 the Glen Line had been making fortnightly sailings from London to the Far East.[291] Allan Gow McGregor – who seems to have taken over the day-to-day running of the firm after the death of his father[A] – disposed of several of the older steamers and replaced them with vessels of much larger cargo capacity.[291] *Glenroy*, launched 6th December 1900, was the twentieth ship built for the Glen Line by the London and Glasgow Company.[533] But times change and inherited loyalties attenuate.[A] Orders for steel ships were being placed at five guineas a ton, the lowest in the history of iron and steel tonnage,[535] and money counts; by the time the last of these new ships came along in 1905 other shipbuilders had been made responsible for their construction.[534]

On 12th May 1910 the Glen Line (McGregor, Gow & Co.) Ltd. was registered, with a nominal capital of £225,000; subscribers included Allan and Bertram McGregor, and Leonard Gow, Junior.[271] Early the following year a controlling interest was purchased by Elder, Dempster and Co., Ltd., and what had been a two-family concern became a small fish in an ever-increasing sea of big business.[291] Elder, Dempster were themselves merged with the Royal Mail Steam Packet Company to form what was, by the end of 1911, the largest shipping combination in the world.[536]

The management of the Glen Line was largely in the hands of its brokers McGregor, Gow and Co., Ltd., which firm had been bought, along with the goodwill and the exclusive right to the use of the name "Glen Line", by Elder Dempster's.[271] As yet another business deal the R.M.S.P. Company in 1911 acquired all the shares in the Shire Line, a Company whose ships all bore the names of Welsh shires. Because of the similarity in trades and the common directorship, the Glen and Shire Lines thereafter operated a joint service.

During the 1914–18 War the Glen Line lost six ships by

6.12.00

12.5.10

enemy action[291] – a bald statement covering much individual pain, disaster and bereavement.[A] Allan McGregor died,[291] being succeeded as General Manager by his son Cameron D. McGregor.[504] This period coincided with an interest in the marine diesel engine, with *Glengyle* the first of the Company's motor vessels to sail to the Far East.[291] *Glenapp* of 10,000 tons dead weight and 6,600 horse-power was, in September 1918, the largest and most powerful motor-ship yet built.[537]

8.1.16

In 1920 the Shire and Glen Lines were merged; the Shire boats put under the Glen Line flag,[291] and the name changed to Glen Line Limited.[271] *Glenogle* was the first of five large twin-screw motor-ships which by 1924 had brought the fleet up to a total of 16 vessels. Of these 11 were motor-ships built at Govan by Harland and Wolff, Ltd.,[291] incorporators of the London and Glasgow Company; the wheel of loyalty, or self-interest, had turned full circle.[A] The very high cost of these ships, and a devastating slump in trade which had begun in 1921, created a severe financial strain on the Company.[291] They were not the only one in difficulties.

The chairman of the Royal Mail Steam Packet Company had an arrangement whereby he received a basic amount annually, plus a commission of $\frac{1}{2}\%$ of the gross takings, provided a dividend of 5% were paid on the Ordinary Shares of the Company; the difference to the chairman being that between £3,000 and roughly £30,000.[353] In seven of the eight years 1920–27 this minimum dividend was paid, or exceeded,[354] but at a cost of over five million pounds produced from reserves earned during the War, refund of Excess Profits Duty, a decision not to provide for depreciation,[355] and the sale of one wholly-owned subsidiary Company to another wholly-owned subsidiary Company at a paper profit of £300,000.[354]

In June 1928 a two-million pound issue of Debenture Stock was made to cover the repayment of loans; this was over-subscribed on the strength of the dividends paid during the preceding ten years.[356] The *denouement* came in 1930 when the Royal Mail Company had to apply to the Government for a loan guarantee to be continued; whereupon an independent investigation was made to justify the use of taxpayers' money.[357] As a result, Lord Kylsant was sentenced to 12-months' imprisonment for issuing a false prospectus.[358]

Ordinary shareholders' capital was totally lost in the associated collapse, but a Royal Mail Realisation Company was formed to liquidate the remaining assets of the Royal Mail empire for the benefit of the Debenture stockholders.[360] The Glen Line, although its shares were held by the R.M.S.P. group of companies, had led a separate existence,[504] and under the Scheme of Arrangement announced by the liquidators the *status quo* would be maintained until 31st December 1934.[359] Late in March 1935 it was rumoured that Alfred Holt and Company were negotiating for the purchase of the Glen Line.[503]

Boardroom discussion of the subject could conveniently have concentrated on the benefits of the likely extension of trade,[95] with little time being spent on the possibilities of managing the Glen Line more efficiently since the existing organisation was excellent.[504] A regular service was maintained from London, Middlesborough and of course the Continental ports,[503] and the Glen Line had an arrangement[19] – an echo of the China conference[A] – with the Peninsular and Oriental Steam Navigation Company whereby the P. & O. did not trade with the east coast of England, whilst the Glen Line did not trade with the west. Buying into the latter firm would enable Alfred Holt's to trade outside their existing limits by arranging a charter to the Glen Line whenever necessary at a notional rate.[19] The two general managers could be re-appointed managing directors.[504] Another minor matter was the retention of the red funnels and the distinctive house flags of the Glen Line[439] to please the shippers, who could not conceive of any changes in outward appearances or established routine.[95] Negotiations were completed in June, and an announcement made that a controlling interest had been acquired by the Ocean Steam Ship Company Limited.[439] A new career for the Glen Line was about to begin.[504]

Alfred Holt had started his career as an engineer, but in

30.7.31

4.3.32

1864 he and his brother had founded an enterprise which thereafter followed the guiding light of engineering efficiency. Holt's ships were in a class of their own, and since 1874 had carried their own insurance. For an obvious reason the Ocean Steam Ship Company and its associated companies were known universally as, "The Blue Funnel Line". Their managing owners were Alfred Holt and Company.[291] Sir Richard Durling Holt, Bt., chairman of both the Ocean Steam Ship Company and a transmuted Elder Dempster Lines, became chairman of the Glen Line, and his fellow directors joined the Board.[504] Head office would remain in London but would be concerned only with the booking of passages and the handling of cargoes. Liverpool would be responsible for the design and maintenance of ships; also routes and crewing. Glen Line uniform would continue to be worn by officers, but the individuals would gradually disappear through retirement and death.[64]

To the sea-going employees the change-over would mean more paid leave, full pay when standing by ships laid up during trade depressions, and better treatment generally; in return all Alfred Holt's expected was that each man did his job.[31]

Next item on the agenda: reorganisation of the Glen Fleet. The two Shire boats were overdue for the scrapheap.[A] Of the Glen ships one could be sold to the Greeks,[506] another to her builders under an existing agreement,[505] and the pioneer motorship *Glenamoy*[508] should, albeit with some regret, be sold for £12,000[507] – to take advantage of the Scrap and Build Act which offered financial inducement to shipowners to order one new vessel and scrap two of equivalent tonnage.[495]

Which brings us, gentlemen, to the question of replacements.[A] Four Blue Funnel ships of mature years could be transferred to the Glen Line,[291] but what was needed fundamentally was a complete class of new ships: fast and powerful enough to anticipate further expansion by rivals,[507] attract the best cargoes and form an advertisement for the owners.[70] Running economy had increased so much in the fifteen years since 1920 that it might even pay to abandon eventually *Glenogle* of that year and her four sister-ships, even although they were capable of some years' service.[494] It is agreed, then, that our naval architect designs a new ship:[64] 18 knots, 10,000 tons deadweight, and we shall probably need eight of them.[507] In the meantime, no comment to the Press.[503]

Harry Flett had become Holt's Chief Naval Architect in 1924 at the age of 34; since then he had seen to the design and construction of twenty-four ships for the Blue Funnel Line.[476] It was now his responsibility to rough out a design to suit the given conditions.[95]

In the first analysis a ship is a steel box girder,[595] but a girder whose centres of gravity and buoyancy are important factors. This box girder has to be moved through the water, so the hull shape and the power source are important. Lastly, it has to be capable of carrying and handling goods. In his approach to this problem, the naval architect is powerfully influenced by his previous experience in which much the same requirements have been examined and a solution found. He is constrained too by the rules of the Classification Society under which he chooses to work – in this case The British Corporation Rules and Regulations. Thus a new ship emerges which improves – marginally – on previous designs, corrects past mistakes, and contains, perhaps, a little of the personality of its creator.

For the propulsion the marine engineer must be approached. Given the approximate size and speed of the proposed vessel, he can estimate the probable horse-power and engine room space required.[95] The main quality of a marine engine is reliability, and one of the ways to ensure reliability – and achieve high power – is to adopt a twin-screw arrangement. By 1935 the oil engine was as reliable as the steam-engine and twice as efficient;[502] Alfred Holt and Company had been almost as early as the Glen Line in their adoption of the Diesel engine for cargo liners.[291] Generally the Blue Funnel Line had concentrated on Burmeister and Wain motors constructed in Copenhagen.[70]

Dr. Diesel had made an agreement in January 1898 whereby the Danish firm was licensed to construct Diesel engines,[501] but it was fourteen years before the builders produced a practicable engine large enough for a sea-going ship.[596] Development in the Blue Funnel Line progressed from the 4-stroke single-acting engine in *Tantalus* of 1923 through the *Agamemnon* and *Menestheus* class of 1928–29 – which were supercharged on the insistence of the owners[538] – to the emergence of a double-acting two-stroke engine for *Stentor* in 1931.[108] This latest arrangement, with airless injection, was by 1935 the standard on all fast single-screw motor liners and to an increasing degree was being introduced on twin-screw ships.[513] For the latest enquiry from Holt's calling for even greater power from less space, the design selected was the "Stentor" type and size, but for the twin-screw installation some modifications would be necessary.[538] The engine builders, having decided on a suitable development of their current design, reply to the enquiry from Holt's. The latter's directors, armed with reports from naval architect and marine superintendent, preliminary drawings and estimated costs, then satisfy themselves on the financial viability of the venture, decide to build the ships and give them a class name. Now the naval architects can revise calculations, check capacity sums and complete the general arrangement drawing which gives different views and a midships section of the proposed vessel.[95] Into the 507 feet 8 inches between raked stem and cruiser stern there had to go a hull shaped to cleave the water with minimum resistance, inside this hull had to be found space for six holds and 'tween decks totalling 653,000 cubic feet – including about 1,180 tons of insulated meat and fruit – tanks for 400 tons of fresh water, 1,000 tons of fuel, 2,200 tons of water ballast. And accommodation: better than average for officers and crew, luxurious for twelve passengers.[497] All the major sections of the hull would require to be sub-divided into watertight compartments, with the biggest of these forming the engine room. There the marine superintendent held drawing-board sway.[595]

Not only has the engine room to house the main engines, it has to produce power for the electric life of the whole

organism that is the ocean-going ship.[597] Power for the
windlass to hoist the 5-ton anchors,[297] power for winches to
handle derricks and mooring lines, power to operate fuel,
water and air pumps, power to light the entire ship, power to
cook the food and refrigerate perishable cargo; hence the four
8-cylinder 2-stroke diesel auxiliary engines each driving a
350 kilowatt generator,[538] and for emergencies one little
generator of 40 kilowatts.[297] This machinery had to be
located within a few feet of what were likely to be the most
powerful marine diesel engines in the world;[70] transmitting
torque to twin shafts nearly 18 inches in diameter, their
intestinal turnings manifested in manganese bronze
propellers measuring 17 feet across the tips of the blades.[297]

20.10.36   On 20th October 1936 the Board of Directors decided to
increase the capital of the Company by the creation of
2,271,250 Ordinary Shares of £1 each[271] – enough to pay for
the first five ships of the new class.[411] A few weeks later the
managers invited tenders for these five,[500] and in Scotland
alone estimating departments of four different firms squared
up to the task of yet another pricing job.[510] Shipbuilders were
asked to tender on the basis of (a) Holt's General
Specification for Materials and Workmanship, (b) a
specification particularly applicable to the new class of ship,
(c) the drawings.[95] Information regarding nominated
suppliers of engines and other equipment would also be
included. Holt's standard requirements were well known:
plates thicker than Lloyd's A.1, and so on.

A design, based on these documents, is roughed out for
weights of steel, stability and dead weight.[49] Enquiries are
sent out for pricing various items and a first study made of the
availability of berths capable of taking the size of vessel to be
built.[517] All the work rising to a climax[49] in the last-minute
rush before handing in completed drawings and signed
tenders bearing the price and the all-important delivery
date.[539] Then the aftermath, with pressure being brought to
bear on an otherwise favoured contractor to adjust the price
downwards in order to get the job;[95] hence the confident
predictions that two Scottish firms would be successful.[511]

Otherwise no prior knowledge is vouchsafed to the shipbuilder, though enquiries from nominated sub-contractors may act as straws in the wind.[49]

Eventually, in December 1936, it was announced that two of the new ships would be built at Hong Kong, one at Amsterdam, one by Scott's of Greenock and one by the Caledon Shipbuilding and Engineering Co., Ltd., of Dundee.[512] Alfred Holt owned shares in the Caledon Company; a relationship exploited by the former, with the extraction of all sorts of services and concessions on the strength of past acquaintanceship, present contracts and future prospects.[95] The tender price for the hull, including the electrics, of the seventeenth vessel to be built for Alfred Holt[509] and Company was £263,000 with the installation by Caledon of the engines built at Copenhagen bringing the figure up to £350,000.[49] For this one ship complete with engines the bill to Alfred Holt and Company would total £440,000.[23]

At the end of the year the Caledon Company had seven orders in hand;[513] when the steam coaster *Aboyne* took to the water on 28th December she was the twelfth vessel launched from their yard during 1936.[313] The new contract was given the ship number 368.[49] With the documents signed, the first task would be for the drawing office to produce the general design plan of the vessel and the plans required for the British Corporation. At the same time, all the design calculations must be checked. Next the plans required by the engine builders, and the drawings of the stern casting, to avoid crucial delays later. High on the list of priority drawings are those giving the principal construction arrangement; from the keel and double bottom to the main details of accommodation – all inter-related drawings which must proceed simultaneously.[539] When the essential parts of these 10-foot long documents[619] have been completed on serried ranks of drawing boards they form a comprehensive layout of the whole ship, from which to order the bulk of the material.[539]

All this takes time. Time is required too for the preparation

28.12.36

of specifications, and the consideration of sub-contractors' quotations before the wave of orders goes out: for steel from Dundee,[49] a donkey boiler from Dumfriesshire,[297] propellers from Birkenhead,[95] propeller bracket and stern frame from Skoda, Czechoslovakia, rivets from Dusseldorf in Germany.[59] While these materials are being manufactured the more detailed work on the drawings can proceed. At the same time the mould loft is busy, since templates are required in the shipyard at the same time as the plans.

Once the steel deliveries commence the Machine Shop starts punching, shearing, counter-sinking, planing, bending, rolling, joggling and flanging;[539] in the platers' shed the bending rolls curve plates cold, while furnaced plates are bumped into shape by hydraulic hammers[541] – all this in the endeavour to anticipate the lag between the production of finished materials and the rate of erection on the building berth in the early stages of construction.[539]

As the preliminary work gets into its stride, life in the Stannergate Yard goes on. First launch of the year 1937 is the cargo steamer *Bungaree* for the Adelaide Steamship Co., Ltd., on 9th February.[327] After the debris of launching is cleared away preparation of the berth for the construction of the next vessel can commence,[49] with the keel blocks of concrete and the 12″ × 12″ timbers carefully re-set to new lines and levels.[2] Six weeks after the launching of *Bungaree* Alfred Holt and Company place an order for two more ships; repeats of No. 368.[514]

14.4.37   14th April 1937.[49] The keel of the new ship is laid in Berth No. 3,[138] and the erection of No. 368 begins. Construction of the keel and centre girder is a straightforward business, and while the riveters make good progress on the bottom shell plates, immediately behind them appear the tank girders and tank top plates: the spearhead of a shaft of prepared materials stretching back to the sheds; a veritable river of steel wending its way irresistibly to the sea[539] – until someone at the steelworks turns off the tap.[A]

It was a common complaint of shipbuilders that their attempts at organised production were repeatedly frustrated by the confusion of deliveries from the steelworks.[539] The shortage of steel was chronic, and supplies were only obtained piecemeal and in hand-to-mouth quantities.[314] Adding injury to insult the price of steel delivered after 31st May 1937 rose by 37/6d. a ton, even although ordered before that date. The rise had been anticipated, but only to the extent of 10/- to 20/- per ton.[253] Difficulties are tests of man and management.[A] Construction of the hull was in the hands of Mr. Parker; Mr. Wilson was ship manager with Mr. Dempster and David Taylor assistant managers.[103]

So, to the clamour of the pneumatic hammers the skeleton grows, with frames springing up as fast as the erecting crew can place them;[539] the shipwrights constantly checking that the hull shape is fair, and evenly constructed about the keel; now and again they shore up the ship's bottom if the supports sag under the mounting weight of steel.[541] The surveyor from the British Corporation occasionally helped with problems and ever insisted on the work being done correctly – a discipline which does no harm to workers of high morale and ability.[49]

Now the decks are being plated and the strakes of shell plating grow from end to end, the bulkheads and beams, the deck girders and pillars are all in position and the fabric of the structure securely bound together and faired; the remainder of the material is moving smoothly into place by well-tried methods. The craft as yet lacks both stern frame and bow framing, but the heavy casting that is the former is about to be manoeuvred down the berth, and the material for the latter is on its way.[539] Here we may leave the riveters, falling back[541] on a regular 70,000 rivets weekly, towards the as yet distant total of half-a-million.[539]

On the engineering side Mr. Stewart was Manager, assisted by Mr. McMillan. Mr. Stevenson was Head Foreman with Arthur Murrison chargeman engineer from the time the floors were laid, with responsibility for marking off the engine seats. No welding was permitted on the heavy plates on which the engine bedplates would stand, and an arrangement of cast steel brackets athwartships to stiffen the bedplates had to be riveted down and caulked for watertightness first.[103]

With the after end riveted up and the engineers ready to bore out the shaft brackets, the shipwrights "drop the stern" by slackening shores and keel blocks, to transfer some of the dead loads to the stern structure until no further movement is obtained.[541] While the other workmen are eating their "pieces" and their rattling hammers are temporarily stilled, piano wires are set up and tensioned between the centre of each "A" bracket and the forward end of each engine-seat at the exact height, and on the line of the crankshafts. Proof lines are marked from the wires on the bulkheads and frames to fix the positions of bearings and glands that will accept the shafting.

From this "marking out" the boss and bulkheads were "bored out". Whilst the boring out was in progress a continuous telescopic check was kept, to ensure that the pin-point of light on the engine-seat did not move as seen in the cross wires. No adjustments to the setting of the boring bar were necessary before the final boring cuts. Let no one think that Glen ships were thrown together in haste.[103]

The 17′0″ diameter propellers had bolted-on blades which could be set to various pitches between limits of 15′6″ and 18′9″[23] by fitting (laboriously) "cod pieces" into elongated holes in each blade and making secure. A pitch of approximately 17′ was set while the vessel was on the ways.[103]

1937 becomes 1938. Suddenly, to the casual observer, the bare steel bulk is transformed by gleaming paintwork. To the shipbuilding worker the first real thrill of pride.[539] Here is the last word in perfection: a Holt ship built on the Tay – confirmation that Caledon hulls and designs were world-renowned as the best. That fine Holt ships could leave other rivers was just not possible.[103] "Same again, Jimmy!"[A]

Thoughts turn to launching, and it transpires that for weeks shipwrights have been working unobtrusively,[539] strengthening the hull inside and preparing launching ways outside;[481] now the gradual transference of some two thousand tons weight from the blocks and shores to the ways, as evinced by the tallow's being squeezed out from between the intended sliding surfaces[95] – and a certain feeling of liveliness felt when treading the decks.[517] A ship keen to be off.[49]

Study of the problems of launching goes back to the tendering stage,[517] when a suitable berth had to be decided, and a date chosen from the few days in each lunar month producing sufficient depth of water at the end of the ways.[539] Later came more decisions: the spacing, slope and camber of the launching ways, the taut calculations of pressure and load on the fore poppet, the assessments of the points of maximum tipping and stern lift; all responsibilities pressing on the brow of the contractor's naval architect.[481] The launch was fixed for 3.45 p.m. British Summer Time on Wednesday, 29th June 1938;[328] that is 47 minutes before high tide,[143] giving 4″ less water but a margin for unforeseen delays before the rapid drop of the water's level after high tide.[49] High winds in the days before the launch justified summoning the more powerful tug *Grangeburn* to help the local *Gauntlet* and *Mentor* get No. 368 under control after her release upon the waters.[329]

The day dawns, work starts. Male guests from London and Liverpool are shown round the yard, then repair to lunch.[163] Imperceptible movement of minutes meter the afternoon. Yard employees assemble; office girls drift down to watch. Naval architects with stop watches choose a promontoried point of vantage. The few men with physical work to do operate in a controlled and confident manner, removing the side bilge blocks to the ribald remarks of the idle onlookers. Pins are knocked out, plates and dogshores pushed over; paint quickly applied to the patches of exposed steel.

Almost unnoticed by the crowd on the ground,[A] the platform party have arrived and await the guests of honour, C. E. Wurtzburg,[163] a Holt's man since 1913 and the new Managing Director of the Glen Line,[485] and his wife who, fresh from her morning drive to Glamis, is to perform the launching ceremony. They mount the stairs and Mrs. Wurtzburg is introduced to the designer, the bowler-hatted builders of the ship soon to be launched, the owners of

29.6.38

other ships being built, my Lords, ladies and gentlemen. Presentation of a bouquet of red carnations, white carnations and blue cornflowers. Mr. Henry Main of the cherubic countenance, and Managing Director of Caledon, takes her in hand and explains the procedure.

Quite simple really. Miss Paterson, my secretary, will hold your bouquet. The bottle of champagne within its striped red, white and blue cover is proffered by a disembodied arm. The white brassard round the bottle reads "Success to Glenearn". While Lawrence Holt behind explains the finer points to your husband, you take careful aim at the towering bow, the steadying hand of Mr. Main on your elbow and his last word of advice in your ear.[163] Swing up, down, away, smash. Sensation! The shattered bottle swings back into your catching hand,[315] spraying champagne around. Miss Paterson instinctively turns her head away, then reaches out in an attempt to stop the drips falling on your coat.

Now Mr. Main hands you the polished wooden mallet with the ship's name and the date inscribed on a small silver disc, and you quickly move over to where the cutting blade rests against the cords. You have been told not to worry if you didn't cut at the first hit, but "they" did not know you were used to hitting tennis and hockey balls pretty accurately, and one steady hit was enough...[163]

The cords cut, the end of the steel wire rope is released. The relief of tension is transmitted through many changes of direction to down below the hull, where the last blocks have mysteriously disappeared. The triggers drop. For an eternity that is a fraction of a second nothing happens.[2] Out on the jetty one's fear changes on the instant from the ship's launching herself prematurely to not launching herself at all.[49] The groundlings' eyes are riveted to the surfaces in contact. No movement, slight movement? Silent movement, swift movement. Bell ringing. Cheers of relief.[2]

Up on the platform Mrs. Wurtzburg was amazed how quickly *Glenearn* moved and so she rapidly pronounced, "God bless this ship and all who sail in her", as the vessel gathered momentum. There was much cheering from below.[163] From that level the largest vessel built on the Tay since 1923 had towered above everything else in the yard,[315] except perhaps the understandable pride of her builders.[103] Even now, a serious tradesman leans out with a hand in the grease to sight down the launching way to check that all goes well.*

Further away, an individual largely responsible for the safety of the vessel, but temporarily powerless, can only watch, hope and pray[49] as several thousand tons of steel are transferred from land to water at twenty miles per hour, giving him successive causes for anxiety: will the forefoot pivot, will she break her back, will the poppet fail or the forefoot ground?[481] Meanwhile the object of these various concerns is sliding smoothly into her element, producing no greater signs of distress than the wisps of greasy smoke left rising from the launching ways.[95] On deck near the bows a man ups a Dundee bonnet* as with beautiful ease and grace *Glenearn* reaches into the water, then, as a nice acknowledgment to her constructors, she makes a little curtsey, a dipping of her bows.[163]

Now there is nothing to stop her but the sheer resistance of the waters, and even as the tugs nose through the flotsam to take charge, even as the stop-watchers bend over their notebooks, and the launching squad start knocking out wedges and dropping shores, as their mates dander away back to their jobs[2] and the guests retire to tea, presentation and speeches,[315] the object of all their passing interests is a free entity. Afloat. Alive.

* Frontispiece.

CHAPTER 3

WINSTON IS BACK

After the launching *Glenearn* was taken up-river to the 130-ton crane capable of lifting her engines. B. and W.'s machinery had been shipped across from Copenhagen in a coaster, unloaded at the Caledon jetty, and was ready for installation.[72] During the building of the main engines – in which the exhaust pistons would be operated by eccentrics instead of a lay shaft[108] – it was thought that there might be trouble with the bottom exhaust liners due to the less flexible motion. When the test on the second engine had confirmed these suspicions, the builders were asked to design a new bottom exhaust liner of cast molybdenum steel. With a cast iron insert which could be replaced after normal wear a very much cheaper arrangement resulted.

The piston rods called for the greatest possible care in their manufacture; each rod was a separate casting forged from steel of 28–32 tons tensile strength, with threads cut with the finest precision. A special spanner was used to tighten the nuts to a predetermined strain in the rod. A further improvement was the tightening of the stay bolts by hydraulic jacks instead of the laborious hammer and spanner method.[538] Alarm mechanisms made by Monitor Patent Safety Devices Ltd. were to be fitted for the protection of the propelling machinery.

While lowering an engine bedplate weighing about 70 tons into the forward hold the load dropped about two feet, due perhaps to slippage of the slings. There was some slight damage; the buckling of a flange. William Kerr the Chief Engineer telephoned Mr. Freeman in Liverpool. He came up and said that as it was a new ship the defect should be put right. Burmeister and Wain flew a man over who measured up the damaged piece; in due course a replacement arrived which fitted perfectly.[72]

Installation of both the main and auxiliary engines was

supervised by their builder's erector, Mr. Karlsen.[108] He was everyone's friend and did everything he could to interest everybody in what was going on, and to explain all the operations to anyone who asked about them. But since 1930 all machinery had been built by "outside" firms, with Caledon engineers responsible only for the fitting and installation; as a result they did not have the same pride in building even Holt vessels as the ship construction men. However, this attitude of the fitters did not affect their workmanship. Very few of them were trained in marine practice, having worked in local factories and engine shops on weaving and spinning machines. Though well-enough trained in handling tools accurately, many of them accepted that they were too late or too old to learn about the building of large engines and just got on with the work as instructed.[103]

Under the crane Glenearn's masts, derricks and boats' derricks were erected and all rigging fitted.[541] Then just down stream to the fitting-out basin for finishing.[49] The men employed in the finishing trades had not been getting much to do until after Glenearn's launching.[328] Although only a dozen passengers were to be carried the cabin space and furniture had been carefully planned. All the panelling was in Australian maple cut into rectangles separated by a green line about 1″ wide;[411] one could be excused for thinking one was back on Merseyside in a public house owned by Bent's Breweries.[23] Three-mirrored dressing tables, green wash basins. Hot and cold running water were supplied not only to the passengers but to the quarters of officers and crew.

Green, too, were the chairs in the dining room next the galley – the galley with its frigidaire systems, its toaster capable of taking forty pieces of bread at a time, and its "iron cow" for reconstituting milk from powder. Furnishing of the lounge was completed with a baby grand piano and a combined radio/gramophone.[411] On the walls photographs of Glenearn's geographical namesake near Bridge of Earn, Perthshire.[547]

Everything was planned to be ready some time before the trial trip, to allow for testing of all piping systems, derricks

and winches; also a quay trial of the propelling machinery.[539]
During the mooring tests difficulties arose with the pistons of
the auxiliary diesel engines[108] – engines on which the
economy and safe working of the ship would depend[597] –
engines for which one spare crankshaft had been provided in
case anything should befall the suppliers...[70] Thirty-two cast
iron pistons were returned in great haste to Copenhagen for
replacements having a screwed-on top of chromium steel.[108]

After the machines, the men. From Captain P. L. Saunders
– thirty-five years' service with the Glen Line, ten as Captain
of *Glenshiel*[411] – to Lascar greasers and Chinese stewards;
joining the Chief Engineer and Sydney Cowan the Chief
Steward, both of whom had been at Dundee since before the
launching.[31] Three men from Burmeister and Wain came
over;[108] together with A. G. Arnold, Alfred Holt's Resident
Superintendent Engineer at Copenhagen since 1923.[5]

6.12.38   Sea trials took place on 6th December 1938.[108] *Glenearn*
was put through her paces on the measured mile off the
Northumbrian coast north of Whitley Bay.[5] Mr. Knud
Hansen, B. & W.'s test engineer who had already tested the
engines in their erecting shop at Copenhagen, was in charge of
the technical tests on the main and auxiliary engines.[108] The
trials passed off successfully,[72] with the main engines working
softly and smoothly just like steam engines,[108] the ship having
no trouble attaining full power,[72] and reaching $19\frac{1}{2}$ knots
against the 18 of the Specification.[103] *Glenearn* having
satisfied all concerned, the Caledon colours were symbolically
struck, and the flag and pennant of the owners hoisted in their
stead.[539]

After the new ship had sailed for ‿ Middlesborough it
remained only to finish off and date the working drawings,
and to complete the ten-foot model of the ship built for no
other reason than pride in workmanship: the yellow pine hull
sandpapered smooth as steel. Window portholes were made
from pieces of mirror. Plated brass fittings were supplied by
the Sunderland Model Company at a cost of over £1,000;[138]
all so that, however far *Glenearn* might wander, something of
the vital spirit hammered into her[A] – even as into a *Glengyle*

presently rising on the stocks[315] – would always remain at the place of her birth.

Having dry-docked at Middlesbro' and been surveyed there, *Glenearn* arrived at London on 19th December[300] and started loading for the voyage to Yokohama.[72] She was due to sail on the 24th, but Lawrence Holt delayed the sailing so that they could all have Christmas at home.[31] Then the arrival of the passengers – £60 to Hong Kong[410] – the official inspections by the superintendents of each department and by the Company's Directors, the formalities at the Customs House[597] before sailing on the 3.36 p.m. tide of 28th December 1938.[290]

19.12.38

28.12.38

First port of call was Port Said; only a few hours were spent there, including 50 minutes searching for a missing Chinaman, before moving on and into the Suez Canal. Fourteen hours to Suez, then on to Penang, Singapore and Seletar on the north side of the island.[290] The standard of catering was very good, the stewards experienced; passengers were always satisfied as long as they had good food and drink.[31] On this the maiden voyage of the named ship of a new Class, *Glenearn* was of interest to shippers who were brought on board at each port and dined;[72] and no doubt, wined.[A] Hong Kong was reached about noon on 31st January 1939, thirty-four days out from London; the new Glen liner berthing at Holt's Wharf, Kowloon – just across the harbour from Taikoo Dockyard where two sister-ships were building; one, the *Breconshire* due for launching in 3 days' time.[411]

31.1.39

On to Shanghai, though trade with China had sunk to a low level due to the war with Japan.[516] Not so with the aggressor country in the conflict; Kobe, Yokohama and Nagoya were each favoured by a visit before *Glenearn* turned for home, returning by way of the Philippines, Saigon, Belawan in Dutch Sumatra, and, after Singapore again, Colombo.[290] At Port Said, boiler oil was offered as fuel for the diesels, but Mr. Kerr refused it and *Glenearn* returned two or three days late running at reduced speed on diesel oil.*[72] Two

19.2.39

* *Glenroy* faced somewhat later with a similar choice, suffered some damage to glands and stuffing boxes due to overheating.[72]

days out of Marseilles on the last day of the homeward voyage,[290] *Glenearn's* engines were taken up to full power, producing 14,390 indicated horse power at 17.77 knots loaded.[179] London was reached at 4.20 p.m. on the 5th

5.4.39 April.[290]

From London the Chief Engineer was sent back to Dundee to supervise the installation of machinery in *Glenartney*; Mr. J. Cahy,* who had been Extra Second on the maiden voyage, became Chief Engineer.[72] After coasting to Dunkirk and Amsterdam, and dry-docking at Antwerp, Voyage 2

14.5.39 began;[290] the name ship of the Glenearn Class was all set to slip into an unexciting and profitable routine of not unpleasant monotony. Apart from the odd day or two in the same foreign ports the deck officers could look forward to a lifetime of standing on watch, while down below the engineers would make their methodical rounds of inspection, never wholly unconscious – even off-duty – of the steady thump, thump, thump of the engines.[A]

Voyage 2 ended at 8.52 p.m. on Tuesday, 22nd August

22.8.39 1939,[290] *Glenearn* arriving at London amidst the greatest sensation since August 1914. The day before, Germany and Russia had concluded a non-aggression pact,[440] and the news broke on the world like an explosion. There was nothing now stopping Hitler from invading Poland, and that would bring France and Britain, however reluctantly, into another conflict with Germany.[R] To meet the extreme crisis of war Parliament was recalled to pass legislation investing the Government with full emergency powers. Without waiting for Parliament the

23.8.39 calling up was announced of some of the armed forces; also the A.R.P. and Civil Defence organisations.[441]

In view of the threatening situation, it was decided to abandon the rest of the voyage to Hamburg,[523] to avoid the fate of an earlier *Glenearn*, also brand new: seized by Germany on the outbreak of war in 1914.[525] On board the latest ship was a consignment of latex with the German port as its destination. There were no ships sailing to Hamburg and the German Company telegraphed that a firm called

* Name changed.

Revertex Limited should accept the consignment in exchange for a similar quantity at Genoa.*[522]

In the days that followed, the pace of the march to war quickened. Cruise liner sailings were cancelled, hop-pickers were advised to take their gas masks with them,[442] American tourists left, German ships loading at north-east coast ports received instructions from their owners to return home not later than Saturday the 26th.[443] That day there was an evacuation rehearsal, and at midnight the Admiralty assumed control of British shipping.[444] Paragraph 46 Part II Section 3 of the Board of Trade War Book (Revised Edition) requires that in such circumstances the Liverpool Steamship Owners' Association must be informed. A note to this paragraph states that measures affecting the security of ships against enemy attack would be provided for in the Defence Regulations.[264] Under these Regulations the Admiralty then issued a series of orders on the night of Monday 28th August; orders which came into force immediately: lighting regulations, the dimming of navigation and anchor lights, darkening of vessels in harbours where air-raid precautions were in force.

These instructions could hardly have taken the shipping industry by surprise;[520] since 1937 the stiffening of decks of merchantmen to carry guns had been going on, while over 9,000 officers of the Merchant Navy had gone through convoy and gunnery courses.[519] Most phases of national life were being organised to meet the emergency that it was still fervently hoped would not come.[520] At the same time, arrangements were being made to begin a new war at the point where the old war had left off.

Poland was attacked by Germany at dawn on 1st September.[R] In Britain general mobilisation was proclaimed[445] and by 11 a.m. on Sunday, 3rd September, Britain was once more at war with Germany.[R]

In the King George V Dock, London, *Glenearn* was commandeered by the Ministry of Shipping,[85] painted grey

28.8.39

3.9.39

---

* The question of the unpaid freight on this parcel of enemy-owned goods had eventually to be settled in the Prize Court. On 4th December 1941 compensation of £141 7s. 7d. was allowed out of the proceeds received for the goods as lawful prize, as against £150 1s. 9d. claimed.[523]

7.9.39 overall,[64] and sailed on charter* at 5.33 p.m. on 7th September. Arriving at Southampton on the 9th[290] – the same day as the first convoy of troopships had left, taking the British Expeditionary Force to France[R] – *Glenearn* loaded up with tanks and motor vehicles[85] before sailing again two days later.[290] It was a slow convoy, and *Glenearn's* engineers had great difficulty in running the engines at the required speed.[85] The voyage to Brest took 41 hours, and the return journey was not much better.[290] In the 25 years since the original B.E.F. passed through Southampton much of the emotion and excitement of sailing away to war had died. This time there were no military bands, tearful women and last farewells; troopships sailed to schedule, with dock workers the only watchers.[407]

After an even slower voyage to Brest,[290] on return to Falmouth representations were made to the Ministry of Shipping, with the result that *Glenearn* was included in a fast convoy, and successfully kept station on ships capable of twenty-two knots.[85] On this occasion Brest was reached in 14 hours and the return to Southampton made in the same time. After waiting four days at Southampton and another four at Plymouth, *Glenearn* returned to London, arriving on the 12.10.39 afternoon of 12th October.

October became November and *Glenearn* was requisitioned by the Admiralty;[290] what for, was not known, except that three sisterships were to be taken over too. *Glenroy* after completing two Far East voyages, *Breconshire* after her maiden voyage from Honk Kong, and *Glengyle* still at the fitting-out jetty at Dundee.[610] In due course *Glenearn* went to Palmer's Shipbuilding yard, Hepburn-on-Tyne, "for armaments".[290]

Then began a tremendous conversion – heart-breaking in its ruthlessness and its disregard of material[85] – to a special fleet supply ship. All the cork and well-seasoned timber of her refrigerating capacity was ripped out, along with the

---

* The rate of hire applicable to a liner of *Glenearn's* gross registered tonnage and refrigerated cargo space was agreed retrospectively to be just under £3,600 per month, together with an allowance for depreciation and return of capital of 10% per annum on the first cost of the ship.[255]

refrigerating machinery.[610] The lower decks forward were removed, and intermediate bulkheads and coffer dams fitted, to convert the forward holds into oil fuel storage tanks complete with pumping and heating arrangements for work in Arctic conditions. The after end of the ship was changed into storage space for ammunition.[558] Her centre-castle was now to have workshops on one side and naval mess decks on the other,[85] while her upper and bridge decks fore and aft were armoured against air attack.[558] *Glenearn's* funnel was lowered 11 feet, the rear mast 40 feet. The foremast was replaced by a derrick post, and a central aerial mast was fitted just forward of the funnel.[620]

It was obvious that *Glenearn's* function would be to rendezvous the ships of the Fleet at sea and eliminate the necessity for their returning to port, thus keeping them on patrol for longer periods than normally possible.[85] In which parts of the world the Glen ships would be functioning was anybody's guess. It was believed at the Admiralty that at least one German pocket-battleship was on the high seas, and groups of French and British warships had been formed to track down such commerce raiders;[R] perhaps the converted Glen ships were intended to supply these far-ranging hunting groups. In the South Atlantic, yes – but in Arctic conditions? Surely not. The true nature of the enterprise for which such expensive preparations were being made remained veiled in secrecy.[A]

On 3rd September 1939, Winston Churchill – for years the voice of rearmament crying in the political wilderness – had been reappointed First Lord of the Admiralty, the post he had held on the outbreak of War in 1914. Within days he was preparing a plan for establishing a naval force in the Baltic Sea.[567] The Director of Naval Construction thought it would be possible to hoist up an old battleship of the *Royal Sovereign* Class a distance of 9 feet, in order to avoid grounding on the way in. Enormous caissons would be required but would serve an additional purpose as anti-torpedo bulges.[216] Churchill was strongly supported by his Admirals: Lord Cork and Orrery considered the undertaking perfectly feasible, Admiral Bruce Fraser Third Sea Lord and Controller advised the addition to the assault fleet of the four fast Glen ships.[567] Although it was pointed out that four "Glenearns" could import 120,000 tons of food annually, it was decided to proceed with the requisitioning. The conversions were expected to take about four months, including three months in dry dock.[216]

And in truth, after months of tearing apart and rebuilding, there did emerge something worth while in the way of a supply ship;[85] one capable of carrying 4,600 tons of cargo oil fuel and 5,000 tons of ammunition. Defensive armament against air attack included an 8-barrelled and a 4-barrelled pompom, also two 0.5″ quadruple machine guns; "offensive" armament was four 12-pounder guns.[620] After much strenuous work under pressure[558] *Glenearn* dry-docked at Newcastle-on-Tyne in February, and was surveyed there.[290] Her under-water lines were the subject of admiration, particularly the stern tubes, rudder and the curves of her stern.[85] Early in March she started loading ammunition for her own magazines.[216] Captain E. W. R. Sim, RN, had been earmarked as her Commanding Officer,[558] but the venture had long since been abandoned.[568]

In the interval taken up by the conversion the international political situation had changed, and exigencies of the Senior Service had prevented the preparation of the battleships and cruisers against air attack;[216] indeed, the problem of making ships comparatively secure against aircraft had not been solved.[568] And the Glens – the only suitable British merchant ships – had the disadvantage of drawing 29 feet fully loaded; they would have had to go in carrying only 2,000 tons of stores and expecting to fill up with oil from Sweden.[216] A forlorn hope.[A] *Glenearn*, after a few modifications to suit her owners, was handed back to them;[85] as were *Glenroy*, *Glengyle* and *Breconshire*.

30.4.40 With J. P. Williams as Master, *Glenearn* sailed from the Tyne on 30th April 1940 and arrived at Liverpool on the 3rd May.[290] The four ships presented a very awkward problem: while the Admiralty wanted the vessels to be within call, the

Ministry of Shipping thought they should be put to good use. Alfred Holt's suggested that T. & J. Harrison might operate them, taking a limited general cargo out to the West Indies and bringing fuel oil and sugar back.[610] *Glenearn* sailed on the 5th May for Port of Spain, arriving on the 14th. From there to Brighton, Point Fortin, San Fernando and back to Port of Spain before sailing for Liverpool.

20.5.40

Another similar voyage in June passed off[290] without problems other than that of getting out the heavy oil carried between the double bottoms; with no heating elements there it was a terrible job to get the last of it out.[71] Apart from the official cargo, at least one member of the crew brought back a useful contribution to his family's sugar ration; the newly-appointed 2nd Engineer imported a 100-lb. bag in this way.[1] A comparatively peaceful and useful occupation was short-lived, for on completion of the second voyage to Trinidad on 28th June *Glenearn* was once again taken over by the Admiralty and handed over in turn to Grayson, Rollo and Clover of Liverpool for another conversion.[85] Of the four ships, only *Breconshire*, last back from the West Indies, was to be spared.[610]

28.6.40

CHAPTER 4

ALERT AND CONFIDENT ENERGY

The use by the Japanese of landing ships and craft against the Chinese in 1937 came as a surprise to the British Intelligence Services. Although it was considered that air power would probably make amphibious operations in Europe impossible, in July 1938 the Inter-Service Training and Development Centre was set up to study the subject of inter-service operations. A list of merchant ships suitable for conversion to landing craft carriers was drawn up in March 1939,[237] and in May of the following year it was recommended that immediate steps be taken to have ships made ready; special gravity davits should be installed in two of the new Glen liners *Denbighshire, Glenartney, Glengarry* or *Glenorchy*, and fitting them for carrying troops. Anti-aircraft armament would also have to be provided.[164]

By the time this memorandum was typed Denmark had been over-run and *Glengarry* captured within hours of first putting to sea; most of Norway had been occupied,[601] and another "blitzkrieg" had ruptured the Allied front in France. Meanwhile, four spare Glen ships already armed and armoured were filling in time making voyages to the West Indies.[A]

For the expedition to Narvik the War Office raised twelve Independent Companies, but only six found their way to Norway. Two landings were made in May, the first Allied combined operation of the war, and the first occasion in history in which tanks were landed. The craft involved totalled four for landing infantry and two capable of carrying vehicles;[237] all brought out by the Blue Funnel *Cyclops*.[601]

The Dunkirk evacuation accounted for all but a handful of the Navy's remaining landing craft, and although enough were building to land one infantry brigade no naval organization had been set up to man and serve them. In the middle of June, however, Prime Minister Churchill created

44

the post of Director of Combined Operations and shortly afterwards the three ships *Glenroy, Glengyle* and *Glenearn* were taken in hand for conversion[237] to Landing Craft Carriers.[234]

The firm of Grayson, Rollo and Clover Docks Ltd. was not a shipyard in the accepted sense, but a specialist repair company whose work on the Liverpool side of the Mersey was carried out in the public docks. *Glenearn* arrived after the first rush of wartime conversions had settled down to regular employment for Merseysiders – a satisfaction not experienced for nearly two decades. This, together with the "Dunkirk spirit" had raised morale, and labour relations within the port appeared to be exceptionally good. After unloading, *Glenearn* was berthed at the west side of Langton Dock. In accordance with the firm's policy, everything not part of the finished design was removed, also anything to allow access was taken away before fitting any new materials.[128] The bulwarks aft of the forecastle were removed to allow easier handling of the landing craft.[85]

Technical problems created by the proposed conversion were fairly straightforward, and consisted mainly of deciding on the best groupings of davits and the arrangement of the troops' accommodation.[540] Another major operation was the protection against magnetic mines by 'degaussing', which involved circling the hull internally with cables encased in 6″ steel tubes.[128] The broad plan may have been understood, but many details had to be decided on the spot. Three times the firm of Welin-Maclachlan Ltd. were given the weight of the landing craft their davits were to house; in the intervals the weight had increased and each time the davits had to be strengthened.[85] To handle the final load of 14 tons compared to the original figure of 10 tons, the trackway had to be reinforced, the winch-motors replaced, new controllers fitted and rewired to the switchboard. Six weeks delay.[235] War teaches, amongst other things, patience.[85]

Glenearn was being fitted out to carry twelve assault landing craft (ALCs) and two motor landing craft (MLCs); the latter to be deck cargo and hoisted out by derricks. In July it was decided to stow a whaler on deck also, so that the parent ship could go to a buoy. Deck stowage was also required for an SLC or support landing craft[238] – an armed adaptation of the ALC – for training and operations.

The military force to be carried amounted to 34 officers, 36 Warrant Officers and Sergeants, and 627 other ranks.[235] Extra fresh water and toilet facilities for these increased numbers aboard called for changes in the uses of existing tanks, with considerable adaptation of pipework and the provision of extra pumping arrangements. Grayson, Rollo and Clover had to produce the parts required. It was often a case of modifying and using what was readily available rather than waiting for exactly the right piece of equipment to arrive.[128] Such conditions presented opportunities for a little private venturing by the well-connected; the Second Engineer had to resist strong pressure to accept a piece of mechanical plant that was patently too large for the opening it would have had to go through.[1]

For the rapid embarkation and disembarkation of troops, accommodation ladders with a platform at the foot were to be provided; also an embarkation port constructed on each side of the ship as near the water line as practicable. Suggestions, discussions and instructions by, with and from the I.S.T.D.C. and D.C.O. formed a steady stream: hammocks for the troops were to be provided by the ship, also sufficient crockery, cutlery and cooking utensils. And lifebelts. Accommodation to be found for hammock stowage, kit-bag storage and rifle racks. 100 yards of reinforced army track, plus coconut matting, hooks, mild steel bars and holding-down plates to be loaded and stowed away ...[235] Grayson's men worked a seven-day week with three or four evenings' overtime thrown in,[128] trying to meet the completion date of 15th October.[235]

A few bombs had been scattered over Merseyside at the end of July, while at Birkenhead on the night of 8–9th August the first casualties were inflicted on the civilian population.[365] A few days later an aerodrome near Liverpool was attacked in daylight, and *Glenearn*'s war entered a new dimension of 39 18.8.40 minutes past midnight on the 18th when a high-flying

German aircraft dropped a stick of bombs down the line of docks damaging railway tracks, a grain store, sheds and a graving dock; all well away from *Glenearn*. A small bucket dredger was hit, turned turtle and sank.[241]

A quiet spell followed[365] and the work went on. *Glenearn* went into one of the Langton graving docks for examination of stern bush wear, down cleaning of sea intake gratings and scraping and painting of the hull. For a short period she was at a berth known locally as the "Tin Sheds".[128]

The raids started again on the 28th and continued for four nights, with the German planes loosing clusters of incendiaries along with their high explosive bombs.[366] On the 31st the attacks began shortly before 11 p.m. and concentrated on the Liverpool Docks. Many high explosive and incendiary bombs were dropped, and the Customs House was set on fire.[243] Probably attracted by these fires at Anston House, a second attack developed at midnight and went on for three hours;[241] many shipbuilding firms in the district were bombed.[243] Two tankers at Birkenhead were damaged.[561]

In the first hour or so of Thursday, 5th September, about thirty-five HE bombs exploded in the immediate area around *Glenearn*. Between Nos. 1 and 2 Langton Graving Docks there was damage to water, gas, electricity and hydraulic mains; roads and a railway adjoining Brocklebank Docks were also affected.[243] *Glenearn* was hit by a small bomb on the after well deck, or more precisely on a winch on the starboard side forward of the stern.[63] The winch, worth £1,200, just disappeared; pieces of hardened steel bomb casing were scattered about the deck.[*1] Otherwise, there was not much damage,[63] and repairs were carried out simultaneously with the work of conversion.[85]

On the evening of 7th September the signal "Cromwell" went out from GHQ Home Forces; this was the code-word that the invasion had started, or was imminent, and that the troops must go at once to their battle-stations. In Liverpool, the Home Guard led by veterans of the Great War who had

28.8.40

31.8.40

1.9.40

5.9.40

7.9.40

* The precise dating of this incident is uncertain.

"beaten the Germans once before" were called out; although it took about eight hours to round up 200 out of 400 in one battalion. A day's ration issued was promptly eaten for breakfast, so there was no unexpired portion left to return when it transpired that the executive order had applied only to military command areas on the south coast of England.[98]

A week after *Glenearn* was hit it was *Glenroy*'s turn.[561] On the 12th an incendiary bomb penetrated the deck and started a fire. Willie Ramsay, the Third Engineer of *Glenearn* and some of his men ran along and put it out.[113] *Glenroy*'s approximate completion date had been put back to 25th September, with *Glenearn*'s unchanged as 15th October, but even on official correspondence these expectations drew the comment, "What a hope!"[231] There was speculation among the few remaining members of the original ship's company about what sort of desperate enterprise the future held for them: would *Glenearn* be well escorted? Would there be air cover? Chances of survival were better not discussed, but this party was bound to end in a rough house. It was some consolation to think that if they "went" it would be in good company.[85]

The September raids continued. On the night of the 14th the docks again seemed to be the main target. At 8.20 p.m. Mersey Docks and Harbour Board circulated a warning on their own initiative on account of gunfire heard. Just before 11 p.m. a stick of bombs dropped in a line from north to south, the last one falling in the roadway on the west side of Alexandra Dock. A string of incendiary clusters fell on a parallel line farther to the east. Two nights later gunfire and explosions were heard before 7.35 p.m.; the raid thus heralded was aimed mostly at the centre of the city.[241] In the raid of the 26th many bombs fell in the far south of Liverpool's dock area; the L.N.E.R. Goods Yard, Bibby's Yard, Elder Dempster's Store east of Brunswick Dock, and Dock Station were all burnt out, as were all the buildings or warehouses west of the Dock.[195] In King's Dock there was a large fire where four ships and two warehouses burned throughout the following day; seven other fires were extinguished.[243] Two more air raids brought Liverpool's total for September to twenty.[365]

October was fairly quiet,[63] if one disregards a German bomber firing on a bus in daylight[365] and discounts the night of 11–12th when nineteen HE bombs of 50 kg. and two incendiary clusters landed within 700 yards of *Glenearn*, including one of the former close against the dock wall.[240] Four ships were hit.[561] *Glenroy* experienced the raid from a different angle; her ship's company having arrived earlier in the month she had sailed on the morning of the 11th to carry out speed trials and returned the following forenoon.[165]

11.10.40

12.10.40

By this time, too, some naval appointments had been made to *Glenearn*. A retired Captain RN, Laurence B. Hill, had been given the command, with Lieut.-Com. Venables RN (retd.) 1st Executive Officer.[299] Lieut.-Com. Best RNR (retd.) would take charge of the landing craft when they arrived.[136] Two more Lieutenant-Commanders RNR were appointed in September: L. E. Foster and Thomas Hood. The senior deck officers were thus a mixture of Royal Navy (retired) and Mercantile Marine, some active, some retired.[299]

For the staffing of the engine room the Navy had a problem, having no experience of marine diesels;[63] but by a special arrangement involving the Admiralty, Alfred Holt and Company, and the individual engineers, the latter stayed on. All, without exception, signed T 124 Agreements[610] whereby they were engaged by the Director of Sea Transport on their existing Mercantile Marine terms, but were placed under naval discipline and became, "Members of the Naval Forces of the Crown" for compensation, sick pay and hospital treatment.[193] Each engineer was granted a temporary commission in the Royal Naval Reserve with appropriate ranks from Lieutenant-Commander (E) down.[299] As the RNR made no provision for electrical engineers William McKenzie was commissioned sub-lieutenant (E) in the RNVR.[85]

Until *HMS Glenearn* commissioned, all the personnel old and new had to stay in hotels, or "digs"[63] or with relatives.[1] As a result of this nightly dispersion everyone had their own bomb stories to add to the shared experiences on board while on duty fire-watching.[A]

28.11.40 When the sirens sounded at 7.23 p.m. on the 28th November the 58th attack on Liverpool began, and the planes came over in waves. This was the night of the "land mines"; huge containers of explosive which floated down supported by silk ropes attached to green parachutes. An army sergeant charged one with bayonet fixed thinking it was an enemy airman. Flares and the moonlight made the streets almost as bright as day,[366] but indoors the very loud bangs were thought to be from an unusually big anti-aircraft gun. *Glenearn*'s 2nd Engineer was staying in a house in Childwall, sleeping in front of a ground-floor fireplace. When a mine went off about 200 yards away the blast came down the chimney and blew soot all over him, the mattress and the room. The crater made by this mine measured 40–50 feet across and was about 20 feet deep.[1] By 4 a.m. more than 200 people had died and a greater number had been injured.[366]

HMS Glenroy had commissioned and sailed earlier in November;[166] now, just into December, officers and ratings were arriving every day.[136] The old originals now messed on board, joining Lieut.-Com. Venables who had been bombed out of his hotel; Lieut.-Com. Hood was glad to have finished with sitting through raid after raid in a jerry-built brick "pub".[63] Newcomers spent the first few days becoming familiar with the strange-looking ship, the officers and the crew. It was amazing how quickly Captain Hill got to know the surname of every man aboard, and never spoke to any officer or rating without calling him by name and rank. More than any other single act, this ability of his gave everyone a sense of belonging, and helped enormously in getting everyone settled down. It also earned him the immediate respect of all on board.

But it soon became very obvious that, of the large ship's company, very few below decks had ever been in a ship before. Of those that had, their experience was of men-of-war, not what was still very much a merchant ship.[124] The mercantile mariners, on the other hand, had to try and adapt themselves to the Navy's ways. The 2nd Engineer submitted a parsimonious list of materials required by his department, to be told that he must think in much larger quantities in future.[3]

The Admiralty Board had directed that His Majesty's Ship GLENEARN was to be commissioned on Friday the 13th, but Captain Hill refused to do so on such an inauspicious date;[63] so the white pendant with the red cross of St. George was run up to the masthead[287] on Thursday, the 12th of December 1940.[63]

12.12.40

Meanwhile the ship was still in the hands of the Dockyard. It was hoped that by working day and night the refit might have been completed by 15th December,[230] and there was the usual rush to finish, exemplified in the case of one small cabin about 8 feet by 7 feet containing a built-in bunk and a chest of drawers. Two painters were painting the deck head, a joiner completing the woodwork, a plumber fitting a washbasin, and another man laying the lino[128] – all, as it transpired in vain since the latest completion date was not met, and had to be put back to the 27th.[230]

On the 18th King George VI came to Liverpool and visited the docks.[559] Two days later the full moon brought other visitors at 6.30 p.m.,[243] sweeping over the area in repeated waves.[364] By 9 p.m. there was a serious fire at Canada Dock No. 1, a high explosive bomb had burst in Langton Graving Dock[243] and another had fallen between *HMAS Australia* and the wall of Brocklebank Dock without exploding.[241] Royal Naval ships in Gladstone Dock to the north were firing at parachute flares with their heavy machine guns,[196] the tracer bullets cutting patterns in the night sky.[364] About midnight fire parties were ordered to land[196] and take over the fire fighting from the exhausted shore crews.[124] They worked under a canopy of bursting shells and sweeping searchlights.[364]

18.12.40
20.12.40

By 4 a.m. on the 21st Merseyside had experienced its heaviest raid. Incendiaries had hit the Town Hall, the Municipal Offices, the Central Police Offices, Prince's Parade and the landing stage. Fire had broken out at the Cunard Building; the Dock Board Office and the Waterloo Grain House were alight.[367] Liverpool Exchange Station was blocked,[243] and the Leeds–Liverpool Canal breached; water

21.12.40

from a one-mile section of canal poured into the Canada Dock Station.[241] But the working of the Docks was not seriously impeded, although some delays were caused by the fires in timber yards and by the hose pipes of the fire service.[243]

Glenearn's main armament had consisted of four 12-pounders[620] which had seen service in the 1914–18 War and subsequently been modified for use as High Angle/Low Angle guns.[124] In the current conversion the forward pair had been removed and one remounted at the bows;[63] an otherwise suitable mounting right aft was being prepared to receive a steel hut containing special apparatus leaving no place for a fourth gun.[230] The remaining three were now required to supplement the failing barrage of shore-based anti-aircraft guns which, after putting up their best fire so far, were running out of ammunition.[124] The raids started again at 6.30 p.m. and soon the incendiaries were showering down. Parachute flares illuminated the whole dock at 9 p.m. and for the next hour most RN ships fired close-range weapons at them; several were hit and five shot out. Many bombs fell in and around the basin; some did not explode, others did but caused no damage but making the ship roll.[196] There was no proper fire-control for *Glenearn*'s 12-pounders, so all that could be done was to point them upwards and send the shells into the sky in the hope that the enemy might be deterred from flying too low. What was perhaps more important, it gave the ship's company the feeling of doing something to hit back at their tormentors. During one of the calls to action it was noticed that one of the gun crews was absent from his place of duty.[124]

This night's raiding was even worse than the previous night's. By 10.30 p.m. naval fire parties were needed at Alexandra Dock where on the west side work had stopped. Berths at the south side of Brocklebank Branch Dock and south west No. 3 Canada Dock were also out of commission.[243] There were huge fires round *Glenearn* and incendiaries fell on her; she went on fire forward but this was quickly put out.[63] There was a wind from the north and sparks and burning matter were blowing across the basin; hoses had to be kept running on deck.[196] Fire was spreading from adjoining premises. Grayson, Rollo and Clover's fire watchers dealt with seventy incendiary bombs.[241]

By 2.20 a.m. on the Sunday[196] most of the warehouses on the dockside were being gutted by fire, and the city's anti-aircraft guns seemed to have run out of ammunition. Sub-Lieut. Scott was in charge of a fire fighting team when German planes came down to a low level and machine-gunned the docks in the direction of the fires.[124] Destroyers in Gladstone Dock returned the fire.[196] During one such attack a stream of sparks streaked down the dockside towards *Glenearn*'s fire fighting team – who made headlong dives under some railway wagons alongside the blazing warehouse. When they emerged they were surprised to see Surg. Lieut.-Com. Johnston in the roadway where the bullets had been sputtering, tiptoeing amongst the hoses and trying to avoid the water and debris. When asked why he had not taken cover, he said that he had a new uniform on and it would have been a pity to spoil it.[124] He and Surg.-Lieut. Tait had been dining ashore.[136]

At 5.25 a.m. the "all clear" sounded.[196] It was then that the missing member of the gun crew was discovered; he had locked himself in the "heads" from sheer fright. Later the same day he was brought up before the Captain on defaulters and the Master-at-Arms was told to read to the young offender the punishment for deserting in the face of the enemy – death. The poor fellow fainted, but he might yet become a useful member of the crew.[124] He was not the only one getting jittery: some of the officers spent a great deal of time below decks under chairs, tables or anything else available. It was said that the planes carried three bombs, and long hours were spent counting them as they landed: one, two, three – always hoping that the third one would miss.[136]

The north end of the docks had taken a hammering.[367] The dock gates had been damaged and at low water the ship settled on the mud.[85] The raid of 22nd–23rd December caused a fire at Langton Double Storage Shed next the

22.12.40

23.12.40

Graving Dock.[243] It was obvious that if the ship did not leave soon she would never get away. So it was decided that, completed or not, she must leave.[85] *Glenearn*'s officers had to make their own arrangements for embarking the landing craft, as the port services were still disorganized.[61]

The LCMs were meant to be launched by lifting them outboard on jumbo derricks suitably secured with topping lifts to the top of the mainmast. Captain Hill decided that the fore topmast was unnecessary and should be taken down, telling Sub-Lieut. Scott RNR as Officer of the Deck to get the job done. Having called out one watch under a Petty Officer he described what was required and how the Warrant Officer might go about it. There seemed to be far too many men to do the job, but if that was the way the Navy worked...

After spending the best part of the day at it the mast was still in position aloft, so as darkness was fast approaching the officer took charge of the operation, dismissing all the hands except the Petty Officer, two experienced seamen and one winchman. Going aloft with one seaman they rove the necessary mast rope, secured the steadying guys, and with the aid of the two men on deck lowered the mast in about an hour. Scott missed his dinner that night but relaxed in the wardroom over a pink gin and was feeling very pleased with himself when Captain Hill came over and spoke to him, congratulating him on having got the fore topmast down, and then gave him a ticking off for doing the job himself.

25.12.40   The day before the ship was due to sail, it was found that to lower the LCM off the foredeck with reasonable clearance between the craft and the ship's side, a ring bolt riveted to the boat deck needed to be moved some three feet outboard. The Chief Engineer was consulted; he detailed the Second Engineer to carry out the work. Lieutenant (E) Aiken arrived on deck with two stokers, some oxy-acetylene cutting tackle, a drilling machine and two rivets. Very soon they had the ring-bolt removed. They were about to start drilling two holes in the new position when someone drew the attention of the dockyard to the fact that the ship's company were doing the job themselves. An immediate walkout of all the dockyard men was called, and a strike threatened. Eventually Captain Hill had to give way and allow the job to be carried out by the dockyard men. And so it was, by some fourteen of them: boilermakers and mates, shipwrights and mates, riveters and mates, fire boys and mates – all the conglomeration of union demarcation in the midst of a war of national survival.[124]

Boxing Day 1940.[61] Hands fall in. Prepare ship for sea. Stand by engines.[166] *HMS Glenearn,* lacking handrails and ladders, and festooned about with cables,[85] cast off from the quay, entered the lock, proceeded out of the lock and into the River Mersey. That same afternoon they weighed anchor and set course 288° down the swept channel.[166] Putting out the paravanes in pitch darkness was pure hell, and took two and a half hours. Lieut.-Com. Hood dared not let any of the "hostilities only" ratings do anything without making sure personally that it was O.K. Captain Hill was not pleased, to say the least of it, and they would spend the next day practising the operation.

26.12.40

They were all glad to get out of Liverpool. Liverpool with its five hundred fires. The enormous sheds of timber burning were a terrible sight, particularly when there was no need for it to be stored at the dockside at all. In truth Liverpool was not really ready for the raids. Earlier on Lieut.-Com. Hood had rigged a wire from *Glenearn* across to the other side of the dock, so that if the nearby shed caught fire the ship could haul herself off immediately. The wire was doing no harm on the bottom of the dock, but the authorities raised hell, and it had to be taken in.*[63]

Serious deficiencies had been revealed in the readiness of some merchant vessels to deal with fires on board, or indeed to take any action at all to safeguard the ships. Four, including one of the new Glen ships and a "Blue Funnel" boat, had been saved in Gladstone Dock by parties of sailors from nearby RN destroyers. While the bluejackets went forward to deal with the fire there and the Chinese seamen concentrated on donning lifejackets, an officer on the stern of

---

* In 1941 it was an order that all ships should rig such a wire.[63]

the Glen Line vessel had refused to give a line to a tug, just in case the tug claimed salvage.

Shortly after *Glenearn*'s departure, Rear-Admiral J. S. M. Ritchie, Flag Officer in Charge, Liverpool, wrote to the Secretary of the Liverpool Steamship Owners' Association, mentioning the four ships by name and commenting that the state of affairs on board these vessels was not as it should be. In addition to this, the spirit evinced by one or two officers was unworthy of the great tradition of the Merchant Navy. "... it is essential in these times of National Emergency that all possible steps should be taken to maintain a spirit of alert and confident energy...".[196]

No one knew what opportunities the future might hold for redeeming the reputation of the Merchant Service. A new contender buckles the tarnished shield; ordeal by fire may yet bright honour yield.

CHAPTER 5

CONFUSED OPERATIONS

On 17th July 1940, the Prime Minister had appointed Admiral of the Fleet Sir Roger Keyes to be Director of Combined Operations. Shortly after, Mr. Churchill had asked him to outline three or four raids by five to ten thousand men which might be mounted in the autumn. The next few months had been devoted to building up an assault fleet and the Commando units. In August a Combined Training Centre (CTC) at Inveraray had been started.

At one of their meetings in September Churchill asked his Director of Combined Operations if he had ever considered the possibility of capturing the Italian island of Pantellaria. Keyes, leader of the Zeebrugge Raid of 23rd April 1918, told him that he had thought a great deal about it, and considered the operation to be quite feasible. In the same month, however, all the Commandos and Independent Companies were placed under command of C-in-C Home Forces as part of the anti-invasion measures.[237]

With possession of the Atlantic coast of France, it was thought that the Germans might attempt to capture some of the Spanish and Portugese islands in the Atlantic in order to threaten the British convoy routes. Furthermore, if Spain were invaded – or joined the Axis Powers – so that Gibraltar were effectively lost, the islands were the only alternative points from which to command the western approaches to the Mediterranean and protect the vital route to Egypt around the Cape of Good Hope. From the 6th October troops were kept standing by to carry out Operation BRISK – code-name for the capture of the Azores.[224]

Early in November the Chiefs of Staff, after considering various proposals for the offensive use of Commando troops, expressed a preference for the Pantellaria project – codenamed WORKSHOP.[237] There the matter rested until the 19th, when a meeting arranged by the Director of

Combined Operations was attended by the three Chiefs of
Staff and the three Defence Ministers. The WORKSHOP
proposal was unanimously approved, and Churchill told his
D.C.O. that he wished Keyes to command the operation.[224]

But this decision created a problem. The Azores expedition
– BRISK – if mounted, would require at least one Glen ship,
among others, and *HMS Glengyle* commissioned on 10th
September had been allocated to it. Pantellaria –
WORKSHOP – called for two Glen ships, and while *Glenroy*
was expected to be completed and ready for action by the 12th
December, *Glenearn*, even if finished to time on the 15th,
would not be ready for operations until the 30th.[230] The
forces for WORKSHOP were due to sail on the 15th, and the
Defence Committee had stipulated that there must be no
period during which it would be impossible to carry out
Operation BRISK.[224] The dilemma was resolved by accept-
ing a temporary reduction in the scope of BRISK; from 13th
December, when *Glengyle* would have to be withdrawn, until
the end of the year when *Glenearn* should become available to
take over the other Glen ship's duties.[230]

In spite of the fact that the capture of Pantellaria was a
policy approved by both the Prime Minister and the Chiefs of
Staff, the Joint Planning Staff and the Executive Planning
Staff raised every possible objection, and persistently derided
the idea of the operation in a most improper manner. At the
highest levels, however, it was settled that the preparations
should proceed as quickly as possible, with the Commando
troops doing their training at Lamlash on the Isle of Arran.
The plan proposed attaching *Glengyle* and *Glenroy*, each with
950 Special Service* troops on board, to a fast convoy –
codenamed EXCESS – taking personnel and stores through
the Mediterranean to Malta and Greece. Near Pantellaria the
Glen ships and their escort of four destroyers would break off
and assault the island. After the disembarkation all ships
would withdraw to Malta.

Approval for the Force to assemble at Lamlash and sail
with the convoy on the 18th December was given on the 9th.

* That is, Commandos.

On the 14th, however, the Prime Minister told Admiral Keyes that operation WORKSHOP would be postponed until the following month; in the meantime the striking force, now called Force 103, was to be held at three days' notice as it might be required elsewhere. The three ships *Glengyle*, *Glenroy* and *Royal Scotsman* embarked landing craft at Greenock between 17th and 19th December. In the early hours of the 20th, a full dress rehearsal was carried out, so that the D.C.O. was able to report that Force 103 was ready to carry out WORKSHOP; or any other offensive operation required of it. At this point, due to an accident to another landing craft carrier *Ettrick*, Admiral Keyes was ordered to hand over *Glengyle* to take over *Ettrick*'s stores and role in operation BRISK. Thus both striking forces were temporarily immobilised.[230]

Just after Christmas the Deputy Director of Combined Operations in London was led to the belief that WORKSHOP had increased in popularity, and there was no doubt in his mind that the WORKSHOP forces would be sent through the Mediterranean in January 1941. As there was no hope of *Ettrick*'s being ready before 15th January he was convinced that the Royal Marine stores in *Glengyle* (ex-*Ettrick*) should be transferred to *Glenearn* as early as possible; say by the 2nd or 3rd of January. *Glenearn* with her partially-trained ship's company would be good enough for BRISK, and she should be held in readiness for that operation. At this time, too, the Assistant Chief of Naval Staff (Foreign) was suggesting that *Glenearn* should join the other two Glen ships in WORKSHOP.

Then at the end of December the Chief of Naval Staff announced that no destroyers were available for WORKSHOP and it had been decided to delay the expedition's departure until the 17th February. Keyes was asked if he would like his force to sail with a convoy leaving England on 7th January for the Mediterranean via the Cape. Sir Roger preferred this to keeping the troops waiting in Arran; and so it would have been agreed, but the Prime Minister did not approve. At this the Force Commander pointed out that the previous postponement had shaken the confidence of his men, that the latest postponement would entirely dissipate the offensive spirit of the Commando troops presently trained to such a high pitch; it would be better to return the men to their units.

Then the Executive Planning Section of the Joint Planning Staff came up with a memorandum re-allocating the ships for the Pantellaria operation and the truncated Azores expedition TRUCK. *Glenroy*'s duties were unchanged, while *Glengyle* was still to be held at 48-hours' notice to sail on TRUCK. *Ettrick* was expected to complete repairs by the 11th January, after which *Glengyle* would unload *Ettrick*'s stores and reload with Force 103's and again become available for WORKSHOP training at Lamlash...

At a meeting on the 3rd January 1941 attended by representatives of the Admiralty, the War Office and 1st Corps, it was decided that amphibious training should re-open at Inveraray on 15th January with one battalion of the 4th Brigade going on board *Glenearn*, to be followed by battalions of the 1st Infantry Brigade (Guards).

After a number of incidents involving the troops at Lamlash resulting in a report by the civilian police to the D.C.O. the Commandos were sent on 14-days' leave. While they were away, the Director of Combined Operations submitted to the Chiefs of Staff Committee a revised naval and military plan for WORKSHOP on the assumption that *Glenearn* and *Karanja* would be available in addition to *Glengyle*, *Glenroy* and *Royal Scotsman*. In this scheme the three Glens and *Karanja* were to land a first flight of 1,860 men.

17.1.41   The following day the Joint Intelligence Sub-Committee of the War Cabinet presented a new report on the scale of enemy attack to be expected after Pantellaria had been captured. It was concluded that there would be heavy, if intermittent, naval bombardments, air attacks by 400 German and 100 Italian bombers, and a possible attempt to re-occupy the island by a sea-borne operation in conjunction with German parachute troops.

Meanwhile, German dive-bombers had arrived in Sicily and very roughly handled convoy EXCESS after it had been held at Gibraltar until the 6th of January.[230] The entire British naval strength from both ends of the Mediterranean had been engaged on this operation, the aircraft carrier *Illustrious* receiving several hits from heavy bombs; the cruiser *Southampton* had been sunk and *Gloucester* damaged.[R]

On the 21st January 1941 the Chiefs of Staff Committee recommended the abandonment of WORKSHOP and the despatch of the three Glen ships to Egypt.[230] This move round the Cape was to be known as operation ACONITE.[223]

*   *   *

Of these waves of controversy *Glenearn* received only the occasional backwash.[167] Having joined *Glenroy* at Dalmuir yard the refit was finished off by Messrs. John Brown & Co., Ltd.[85] Snags were found when *Glenearn* did trials. Although she had three excellent anchors – a spare bower was stowed on the bulkhead abaft No. 2 hatch – they would not house properly in the hawse pipes; a fault in the original design of the bows. Juggling with a wire could flip up the flukes, but it was a laborious business; also the paravane wires fouled the anchor when the shoe was lowered down the stem post. Both of these defects would cause a great deal of work every time the ship left harbour when there was no time to spare.[63]

With the refit completed *Glenearn*,[124] while still at Dalmuir Basin, embarked the 2nd Battalion the Norfolk Regiment, which arrived in two trains during the forenoon of 15th January. At 1500 *Glenearn* weighed anchor and steamed down the Clyde while the troops were still settling in.[245] There was in *Glenearn* a device involving bevel gears and rods which enabled the man on the bridge to indicate to the engine room the r.p.m. required; turning the handle moved the pointer over a scale, with a corresponding display below. Down on one of the troop decks, however, a soldier had slung his hammock from one of the horizontal connecting rods instead of from the hooks provided, then climbed in. Up on the bridge the Captain ordered an

15.1.41

increase in speed, the handle of the revolution indicator was cranked rapidly and the poor fellow in his hammock was wound up towards the roof like the victim of some mediaeval torture; then the thing jammed.[1]

At Greenock *Glenearn* anchored for the night;[245] *Glenroy* was already there.[169] Next day at noon *Glenearn* weighed, steamed further down the Clyde then up Loch Fyne to Inveraray.[245] All the stark grandeur of Argyll in January; it was a most beautiful spot.[136] Sir Roger Keyes came aboard to ensure that Captain Hill would train the landing craft crews in the manner already laid down for the other two Glen ships. He emphasised that success in amphibious warfare lay in training the soldiers and sailors to work together and learning to trust each other.[231] In the evening the Norfolks practised boat stations.[245]

Moorings had been laid for the three Glen type landing craft carriers and other converted merchant ships.[234] One of the snags was that *Glenearn*'s merchant service buoy shackles did not fit the ring of the naval buoy; the only practicable quick release was to rove the huge cable through the ring of the buoy and bring it inboard to the Blake slip stopper.

The weather was bitterly cold.[63] But by this time just about everyone was aboard, and new friends were being made day by day. From the troubles in Liverpool had grown a certain *esprit de corps*;[136] here they were free from air raids and able to shake down into teams for the day-to-day running of the ship. Boats' crews were busy getting their craft ready for use, and practising the lowering of the ALCs from their davits; then the none-too-easy job of picking them out of the water to recovery positions. Launching the MLCs was a more formidable task – what with "action stations" and gun drills, a sense of purpose pervaded the entire ship; a desire to see themselves a reasonably efficient unit, to find out the pitfalls and put right the mistakes.[124]

The troops had the experience of living on board and being carried in the assault landing craft. For the sailors it was a week of training the infantry and themselves;[63] forming up the craft into two divisions, running in at 10 knots with 35

16.1.41

soldiers apiece sitting on the low benches waiting for the ramp to drop.[238] The beaches were totally unsuitable for landing troops, being steep-to and rocky, but the soldiers carried out some very spectacular exercises; climbing over the surrounding mountains at all times of the day and night, finding their way over difficult and dangerous country by map and compass – often soaking wet and nearly frozen stiff with the cold. Occasional tots of navy rum kept up their really magnificent morale.[124] It was not the first time in their history they had combined with the Navy, and they were proud of this fact. They were a good bunch; the ship liked working with them and made some good friends.[85]

The Norfolks left at 0900 on the 21st, sailing for Greenock in *t.s.s. King George V*.[245] It had been mostly night boat work with long hours for the upper deck crowd,[124] but the engine room had not been much affected; the ratings even managed to play a game of football. Surg.-Lieut. Tait was co-opted to make up the numbers, and felt suitably honoured.[136] Some familiarity with the licensed premises of Inveraray was also gained about this time.[124] 21.1.41

The 2nd Bn. the Hampshire Regt. arrived by road from Dalmally but had time to carry out only one day's landing exercises before *Glenearn* was ordered to proceed to Greenock; there the infantry disembarked, to return to their winter training area in the south.[244] *Glenearn* sailed to Dalmuir to correct minor defects.[61] 22.1.41 24.1.41

The ship's company were allowed weekend leave to Glasgow. Many sneaked on to trains for their homes farther away; Sub.-Lieut. Scott had a wretched journey dogged by bad luck, arriving in Birmingham about eight hours late and in the middle of an air-raid. He had to walk the eight miles to his home and reached there just in time to have breakfast before catching the next bus to town and the train back to Glasgow.[124] Lieut. (E) Aiken, whose home was there, was more fortunate; he spent his time improvising a shelter in the cellar for the raids yet to come. Shortly before leaving on what was likely to be some desperate venture he took his 11-year-old son aside, then going down on one knee placed on the boy the responsibility for looking after the rest of the family while his father was away.[2]

30.1.41   From Dalmuir to Greenock. *Glenearn* anchored off the Tail of the Bank while 750 passengers,[223] mostly Army drafts,[61] but including a few naval officers and a lower deck naval draft of 240, embarked.[46] Tropical gear came aboard along with other stores,[136] so it was figured that they were bound for

31.1.41   some foreign climate.[90] Next day the ship passed the boom across the Clyde and steamed to Lamlash[46] where *Glengyle* and *Glenroy* were still taking on stores for 7, 8 and 11 Commandos.[223] Eighteen officers, mostly from 11th Scottish Commando, were transferred to *Glenearn* for accommodation.[231] All three ships – now known as Force "Z" – topped up with water.[223]

A disagreement broke out among the three Captains over who was rightfully Senior Officer of Force "Z".[119] Although Sir James Paget, Bt., of *Glenroy* had been specifically mentioned in the Admiralty message of 22nd January,[223] both he and Hill of *Glenearn* were retired Captains RN recalled to duty.[119] Petrie of *Glengyle* had been retired with the rank of Commander more than ten years before the outbreak of war[299] – however, officers re-employed from the Retired List had no seniority.[46] *HMS Glengyle* had commissioned first,[610] but Petrie her second captain had been appointed last.[231]

In the resulting confusion Colonel R. E. Laycock, the senior military officer, embarked in *Glenroy* under the impression that he was on the flagship, but in the event Captain Petrie's claims carried the day. Commander I. C. Robertson, RN, who had some experience of staff work, was appointed, "... to *HMS Glengyle* for passage and for staff duties with Senior Officer Force 'Z'."[119] Of the three ships *Glenearn*'s position was in least doubt; by all the criteria except moral stature of captains, she was the junior[A] – although one of her passengers was convinced that Hill should have been commodore by virtue of his initial standing highest in the alphabet.[46]

At 1650 the cruiser *Kenya* arrived in the anchorage. The

slow process of preparing to sail continued. Some time after dark the pom pom crews closed up, then an hour before midnight the signal "stand by engines" was rung down to the engine room. The anchor was raised, wet and dripping. Both engines went slow ahead. Clear of the Lamlash boom, course was set 147°, the destroyer escort met[172] and the convoy proceeded down the Clyde estuary at 15 knots.[173] Although the time spent on combined operations training – "confused operations" – had generally been enjoyed, most of Glenearn's ship's company were glad to get away.[63]

1.2.41

*　　*　　*

While wardroom vocalists harmonized on the attributes of the barmaid at the inn at Inveraray,[124] the Director of Combined Operations was posting off letters about the breaking up of his commando force into two parts, each too weak to take a decisive part in operations either east or west of Malta. To Churchill, pleading with him to stop the Glen ships now that the Naval Staff had recommended a plan to raid Sardinia;[217] to the Chiefs of Staffs Committee suggesting that the three Glens should be berthed alongside at Cape Town and the whole of 11 Commando transferred to Glenearn, so that ships and soldiers would arrive in the Mediterranean ready for immediate service – having by Admiralty instruction been denied direct access to information about the sailing of Force "Z", he had assumed that to transport three Commandos in three identical ships one unit would have been allocated to each. Not so. No. 11 Commando had been divided between Glengyle and Glenroy; crowded into these two ships, separated from any landing craft that might carry them to an enemy shore.[231]

All these efforts were in vain. The Joint Planning Staff, having frustrated WORKSHOP, turned their attention to the arrangements for TRUCK. They declared that the forces allocated were unsuitable for both an unopposed occupation and an operation to eject the Germans from the Azores; concluding that the project should be cancelled. Operation WORKSHOP was not formally cancelled; it just faded away.*[230]

* On the 11th June 1943, after heavy air and sea bombardments, the island of Pantellaria was assaulted by British amphibious forces. As the landing craft headed for the shore white flags appeared and the garrison surrendered.[R]

CHAPTER 6

A WORLD FAR APART

Force "Z", consisting of *Glengyle, Glenroy* and *Glenearn*, [198] was accompanied by the cruiser *Kenya*[198] and an anti-submarine escort of four destroyers of the 5th Destroyer Flotilla:[223] HM Canadian Ships *Restigouche, Ottawa, St. Laurent* and *Skeena*.[198] The order to sail had come long before *Glenearn*'s men were properly trained as a cohesive unit. Sailing with other ships and keeping station with them was a new experience for most of the ship's company; made somewhat easier as the three identical vessels, by making similar propeller revolutions, sailed at almost the same speeds.

However, as they steamed north-west up the Irish Sea the weather deteriorated and they ran into the "father and mother" of a gale;[124] wind force 8–9 from the north-west.[173] Quite a lot of damage was done to the landing craft when their receiving gear proved faulty,[61] and some of the naval passengers spent a horrible night wrestling with cables and shores, helping the crew to lash the craft more securely; to prevent them breaking away from their davits again. Some of the davits themselves almost carried away, but no boats were lost.[46]

Glenearn's paravanes had already carried away, to the relief of Lieutenant-Commander Hood.[63] Some gear in the steering compartment came adrift and put the telemotor gear for the rudder out of action for several hours. As a result, the ship had to be steered by the engines; not easy in a rough sea while zig-zagging.[61]

The ship's corkscrew motion continued all day;[71] *Glengyle* and *Glenroy* were both pitching a third of their lengths clear and *Glenearn* must have been doing the same.[63] Sea-sickness was rife. Most of the troops were very ill indeed, as were more than half the ship's company. Conditions on the troop decks were appalling, with the soldiers too unwell to clear up after themselves and the situation deteriorating.[124]

South-west of Skerryvore the convoy was joined by the Cunard White Star *m.v. Georgic*.[223] At the height of the weather daylight could be seen under the keel of the 28,000-ton liner as far aft as the foremast.[46] In the afternoon several slight changes of course were made, until the convoy was heading due west, straight out into the Atlantic.[173]

2.2.41 During the night the wind moderated,[61] and daylight on the Sunday brought calmer and warmer weather.[71] Normal ship-board life returned.[124] The destroyers parted company at noon to meet *HMS Furious* and escort her to the Clyde,[223] and shortly after this a "Lerwick" flying boat was sighted in

3.2.41 the north. In the early hours of the morning the convoy had to avoid a hospital ship, then, having reached a distance of 600 miles from the Irish coast, course was changed for Freetown.[173] While Force "Z" headed south,[198] *Georgic* departed for a separate destination.[223]

Before long all hands recovered and discipline was restored; the Army doing physical training and sharing lookout duties with the sailors, while the ship's company were kept busy with gun-drill, fire-drill, and night action stations as well as the normal daily tasks[124] – also brought to the point of resignation from the Service by the skirl of bagpipes.[X]

5.2.41 The three ships advanced in various formations, and carried out signal exercises with *HMS Kenya*. One afternoon the Azores were sighted in the west, and *Glenearn* was given a turn as guide of the fleet.[173] While thus temporary commodore the signal was made to *Glengyle*, "You are steering an erratic course. Please endeavour to keep station." To this lunge came the riposte, "Authorised Version, Matthew XV, 14." *Glenearn*'s chaplain had only the Revised Version, but a scurry among the passengers produced the key. The text was, "Let them alone: they be blind leaders of the blind. And if the blind lead the blind both shall fall into the ditch."[46]

6.2.41 With *Glengyle* once more guide of the fleet and guns crews closed up it was signalled that gun practice would be carried out;[173] each ship firing successively at a smoke-float dropped from *Kenya*. When *Glenearn*'s turn finally came the target was almost two miles distant, but the starboard 12-pdr. sank it with one shot over open sights. It was a one in a million chance, but no one would ever convince that gun crew that it was anything other than sheer good gunnery, and the enemy had better watch out.[124]

In contrast to the first few days, the voyage had become something of a pleasure-cruise;[71] at least for the officers. With more time to get together in the ward-room, Captain Hill spent as much time as possible with them.[124] It became his custom, too, to invite different ones each evening to his cabin for dinner – a nice gesture, which gave the medical officers, and others who did not come into contact with him too often, a chance to meet and get to know him. Evenings otherwise were spent in the ward-room; tombola was organised by "Guns" – L. W. Fulford, RN – with great success.[136]

The commissioned naval passengers were a mixed a bag of RN recalled from retirement, RNR and RNVR. Of the soldiers, Captain Fleming of the Guards was the most impressive; a dark retiring man, he kept company mostly with a few other Guards officers who set themselves rather apart from the common people. The only naval type who frequented the Guards' circle was a junior deck officer with an aristocratic title.[46] Peter Fleming had travelled through foreign lands in great discomfort and occasional danger, subsequently writing best-selling books about his adventures.[A] In one of these, "News from Tartary", he had complained that he knew only one game of patience and did not particularly like it; *Glenearn*'s 2nd Engineer took an opportunity and taught him another.[1] Fleming organized a series of talks in the anteroom during the dog watches, but did not give one himself.[46]

At 0645 on the 7th a convoy appeared on the starboard beam, and three hours later Force "Z" was joined by *HMS Dorsetshire*; at the same time as two other cruisers *Devonshire* and *Norfolk* were sighted carrying out a search for a disguised merchant raider.[198] Next afternoon *Dorsetshire*'s aircraft, a "Walrus" amphibian, carried out a dummy dive-bombing attack on the ships of the Force.

One morning the destroyers *Forester* and *Faulkner* turned

7.2.41

8.2.41

9.2.41

up to escort[173] the Glen ships to Freetown, Sierra Leone –
"The White Man's Grave".[71] A full day's steaming before the
buoy marking the outer end of the swept channel was sighted

10.2.41   at 0915, and 40 minutes later land appeared on the port bow.
After passing through the Freetown Gate the ships dropped
anchor. In the hours that followed there was much activity:
oilers and waterboats came alongside, postmen left for the
shore.[173] Some of *Glenearn's* passengers left too.[47] Natives in
canoes came out yelling things like, "What about a Glesca
tanner?" while another played "South of the Border" on a
mouth-organ.*[114] There was to be no shore leave, but the
lights of Freetown were entertainment enough after 18
months of "the blackout".[579]

11.2.41   Force "Z" weighed anchors early in the morning and, after
passing the boom,[173] took up line ahead formation
accompanied by *Dorsetshire*, with *Faulkner* and *Forester* as
local escort.[198] After reducing to 7 knots to put out paravanes
– where available – speed was worked up to 17 knots; later they
started zig-zagging. At 2000 the starboard destroyer reported an
undersea contact, and went off to investigate. Twenty minutes of
suspense before it was decided that whatever had causes the echo
in the Asdic receiver was not a U-boat.

12.2.41   Half an hour before midnight clocks were put forward 30
minutes, and two hours and ten minutes into a new local day
a darkened ship was sighted bearing 205°. *Dorsetshire* went to
investigate. Star shells were fired over the stranger, and a
searchlight, among other things, trained on her. She spoke: a
merchantman bound for Freetown from Cape Town.

13.2.41   Force "Z" crossed The Line in the early hours of the
13th.[173] On board *Glenearn* there was no official ceremony,[46]
but the "Freedom of the Seas" was conferred upon initiates in
the form of an illuminated scroll, signed and sealed by both
Davy Jones and King Neptune.[2] The equatorial latitude was
reflected in the weather; at times the engine room was almost
unbearable.[71]

15.2.41   Every unknown ship was investigated by *Dorsetshire* or by
her aircraft,[173] and an exercise was carried out simulating an

* Based on a later visit of *m.v. Stirling Castle* on 4th April 1941.[114]

attack by enemy surface craft, with the Force breaking formation and retiring behind a smoke screen laid by the cruiser.

It was estimated that Cape Town would be reached on the morning of the 19th; everyone was eagerly looking forward to going ashore.[71] Several vessels, some showing lights, were sighted ahead as the searched channel was approached. The Glen ships anchored briefly in the harbour – Table Bay – awaiting the arrival of the pilots, but by 9 o'clock *Glenearn* had entered the basin and secured a berth in Capetown Docks.[173] During the next two days her davits were straightened and strengthened,[46] the landing craft repaired,[61] and new paravane gear brought on board.[63]

19.2.41

Throughout the short stay libertymen were allowed ashore at various times throughout the afternoons and evenings.[173] Cape Town was a beautiful place. After dark it was ablaze with lights and neon signs: so strange after leaving the home country in darkness. Cape Town's white people were largely of Dutch extraction, and very hospitable. Some of the younger officers went to a roadhouse called "The Blue Moon" for an evening's dancing.[71]

All too soon came the order to prepare for leaving harbour. At 0845 the pilot came aboard, and after a short delay while the tug was made fast, the ship was pulled round and out of the basin.[173] After dropping the pilot Force "Z" formed line ahead with *Dorsetshire* following,[198] and set course for the Indian Ocean.[71] For the remainder of that day they stayed within sight of land, and were briefly covered by an Avro "Anson" aircraft; *Dorsetshire* investigated the few ships encountered. With the coming of daylight there was sighting after sighting: one the Japanese *Kano Maru*, another a Jugoslav merchantman. An "Anson" accompanied the Force again as they sailed along close to the coast after rounding the Cape.[173]

21.2.41

22.2.41

Sensation![71] Following a raider report from a Dutch ship being attacked at the northern end of the Mozambique Channel[R] the cruiser *Glasgow*'s aircraft[170] had sighted the German pocket-battleship *Admiral Scheer*.[71] Within hours, an aircraft carrier, three heavy cruisers and two light cruisers were converging on *HMS Glasgow*, and the Admiralty released other warships from escort duties to join in the hunt for the raider.[R] At 0300 *HMS Dorsetshire* left on the orders of the Commander-in-Chief East Indies; Force "Z" was ordered to proceed unescorted to Durban.[198] On board *Glenearn* the reaction to the last piece of news was a rush for clean "bib and tucker" in case of shore leave.[85] At 1430 a wireless message from *Dorsetshire* ordered the Force not to enter Durban, but to rendezvous in 28°S 34°E. Disregarding this the squadron pressed on, and two hours later were off Durban in visual communication with the shore.[198] The three ships slowly circled round in full view of the port[85] while cypher messages were received;[173] with a German commerce raider loose in the Indian Ocean, for once no one complained at having to take a turn on cypher watch.[46]

By 1830 a message from the Commander-in-Chief Mediterranean had been received from the shore signal station, and a reply from the Senior Officer Force "Z" passed for onward transmission. The decyphered orders[198] confirmed that they would sail without escort,[71] and so at 2000,[173] after three full circles,[85] the squadron set course 049°, and proceeded at 18 knots;[173] the lower deck concluding that the three Glenships were being used as decoys.[127] On board *Glenearn* Captain Hill held a discussion on defence. With her three 12-pounders – one said to bear the date 1896 – and a few 0.5″ machine guns against the 11-inch armament of *Admiral Scheer*, any resistance would be merely a gesture.[46]

At 0520 the masts of a warship appeared over the horizon, but she was soon identified as *Dorsetshire*.[173] It was learned that *HMS Glasgow*'s aircraft had not regained contact with the enemy ship, which had disappeared into the broad expanse of the Indian Ocean. The two cruisers had broken off the search, and the other ships engaged in the hunt had dispersed, back to their various duties.[71]

During the next few days *Glenearn* carried out gun trials. *Dorsetshire*'s "Walrus" made dive-bombing practice,[173] and exercised dropping a message on *Glengyle*; the latter's machine gunners fired at sharks for want of better targets.[71] The cruiser kept in station except when investigating the occasional unknown ship on the horizon.

On the morning of the 28th the ship sighted bearing 060° turned out to be *HMS Glasgow*.[173] This cruiser had been hit by two torpedoes from Italian 'planes in December 1940 and had lost one propeller, but could still manage about 25 knots on one engine.[63] *Glasgow* took station 3 miles ahead of the convoy, with *Dorsetshire* another 5 miles beyond; the former's colours were half-masted for an hour in the late afternoon when the funeral took place of a stoker.[170]

28.2.41

The heat was killing as the Equator was recrossed. They were now off the coast of Italian Somaliland, or what was left of it,[71] so there was a possible danger of bombing. Aircraft lookouts were posted[579] – although the Italian colony was being rapidly overrun by Imperial forces; mainly white South Africans and African native troops. Mogadishu, the capital and seaport, had been occupied only a few days previously.[R]

1.3.41

Early next morning *HMS Glasgow* turned away into the rising sun, then opened fire with her main armament at *Dorsetshire* – but with a 6° throw off ahead – for practice.[171] Later, as the sun was setting, the County Class cruiser, Force "Z"'s faithful protector, parted company for service elsewhere.

2.3.41

Land sighted on the starboard bow[174] proved to be Socotra Island, said to be the last resort of the world's cannibals. Thus out-posted, the Gulf of Aden was entered; another corner turned on the long trail winding to war.[71] *Glasgow* tried to fly her kite target for *Glenearn*'s high-angle guns, but it would not fly until it was towed across wind.[171] A day later, with *Glengyle* heading the line the other two ships carried out gun trials. Whilst the firing was in progress the Force was joined by the destroyer *Kandahar* overtaking at high speed, and within the hour by the sloop *Flamingo* approaching from the starboard quarter.[174] After the completion of the firing practice, the convoy ran into a school of porpoises leaping out of the water in their thousands.

3.3.41

4.3.41

The day turned into a dismal afternoon, with peasoup fog.[71] Paravanes were put out, and speed increased to 17 knots, with *Glenearn* in station 3 cables astern of *Glengyle*. During the night they passed through the Straits of Bab-el-Mandeb into the Red Sea,[174] which was bounded on one side by the enemy coast of Eritrea. At the port of Massawa ahead there were several Italian submarines and destroyers, which could be a serious danger – if they ever came out. Even so, to someone with training in submarines the constant zig-zagging seemed a pretty useless manoeuvre.[63]

During the voyage there had been the usual run of mild cases on the daily sick report; also an acute appendicitis, on which the doctors had operated successfully.[136] But the heat was illness enough.[A] In the tropics even a makeshift swimming pool was considered a great idea; a canvas contraption held in place by ropes and things, it obviously had its inspiration in the engine room department where working conditions were worst. The pool was enjoyed by all who could get into it, even when the canvas sprang a small leak. But the leak became a rent, and the canvas burst asunder; the resulting tidal wave carrying with it all who happened to be in it at the time, together with others who were asleep or reading on deck. Fortunately no one was swept overboard.

With the demise of the swimming pool the only entertainment left was the gramophone which the younger members of the ward-room still played with interminable enthusiasm. "Begin the Beguine" was heard so often that one evening the First Lieutenant – Venables – strode in with, "How the hell can you chaps listen to such drivel?"[136] The pleasure cruise had turned into a long, weary trip.[124]

Endless days of zig-zagging up the Red Sea, with little to break the monotony or punctuate the slowly passing hours: a hospital ship to starboard, a light to port. Another hospital ship. Land on the starboard beam. An island to port, a light to port. Another light to port, another. Alteration of course to pass the swept channel buoy. Alter course, alter course. Slow both. Alter course, alter course. 10 knots. Alter course, alter course; half astern both. Let go starboard anchor. Cable secured.[174] The long voyage was over; Force "Z" had reached Suez.

The anchorage was so full of shipping that *Glenearn* had had to anchor in a prohibited area[61] about three miles off-shore.[71] Darkness fell. Over on *Glengyle* Captain Petrie prepared his "Report of Proceedings of Force 'Z'". As the distance run – 12,860 miles – was totted up, the average speed through the water – 16.9 knots – worked out, and the average fuel consumption – 1.88 tons per hour – checked,[198] his off-duty subordinates and the passengers got together for a sing-song. The voices of men singing carried over the water, to be answered by Australian soldiers on a troopship not far away.[71]

On board *Glenearn* the voyage was already slipping into the past, a little Odyssey about to be over-shadowed by the demands of war,[A] but always to be associated – by some – with a vocal setting of Chopin's Waltz in C sharp Minor, Opus 62, No. 2. In retrospect, it seemed to have been on the gramophone every time one went into the anteroom:[46]

> So deep is the night
> No moon tonight
> No friendly star
> To guide me with its light
> Be still my heart
> Silent lest my love should be returning
> From a world far apart.*

* For details of copyright see Appendix B.

CHAPTER 7

TWO BLOCKS OFF BARDIA

8.3.41   After a lazy day lying at anchor,[71] the Glen ships moved to a safer anchorage at Ras Baku Rock, 80 miles from Suez.[174] It was an awful place – nothing but sand as far as the eye could see.[71] The Germans had been making nightly air attacks,[124] dropping mines in the Canal,[63] and sunken ships had kept it closed since the 15th February.[R] Force "Z" would just have to wait.

10.3.41   Not long as it transpired. Shortly after midnight anchors were aweigh, paravanes streamed and course set for Suez; *Glenearn* and *Glenroy* keeping station on *Glengyle*. Between No. 1 and No. 4 Buoys they stopped to await the Canal pilots.[174] Then, although she was the junior ship, *Glenearn* was ordered to go first; a rare honour that some found wryly amusing.[63] So *Glenearn* passed the breakwater and entered the Canal.[174]

On the banks were Egyptian soldiers and, at intervals, RAF lads manning the balloon barrage.[71] Anti-aircraft defences consisted of an assortment of weapons, the most spectacular being a rocket which paid out a length of thin wire and a parachute; the idea being that the rocket carried the parachute end to a considerable height, and the enemy 'planes got caught in the wire. There were no signs of any crashed aeroplanes, but plenty of wire drooping about.[124]

Ahead appeared the funnel and bridge[71] of the *Aghios Georgios*.[285] The sunken Greek ship narrowed the passage so much that there was barely room to squeeze through; the buoy marking the wreck was only about 6 feet clear of *Glenearn*'s side. And so into the Bitter Lakes;[61] by midmorning they were secured to a buoy off Kabrit.

In the afternoon a small party of high-ranking officers boarded *Glengyle*. Shortly after their departure there was an air raid warning, and the guns crews closed up for three-quarters of an hour. Later the three ships got under way and

Also by Alex. Aiken:

COURAGE PAST

The Glasgow Highlanders (9th Bn. H.L.I.) at High Wood, July, 1916; an incident in the Battle of the Somme. Compiled from survivors' accounts and contemporary documents.

159 pp, 10 pp photographs, 1 map.   ISBN 0 9502134 0 3.

"... somewhat amorphous and disjointed ..." Times Literary Supplement.

"... unpolished in places ..." Glasgow Herald.

"... leaves something to be desired ..." College Courant.

"... amazed at the fidelity ..." Walter Pryde, DCM.

"... how you express my own thoughts ..." T.M.G. Robertson.

"That is what it was like ..." C.E. Carrington, MC.

<u>Courage Past</u> was published by the author, and is priced at £4 (post free).

48, Merrycrest Avenue,

passed into the Great Bitter Lake, anchoring a mile off Fanara in 5 fathoms of water. There the pilots left.[174]

On the shore opposite there was a prisoner of war camp, said to contain 52,000 Italians captured during the recent desert campaign; after dusk the whole place was lit up like a town pre-war. In the early morning German 'planes dropped four bombs not far away, apparently in an attempt to hit the RAF aerodrome.[71] During the day the hands were employed de-storing ship. MLCs and ALCs were hoisted out, and disembarkation of the military began.[174] The commando passengers went first, and were landed at Geneifa;[579] from there making their way to Kabrit where a Combined Training Centre had been set up.[239]

11.3.41

For the next day or two, apart from landing craft exercises in the forenoons, there was not much activity.[174] However, in the afternoon of the 13th a naval draft left for Alexandria. Whilst they were waiting for the train at Fayid Station, warning was received that General Wavell was coming. After quickly tidying up the immediate area the draft fell in, and the officer in charge – Sub-Lieut. G. I. Finkel RNVR – contrived to delay the Commander-in-Chief Middle East and the Chief of the Imperial General Staff while one of the signallers flagged a message to the ships telling of the unexpected visitors. The improvised formalities were spun out until the landing craft arrived, and the great soldier[46] – whose force equivalent to two divisions had totally destroyed an army of ten[R] – was taken out with his staff and his guest to inspect *Glengyle*.[46]

13.3.41

At 0800 a sandstorm warning was received, after some of the landing craft had left for exercises. The wind at this point was from the north, Force 2, and the sea calm. By 1200 it was blowing from the SSE Force 6, and the waves were 34 feet high. With engines at "stand by",[174] an anchor watch set and the cable veered out *Glenearn* awaited the return of her craft through the foul weather lashed up on the lake. There were some narrow escapes amongst the landing craft and their crews, but in a way it was good experience for boats crews who were getting really skilled at their work.[124]

14.3.41

This terrible sandstorm continued,[71] with the wind

reaching Force 7 between 1800 and 2000.[174] Everything, even indoors, was covered with sand[71] by 2200 when the sandstorm blew itself out.[174] To add to the misery, the BBC's Overseas Service announced that a mass air-raid on Clydeside had taken place; everyone from that airt was worried about their folks at home.[71] In the days that followed some of these doubts were resolved – by cablegram.[1]

17.3.41   Monday, 17th March 1941. Combined operations training began, with the Glen ships embarking the battalions of 22 Infantry Brigade of 6 Infantry Division.[239] *Glenearn*'s assault landing craft proceeded inshore and returned with men of the 2nd Battalion Scots Guards.[63] Military boat stations, with the ALCs circling the ship before being re-hoisted, were exercised by day and by night. There then followed a complete landing from ship to shore and an attack.[174] The Scots Guards were most impressive,[85] and not just for their superb physique. Their discipline was incredible; not a sound or whisper in the darkness and the bitter cold.[63]

For their part the ship's company where shaping up quite well too. Hoisting out an LCM required the use of a 50-ton main derrick. Four guy winches had to be manned, as well as the topping lift and main purchase winches. None of the winchmen had ever been to sea before, and if any Chief Officer in the Merchant Navy had been asked to hoist out a 30-ton load, of awkward size and shape, in silence in the dark with boys off the street on the main derrick winches, he would have said it was impossible. But Captain Hill, who was a real sailor, had said that the officer in charge would have to trust his winchmen, and eventually they had become a good team.

While this heavy landing craft was being unloaded by the forward main derrick, Captain Hill noticed that the main sheave at the top was not turning. Lieut.-Com. Hood, RNR, was in charge, and had the sheave taken down – it had jammed, and the bush was ruined. The warrant shipwright, whose responsibility it was, said, "That's a shipyard job." But there was no shipyard. Without the derrick one of the two LCMs could not be operated and the efficiency of the ship would be seriously reduced.

Lieut. (E) Aiken said that if a piece of brass could be found it could be turned to fit. There was nothing on *Glenearn*, and indeed there did not seem to be a piece that size in Egypt. Having always had faith in the ability of marine engineers to mend and make do, Hood persuaded the Captain to let the Chief and Second Engineers look around. The latter suggested *HMS Illustrious* which was not very far off, waiting to go south through the Canal once it had been cleared of mines.[63] The aircraft carrier had been badly damaged in the Mediterranean, although judging by appearances was very little the worse for her experiences.[71] *Glenearn*'s deck officer did not know exactly what was required, so the engineer went over.[63] *Illustrious* had been hit by six bombs and suffered three near-misses while covering convoy EXCESS in the previous January.[R]

Aiken returned with a piece of phosphor-bronze of about the right size from their stores. Junior engineers then took over and turned it down, shaped it, cut the grooves, drilled holes and then fitted the new bearing. The whole business had taken several days, and the willing way the whole engineering department, from Lieut.-Com. (E) Cahy downwards, turned to and helped was a revelation to some of the naval men. Yet the senior RNR hands, who were all in the 35–45 age group, felt very old comparing themselves to the boys in the landing craft.

The Scots Guards departed fit, keen and perfectly disciplined,[63] to be replaced by 3rd Battalion Coldstream Guards cast in the same mould;[244] the only difference being that whereas the Scots Guards had previously been deployed on mine-watching duties along the Canal,[63] the Coldstreams had fought in the Western Desert culminating in the Battle of Sidi Barrani and "about five acres of captured officers and two hundred acres of other ranks".[569]

Having already had a few days' training from *Glenroy* the Guards embarked on *Glenearn* and went straight into full-scale landing exercises; by day then in a night operation.[246] This could have been the very dark night when one of the LCMs gently grounded on a sand-bar in the tideless lake, and

26.3.41
27.3.41

the craft commander, thinking he was on the beach, gave the order to lower the ramp. The Bren gun carrier then drove off and into eight or ten feet of water.

Another night operation was that carried out on Sub.-Lieut. de Kock's finger, after it was crushed between his ALC and the side of the ship. Only the tip of one finger was involved, and it was successfully amputated by Surg.-Lieut. Tait, RCNVR.[136]

29.3.41 After their strenuous course of training the Guards returned to Kabrit Camp.[246] For the ship's company it had been wearing work, because they had the ship to run during the day and boat work all night. All the soldiers had been very keen, but they had only had a week of it, while the sailors could see themselves doing it for months.[63] The strain was beginning to tell, and the weakest showed it most; the day the last Guardsman left *Glenearn* Lord Livingstone of Guernsey,* serving as a landing craft officer, was court-martialled for sleeping on watch after a party, and dismissed his ship.[71]

With the completion of training of what had become 22 Guards Brigade[599] there was a pause in the proceedings and the ship's company relaxed while they could.^ Someone had a thing called an "aqua-plane" on which one could be towed behind an ALC. Permission was asked of the Captain, who seemed interested – so much so that he even appeared on deck in a black and white striped bathing suit left over from a silent film. He made a few turns around the ship then said, "Carry on, chaps – have a good day," and returned to his quarters.

Another popular officer was Lieut.-Com. J. W. Best, RNR, who was in charge of the ALC crews. He was very fond of fishing, and whenever he got the chance he would have a line out. Of course, eventually the inevitable catch was an old shoe tied on by some rating. So all things considered *Glenearn* was a very happy ship.[136]

Glengyle and *Glenroy* had already sailed further through the Canal to the town of Ismailia for four days' leave apiece, and now† it was the turn of the junior ship.[174] Just before entering

* Title changed.
† About 31.3.41.

Lake Timsah they passed the *s.s. Ranee*, which had been mined and sunk in a very awkward position, partially blocking the fairway,[71] but by dredging and pulling the wreck to one side a passage had been cleared.

Glenearn anchored in Lake Timsah off Ismailia, and each watch got 48-hours' leave.[63] Ashore it was quite nice, with coffee at "The Copper Kettle",[114] afternoon tea at the Greek Club and dinner at the French Club; finishing off the evening at a cinema.[71]

Some of the officers went to Cairo, a distance of over 100 miles taking $3\frac{1}{2}$ hours in the train. Lunch at Shepherd's Hotel and from there by car to the Pyramids; then by camel to the Sphinx where photographs were taken. Back to the Great Pyramid of Cheops and a strenuous half-hour's climbing the seemingly endless steps inside to see the Pharaoh's tomb. A visit to Cairo Zoo and a perfect if tiring day was rounded off at one of the better Egyptian cabarets, even if no word spoken or sung were understandable. After a night at the Victoria Hotel a day of sight-seeing, visiting the native bazaars, the old mosques and the museum, before entraining for Ismailia, and so back to the ship.[71]

When *Glenearn*'s company had started their well-earned rest the war picture of Africa had been very bright indeed: Admiral Cunningham had just sunk three Italian heavy cruisers and two destroyers in a night encounter off Cape Matapan. On land the desert flank in Cyrenaica had been quiet for weeks, but in Eritrea Imperial troops were advancing on the capital Asmara, while in Abyssinia Italian resistance had been brushed aside in the race to Addis Ababa.[446] However, in a few short days the situation had changed crucially. German troops had appeared in Libya and the British were in rapid retreat;[448] Benghazi had been evacuated.[449] In the Balkans tension between Germany and Jugoslavia was growing.[447]

In *Glenearn*'s absence the training of 16 Inf. Bde. had begun with the 1st Bn. Argyll and Sutherland Highlanders split between *Glengyle* and *Glenroy*.[247] The Argylls were under the impression that they were training for the invasion of

Sicily,[580] although detachments of the brigade artillery and the Bren carriers had been withdrawn for handing over to 22 Gds. Bde.[247] It was also said that General Wavell had been back again and there was something in the wind; the state of affairs in Libya could mean action soon for the Glen ships.[71]

On *Glenearn*'s arrival at Fanara *Glengyle* returned the Support Landing Craft and the crew that had been victualled by the senior vessel for the preceding few days and sailed for Ismailia again,[175] leaving the two junior ships to take on the 2nd Bn. Leicestershire Regiment between them. *HQ, B* and *D* Companies were brought out by ALC and MLC at 1345, but about 5 o'clock orders were received cancelling the training; so after tea on board ship the Leicesters climbed down into a tank landing craft bound for Kabrit Point.[248]

7.4.41

News of the day was that Jugoslavia and Greece had been invaded on the 6th, and that British, Australian and New Zealand troops had been on Greek soil for some time.[450]

Through to Lake Timsah again; there the second half of *Glengyle*'s libertymen had been recalled from as far away as Cairo and were fully expecting to sail into action at any time.[71] Stores, equipment and soldiers were embarked[85] on the morning of the 8th, *Glenearn* getting the 11th Commando – now redesignated "C" Battalion of "Layforce".[579] So the ships waited at the ready, fully loaded with troops, for word to move; it was rumoured that they were bound for Greece.[71] Twenty-four hours later they were still waiting to start their first real job.[85]

8.4.41

Eventually in the early afternoon anchors were weighed, engines made slow ahead and Force "Z" entered the Canal. With the ships gliding along at a steady 10 knots progress was measured by the railway stations on the bank of the long straight waterway. Then the town of El Qantara drew abeam, followed by more desert. Only one other ship was seen: the *s.s. Rinda*, and Port Said was reached about 1800.

9.4.41

Next day was one of daily harbour routine, with store boats coming alongside, comings and goings to and from the shore and shore leave for naval and military alike.[175] For the former it was typical matelot stuff ashore: sight-seeing, buying souvenirs, bartering with the Arabs, getting drunk.[114]

Good Friday was given over to Sunday routine,[175] with still no sign of a move; by Saturday night the permitted pleasures of Port Said were beginning to pall.[71] Easter Sunday and Holy Communion; Roman Catholics went ashore with the postman, while for the Protestants it was "Hands to Divisions" and the military to church. At 1650 the special sea duty men closed up and 40 minutes later the ships passed the breakwater at 15 knots. Speed was reduced for paravanes to be streamed and about 15 miles out from the coast course was set 326°. Force "Z" zig-zagged towards the setting sun.

11.4.41

13.4.41

Morning found the Force outside the naval base of Alexandria. After passing the boom the ships anchored in the outer harbour awaiting tugs;[175] by nightfall they were made fast to buoys amidst the battleships *Warspite*, *Barham*, *Valiant* and the new aircraft carrier *Formidable*, all of which had taken part in the recent destruction of the Italian Navy. In *Glenearn* excitement mounted, as rumour was followed by counter-rumour.[71]

14.4.41

Next morning before 9 o'clock, boats came alongside and all the stores, equipment and troops were taken off.[175] Bemused sailors barely had time to read their first letters from home[71] before the soldiers were brought back again. That night, as a succession of store boats, lighters, oilers and finally ammunition ships came alongside,[175] it was announced that they would sail in the early hours of the morning with ships of the Mediterranean Fleet. For action.[71]

15.4.41

The whole of *Glenearn*'s company were at concert pitch, and ready to carry out whatever task was in store.[124] Shortly before 0100 the hands were called, special sea duty men closed up and the gangway hoisted. *Glenearn* and *Glengyle* slipped their buoys and passed through the gate[175] on their way to an unknown destination.[71] With an escort consisting of the anti-aircraft cruiser *Carlisle*[279] and the Australian destroyers *Stuart*, *Voyager* and *Waterhen*[236] the landing ships sailed westwards along the Libyan coast at full speed,[280] slowing

16.4.41

down only momentarily at 0630 to take in paravanes before resuming their zig-zag course.[175]

The morning hours passed with practice "Action Stations",[71] gunnery trials, and the sinking of a floating mine by *HMAS Stuart*. Throughout the day there were air-raid alerts, and at 1112 a 'plane was actually sighted on the starboard beam. Warnings continued almost at hourly intervals;[175] it was obvious the force was being shadowed.[85] At 1905 a ship was sighted bearing 210°; this turned out to be a *Seine*-class tug.[175]

Throughout the afternoon the weather had been deteriorating;[124] by sunset the seas were rising and falling 24 feet.[175] It was obvious that the landing craft would not stand any chance of putting the troops ashore. Indeed, it was unlikely that the craft could even be lowered without capsizing.[124] At 1955 course was altered to 090°,[175] and it was a rather disheartened crew that retraced its route back to Alexandria.[124]

By 1410 on the 17th April *Glenearn* was back at her buoy. Later the stores, troops and equipment were disembarked;[175] the third time this sort of thing had happened in little over a week. Things were being said that could not be placed on record, and a notice appeared briefly on the notice-board echoing Winston Churchill's words, "Never in the field of human conflict have so many been '- - - -' about by so few."[85] The lower deck was "two blocks", "chocker", "chock-a-block", and just plain fed up.[114]

From the peak of excitement the pace of life on board changed back to the organized boredom of harbour routine. Out in that harbour other ships went about their business. *Warspite*, *Valiant*, *Barham* and *Formidable* left; *Glenroy* 19.4.41 shifted her berth. At 0240 *Glengyle* weighed anchor and sailed[175] with the cruiser *Coventry* and the same destroyer escort as before,[233] but *Glenearn* was left behind – two ships must have been considered one too many.[61]

20.4.41 Late on the 20th, the force returned,[175] having raided Bardia on the Libyan coast. The town and the immediate area around it had been found to be unoccupied, but after a dump of old motor car tyres had been set alight[236] two enemy motor-cyclists had come along to see what was wrong. Instead of firing at them a sentry had challenged; whereupon they turned around and drove off. A grenade thrown after them wounded two commandos. One officer was shot through the eye by another sentry for saying, "It's only me" instead of giving the password. One landing craft could not find the beach; another found the beach but could not find *Glengyle*.*[63] About forty-five soldiers had been left ashore and one damaged ALC had been destroyed.[236] The men who had taken part in the raid,[579] and some who had not,[63] looked upon it as something of a fiasco, and there was general disappointment.[579]

The shot commando officer died in the morning and his funeral took place in the afternoon with full military and naval honours. It was an impressive sight, with the large party of soldiers and sailors leading the cortege to the British Cemetery in Alexandria,[71] but well might the humble seaman on *Glenearn*,[A] as he turned back to his painting,[175] sing his contemporary sea-shanty: 21.4.41

"Roll on the *Nelson*, the *Hood* and *Renown*, this one-funnelled bastard is getting me down."[114]

A Note on Chapter 7

The training in combined operations of 6 Inf. Div.[239] at the time gave the impression that the target was Sicily, and objectives on the south-east coast of that island were actually allotted.[580] This was a cover-plan to conceal the real objective, which was Rhodes.[239] A plan to capture and hold the island was first asked for by the Prime Minister on 30th October 1940. On the 21st December the Chiefs of Staff sent a cypher telegram to the C-in-C Middle East requesting him to prepare alternative plans for the capture of the Dodecanese (a) with the forces and craft then available, (b) with the addition of two Glen ships, their landing craft and two special service battalions.[226]

* Because of a faulty compass. It sailed to Tobruk harbour.[236]

The Prime Minister's instructions to the Foreign Minister on his mission to Egypt dated 12th February 1941 included the admonition that the operation should be carried out at the earliest possible moment, including, if necessary, the re-loading of the Commandos at Cape Town, ready for an opposed landing.[570]

Because of the German intervention in Libya, the decision to postpone the landing was taken by General Wavell on the 3rd or 4th of April.[R]

Churchill's directive of 14th April to the Chiefs of Staff stressed the importance of raiding the coastal road between Tripoli and Agheila using forces landed from the Glen ships,[571] but El Agheila is more than 48 hours' steaming from Alexandria; most of it parallel to an enemy-held shore line. The raid on Bardia was perhaps the most that could be attempted with a fair chance of survival for the ships taking part, and this would explain the sudden return of the troops on 15th April. But the reason for "Force Z's" earlier move from Ismailia to Alexandria remains shrouded in the fog of war.[A]

CHAPTER 8

"WHOOPS, CHAPS!"

A peaceful strand. The hot Egyptian sun blazes down from 21.4.41 a cloudless sky upon the magnificent anchorage, creating an atmosphere of serenity and tranquility. Dotted about the water are grey-painted ships: stationary, immobile. In the foreground a group of naval officers are spending a lazy day on the beach, sunbathing. Late afternoon gives way to early evening before they feel obliged to pack up and make their way back.

On coming aboard they are told that all further leave is cancelled; the ship is under sailing orders. "Buzzes" are flying around, giving speculated destinations for and purposes to the imminent venture. Later, all are put out of their uncertainty when it is announced that they are sailing the following day for the island of Crete. This is greeted with approval, even enthusiasm. Youthful memories are ransacked for something of the island's history, other than the vague recollection that it had some importance to the ancient Greeks and Romans.[136] Of mainland Greece the general knowledge is more immediate: the military situation is serious, and thousands of colonial – no, Commonwealth – troops have to be evacuated.[71]

At 1340 Convoy "AG 13", consisting of the three Glen ships 22.4.41 and the Store Carrier *HMS Ulster Prince*, sails.[168] *Glenroy*, not affected by the recent comings and goings, leads the way out of the harbour, followed by *Glenearn*. *Glengyle*,[63] slipping from the quay where she has been disembarking troops,[175] brings up the rear. Outside the harbour a dredger is working in the main channel as *Glenroy* turns and heads out the North Pass, a way not used by big ships.[63]

At 1425[175] Captain Hill notices that he is overhauling the leading ship. When he sees mud coming up from *Glenroy*'s propellers he says, "I don't like this, pilot. Full astern, both."[63] A light from *Glenroy* flashes that she is aground; *Glenearn*, still going full astern, starts signalling to *Glengyle*.[85] *Glenearn* backs out, turns, goes past the dredger and so out to sea.[63] Thus, before even leaving port, one of the ships is already out of action; this can only mean more work for the others.[71] Quick thinking by a real sailor had saved *Glenearn*.[63]

Course was set, and the three surviving transports took up line ahead, with *Glengyle* leading and *Ulster Prince* bringing up the rear;[175] the escort consisted of the destroyers *HMAS Stuart* and *Voyager* and the cruiser *HMS Phoebe*.[593] In the early evening *Calcutta* was sighted overhauling on the starboard quarter; thereafter the anti-aircraft cruiser kept company with the convoy. The only other vessel seen was a hospital ship coming the opposite way, after dark.

23.4.41   In the morning *Phoebe* parted company. Good progress was made, with nothing larger than a rowing boat to record before land was sighted bearing 072° in 1754. There were a couple of distant aircraft sightings before sunset, and at 2058 a submarine contact was reported by *Stuart* – the ships went to "Action Stations" for the best part of quarter of an hour – before Suda Bay was entered an hour before midnight. At

24.4.41   0001 the first of three booms was passed.[175] The entrance was not easy, as the light buoys all had different characteristics from those laid down in the sailing instructions, and there were two merchant vessels in the channel at the entrance gate. After the convoy had entered harbour the destroyers patrolled outside for a while before anchoring, then the naval base settled down for the night.[61]

Judging from a shipside view, Crete seemed a lovely place.[71] Suda Bay was an excellent harbour sheltered by high hills – but it was difficult to admire the scenery in a state of high excitement. Nearly everyone had some idea of what might lie ahead: the troops in Greece had been driven down to the sea, and the betting was odds-on *Glenearn*'s having some part in the rescuing of them.[136] Another reminder of the war was the 8-inch cruiser *York*, severely damaged by an Italian explosive motor-boat,[R] and now being tended by the salvage ship *Protector*.[63]

While the hands were at breakfast[175] there was a "Red"

warning lasting 15 minutes.[168] The ship sailed at 0905. An hour later *Glenearn* was in station with *Glengyle* to starboard and *Ulster Prince* astern; *HMS Calcutta* following *Glengyle*.[175] The convoy's escort had been strengthened by two of the new "corvettes" *Salvia* and *Hyacinth*.[593] At 1152 while still in sight of land, five aircraft were sighted in the direction of Suda Bay, but they did not close.[168]

Glenearn's three doctors were busy putting the finishing touches to their arrangements for handling the large numbers of wounded anticipated. Besides the Sick Bay with its eighteen cots and the two Medical Distributing Centres below the main deck, the Chief Petty Officers' and Petty Officers' Messes had been cleared out, to be used solely for stretcher cases. As far as possible, everything and everybody was ready for any emergency.[136]

On sailed the force; morning gave way to afternoon. At 1450 *Voyager* made a submarine contact on the starboard side and charged over to deal with it; twenty-five minutes of activity and three patterns of depth charges later[175] the destroyer hurried on after the others, but with no definite results.[280] The "buzz" was that 17 survivors had been picked up.*[71]

Off Phalconera Island[61] at 1703 the convoy divided. *Calcutta*, *Glengyle* and *Salvia* setting course for Porto Raphtis whilst *Glenearn*, *Ulster Prince* with *Stuart*, *Voyager* and *Hyacinth* went on to Nauplia.[593] The weather was Mediterranean at its best: brilliant sunshine, no cloud and the temperature just right – for a holiday.[85] Visibility was 7 to 8 miles, and as the ships were standing towards the coast of Greece,[61] some of the individuals on deck were admiring the distant scenery.[136]

Everything was very peaceful, so, knowing that he would get no sleep that night, Captain Hill went down to his cabin for a short snooze.[61] *Glenearn* chugged along doing $15\frac{1}{2}$ knots on a course of 283°, the steady beat of her diesels reverberating in the funnel;[200] from the bridge the noise was

---

* No enemy submarine was lost on 24 April, 1941.[R]

like that of an aeroplane.[63] Three-quarters of an hour after retiring, the Captain was rudely awakened.[61]

1742   First indication that anything was wrong was a roaring sound, coupled with machine gun fire. Everyone on deck ducked instinctively; at the same time the alarm buzzer for "Action Stations" went off.[136] It took several seconds to realize that they were being dive-bombed, and very competently.[85] The bombs – three of them – burst close astern.[200] Then and then only was the aircraft seen;[199] it was a Junkers 88, a twin-engined bomber.[177] He had made a very good dive, right out of the sun.[200]

There was a sudden scamper to put on tin hats and "rubber tyres", then to get to battle stations.[136] Captain Hill was fully dressed, so it did not take him long to get on the bridge; just in time to put the ship hard a-starboard for the second 'plane's attack. This one too did a very good dive, and although he could be heard, could not be seen.[61] His bombs were released at about 1200 feet on a line 20° off to port and were meant to straddle the ship's bow.[200] Captain Hill could see that four of them would miss, but the last one looked dangerous.[61]

Lieut.-Com. Hood had reached the 12-pounder on the forecastle* and the gun's crew were climbing into the platform
1747   when the bomb burst just below them – 20 feet away at most. It had hit the forecastle just before the windlass, penetrating the deck on the port side and exploding in the Paint Store.[63] The port anchor and hawse pipe vanished, taking part of the side plating with them; the compartments in the vicinity caught fire.[199] Two of the gun's crew who were late in reaching their station were wounded, and a piece of the cable compressor, weighing about 100 lbs. landed inside the gun platform just beside Lieut.-Com. Hood.[63] It had been quite a small bomb, weighing about 150 lb.[200]

The pilot had pulled out of his dive about 700 feet up;† a few rounds were fired after his retreating shape by *Glenearn*'s close-range weapons,[200] while *Stuart* and *Voyager* hotly engaged him. At the same time the cruiser *Phoebe*,

* "A" Gun.
† See photograph No. 8.

approaching the convoy from the south, opened fire from 8 miles away on the other bomber circling the convoy.[177] One of the 'planes left the scene emitting a lot of smoke, but nevertheless the quite extensive barrage put up by the ships had not seemed to cause the enemy fliers much concern.[124]

The terrific crash forward had shaken the ship from stem to stern; everyone exclaimed in effect, "Whoops chaps! We've caught one".[136] A not-too-near-miss on the starboard side amidship had rattled the engine room and put a few splinters through the superstructure, and the machine gun attack had made a few more holes in diverse places, but done little or no real damage.[85]

While efforts were being made to put the fire out two smoke floats went off in the forecastle; the damage control parties were driven back by the choking fumes[63] until the Captain turned the ship downwind and stopped.[61] The rest of the convoy went on, but *HMS Phoebe* stayed and covered *Glenearn* whilst the fire was brought under control.[177] Lieut.-Com. Hood was laid out by the fumes and dragged to the Sick Bay where he soon recovered. It was necessary to decide whether to flood the forward magazine, and Lieutenant Peters was sent to find out;[63] he had to climb down a long trunkway from which smoke was issuing.[85] Having made his inspection he managed to climb back up and was pulled out semi-conscious.[63] As a precaution the magazine was flooded.[61] After about half an hour the two ships went on again.[177]

1845

Apart from the two or three people partially suffocated by the smoke,[136] four ratings had been wounded but none dangerously;[199] all had badly lacerated scalps and faces from flying splinters, and one had a fractured femur. These cases were promptly treated by the medical staff.[136] But the material damage was serious enough: the electric windlass was completely out of action, they had only one anchor left – and no way of recovering if once they dropped it. Hill and Hood discussed what to do at Nauplia – they would have to anchor, and this meant they would have to slip.[63] The starboard gypsy was still able to turn, and the magnetic brake which took control if power failed the windlass was still intact, so the remaining anchor could be dropped successfully.[85] Hood said he could slip the anchor from the compressor bar; the Captain was doubtful, but left it to his confident subordinate.[63]

Accompanied by the cruiser,[177] *Glenearn* went full speed ahead for the Gulf of Nauplia.[61] At 1955 the hands went to dusk "Action Stations", and less than an hour later they were entering Nauplia Bay.[177] Captain Hill had intended to go in very close to save boat work, but there was a burning wreck in the way, so he stopped two miles out. When their anchor went down they were only about half an hour late.[61] All the landing craft were at once sent in to the harbour;[199] Admiral Cunningham had signalled that the object of the evacuation was to embark men, if possible with arms, but no material was to take precedence to men.[375]

There was no moon, and the only light came from ships burning in the harbour and from fires ashore.[85] Out there in the darkness were thousands of men who had waited among the olive groves for up to three days[15] watching the German Air Force bombing and machine-gunning everything at their leisure: ships off-shore, "Hurricane" fighters on the aerodrome, houses on the hillside. Now the troops, having wrecked their surviving transport, were making their way on foot, some in twos and threes,[157] some in parties of twenty-five or so[15] – some RAF types swinging along in column of threes[157] – down to the town where the naval beach master had organized three inevitably slow-moving queues leading to quayside and beach.[15] *Glenearn*'s landing craft embarked personnel from both places.[15,99]

The laden craft chugged off into the blackness until the dark mass of the parent ship loomed out of the night. By the flickering light some of the passengers noticed the jagged hole at the bow,[142] before their attention was concentrated on the square aperture in the ship's side with short wooden ladders fitted below it – the soldiers were told to throw their rifles up first, then, standing on the gunwhale, jump for a ladder as the craft lifted on a wave.[157] This experience was rather unnerving for some non-sailors, and a few nearly came to

(margin notes: 1955, 2045, 2155)

THE FIFTH *GLENEARN*
2. 29th June, 1938.

THE LAST
3. Taken in June, 1972.

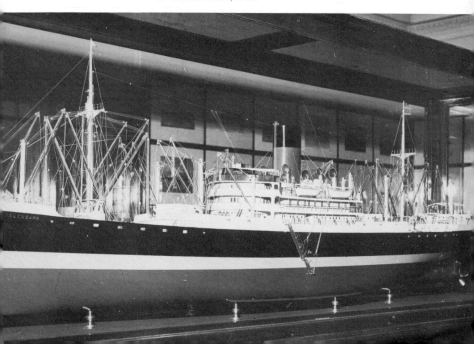

LANDING CRAFT CARRIER
4. Loch Fyne, January, 1941.

HEAVY CRUISER
5. *HMS Glasgow* off Durban, April, 1941.

WRECK OF THE *RANEE*
6. Suez Canal about 31st March, 1941.

ANTI-AIRCRAFT CRUISER
7. *HMS Coventry* at Alexandria.

THE BOMB ON THE BOW

8. As seen from *HMAS Stuart*.

9. Surface damage.

25th APRIL, 1941

10. Centrecastle starboard side.

11. Hoisting out an MLC, Suda Bay. *HMAS Voyager* beyond.

14th JULY, 1941

12. *Georgic* aground. Taken from *Glenearn*.

13. *Glenearn* aground. Sub.-Lieut. Scott on the forecastle head. Taken from *HMAS Hobart*.

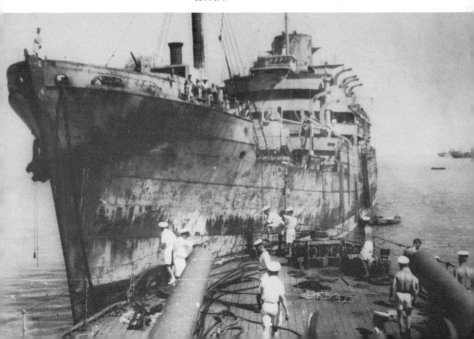

HMS GLEN,
14. 22nd October

ROYAL NAVAL RESERVISTS

15. Lieut. P. W. Scott and Lieut.-Com. T. Hood.

16. Lieut.-Com. J. W. Best.

HOLT'S MEN

17. Sub-Lieut. (E) McKenzie, RNVR.

18. Lieutenant (E) Aiken, RNR.

grief,[142] but all were grabbed by the cheerful bluejackets and bundled unceremoniously inside.[157] Others had used rope-ladders to climb aboard.[48]

Everything was functioning very smoothly,[61] and the harbour seemed to be alive with craft and small boats.[85] Then *HMS Hyacinth*, passing up the port side too close to *Glenearn* rammed ALC No. 9, which capsized and sank.[199] The soldiers, thrown into the water wearing heavy equipment and still clutching their weapons, had little chance on their own.[85] Two of *Glenearn*'s sub-lieutenants released a Carley float apiece, then dived in after them and helped one soldier after another to safety.[124] In this way many, but not all, were saved. After the two rescuers had returned on board they were sent for by the Captain and reprimanded for leaving their posts.[85] It was made very clear that they were doing more good ensuring the safety of the many who were already on board, than by attempting to save a few who had failed to make it. Thus the hard face of discipline;[124] but after the event, unspoken the lasting regret for the poor fellows who were drowned.[61]

An "A" lighter, or tank landing craft, which had been hiding somewhere during the day, was also present, but arrived late and took a long time even to partially fill up and clear the harbour; its trips to *Glenearn* were few and far between.*[199] Whereas *Glenearn* had anchored some distance out, *Ulster Prince* the fast Irish Channel steamer, had been ordered to embark her troops from the stone quay at Nauplia. Watching her approach through the haze of smoke were medical officers and other male personnel of 2/6th Australian General Hospital A.I.F. About 200 feet from the quay *Ulster Prince* stopped moving; she had run aground.† The doctors were ordered to throw their surviving pieces of first aid, blood transfusion and specialised neurosurgical equipment into the water and take to the landing craft. By the time they arrived on board *Glenearn* it was about 0100 on 25th April – Anzac Day. If 25th April 1915, had been the birth of the Australian

25.4.41

---

* Only two between 2230 and 0330.[199]
† Having already been aground from 2125 to 2207 at the head of the Bay.[279]

Imperial Force at Gallipoli, April 25, 1941, seemed like the death of it.[99]

The night seemed endless. Troops were crowded into every conceivable part of the ship:[124] mess decks were filled with sleeping men sitting on benches with their heads and arms resting on the tables, while others had squeezed into spaces on the deck between the legs of tables and men alike.[157] Many of the passengers were reluctant to go below, and had to be persuaded to clear the upper decks sufficiently to enable the sailors to fight ship on the voyage back to Crete.[124] In this way some were pushed down into the bowels of the ship;[15] even into the magazines.[124]

Army officers filled all the cabins; the Captain's had two brigadiers and three colonels in it.[61] One of the latter, after dumping his gear on the bunk had gone down to the Sick Bay where an operating theatre had been set up.[99] The ship's medical department found itself with over 200 wounded men, and were wondering how they would ever get these sorted out and dealt with.[136]

Captain Hill's orders were to leave by 0330 so as to be clear by daylight, but by 0230 the congestion on board was so great that he was compelled to stop embarking troops.[199] Landing craft were hoisted, and the space between the forward MLCs promptly filled by soldiers.[48] The numbers on board totalled about 5,100 including 30 cot cases of wounded, two German prisoners[199] and a female night-club entertainer from Athens smuggled aboard by a war correspondent.[556] Units represented included ANZAC Corps Headquarters, 6 Australian Div HQ, the 4th Survey Regiment, 16th Heavy Anti-Aircraft Battery and some base details;[573] also a small detachment of Royal Engineers, who earlier had refused a flight to safety in a "Sunderland" flying boat, in order to carry on with the task of ferrying casualties of the afternoon's air raid. In addition to wounded personnel,[79a] the Royal Air Force was represented by ground staff of Nos. 11[157] and 80 Squadrons.[48]

0315   About 0315 the anchor cable was cut through with an oxy-acetylene burner,[85] and the blacksmith ordered to hit the compressor bar with the heaviest hammer in the ship. The 2-

ft. by 5-inch square bar of steel flew up on its hinge, and the cable disappeared down the hawse pipe, to join the anchor on the bottom of Nauplia Bay. They were off.[63]

Glenearn sailed, followed by the cruiser *Phoebe*.[177] After leaving Nauplia Lieut.-Com. Hood left a sub-lieutenant to take the bridge until dawn. The former had offered his bunk to an army captain who would not take it, but had accepted the settee. Before taking over the bridge again at breakfast time Hood put another army man in the bunk, and loaned him a razor and towel.[63] All the soldiers wanted to do was sleep, and they slept[85] – or dozed fitfully,[157] depending on the relative comfort of their surroundings. 0335

The Sick Bay was full of wounded from recent bombings ashore, and men suffering from lung and abdominal blast injuries sustained in the water after their ship had been sunk. R. A. Money, Commanding Officer of an Australian Hospital Unit and a surgeon himself, assisted the Naval surgeons until about 0600, when he returned to the Captain's quarters to find[99] Brigadier E. F. Herring, CRA of 6 Australian Division and Brigadier C. S. Steele, CRE of 1st Australian Corps[283] sitting up on chairs in the day cabin and the bunk still unoccupied. Money, a mere lieutenant-colonel, turned in and slept.[99]

Others were beginning to stir. By about 0800 some of the deck passengers were awake and wandering about the ship.[157] They were all desperately hungry,[15] but the Accountant Staff had risen to the occasion.[61] Some half-dozen Soyer stoves appeared on deck and, depending on which queue were joined,[15] imperturbable sailors served out breakfast sausage,[157] hot soup[48] and the most delicious stew the customers had ever tasted; the tin hats the last item was served into may have had something to do with it.[15]

The other half of the evacuation fleet had been first sighted at 0740;[168] *Glengyle* had come through unscathed with more than 5,000 troops on board. Now it was a race to Crete.[71] *Calcutta* took up station on the port beam of the combined convoy,[170] and *Phoebe* on the starboard.[177] Shortly before 0900 the "Action Stations" sounded, and a few minutes later 0901 the escort opened fire on two Ju 88's, but no attack developed.[279] By 0916 it was "All Clear" again.[175]

Although the soldiers were exhausted by their experiences,[124] and spent their spare time lying somnolently in passages and between life rafts,[157] they were a fine lot – mostly Anzacs – and still full of fight.[61] And they had come off to the ship with all the arms and equipment that they could carry.[124] Despite their fatigue and lack of sleep the troops rallied every time an aircraft came near: grabbing their rifles, Bren guns or whatever they had, to fire into the sky in a magnificent display of fighting spirit in adversity.[136]

1157

Calcutta opened fire on three aircraft,[165] and minutes later one of the Junkers 88's attacked *Glengyle* from dead ahead, dropping three bombs which missed by 50 yards.[175] Then it was *Glenearn*'s turn.[61] Three 'planes came over close together. The ship's armament of 12-pounders, single pom-poms and Hotchkiss machine-guns made quite a racket on their own, but to which was added about fifty Bren guns manned by the troops.[142] All kinds of small – and some not so small[48] – arms were being fired, from riflemen lined up along the deck[15] – others sitting, some lying on their backs, cursing and swearing at Gerry all the while[136] – to Australians firing anti-tank rifles held braced against the ship's superstructure[48] and Seaman Shaw manning a 0.5-inch machine-gun on the Support Landing Craft, when he should have been down below with the damage control parties.[127] Everyone on board seemed to loose off at the enemy, and some in *Glenearn* feared for those in *Glengyle*.[63]

When two of the 'planes went on to shoot down the third[48] it was realized that the former were short-nosed "Blenheim" fighters of the RAF,[157] but the lads had fired at the lot.[61] After this excitement things quietened down.[A]

As senior medical officer on board, Lieutenant-Colonel Money had called a conference of all the doctors to organise the care of the wounded and the sick.[99] As a result of this team effort involving nearly twelve hours of operating,[61] every casualty had been treated. There had been two deaths: a young RAF lad with a penetrating chest wound and a sudden reactionary haemothorax; the other a Greek soldier. A hasty post mortem examination confirmed extensive lung and abdominal blast injuries.[99]

A Petty Officer was detailed to sew up the corpses in canvas; he was not very happy about the assignment, but when offered a tot of rum for each one, ended up going around asking if there were any more to do.[124] As the force neared the swept channel leading to Suda Bay *Glenearn*'s colours were half-masted and the dead committed with due ceremony to the deep.

The convoy ceased zig-zagging, and the ships formed single line ahead to enter harbour *HMS Phoebe* leading.[168] *Glenearn* arrived at 1640[199] but could not anchor,[124] as the spare was being saved for one last emergency,[85] so the troops were disembarked while the ship manoeuvred in the harbour.[124] As men were climbing into the boats a Cockney voice was heard saying, "Any more for the Skylark?" "Round the battleship twopence." There were many grateful expressions in the faces turned up from the craft as they left the ship's side, causing a surge of pride in navy men lining the rail.[136] The army "captain" who had shared Lieut.-Com. Hood's accommodation turned out to be a full colonel; Hood had been rather rude to him.[63]

Casualties were taken off from 2030 onwards;[99] – some wounded Aussies from their barge singing, "Oh, I do like to be beside the seaside"[136] – and the disembarkation completed by 0100.[199] The ship was in a mess: the decks littered with the refuse of the departed troops, and small arms ammunition left all over the place.[124] In a fix too was the medical department; they had used up practically all their supplies – what was to be done for the next batch of wounded was the problem. However, they could at least get things cleaned up in the meantime.[136]

One of the "Blenheim" fighters had had to crash-land with a damaged undercarriage, so the shooting must have been fairly good. *Glenearn* remained under way all night, moving now and then to keep clear of the beach. No one got more than a little sleep,[61] and it was a very weary ship's company

1640

2030

26.4.41

0700   that sailed[124] with *Glengyle* escorted by *Calcutta* and the destroyers *Stuart, Diamond* and *Griffin*. This time they knew what to expect.[61] As they set off for Greece again Sub-Lieutenant (E) McKenzie, for one, was convinced that this time the ship would be sunk.[85]

CHAPTER 9

MR. HOLT'S HAWSER

In the early afternoon of 26th April, 1941, a hundred miles or so north of Suda Bay,[175] a great concourse of shipping was dividing itself into several separate convoys, in preparation for the forthcoming night's work. All told, there were eight transports, eleven destroyers and two anti-aircraft cruisers, as well as three cruisers of the battle-fleet.[593]

On their way to this concentration area the Glen ships had passed a south-bound convoy returning troop-laden from the mainland.[71] It had been under air attack at the time, but the only involvement in this action had been when *Calcutta* had opened fire on a single Messerschmitt 110. Now, having approached – indeed passed – the area of assembly, they stopped zig-zagging and formed line ahead before turning to a southerly course.

When just about to join up with a group of six merchantmen, the buzzers sounded "Action Stations". As this combined convoy altered course to 120° two Ju 88's appeared in the sky to the NNW and were engaged by *Carlisle*.[168] The force divided, *Glengyle* and another ship being led away to the NNE by *Carlisle*[175] whereas *Glenearn* with the two merchant ships *Slamat* and *Khedive Ismail* followed *Calcutta* southwest, before taking a more westerly course once clear of the area.[168] Their destroyer escort consisted of *Diamond*, *Griffin*, *Hotspur* and *Isis*.[593]

Later, *HMS Isis* opened fire on a Junkers 88 away to the north-west, and minutes afterwards another was seen in the same sector. As course was being changed to 340° the corvette *Salvia* was sighted bearing 250°, and a few miles further on a ship, apparently on fire, was passed to westwards.[168] *Glenearn*'s destination was again Nauplia, but this time more care had been taken over the choice of course; they were now keeping in fairly close to the coast of Morea, in the hope of avoiding detection.[61] Nevertheless the speed of the convoy was under 12 knots;[168] they were "just asking for it". How the lack of *Glenroy* was cursed![63]

An afternoon of red warnings[61] stemming from *Calcutta*'s radio direction finding equipment was added to the experiences of the previous day;[63] some of those in *Glenearn* were getting a bit "jittery". However, it had turned into a quiet enough day, and now the sun full on the port beam was beginning to dip towards the horizon; perhaps they were going to be lucky after all. Then the alarm went off.

The gun's crews had been closed up all day; now the remainder of the ship's company are all at their posts.[136] There is the usual awful pause; everybody waiting for something to happen, and feeling more and more apprehensive.[63] As the stomach sinks and the skin shrinks, the brain repeats a random phrase, or a snatch of tune, as if one's life depends on it; another's brave attempt at humour fails to register and disappears without trace. Time stands still.[A]

The "Huns" came over very high and not in the sun;[61] there were about twelve of them. All the ships were ready as the planes came right overhead;[63] then down they came.[61] A good barrage.[63] Aircraft engines in crescendo, guns firing, shells bursting, the shriek of a falling bomb through the pumping of pom-poms and the rattle of a Lewis gun; a shattering detonation. Then, without stopping, the mad music repeats itself. In some ways it was worst for those down below with no job yet to do – with the unholy row going on up top the suspense was terrible; one began to wish they could be hit somewhere and so put an end to it.[136]

The attackers were Messerschmitt 109's with yellow noses,* each carrying one bomb of about 500 lb.,[63] and they came in two waves.[168] It was not a very determined attack, as the gunfire appeared to upset the pilots. They came in over the starboard side and from astern, releasing their bombs at about 2,500 feet.[200] There were bombs all over the place;[61] one near miss on the port side blew splinters upwards through the side-plating of the engine room.[85]

Glenearn's engines had been put to "full ahead both" as part

1825

* *Calcutta*'s log says nine Ju 88's and 87's.

of her avoiding action,[200] and on the bridge Captain Hill – called "The Tiger" when out of earshot[63] – had a signalman whose sole job was to watch the fall of the bombs and call out where he thought each one was heading.[136]

After a hectic five minutes the first attack was over. Then the second wave broke formation and it all began again.[168]   1830
One plane dived on the starboard bow[63] – the pilot could be seen hunched up in his cockpit[1] – and released his bomb at about 200 feet, but missed by a hundred yards. Another dived, but they were ready for him. The pom-poms held their fire on the "Tiger's" personal orders; when they did open up, the bursts were right in front of him – he pulled up and did not come back. One aircraft seemed to be doing a pointless figure of eight over the convoy, but he attracted much of the AA fire.[63]

By 1837 the attack was over. *Slamat* and *Khedive Ismail*   1837
had, like *Glenearn* been only slightly damaged.[168] It was a moment for profound relief, a feeling of corporate pride and even for a little, honest self-satisfaction; they had survived.[A]

No one noticed until *Calcutta* opened fire.[168] The 'plane   1844
carried out a beautiful vertical dive...[61] the bomb sounded like an express train as it came down...[63] the signalman stood frozen and speechless...it seemed to be heading straight down the funnel...[136] just missed the heads of those on the bridge...an officer flattened himself against the armour plating...[63] it fell ten feet from the starboard side just abaft the bridge,[200] to burst under water.[61]

The ship staggered with the shock[63] and lurched to port,[85] taking a $10°$ list[61] and remaining over. Down in the engine room the main injection pipe-casting fractured and fell away; a solid jet of water about $24'' \times 18''$ in cross-section poured in, with the green light of a Mediterranean day shining through it.[85] *Glenearn* began to settle.[136] The Chief Engineer went up to the bridge to say that the engine room was flooding and the engines would soon be stopped.[63]

Captain Hill had all the boats turned out in case the list became worse; a risky order had discipline been less than perfect. As it was, there was no sign of panic, although three men who had been in the ship just two days tried to get into them; they were promptly hooked out again.[61] The senior officer of the convoy in *Calcutta* signalled to prepare to abandon ship,[63] and there were those on board who thought, "Here's where we swim for it,"[136] then, looking at Greece 12 miles away said, "I can't swim *that* far."[63] The Captain to the Chief Engineer, "Will she float, Jim?"* "Yes."[85] So the Tiger replied to the signal, refusing to abandon ship, "My ship will float and can be towed." So another signal was made for *Griffin* to take *Glenearn* in tow, while the rest of the convoy would go on.[63]

About twenty minutes after the bombing the ship had righted herself and there was time to look around. She had settled by the stern and gone down 10 feet, but appeared to be fairly comfortable and was not going to sink,[61] so that was something to be thankful for; they could only pray that Gerry would not come back and finish them off as they lay floating idly on the ocean.[136] They were really almost helpless: with the engines stopped, all the lights had gone out[61] – but the emergency lighting came on, and was quite effective.[136] As all the cooling was electric, however, there was none now.[61] Amazingly enough, there had been only one casualty; a rating with a piece of shrapnel in his buttocks.[136] The only disgraceful incident to come to light was that the ward-room wine store had been broken into – apparently when the "Abandon Ship" signal had been received, and a lot of bottles were going about; the Warrant Shipwright was blamed, but nothing could be proved.[63]

Griffin closed to take *Glenearn* in tow.[76] Lieut.-Com. Hood and Sub-Lieut. P. W. Scott were responsible for preparing and making fast the tow; it was going to be no easy task with no electrical power to assist them.[124] Two shackles of anchor cable had been pulled out of the locker to be used in lieu of an anchor at Nauplia, and Hood wanted to use this for towing, but against his better judgement allowed the 1st Lieutenant to cut it away with an oxy-acetylene burner and let it go overboard. It was proposed to use *Griffin*'s $3\frac{1}{2}''$ wire,† which

---

* Name changed.   † Rope is measured by circumference.

Hood doubted would be strong enough,[63] but the light wire would get the tow started quickly.[61]

Two more shackles of anchor cable were pulled out and the end passed to *Griffin*.[63] Meanwhile temporary leads were run out from the emergency dynamo to the steering gear, and by 2000 *Griffin* and *Glenearn* had got going. All went well but slowly;[76] *Glenearn*, although very deep, was soon moving through the water. By nightfall they were doing nearly 7 knots in the direction of Crete.[63] Then the emergency generator broke down.[199]

2000

2040

Glenearn sheered off;[76] the hand-powered pump was connected, but with the freshening breeze *Griffin* could not hold the ship to her course,[199] and they had to stop while the dynamo was repaired.[61] While they were waiting Captain Hill decided to send off the boats to assist with the evacuation from Monemvasia further down the coast.[63] It was known that orders had been issued directing all tank landing craft there for an operation the following night, and he judged it best to send his ALCs away at this juncture; before the wind rose any more, and while the ship was stopped anyway.

Ten ALCs were lowered by gravity.[199] The weather had deteriorated and some had difficulty in unhooking. Lieut.-Com. Best and his crews waved their goodbyes as they crashed away; the hollow thumps of their flat bottoms against the waves could be heard long after the darkness had closed around them.[85] They had twenty-six miles to go, and no one expected to see them again.[63] *Glenearn* was left with only some rafts if she sank, but with the destroyer there it would be all right.[61]

2100

Half an hour after the landing craft had left the emergency generator was working again,[199] and after some tricky manoeuvres *Griffin* got clear.[76] They started off again. In the dark it was difficult to watch the direction of the towing hawser,[61] and *Glenearn* was pretty low in the water;[76] the destroyer went too fast and the tow parted.[61]

2130

2140

Now they would just have to get out their own wire, which had not been used as it was very difficult to handle, and it would take some time. The anchor cable was hanging over the

bow and could not be pulled up again, so two more shackles*
were cut away[63] and some more cable got up to connect to
Mr. Holt's special towing wire.[76] This was the largest anyone
had ever seen, and it was believed that all the Alfred Holt
ships carried one. The huge 7" steel wire rope[63] – all 130
fathoms of it had to be flaked out on the fore well deck along
a narrow passageway obstructed by shrouds for the foremast,
by paravane gear and a winch.[199] There was also the hole in
the forecastle. All the work was done without lights and in
perfect silence, which pleased the Captain.[61]

While the wire was being prepared *Griffin* steamed around
in case there were any outside interference. Impromptu
prayers were offered up that there would not be any,[76] and a
momentarily unemployed engineer watching the struggle
going on below commented, "I hope they get it on before
daybreak or we will be a sitting duck."[136]

27.4.41
0030   It took three hours to get ready, which was really very
good,[61] and the tricky job of passing the new tow began.
Griffin manoeuvred her stern immediately under *Glenearn's*
bow,[76] one end of the hawser was shackled to the cable, and
the other lowered over the bow to the stern of the destroyer. It
was so black that nothing could be seen below; when word
was passed that a 7" wire was coming down there was an
awed, "Christ" from the darkness.[63] Thanks to God the eye of
the wire fitted over *Griffin's* towing slip, and the sea was
calm.[76] Lieut.-Com. Hood's men tried to ease out the enormous wire, but the last bight took charge of itself and roared
along the fore deck, up the ladder and out into the night amid
a shower of sparks. Nothing had carried away, and no one
was hurt.[63] Two shackles of cable were eased out, and
0150   *Glenearn* was in tow again by 0150.[199]

Griffin soon had them moving, gingerly at first,[76] but as all
went well speed was gradually worked up until $8\frac{1}{2}$ knots were
being made good;[61] they managed to keep going in spite of
the wind and sea getting up a bit,[76] if with occasional anxious
moments as the great wire tightened into a steel bar. Came the

---

* A shackle of anchor cable is 15 fathoms – 90 feet – long.

dawn and they were still doing well. *Griffin*'s stern was nearly under water, and it was a marvel that her towing slip stood the strain.[63]

But at dawn too, a Hun reconnaissance plane came over and they all thought that this was the end;[61] now they could expect to be blasted out of the water at any moment.[136] But no bombs followed.[61] A convoy from Greece only a few miles away was attacked,[136] but Gerry left them alone,[199] and at 1230 they reached Kisamo Bay at the north-west corner of Crete.[76] Tow-er and towed hove to.

During the passage water had been leaking into No. 5A Hold abaft the engine room, and gaining.[199] It was thought that this could be due to rivet holes in the flooded shaft tunnels; and it was also considered possible that the bilge suction line was not shut off where it passed through the after engine bulkhead. Captain Hill had orders to continue the tow, but as the water was still coming in he replied that he did not think it was safe to go on until his engineers had had time to try and control the leak. The emergency generator had not been thought equal to running a pump as well as supplying power to the steering gear.[61]

As soon as the ship had stopped, hand steering was again connected and the bilge pump started. No. 5A Hold was cleared,[199] and after stopping a leaking rivet or two,[61] no more water came in. The water in the shaft tunnels started to drop and the position was stabilized with a draught forward of 24' and aft 30'-6";[199] the precious emergency generator then managed to work a pump as well as the steering gear.

Captain Hill held a short thanksgiving service[61] acknowledging that although some intervention by the German Air Force had been awaited since dawn, none had come.[76] He also made a speech to the ship's company.[61] *Glenearn*'s crew, with the exception of a towing party, the engineers and the guns' crews, were to be transferred to *Griffin* and then put ashore.[85] None of them wanted to leave; the Chief Steward locked himself in a cabin and only came out when the 1st Lieutenant threatened to shoot through the door.[63] The Master at Arms went along to the Captain's cabin and asked

1230

to see him for a moment, to say that this was the happiest ship he had ever been in.[61]

Meanwhile the sloop *HMS Grimsby* had arrived,[199] and she came alongside *Griffin* to take over the tow,[76] but in doing so got it jammed in a gap in the towing horse, could not turn, got abaft *Glenearn*'s beam and both vessels started to drift across the bay towards the rocks. However, *Griffin*, alongside to take off all the spare men, used her engines and saved the day once more.[61]

Bag and baggage were piled aboard the destroyer;[136] also 150 of *Glenearn*'s complement.[375] 90 were left on board. Now the helpless vessel had to be turned at rest to point seawards. For about two hours the struggle continued. Eventually, having lost most of her fenders and received a goodly number of dents in her foc'sle *Griffin* had *Glenearn* ready to go. Captain Hill gave Lieut.-Com. Lee-Barber, RN, of *Griffin* a large box of Panatellas, and then the destroyer steamed away,[76] her decks crowded with men waving adieu, for they would probably never see their old ship again.[61] The sound of their cheering rang across the water.[85]

1910   The tow sailed at 1910, still with no enemy interference.[199] There was a bit of a wind and sea, and the sloop was rather small for the job as *Glenearn* was now displacing 17,000 tons, 28.4.41   but she did very well.[61] When dawn broke next day Crete was 1000   still on the port side.[85] At 1000, off Gavdo Island, a single bomber made a level attack at medium height.[199] Not being very fond of anti-aircraft fire he did not do very well: one stick of bombs fell 150 yards away and a few splinters came on board; the other was half a mile away on the port side.[61] He was assumed to be an Italian.[124] There were no more attacks, although several scares;[61] but there was so much activity nearer Greece that they escaped.[85] Doing only $4\frac{1}{2}$ knots they were in sight of Crete all day.[63] It was a curious experience being towed – rather like that of a worm on the end of a fishing line.[61] They could do nothing about anything and it was a dead weary business.[63]

With the 40 kilowatt Lawrence-Scott emergency generator reserved for the few essentials, the electric range was useless, so cooking was a problem.[85] It was solved by using the blacksmith's forge for frying and a blow-lamp to boil water. All the fresh water had to be carried from the tanks in buckets. However, they were cooking successfully for 90 men who were getting two good hot meals a day.[61] And to those eligible the ward-room cellar was still open; after 48 hours of sustained effort Lieut. (E) Aiken was staggered by the effect on his wines bill.[1]

At 0915 next day *HMS Protector* was sighted and an hour later the netlayer/target towing vessel was secured alongside *Grimsby*; a little over 30 minutes sufficed to transfer the tow. Speed was worked up to 6 knots,[178] while *Grimsby* became the escort. *Glenearn*'s degaussing gear had been destroyed in the paint-store fire, so they were a bit apprehensive of magnetic mines.[63] On the fourth day a number of loose mines were sighted dead ahead; these had to be sunk as they were approached,[85] and in the afternoon course was altered to avoid another.[178] *(29.4.41 1015)*

As the fifth day dawned Alexandria appeared on the horizon; a truly welcome sight to all on board. While still some distance away from port they were overtaken by a convoy from Crete; to everyone's surprise there was a burst of cheering from one of the ships.[85] *Protector* started working down[178] as they approached safety after a voyage in tow totalling 500 miles.[61] And as they entered the harbour the sirens hooted, and for nearly half an hour every ship in "Alex" paid tribute.[15] *(30.4.41)* *(1.5.41 0600)*

Shortly after 0700 a tug took her to a buoy,[63] the cable was cut,[178] and at 1130 *Glenearn* had arrived.[199] Her two sister-ships were already there, and the harbour was full of enemy-damaged vessels of all sorts.[124] The first person seen was Lieut.-Com. Best who had gone off with the boats to Monemvasia. He shouted that all his men were safe, which was worth a cheer from the parent ship. The rest of the ship's company had just arrived in the early morning convoy having given *Glenearn* a heartening hurrah in the passing.[63] Another interesting piece of information was that Radio Rome had just claimed to have sunk all three Glen ships.[71] *(1130)*

CHAPTER 10

MIRACLE AT MONEMVASIA

27.4.41 In the days that followed the reunion at Alexandria the adventures of the various parties were recounted. How, after a hectic passage of $7\frac{1}{2}$ hours,[85] during which they could not sail a direct course, the flotilla of landing craft had arrived off Monemvasia at 0430.[199] There they came up with the destroyer *Havock* carrying Rear-Admiral Baillie-Grohman, who was in charge of the evacuation arrangements ashore. He and his staff transferred to the ALCs and landed in a small bay four miles north of Monemvasia. There the craft separated and were hidden on beaches about half-a-mile apart,[375] and the crews went into hiding in the undergrowth.[85]

During the forenoon heavy bombing was heard to the north, and enemy aircraft were constantly overhead;[375] some flying as low as four hundred feet. The stone colour of the craft happened to tone in with the sand, and the dried salt marks on the hulls matched the boulders, so they were never spotted by these reconnaissance aircraft.[85] However, one ALC was damaged by bomb blast in the harbour.[199]

As the army was not due until the following night,[85] the crews stayed under cover all day. After dark three of the craft 28.4.41 were sent further away northwards.[199] Early in the morning the reconnaissance 'planes were over again, bringing the dive bombers to some target less than a mile away but out of sight beyond a hill. There were several heavy attacks on the vessel which must have been destroyed, since her ammunition exploded at intervals throughout the day.[375]

*　　*　　*

27.4.41 Meanwhile, the spare members of *Glenearn*'s ship's company had been taken in *Griffin* to Suda Bay, arriving late on the 27th. Just as they were coming up to their anchorage and were preparing to disembark, the destroyer was ordered back up north to search for *Diamond* and *Wryneck*, both of which had failed to arrive at Suda.[136]

The Dutch transport *Slamat*, having stayed at Nauplia embarking troops long after the deadline, with the coming of daylight had been bombed and set on fire. Her troops were taken off by the destroyer *Diamond*, which was duly bombed; she called for help. *Wryneck* had been sent, and had in turn asked for fighter protection, but since 1025 on the 27th – nothing.

At 0230 *Griffin* found one of *Wryneck*'s rafts, and at 28.4.41 daybreak some fifty survivors were picked up. They had been in the water since early the previous afternoon and, surprisingly, the majority were in good shape.

Back at Suda Bay all the survivors were put ashore; *Glenearn*'s quota were tired, dirty, hungry, thirsty and a bit fed up with the whole show. They spent most of their time in slit trenches; there were air-raid warnings almost every hour, and Gerry had a nasty habit of gliding in with his motors shut off, then suddenly appearing around a hill – playing a deadly kind of hide-and-seek.[136]

*   *   *

The bombing near Monemvasia had been aimed at "A" 28.4.41 lighter No. 5 down from Nauplia; the destruction of this large landing craft left the ALCs ex-*Glenearn* as practically the only means of embarking the New Zealand Division.[375] Three battalions of 6 N.Z. Brigade, after a 100-mile road journey through the night, were now disposed at distances of up to twelve miles from Monemvasia, with two platoons of Australians about eight miles further away, to give notice of any German approach. While the New Zealanders got the benefit of a much-needed rest under the olive trees, some near the coast had enough energy to find several small boats and enough initiative to set about organizing an improvised ferry service for the coming night's evacuation when, and if, the warships came. For their part the navy men were confident that there would be plenty of accommodation for the whole Brigade Group in the ships that were coming, but thought that one infantry battalion would probably have to remain behind for another 24 hours, because of the lack of small craft to ferry the troops out to the warships.[281]

After darkness had fallen the ALCs set off for Monemvasia;[85] the first arriving at 2130,[375] to find the troops already waiting.[281] By 2230 no ships had arrived, so one ALC was sent out beyond Monemvasia Island[375]...and met the destroyers coming in. As no suitable beaches existed the embarkation was to take place from the causeway connecting the island to the mainland.[199] *Griffin* closed well in to the small stone jetty in the north side, while *Isis* approached the south jetty, and the embarkation began at 2350 from the five different points, including the wrecked ALC which could not be otherwise used.[375]

First loads carried by the landing craft were the wounded, but the destroyers could not accommodate stretcher cases, so the boats just had to head back towards the shaded guiding lights marking the embarkation points. There was consternation when the military were told that their casualties had to be carried ashore and left, pending the arrival of the cruiser *Ajax*.

The rate of embarkation once it got effectively started was disappointingly slow. Some of the ALCs had not arrived and some of the destroyers had not appeared, may indeed have been sunk; the New Zealanders were warned that only half their force might be taken off.

Eventually the missing landing craft turned up, and shortly after 0100 another pair of destroyers arrived[281] – they had been patrolling off the port as an anti-submarine screen, and waiting for the first two filling up with troops before replacing them[557] – and the operation swung into gear. It was miraculous; boat-load after boat-load left, at shorter and shorter intervals the next batch of men were signalled down to the jetty.[281] The army organization was magnificent and the discipline of the troops superb; *Glenearn*'s craft were handled well,[375] and as for the destroyers – all they had to do was sit there and every few minutes another ALC would arrive with sixty soldiers on board.[557] When *HMS Ajax* came in the stretcher cases were at last taken out.

29.4.41

Meanwhile, the self-help ferry service had transported the equivalent of an entire battalion, and it became clear that the whole force was going to get away, especially as the warships were prepared to stay until 0400 and take their chance with the dive-bombers.

Shortly before 0300, however, the Navy men were complaining that boats were waiting and no troops to fill them. The last craft were taken up by the skeleton Divisional and Brigade staffs, and others of both services who had been supervising the loading.[281] General Freyberg and the C.O. of the rearguard battalion were in the last boat to leave the shore, reaching *Ajax* at 0300 and climbing aboard on scrambling nets.[25]

Orders had been given for the landing craft to be destroyed;[199] in attempting to do so one of *Hotspur*'s petty officers was left stranded on an ALC as another was about to blow up. He was fished out of the water none the worse for his experience, but only one of these two craft was definitely destroyed.[557] One or two others may have been disposed of, but five or six were left afloat[375] – just pushed off when empty[25] – as the Commanding Officer of *Ajax* wanted to leave at once;[199] the burning motor transport ashore was lighting up the ships in the bay, and there was the ever-present danger of submarines.[375] Almost immediately the cruiser was making full speed.[281]

Ajax and her four destroyers reached Suda Bay at 0800.[375] There a convoy "GA15" of seven ships was loading up with personnel and getting ready to sail for Alexandria.[593] Troops in the destroyers were transferred to the transports and the numbers in *Ajax* considerably reduced,[282] although Lieut.-Com. Best and his ALC crew members remained on board the cruiser.[85] Whilst these transfers were in progress and the destroyers were fuelling, several thousand men, and some women, were brought out from the shore;[593] included in this move were *Glenearn*'s spare crew men.[136] They were packed aboard a freighter, the *s.s. Delane*, along with Italian prisoners of war, army troops, Fleet Air Arm personnel and several hundred other "distressed British seamen".

These complicated arrangements were completed in just three hours, and at 1100 the Convoy sailed, with a close escort of the cruiser *Carlisle*, four destroyers, a sloop, and the corvette *Hyacinth*. *HMS Ajax* sailed at 1300 with the covering force of three cruisers and two destroyers. Course was set eastwards.[593]

There were air-raid warnings practically all the time.[136] In the Kaso Strait at the east end of Crete the convoy was attacked at 2315 by E-boats,* and torpedoes were fired but no ships hit. This action continued for almost four hours before the convoy and its protectors were finally left alone at 0300.

30.4.41

In the morning the battleships *Barham* and *Valiant* with the new aircraft carrier *Formidable* took over close escort, and *Ajax*, *Orion* with two destroyers went on ahead,[375] reaching Alexandria at 1800.[282] Convoy GA15, protected all day by the Battle Squadron, proceeded without further incident, arriving outside "Alex" the following morning.[593] There they overhauled *Glenearn* under tow and gave her a cheer in the passing,[63] before going on to finish the voyage safe and well, but somewhat the worse for wear, and needing a wash, a good meal and a lot of sleep.[136]

1.5.41

*   *   *

1.5.41

There was an air-raid on that first night; the guns made a terrific din, and created a fireworks display in the sky.[71] Mines, mostly magnetic, were dropped in the harbour and near the Great Pass; these had to be dealt with before the Fleet could re-enter harbour, each mine making a magnificent splash when blown up by the sweepers.[63] When the Battle Squadron returned[176] *Glenearn* ended up flanked on the south-west by *HMS Warspite* and on the north-east by *Formidable*.[63] The aircraft-carrier arranged a cinema show for Sunday evening, but the entertainment was ruined by another air-raid[71] lasting an hour and a half.[176] Most of *Glenearn*'s company were living ashore, but those on duty that night had never heard such a racket as the eight anti-aircraft guns of

3.5.41

4.5.41

* Enemy motor torpedo boats.

Warspite, or the sixteen of *Formidable* fired right over them;
the waters of the harbour were hissing with hot shell
fragments, and pieces of metal clattered down all over the
ship.[63]

The first few days were spent in catching up with lost sleep
and working to clear up the ship as much as possible.[124]
Glenearn was in an appalling state. The soldiers had left food
all over the mess decks,[63] and when she was put alongside the
Coal Quay to wait her turn for docking,[61] the rats started to
swarm.[63]

Glengyle, like her sister-ship had been near-missed on her
second, and in her case successful, venture into Grecian
waters, but with less dire results – although on entering the
floating dock the underwater damage was revealed as serious   5.5.41
enough. At one point the ship's side had been almost caved in
by the blast.[71] As for *Glenearn*, a working party from
Glengyle's landing craft crews[176] sent to work in her returned   6.5.41
at the end of the day with the impressions that *Glenearn*'s crew
had been sent home, and that the ship herself was bound for
Bombay for repairs. Bombay, with its big floating dock,[71] did
seem the most likely place to have the engine room and upper
deck repairs carried out; facilities at Alexandria were already
overstrained and hope was fading of ever dry-docking in the
one and only dock which was already working to capacity.[85]

As his ship was of no use until she could receive a lot of
attention, Captain Hill was "shoved" into an appointment as
Captain of the dockyard.[61] Before he left, he assembled   15.5.41
everyone on the deck of *Glenearn* and thanked them for being
such a good ship's company, and for the manner in which they
had behaved in action; then he shook hands with each one of
them and wished them luck in the future.[136] Lieut.-Com.
Venables assumed command.

Captain Hill's new appointment gave him certain technical
resources, and as everybody else seemed too busy to bother
about her, he thought he might as well carry out repairs as far
as he could, and so set about patching up his old ship.
Glenearn was still making water, so some salvage gear was
needed fairly quickly to stop her getting dangerously low in

the water;[61] but the main problem was to get the water out of the engine room.

One of the dockyard's divers went down to examine the damage and reported a number of holes which could be plugged. The plugs were duly made, knocked into place, pumps produced and pumping started. It was soon obvious that the pumps were having no effect. The pumps were taken away, divers went down again to search for more holes.[85] Cracked joints in the hull were found and sealed.[61] Pumping was restarted, but the water in the engine room would not go down. This procedure was done again and again with no better results, while the pumping was continually being interrupted whenever the pumps were required elsewhere.[85]

Outside the confines of a half-sunken ship life went on. Shore leave: the British Services Club founded in 1895 and the United Forces Club opened by Lady Wavell in December, 1940.[607] To the Fleet Club in Hospital Street where the beer was sold at half the usual Alexandrian prices and the evening's entertainment – Mrs. Barker's Basket of Beautiful Belles singing and dancing – was free. More typical perhaps, of jolly jack tar ashore were the bars in Sister Street: the "Paradise", the "Black Cat" and the "Lucky Bar". Belly dancers performing for 10 piastres, everyone holding the table while Zuzu's eleven stone of "flab" gyrated on top; the orchestra playing from a platform near the ceiling. With the ladder pulled up they were safe from any serviceman who decided to thump a musician's ear, or wished to "borrow" his instrument as a souvenir; their only contact the tin can for the collection lowered on a string.[114]

There were also reminders of the war still going on. When the official figures of the numbers evacuated from Greece were released, out of a total of 45,000 embarked, the two Glen ships had accounted directly for 13,600. *Glengyle* won the distinction of taking off more than any other ship.[71] *Glenearn*'s landing craft had been instrumental at Monemvasia – another 4,000-odd – even *Glenroy*, holed in two places and having never left Alexandria, had contributed six of her ALCs to the lift from Megara (5,900) and an MLC

10.5.41

taken in *HMS Ajax* to Kithera (820), then towed back to Suda Bay by *HMS Salvia*.[375] If only the three ships had been able to operate together, they might have got half the Army away, and at less risk than going up in separate slow convoys...[63]

Glengyle had come out of dry-dock on the 13th May, and three days later sailed on a quick run to Port Said and back before embarking stores, tanks, ammunition, a lorry and the 1st Bn. Argyll and Sutherland Highlanders. German "paratroops" were likely to land in Crete, and *Glengyle* sailed for there early on the 18th, returning to Alexandria two days later; just about the time, according to the BBC News, that the parachutists and gliders did land on the northern coast of the island. *Glenroy* in turn left loaded with stores and troops for Crete, and later in the afternoon *Glengyle* was ordered to prepare for a similar mission, but at the last minute it was cancelled, and *Glenroy* recalled. When the battle fleet came into port to refuel and take on ammunition, the destroyers brought in German prisoners – survivors of an unsuccessful attempt at a seaborne landing.

That same night came the news that *HMS Hood*, the world's biggest warship, had been sunk off Greenland by the German battleship *Bismarck*.[71] When it was announced that *Bismarck* had in turn been sent to the bottom,* no one in *Glenearn* believed it. They had a saying, "The only news that is true is bad news."[63] *Glenroy* returned after another abortive attempt to reach Crete with reinforcements and supplies; they had been bombed heavily all the time she had been at sea.[71] One of *Glenearn's* deck officers, Sub.-Lieut. De Kock, RNVR, had been seconded to *Glenroy* and had been on the bridge during the bombing. He claimed that each time an attack came in, all the other officers ducked; De Kock ordered, "Hard-a-port", "Hard-a-starboard" as required, only to be roundly criticised after each event.[63]

Once again *Glengyle* prepared to make a "death or glory" run, this time to bring off as many troops as they could. Once again she bore a charmed life,[71] and by 0500 on the last day of

16.5.41

18.5.41
20.5.41

23.5.41

24.5.41

27.5.41

28.5.41

31.5.41

---

* Finished off by *HMS Dorsetshire*.

May was back at her berth alongside No. 75 Wharf,[176] with several thousand troops; some of whom had been rescued once before from Greece by *Glengyle*,[71] and others by *Glenearn*.*[142]

The latter vessel was meanwhile nearer a state of comparative watertightness. Someone had discovered that the low injection was broken off; when that aperture had been sealed by a diver the engine room was pumped out in twenty-four hours. They had wasted weeks.[63] There had been between two and three thousand gallons of lubricating oil on the surface; this had settled on everything as the water level dropped,[85] and it was a horrible sight that presented itself once the pumping had stopped.[124] It was heart-breaking; where once had been heard the sound of powerful Diesel engines, now there was an eerie silence broken only by the dripping of oil and water. This was the pride of the Glen Line.[85]

Other valve holes were plugged from the inside, and small splinter holes welded over;[61] a count on the starboard side, above and below the water-line, was abandoned at one hundred and seventy-five.[85] Now the remainder of the ship's company could move back on board; but not for long.[136] There was no hope of *Glenearn*'s being repaired at Alexandria, so it was no good her just lying there. The main difficulty was the huge amount of electrical work which would have to be done; both Sub.-Lieut. (E) McKenzie, RNVR, the Senior Electrical Officer and Lieut.-Com. (E) Cahy, RNR, the Chief Engineer said the job could only be done in the U.K. or the U.S.A. and it would take at least six months. It had been decided to tow her to India for temporary repair; sufficient to enable the ship to reach home.

A towing party would be left on board under Lieut.-Com. Hood, and all the Engineer and Electrical Officers would be retained to help with the repair work; although Hood thought this a waste of men. The towing party would consist of about 17 officers, 2 Petty Officers, 20 seamen, between 20 and 30 stokers of all rates, 1 P.O. Shipwright, 1 P.O. Writer, 1 P.O.

* The Sappers from Nauplia did not however escape a second time.[79a]

Supply Assistant, 1 W/T Rating, 1 signalman, 1 Naafi assistant, 1 Sick Berth Attendant, together with a handful of cooks and stewards. Eighty would cover everyone; nearly all were picked men from the original crew.[63] The remainder were put ashore, sad at leaving once again what had been a very happy ship, but was now looking battered and rather forlorn at the jetty.[136]

There was much to be done. One fire and bilge pump had to be reconditioned – in order to pump water for fire-fighting; also one main engine turning motor for turning the engines daily to prevent them rusting up. A small generating set was procured to run alternatively with the existing emergency generator for maintaining power on the steering gear.[85] Also a trailer pump for sanitary purposes, and lastly, but by no means least, a coal-fired galley range was supplied by the dockyard.[61]

Lieut.-Com. Hood got the Dockyard sheerlegs to hoist out the spare anchor and to transfer five shackles of cable from the port locker to the starboard; so they could now anchor again – but only once.[63] All this was done at the cost of a great deal of sweat and toil on the part of the Care and Maintenance Party;[85] apart from everything else, the weather was furnace hot.[71]

There were a lot of towing arrangements to be made, and a buoy had to be laid for *Glenearn* at Suez. *HMS Protector* had already recovered the 7″ wire, but the net-layer still had two shackles of *Glenearn*'s cable, and wished to tow with a 5″ wire from each ship and the two shackles in the middle for catenary – which is a good method of towing even if it has snags.[63] But in the end they had got her fit to go away in tow without having had to dock her. Captain Hill was rather pleased; everybody else at the dockyard had said that it could not be done.[61]

There had been more air-raids: a bad one on 30th May, and a hundred people killed ashore on 5th June.[114] On the night of 7th–8th there was another heavy raid;[71] land-mines exploded ashore with spectacular effects and heavy civilian casualties. Alexandria was in a mess as the Egyptians beat it for the desert in tens of thousands. Further out in the same desert the British Army seemed to be just a confused mob on the frontier. Up aloft, much had been read about the Royal Air Force, but little enough seen of its 'planes.[63]

A last look around the harbour. There was *Warspite*: a bomb had written off all her secondary armament on the starboard side.[85] *HMS Formidable* with a hole the size of a house in her starboard bow,[114] and the destroyer *Nubian* with her stern blown off.[85] *HMS Orion* with her "A" Turret gun-barrels bent upwards; Alexandria was full of battered ships.[71] Not present: the three cruisers and eight destroyers lost in living up to the Navy's tradition of never letting the Army down.*

On Sunday 8th June, 1941, *Protector* took *Glenearn*,[85] Lieut.-Com. Venables in command,[63] in train. Just as the towing vessel was taking the strain, a German reconnaissance 'plane was shot down by an RAF fighter. All the ships in the harbour witnessed the heartening sight; it did everybody good to see the enemy getting it in the neck for a change. It screamed down, down, down, down – to crash in the desert. Everyone in all the ships cheered like mad. Whilst these cheers were still ringing across the water *Glenearn* moved slowly out on the second stage of her long tow.[85]

* With the exception of the Highland Division at St. Valery.

CHAPTER 11

"FROM GHOULIES AND GHOSTIES..."

HMS Protector, with *Glenearn* in tow, reached Port Said, and soon they got into a tangle. When *Protector* slowed down, the two shackles of anchor cable at the middle of the towing line dropped to the bottom and effectively anchored her by the stern. This did not stop *Glenearn*; she rode up alongside and the two ships locked together. However, the canal tugs that were taking over the tow sorted them out; *Glenearn*'s wire was recovered, but *Protector* kept the two shackles of cable.

9.6.41

By nightfall the Bitter Lake had been reached. As the anchor in the starboard hawse pipe could not be recovered once it had been let go, the tug anchored and *Glenearn* lay by her. Luckily the wind did not rise. As they continued along the Canal a soldier on the bank shouted, "You are going the wrong way". A.B. Hague: "We'll be back to get you out".[63]

10.6.41

In Suez Bay making fast to the buoy that had been laid for them was a long and difficult business. With no power to the capstan and very few hands to call on, like most jobs it was a case of "Clear Lower Deck". Using the emergency generator a length of port anchor chain was winched to the crosstrees and then gently lowered over the gypsy.*

At Suez Lieut.-Com. Venables, RN, turned over his command to Lieut.-Com. Hood, RNR.[85] They were now no longer under C.-in-C. Mediterranean, and the Indian Ocean side did not seem very interested, so the ship lay swinging round her buoy. As for the proposed journey to Aden, no one ashore seemed to know anything. There were still some repairs to come from Alexandria, so the deck hands unrigged derricks and boat falls whilst they were waiting.

13.6.41

The engineers had already started clearing up.[63] Oil which had coated everything as the pumps lowered the water had been a good thing, as the oil-impregnated parts were kept

---

* Gypsy: the barrel of the windlass; shaped to fit, and grip the cable's links.

from contact with the air, but now everything had to be cleaned; even the gang-ways could not be walked on.

All the Electrical Engineers could do was clean the main switchboard: dismantling the massive tri-pole switches, and then washing each part in petrol before re-assembling. Sub.-Lieut. (E) McKenzie went ashore to ask for wiring to illuminate the ship, and was assured of every help, but nothing was produced. On his way back to the boat by a slightly different route he noticed some cable used in peacetime for dressing ship; it was weatherproof and strong. Without a moment's hesitation McKenzie got the boat to pull in as close as possible before throwing the loot into it. This cable was used thereafter.[85]

At this time the main problem facing the engineers was that when the engine room had flooded, all the auxiliary machinery had been put out of action, as it was driven by electric motors; all the fuel, lubricating and cooling pumps were useless. Also the main engines, if they were to be saved from ruin, had to be turned every day. They were normally started, and could be turned, by compressed air; the compressors were run by auxiliary Diesels and if one of these could be made to go, then they had a chance. They got one stripped down and cleaned, then re-assembled it. There was just enough air already compressed to start it once; if it did not fire first time they were beaten, so everybody prayed. It did – a moment of triumph. Now that they could compress more air all the other auxiliaries could be serviced, and the main engines moved. Now it would be just sheer hard work overhauling the remainder of the machines. Nothing could be done to make *Glenearn* go under her own power until the electric motors had been serviced, as the four main generators weighed about two tons each; this would be a big job.

June gave place to July. Italian 'planes raided at night, but did no damage, hitting the desert mostly; but with the moonlight nights the Germans came, and that was a very different matter. Their aeroplanes flew low to be sure of laying the mines in the right places; the parachutes could be seen coming down and the mines heard hitting the water.[63]

On the 13th July a reconnaissance aircraft flew over in daylight, which meant a raid could be expected that night.[50] There were about forty ships of every age and description in Suez Bay, from the Greek armoured cruiser *Giorgios Averoff* of 1910[63] and the dummy battleship *Centurion* disguised to look like *HMS Anson*,[50] to more effective fighting units such as *HMAS Lismore* a corvette,[144] and the new Australian cruiser *Hobart*. *HMAS Hobart* had arrived at the outer anchorage the day before and berthed near *m.v. Georgic*[275] before entering the Canal on the evening of the 13th, but because of mines had returned to Suez – stern first – and stopped for the time being in the inner anchorage.[273] Meantime the Cunard White Star liner had finished discharging troops and stores after two days of round-the-clock working, and had started loading for the return journey.[363] Other merchant vessels included *s.s. Almanzora* and the Blue Funnel *Euryades*.[475]

It was five minutes past midnight when a "Yellow" air raid warning was signalled. By 0020 it had become a "Red" and several enemy aircraft were being engaged by anti-aircraft batteries ashore; bombs were dropped on Port Tewfik and Suez.[273] This action continued intermittently with individual bombers attacking at intervals ranging from half-an-hour to an hour.[475]

At 0300 groups of aircraft commenced dive bombing the shipping at anchor. They were engaged by the naval vessels including the Greek man-o'-war – but for the most part blindly, as only once did the searchlights hold one for any length of time.[273] *Glenearn* was completely helpless; all she could do was take what was coming to her. All on board were a bit windy by this time. When a bomb came down nearby, Lieut.-Com. Jackson* on the open bridge dived under the wooden chart-table. He got up feeling a bit ashamed, and not helped by the sound of Tom Hood's laughter.[63]

The attack concentrated on *Almanzora*, *Euryades* and *Georgic*[475] lying two miles away down the bay.[63] *Euryades* put up a spirited defence, but it was apparently *Georgic* that

---

* The Paymaster. To avoid the wrong impression, see page 153.

had been selected as the principle target.[475] Of the seven
bombs dropped,[363] two or possibly three hit, and shortly after
Georgic caught fire on all decks simultaneously. She seemed
a hopeless proposition[85] and signalled ... *PLEASE SEND
BOATS* ... to take off her passengers who included a number
of women and children being evacuated from the Middle East
to South Africa.[273] Boats rushed to her from all directions. All
that remained of *Glenearn*'s were a 22 ft. motor-boat, the
engine of which was in pieces, and a whaler; however, the
latter was soon away, under a volunteer crew of young
engineers pulling for dear life.[85] The time was about 0330.[363]

These would-be rescuers had no sooner disappeared into
the darkness than it was noticed that the focus of all their
attentions was under way, and coming up the harbour.[63] Her
Captain had evidently decided to beach her. She was a ghastly
and horrifying sight:[85] listing to port and surrounded by an
immense pall of smoke,[363] her after two-thirds a blazing
inferno, scuttles belching fire like giant blow-lamps and jets of
flame roaring out of the portholes. Everything and everybody
reflected the red glow of this horrible spectacle.[85]

Such was the scene presented to the spectators on the
bridge of *Glenearn* as *Georgic* was about to pass. Then to their
horror as they watched, *Georgic* fell off her course and started
to turn towards the immobile *Glenearn*. The huge black mass
was silhouetted against the fire raging abaft her bridge ... the
enormous bows equalling the height of *Glenearn*'s bridge
approached ... the overhanging stem lunged across the boat
deck towards the feet of the watcher ... it seemed ages before
the crash came.[63]

Down in the engine room McKenzie was walking along a
gangway. Suddenly there was a terrific collision; something
had hit the starboard side with a terrible rending crash, then
followed an awful grinding of steel against steel.[85] *Georgic* had
struck the already battered *Glenearn* at an acute angle just
abaft her bridge ... *Glenearn* staggered and reeled to port ...
Georgic ground up the starboard side with a screaming of torn
steel, a thundering of shaking masts and derricks, whilst
smoke and flame covered the after ends of both vessels.

Georgic hooked *Glenearn*'s buoy cable across her stem post and took her across the bay, buoy and all;[63] with boat davits interlocked the two ships headed towards an invisible shore. *Georgic* was a mass of flames, with portholes like great red eyes, and rapidly setting *Glenearn* on fire too. One of *Georgic*'s lifeboats, hanging by a single burning rope, crashed down ... the roar and the crackle of the inferno ... the terrific heat ... screams for help ... explosions blowing through the sides of both ships. *Glenearn* had no landing craft, some of her portside rafts had been smashed on 26th April, and now *Georgic* had set fire to the Carley floats on the starboard side.[85] There was no water in the fire hoses as the collision had broken the ring main around the ship;[63] the Second Engineer and his men were struggling with a bucket chain, which seemed futile. Willie Ramsay, the Third Engineer, went away to look for a valve to isolate one side of the ring main, broken near the bows.[85] The two ships were locked together and were obviously going to burn out together; the situation was hopeless.

The Captain decided to go to the forecastle with the vague idea that he might slip from the buoy and so break away. On his way there, some *Georgic* men tried to climb aboard, but Hood was so furious that he chased them away. Once on the fo'c'sle it was obvious there was no chance of slipping, but while still there he was astounded to see a huge tripod, fully 40 feet high, coming out of the darkness towards them. It hit *Georgic* full on the stem post and fell over backwards. Then he saw the incredible sight of a twenty-seven thousand ton ship taking a backward jump of about half a cable,* breaking clear of *Glenearn* as she did no. Hood knocked the brake off the windlass and let the buoy cable run out – it had been under great strain – then he stopped to think.

When *Georgic* had ground up their side she had caught their buoy cable and taken *Glenearn*, buoy and buoy anchor across the bay at, say, 7 knots. In the darkness he had not realised that they were making way through the water; the

* A cable equals 200 yards.

tripod was the beacon* on the north end of the Middle Shoal. *Georgic* – by heck! – had hit the shoal and stopped; it was *Glenearn*'s going on he had seen, not *Georgic*'s going astern. As *Glenearn* drew less water, she had gone on to the limit of the buoy cable and then grounded gently on another part of the shoal. *Georgic* was now, at most, one hundred yards away. It was providential that Hood had gone to the forecastle, as he was the only man in the ship who really knew what to do there, and when to do it.[63]

When the two vessels had still been locked together, one of *Georgic*'s officers having been cut off by the fire had jumped from the bridge on to the *Glenearn*. Shaken, he rushed up to Sub.-Lieut. McKenzie asking, "Where is the Captain?" "Forward," said McKenzie, "What's the trouble?" "Get under way at once, No. 8 Hold is full of ammunition, and the fire is in No. 7 now." "We can't get under way, we've no engines." The question everyone was asking everybody else was, "When the fire reaches this No. 8 Hold does the ammunition go up in one big explosion, or a lot of little explosions?" No one seemed to know, but *Georgic*'s 3rd Mate† was telling everyone to get under way to avoid the blast that was imminent.[85]

Lieut.-Com. Hood dashed back to the bridge and found great confusion there; this unknown officer was rushing about giving orders and telling everyone that they must get under way – as if they could. However, after attacking the burning Carley rafts with buckets of fresh water for a while, the broken fire main had been isolated, the pressure restored on the hoses and the fire was soon brought under control.[63] The last bombing raid took place as dawn was breaking.[275]

0350

Things were becoming clearer, but then the rumours started. "We are badly on fire aft," from the Chief Engineer. The Captain got McKenzie, one of the best officers on board, to take a party aft and then report back to him. While Hood was calming down the *Georgic* officer, who was still badly shocked, McKenzie came back to say there was no fire aft,

---

* Two Able Seamen from the cruiser *Caledon*, posted on the beacon as mine-watchers, had had to jump into the water seconds before impact, but had escaped injury.[273]

† Rank changed.

and there had not been any fire aft.

Then the Paymaster said *Georgic* had 300 tons of bombs on board which would go up any minute. *Georgic* by this time was a roaring mass of flames not many yards away. Hood thought, "When the fire reaches that lot, there won't be much left of Glenearn," so he mustered everyone on the fore deck and cut some Carley rafts away.[63] The only thing then left to do was to "wait for it".[85] Then he remembered *Georgic*'s officer and asked him; he said the cargo was 300 cases of condemned 4.7 ammo., which was a very different thing. Just then Hood could have shot both the Chief and the Paymaster.

There was also the worry about the ship's boat, as there were tales of a boat with people in it being washed between the ships in the collision; someone reported that the whaler had been crushed and the volunteer crew lost – but *Glenearn*'s Captain could do nothing about this. He made a signal ashore to report the situation, and sounded round and surveyed the waterline as soon as there was enough light to see.[63]

At 0438 the green "All Clear" warning,[275] and *Georgic* still burning furiously; by 0500 she had been abandoned by all hands – some taken off in their own boats, others in lighters and various small craft.[363] Fortunately, no big explosion took place,[85] only individual blasts wracked the wreck as the 4.7 stuff went off with a grand barrage effect throughout the forenoon.[63] Projectiles of some description whirled out over the desert accompanied by weird noises, "Brrrrrrrrrr..."[1] 0438

Glenearn's boat came back with the entire crew happy. They had hung on to the Greek flagship *Averoff*, and had been wined and dined there.

Damage to the whaler's parent vessel was severe, as her starboard side had been crushed in at the centrecastle on boat deck level, although she had stood up to it well. One of *Georgic*'s big lifeboats was sitting on the bridge gun platform. *HMAS Hobart* was ordered to tow *Glenearn* off the reef at the next high water.[63] First the Australians sent a boat[275] which went all round taking soundings, then the cruiser crept in under the bow,[85] anchored and ran her $5\frac{1}{2}''$ wire to *Glenearn*'s anchor cable. *Hobart* commenced heaving in until *Glenearn* 1000
1447
1515 floated over and off the shoal, assisted by the flood tide* and a southerly wind.[275] Tugs then took her alongside the oil jetty just west of the canal entrance at Port Tewfik.[85]

Georgic remained fast aground, and burned fiercely throughout the day. At 1830 she suddenly took a bigger list to starboard and settled lower in the water by the stern.[273] During the evening and night individuals went on board briefly,[44] and at first light a procession of tugs, lighters and a 30-ton floating crane went out to salvage a German Mark IV tank; the first to be captured in working order.[26] It was on *Georgic*'s fore deck[117] – the only part of the ship not yet burnt out[85] – for shipment to the United Kingdom and detailed assessment of its performance, defences and armament. This rescue attempt had been inspired by a Captain of the Royal Tank Regiment[44] and was carried out by him and a volunteer party of Royal Engineers. The native crews of the various craft were not volunteers; in fact a full show of revolvers was used to get them to go near the ship, which continued burning, with loud explosions, throughout the operation.[26] Apart from the buckled deck – red-hot in places – and the $17°$ list, which made crane access easier,[117] the Sappers regarded it as just another task for the Port Operating Group.†[44] But both the BBC and the British Official Press in their reports of the raid[273] – "A few bombs were dropped, causing one death. Slight damage was done."[451] – lost much credibility in the minds of those who had experienced "Georgic Night".[273]

Hobart had weighed anchor and entered the Canal followed by "*HMS Anson*" and preceded by acoustic and magnetic sweepers, with tugs in attendance astern; for at least thirteen mines had been reported.[275] Later on the 15th Captain Hill arrived. He had been transferred to another job, in Cairo, and had decided to come and see *Glenearn* at Suez. Apparently there was a row going on because they were still there; the collision damage did not seem too bad, and they would probably go on soon if they were seaworthy. After he left, the Care and Maintenance Party set about cementing up all the

1830

15.7.41

* Rise and fall of tide was 6 feet.[U]
† Each of the six soldiers was subsequently awarded the George Medal.[369]

holes they could find.[63]

Shortly before midnight another series of raids on the Canal started, which went on until 0400.[273] These low-flying attacks by moonlight continued, with the oil tanks on the western shore a frequent target. Warnings of air raids were given by the light on the tower at the entrance to the Canal changing its colour.[144] However, nothing fell near *Glenearn* except one mine which dropped in shallow water a few yards from the other side of the wharf; the heavy explosion gave the ship and everyone in her a severe shaking-up.

An expression, "anxiety neurosis" began to creep into the vocabulary.[85] A seaman broke down and had to be put ashore in a Neil-Robertson stretcher; he was seeing dive-bombers everywhere.[63] Nearly everyone was affected in some way: the Second Engineer moved into the Chief's cabin and slept on the couch there. One began to ponder God and religion,[1] wondering what life – now that it seemed likely to be short – was all about;[73] another sought refuge in the bottle,[A] while only the odd individual claimed a succession of unbroken nights of sound sleep.[113]

But all were glad when it was arranged for the Ellerman Line s.s. *City of Kimberley* to tow them to Aden. She was light, but her Captain and Chief Officer were willing to try. Meanwhile *Glenearn*'s Commanding Officer got back the four shackles of anchor cable left on the buoy when *Hobart* had come to the rescue.

During the latter half of July, among the mass of merchant shipping,[63] the anti-aircraft cruisers[144] and the other naval craft at Suez, one or two had stood out: the huge passenger liners pouring reinforcements into Egypt. *Nieuw Amsterdam*,[R] then *Aquitania*;[144] now, as tugs took *Glenearn* down the bay the r.m.s. *Queen Elizabeth* was discharging her khaki cargo. *City of Kimberley* anchored nearby and provided 70 fathoms of $5\frac{1}{2}''$ wire, while *Glenearn* used 120 fathoms of the same size and two shackles of cable. They made a mess of passing the tow, but got under way at last and headed down the Gulf making five knots.[63] It was the 1st of August; they had been at Suez seven weeks.[85]

CHAPTER 12

PAINTED OCEAN; PAINTERED SHIP

The voyage down the Red Sea was uneventful. They averaged six knots which was good, considering *City of Kimberley*'s propeller which was half out of the water, and her best speed, which was 13 knots. Sometimes the towing line was clear of the water, but as both ships were light there was still a big sag in it, so everyone was quite happy. Lieut.-Com. Hood and his acting 1st Lieutenant, Sub.-Lieut. Scott, spent a lot of time brushing up their navigation. One day they seemed to be lost and, according to an exchange of positions, *Glenearn* and *City of Kimberley* had passed on opposite sides of an island, so the tow rope should have caught. On this occasion *Glenearn* was right.[63]

The main problem the Care and Maintenance Party had to contend with was the August heat; with all the refrigerating machinery out of order a cold drink was just a memory.[85] Towards the southern end of the Red Sea the heat became even fiercer and *City of Kimberley*'s elderly Chief Engineer died of heat stroke.[63]

10.8.41   They arrived at Aden on 10th August.[85] As usual, stopping was more difficult than starting, and *Glenearn* nearly went ashore before the tugs came out. With the purchase rigged at the foremast they were able to recover their cable. Again a buoy had been laid for them, three miles out in the outer harbour. *Glenearn*'s boat was broken down, so her Captain was unable to call on *City of Kimberley* to thank them for a fine job during the ten-day passage.

Now it was a matter of trying to arrange a tow across the Indian Ocean to either Bombay or Colombo. But the SW monsoon was blowing, and the navy seemed to think that it would be dangerous to tow; much better to wait until after the monsoons changed in October. As always the trouble was to find out who was to make the decisions and who was responsible for arranging a towing ship. The Captain-in-

Charge, Aden, went home sick as soon as *Glenearn* arrived, so the enquiries got nowhere.[63]

After trying so hard to get the ship functioning, it was soul-destroying to be left in the heat of Aden waiting for the monsoon to pass.[85] As much work as possible was being done in preparation for the coming refit, and the C. & M. Party made a first-class job of the work undertaken, but for all that, everyone became very "browned off".

Glenearn swung round her buoy. It was all very boring. With no frigidaire or ice chest the food was grim:[63] no variety, nothing cold. Even the old standby corned beef suffered from the heat; instead of having to be shaken out of its tin, it ran out and spread in a most revolting manner. Fresh vegetables were ordered daily, but seldom arrived owing to the heavy swell in the outer harbour. The temporary coal fire and range fell to pieces periodically, and in between times smoked the cook out of his galley.[85] One leading seaman, a nice lad whom the Captain had recommended for a commission, had to be discharged to hospital with tuberculosis. It was a bad period.

Glenearn lay a long way out and the boat transport for liberty-men was poor,[63] and in any case there was nothing at Aden to attract men ashore other than organized recreation.[85] They were scared to bathe from the ship because of sharks.[63] Life was dull in the extreme,[85] but occasional bathing ashore kept them sane.[63] Jim Cahy had an air pistol and took pot-shots at the carrion crows which settled on the ship; the pellets did no more than sting the birds, but they hopped away to a safer distance when he came out on deck.[1] A rifle shoot was arranged against the Aden Home Guard; Leading Seaman Heywood had the top score.

Occasional cricket matches were fixed up and played on a matting wicket laid out on the desert. Such games called for a considerable effort on the part of the players[85] – several of them officers, which was not very usual in the service[63] – standing out in the sun with the reflected heat from the hard dry ground striking one in the face, but they were a welcome diversion.[85]

One day it rained! It could be seen coming like a curtain,

and it hit the poop while the bridge was still in sunshine; the rain was so heavy it was difficult to breathe. Next day there was a signal from shore, "Your cricket match is off. Ground unfit for play owing to rain." It transpired that the rainwater had washed out a gully through the cricket "field"; the first rain for two years, it was said.

The October rain was a sign of the breaking up of the monsoons; with the change, *Glenearn*'s Captain again tried to arrange a tow. An armed merchant cruiser *HMS Hector* was there; she was a Blue Funnel ship and would have been ideal – and did not appear to be doing anything particularly useful – but it could not be worked. Others were willing, but with merchant ships it was a question of where do the orders come from, payment, etc., etc. The Naval Officer in Charge said it was nothing to do with him, it was up to the Sea Transport office to do it. They said it was the N.O.I.C.; Hood was getting nowhere.[63]

At Aden they seemed to have fallen between two stools; the Mediterranean Fleet did not want to have anything to do with them, and neither did the East Indies Fleet. Nobody seemed to own poor old *Glenearn*. It was a depressing time. In addition to their discomforts – and their discomfiture – the mails were very few and far between; the ship's company began to feel that they were "forgotten men".[85]

Signs of the distant war were rare enough to be remarkable:[A] the new light cruiser *HMS Euralyus* on her way to the Med.,[85] or the visit by a veteran – Lieut. G. I. Finkel, RNVR – of the voyage round the Cape down from Egypt.[46] The two more or less sound Glen ships had been retained in the Middle East and *Glengyle* for one was back on the Bitter Lakes training British, Australian and New Zealand troops in combined operations.[610] Of the Commando units brought round the Cape for this very purpose two had of course been destroyed fighting as the rearguard during the last days on Crete; the other, "Scottish" Commando – or rather half of it – was back on garrison duty in Cyprus[579] after their part in the Syrian campaign when they had been landed by *Glengyle* at the Litani River.[610]

16.10.41

Eventually the s.s. *Afghanistan* was ordered to tow *Glenearn* to Colombo, but first the towing vessel's Captain wanted ballast; 2,000 tons of it. With all the sands of Arabia available, Lieut.-Com. Hood did not think this would be much of a problem, but Sea Transport refused to agree. Cowasjee Dinshaw & Bros. (Aden) Ltd., the big firm of ship chandlers said they could provide 2,000 tons of salt at 24-hours' notice, but they would require an order from the Navy ... As a last resort a call was made on the Admiral's Secretary. He thought there was a signal somewhere, so Hood made the Dept. of Sea Transport, Aden, check their files. A month-old signal was found saying Sea Transport, Aden, were to arrange towing and ballast for *Glenearn*. A 'phone call to Cowasjee Dinshaw and the salt was on its way. Several weeks lost – maddening.

As it was going to be a possibly 30-day trip, the handing room* was filled with ice and meat. This had been done for the Red Sea passage and the meat had kept for twelve days. Some live chickens and a score of sheep were penned on the after well deck and one of the stokers detailed to do the butchering. About ten native boys were brought on to help the cooks and stewards, do the cleaning and so on. A pair of engineer officers appeared, and two Australian Leading Seamen hoping for a lift on their way down under came aboard.

The Captain and Chief Officer of *Afghanistan* were fine competent men, and arranged the tow well. They brought their cable right along the deck to the poop so that the final strain would be taken by the anchor in the hawse pipe; a lot of work, but very effective.[63] As for *Glenearn*, the hands were never so willing as when piped to make this tow fast;[85] by this time they were getting rather good at it and passed the tow easily. They were all so glad to see Aden disappear astern. *Glenearn* was so foul with weed and barnacles that they could only do $4\frac{1}{2}$ knots, but it was cool at sea.

Two days out the Captain was called at dawn, to be told

22.11.41†

---

* Handing room: a small room outside the main refrigerated space which was cool, and normally used for cutting up and distribution.[63]

† Approximate date.

there was a signal from *Afghanistan,* "Have broken a blade off my propeller and must go back to Aden." The horror and dismay was almost tangible. All the struggle to get away was wasted effort, and it would all have to be done again. Not for the first time, Thomas Hood was very sick of *Glenearn.* Wearily they turned,[63] and to everybody's disgust made for Aden.[85] They crawled back at 3 knots[63] and *Glenearn* made fast to her buoy just five days after leaving.[85]

28.11.41

The only compensation for their disappointing return was the delivery of the first "Airgraphs" – letters photographed on miniature film, flown to the destination, then enlarged sufficiently to be readable. In the case of the 2nd Engineer – whose wife wrote to him every Sunday – this delivery brought his total of letters received since leaving home to five; although in his case he had been sent a number of "cables" – after air raids on Glasgow, and such like.[1] McKenzie had not been so lucky. Although the birth of his daughter on 28th June had been reported to him by the Admiralty, he had yet to receive a letter written after the event.*[85] On St. Andrew's night a number of functions took place ashore, even if offshore there was little to celebrate.[1]

30.11.41

N.O.I.C. Aden said that, if the Master of *Afghanistan* could be persuaded to change his propeller and tow again, they were to go ahead. Captain Dodds was surprisingly cheerful, and agreed. Aden's only dry dock was not big enough to take *Afghanistan,* but if they got more salt and shifted forward what was already there, it would tip his ship.[63] He got on with the job right away, and something like 5,000 tons of salt were loaded forward to bring the stern clear of the water, and get at the nut. This was done and the broken propeller removed. A spare was produced from within, and all that remained was to fit it.

No difficulty was foreseen, and everything was going well. The spare propeller was lowered gently down until it was in the right position for sliding it on – when the slings broke, and down to the bottom of Aden harbour went the one and only spare propeller; and with it the hopes of *Glenearn*'s officers

---

* He had to wait until January, 1942.

who were watching the operation from their boat close by. Consternation![85]

When things are really good they are seldom as good as they seem, and when things are very bad they are never quite as bad as they seem.[A] After some delay, a diver was produced and sent down to examine the propeller. He reported that it was lying flat and undamaged, so new slings were procured, the propeller brought to the surface and carefully fitted. It took several days to unload the extra salt and to trim *Afghanistan*; long enough for Japan to enter the war.

8.12.41

Had it not been for the broken propeller, *Glenearn* would have been in Colombo and the refit probably under way. As it was, they would have to run the gauntlet for twenty-one hundred miles at 4 or 5 knots – what a target for a submariner, and no escort to worry him! Being an old submarine man himself, it seemed obvious to Tom Hood that a sub. off the Gulf of Aden would have rich pickings, and that the Japs would already be at battle stations far and wide.[85] No one could blame Captain Dodds if he quit.

But *Afghanistan* had completed her job and – then the terrible news of the *Repulse* and *Prince of Wales* disaster hit them. Depression settled again over *Glenearn*; this must surely be the blackest day of the war.[63] One remark overheard was, "Cheer up, chums, you'll soon all be in the Free British Navy".[85] However, in spite of everything, *Afghanistan* was ready and her Captain still willing to go, but no one would risk giving them sailing orders. Eventually Hood got the N.O.I.C. to make a signal saying, "Intend sailing *Glenearn*", and off they went,[63] fourteen days after their return to Aden.[85]

10.12.41

11.12.41

Glenearn's Captain had been unable to get a chart of the Indian Ocean, so Sub.-Lieut. Scott and he made one by plotting on the back of another chart the relative positions of places from their latitudes and longitudes in None's Tables, and sketching in the coast lines free hand from an old atlas. With progress barely exceeding a hundred miles a day they seemed to take ages to crawl across the paper.

The only boats they had were a small motor boat and the

whaler. In case of "Abandon Ship" the Captain arranged that the best sailors would go in the whaler down-wind to reach land and ask for help for the rest of the ship's company; or such as remained alive by that time. Sub.-Lieut. Scott would be in charge and he was to be sure and take a certain windy Petty Officer, to save being bottled up on a raft with him. The implications of all this got some of the fellows down – the two extra engineers were useless and would not work – but most took it well enough; the two Australian Leading Seamen were first-rate men.[63]

Whatever it was that was wrong with the chickens, they all died before they could be eaten, and without even laying an egg. Stoker Towel slaughtered and skinned the sheep in a most workmanlike manner; but it was found impossible to recommend Aden mutton for anything – except possibly as a substitute for leather.[85]

Christmas Day was spent at sea.[63] The voyage proved to be quite uneventful, and eighteen days after leaving Aden the tow arrived off Colombo.[85] A corvette, *HMAS Lismore*, escorted them[144] in before the pilot and tugs came out. *Afghanistan* stopped and *Glenearn* recovered her anchor cable, but a mistake lost her the faithful $5\frac{1}{2}''$ wire.[63] Thus in anticlimax the 5,000-mile tow from Greece came to its end;[85] *Afghanistan* went on to receive – if there is a God who looks after such matters – the heavenly blessings reserved for such ships, and for such men as Captain Dodds.

Glenearn was a big ship to be manoeuvred without power in a harbour like Colombo,[63] and as she was being shepherded to her mooring, past the "Ceylon for Good Tea" sign,[144] the pilot wanted to drop the anchor. Tom Hood would not do it, as he could not get it back; his was not going to be a ship without an anchor again. Ever.[63]

28.12.41

CHAPTER 13

McKENZIE'S CATHERINE WHEEL

The day after arriving at Colombo, Lieut.-Com. Hood called on the Admiral's Chief of Staff. He surprised Hood by 29.12.41 producing a letter from the pilot who had brought in *Glenearn*; it was full of admiration for the spirit and willingness of the officers and men – how everyone was hauling on ropes and working, engineer officers included. It was an unheard of thing for a pilot to do. The Chief of Staff asked what the ship's armament was, and on being told it was three high-angle 12-pounders, shook Hood by saying that the anti-aircraft defences of Colombo had as a result just been doubled.

Admiralty overseers should have taken over, but the Royal Navy had no experience of Diesels, so the refit would have to be the responsibility of the ship's staff and Walker & Sons' engineering works.[63] A preliminary conference was held on board. It was at once made clear that any repairs carried out could only be of a temporary nature; sufficient, it was hoped, to get the ship back to a fully-equipped refitting port. This was because (1) skilled labour was very limited and could not be increased, (2) facilities for carrying out certain kinds of work were just not available, (3) the amount that could be done was dependent on stores and materials becoming available. In view of the size of the job, and the limited resources of the workshops, the contractors asked for a minimum of six months; even this estimate assumed that preliminary tests on dismantled electrical gear would prove satisfactory, and that naval supplies would be forthcoming on time. It was a great disappointment about the temporary repairs, but this could not be helped. It was obvious that the electrics were going to be a bugbear.

Glenearn was taken into Walker's Yard and went into drydock, to become a hive of activity. The contractors went to work in no uncertain manner, and the Care & Maintenance

Party worked with them. All the engine room equipment was dismantled and the $2\frac{1}{2}$-ton generators lifted out by crane;[85] at last things were moving. All the guns were taken away.[63]

Bill McKenzie and Tom Hood shared the same room in a house ashore,[85] while Alex Aiken and Jim Cahy lived along with some other officers, at a small hotel called Frangé House about three miles along the coast in the direction of Mount Lavinia.[63] It was the middle of the night when McKenzie was awakened to a message from the port police: "*Glenearn* on fire, Commanding Officer cannot be found." The Commanding Officer was in the next bed.

The fire had been discovered at 0300, and its rate of progress was phenomenal – due to the ship's having been in a dry climate for so long, and all the woodwork consequently as dry as tinder. Almost superhuman efforts of the ship's company, aided by the Colombo Fire Brigade, saved what little there was left of *Glenearn*. All the centre part of the ship was gutted;[85] the top two decks including the bridge, the officers' quarters and the Captain's accommodation with all he possessed.[63]

How the fire started was a mystery. It may have been an acetylene bottle, or more probably an electrical fault.[85] Two Courts of Inquiry could not find out the cause, so the Commanding Officer was blamed: he should have insisted on having more men and posted more sentries so that a fire would have been noticed sooner and less damage done. He was past caring by this time.

What with bomb damage, collision damage, and now fire damage, *Glenearn* was a sorry mess. And uninhabitable, so everyone lived ashore and came down to the ship every morning. The C.O. spent every second night on board as he had only one other executive officer – Sub. Lieut. Scott[63] – after Sub.-Lieut. Clements was posted to Egypt at the end of January.[299] One junior engineer also stayed on board each night.[63]

The fire, of course, added considerably to the amount of work necessary to make the ship seaworthy, but all things considered the work went along very well, except for stoppages on certain equipment because of lack of stores.[85] A Mr. J. L. W. Cowie was Walker's manager; the 2nd Engineer got to know him well, and worked with him most happily. As each new difficulty emerged and appeared insurmountable, Glenearn's officers and Walker's men discussed it and tried any scheme that was suggested.[63] Mr. D. P. Bennett gave almost undivided attention, and never lost his enthusiasm for the struggle to recondition the electrical equipment.[85] Glenearn came out of the graving dock and for a while lay alongside the wharf, before being moved out a ship's length from it.[63]

A brick fireplace was built, with a steel tank on top. Once the water in the tank was boiling, natives pulled stirrers to agitate it around the electrical parts suspended in it. Another wash in fresh water, then baking in an oven, before the final varnishing. The damp atmosphere would reduce the electrical resistance of the insulation very quickly, so McKenzie stipulated that he could only take delivery when he was ready for assembly and starting.[85] While Walker's yard was used for the repairs, all the work on board had to be done by Glenearn's men. While Aiken and McKenzie were ashore organizing things, Willie Ramsay, the Third Engineer worked on board wearing sea-boots, singlet and not much else.[113]

Other vessels at Colombo included such old friends as HMS Dorsetshire, Giorgios Averoff, Hector[63] and two other Blue Funnel ships the Commissioned Mine Carriers Atreus* and Laomedon. Laomedon had been hit by a submarine's torpedo a few hours out of Colombo, but had managed to return to harbour.[113] After the fall of Singapore and the Dutch East Indies, all the shipping which had escaped or been diverted in time was sent to Colombo, until the harbour was packed with ships four abreast at every buoy.[63]

In Burma, Rangoon was abandoned by the British; the subsequent Japanese landing in the Andaman Islands threatened the shipping routes in the Bay of Bengal – and Ceylon itself. Frantic efforts were being made to reinforce the

7.3.42
23.3.42

---

* Lieut. (E) Aiken had served as Second Engineer in s.s. Atreus immediately prior to being posted to m.v. Glenearn.

island: 16th and 17th Brigades of 6th Australian Division, on their way home from the Middle East,[603] and the 16th British Infantry Brigade on its way to India, were diverted there in the middle of March,[283] and *HMS Indominitable* used to ferry fighter 'planes. The other aircraft-carrier *Formidable* and the battleship *Warspite* both put in an appearance towards the end of the month.

Admiral Layton had been appointed Commander-in-Chief, Ceylon, with powers over all the military and the civilians on the island, including the Governor.[603] A dispersal of shipping from Colombo's overcrowded harbour began on Tuesday, 31st March, and within a few days some sixty ships had gone.[197] An air-raid "Alert" sounded on the Thursday morning, and the "All Clear" a few minutes later.[317]

Bill McKenzie had arranged for the officers to attend a cricket match on Saturday, which they did. While they were there, however, a message arrived ordering all naval personnel to return to their ships; a Japanese naval force, including five aircraft-carriers, was approaching.[85] In the evening an intelligence report suggested an imminent air attack,[197] and orders from Admiral Layton called for instant readiness from 0300 on the 5th.[584]

During the night another twenty-five ships, mostly from the outer anchorage had sailed; at daylight there remained in the harbour about twenty merchant ships and a few naval vessels – all either too badly damaged to be moved, or actually under repair. *HMS Hector* had just undocked after reverting to trade[197] and was due to sail next day;[85] she and the submarine depot ship *HMS Lucia* were about half a mile away in the direction of the NW breakwater.[63] Torpedoes were being loaded into the submarine *Trusty*. *HMS Tenedos*, a veteran of the Great War was lying stern-secured to No. 18 Wharf completing a refit,[85] the destroyer filling the space between *Glenearn*'s bows and the quay. Moored parallel to *Glenearn* was a Norwegian oil tanker,[63] the *Soli*.[292] Alongside was *Laomedon* mounting, as it happened, one of *Glenearn*'s 12-pounders. An offer was made to man it, but *Laomedon*'s men would not wear that; *Glenearn*'s armament consisted of

31.3.42
2.4.42

4.4.42

5.4.42

one rifle, so with the main engines still useless they would just have to lie at the buoy and watch proceedings as cheerfully as they could.[63]

Thunder clouds obscured the sun and the sky was almost completely overcast, although the visibility was good, when the Japs appeared.[584] Large formations of them – about sixty 'planes[63] – approached from the south-west, flying at about 7,000 feet. They crossed the coast somewhere about Mount Lavinia, then turned north and dived on the harbour, bombing and machine-gunning; some of them came in as low as 50 feet.[584] *Hector*, attacked by two twin-engined bombers which dropped their loads from about 800 feet, and by three single-engined dive-bombers, was hit four times and caught fire admidships;[214] *Glenearn* sent a party away in charge of Sub.-Lieut. Scott to help fight this.[85]

0800

Anti-aircraft fire was feeble. Then a lone aeroplane came low over the harbour; a Hawker "Hurricane" in difficulties. Such guns as were in action fired at him as he turned south.[63]

As the low-level bombers departed a new attack developed; three flights of six aircraft came over at about 5,000 feet. Each flight was in tight arrowhead formation;[214] to home-trained gunners they would have been easy. Each machine carried one bomb, which they all let go together; a salvo straddled *HMS Tenedos* under *Glenearn*'s bows,[63] two bombs hitting the destroyer aft, with two more near-misses.[197] Another flight and more bombs flew down. A young sailor beside Lieut.-Com. Hood said in a strong accent, "I think they are going to miss us, Sir." All six bombs dropped in the space between *Glenearn* and the Norwegian tanker.[63] By 0835 the sky was clear of 'planes.

0835

Workshops and quays had been badly damaged, but only one merchant ship, s.s. *Benledi*[584] had been hit* and set on fire.[197] *HMS Lucia* had collected a bomb which penetrated eight thicknesses of steel plate before exploding outside the ship's side, but managed to remain afloat.[214] *Hector* burned

---

* The Japanese Navy had a doctrine that the destruction of the enemy's fleet would automatically bring command of the sea, therefore it was unnecessary to destroy merchant shipping.

on in spite of the fire-fighting efforts;[197] after three hours she was abandoned and sank in shallow water. In two and a half years of escort duties the armed merchant cruiser had not heard a shot fired in anger, then just a few minutes were sufficient to end a long career. On their way back the coxswain of *Glenearn*'s boat picked up a good-sized fish; approaching the gangway he was asked by the Quartermaster, "Where did you get that there fish, Jimmy, out o' the water?" With a pained expression the coxswain replied, "No, Lieutenant Scott shot it down."

Tenedos, her back broken, had sunk stern first;[85] fifteen of her men had been killed and eleven wounded.[214] The *s.s. Soli* had settled on the bottom; *Glenearn* had taken the same six near misses well,[63] the only damage being five propeller shaft bearing keeps broken.[85]

The damaged "Hurricane" which had passed over the harbour had gone on to crash-land on the Galle Face green, after which the pilot had walked into the Colombo Club for a well-earned drink.[63] About forty British fighters had taken off and engaged the bombers; in turn they had been attacked by the Japanese fighters.[584] Some dog-fights had been seen over Colombo and the RAF claimed to have shot down between twenty-five and thirty of the enemy, and damaged twenty-five more,[318] but the real hero of the day was Admiral Layton, who had sent the ships up the west coast of India. With a hundred ships caught in harbour the Japs would have stayed and got most of them. No enemy 'planes had been shot down over the harbour, either by the RAF or by AA fire. The gun on *Laomedon* had misfired first shot; now that the raid was over *Glenearn*'s men were told that they could have it the next time.[63]

No sooner had the "All Clear" sounded than *Glenearn* was devoid of workmen. This was their first experience of an air-raid and naturally enough they had not liked it, especially as the ship was out in the harbour. Having gone away, they stayed away;[85] large numbers of the population left for the hills, some even going to India. As a result there was a serious shortage of labour.[584]

A conference was held to decide what was to be done with *Glenearn*. The official attitude was that the ship was a wreck and not worth saving;[113] no one was interested. It was suggested that she should be towed up the coast of India to Cochin, out of the way.[85] To those to whom their ship meant the only way home, this was the last straw;[113] after all their struggles, trials and tribulations she was just to be towed away. It was almost a certainty that to leave Colombo with so much of her engine room equipment in thousands of pieces on shore, she would be out of the war for the duration.[85]

On Thursday 9th the Japanese returned to the attack, striking the naval base at Trincomalee.[604] Again the Air Force claimed to have given them a bloody nose, but it was also said that there were very few British 'planes serviceable after this second raid on Ceylon,[63] and the enemy had not been stopped from sinking virtually every naval vessel they had come across on the high seas: the old aircraft-carrier *Hermes* and an Australian destroyer had gone down under a hail of bombs on the 9th, as had *Dorsetshire* and another cruiser on the 5th.[604] But time would tell.

9.4.42

Fortunately the threatened scrapping of *Glenearn* did not come to pass. After about ten days' absence, during which the oil fuel in *Hector* continued to burn, the workmen started to drift back. One day twelve turned up, the next thirty, the next fifty – then the Air Raid Warning sounded and away they all went for another ten to fifteen days. Into the bargain, all night work was stopped. The native workmen did not like the "blackout" and insisted on stopping earlier so that they could get home before dark; this cut down the man-hours considerably. It was all very depressing.

Hold-ups became more frequent because of lack of stores, particularly insulating varnish; also ball and roller bearings.[85] The completion date of 11th June came and went.[1] In the absence of varnish, aircraft cellulose was used instead.[113] The bearings had not arrived either, so the old ones – although very badly pitted – were refitted with a hope for the best.

When the time came to put the equipment back in the ship the docking programme was full for months ahead, and the dry-dock crane thus not available; it was left to the ship's company to manage as best they could. A derrick was removed from aft and rigged to the samson post on "A" Deck (starboard), and an ALC winch connected to the emergency dynamo for hoisting. The equipment was brought out on a lighter – when one could be procured – and hoisted inboard on the temporary derrick, then lowered through the engine room skylight. Half-way down the engine room the load had to be transferred to the engine room crane; it was a lengthy process. but all the heavy gear was taken on board without damage by this method.[85] No. 3 Generator was started at

4.7.42 0900 on Saturday 4th July.[1] The varnish ordered in January arrived in August; the bearings did not arrive at all.

The heat of the fire in the dry-dock had buckled the deck, and with the monsoon the rain lay in the depressions. So many mosquitoes bred there that the natives burned tow to keep them off.[85] All the officers except Willie Ramsay got dengue fever,[63] so the sick engineers got leave to the hills;

21.8.42 Alex. Aiken left Colombo on 21st August and arrived at Nuwara Eliya the following day.[1] The "Garden of Ceylon" was situated at an altitude of 6,200 feet and its temperature seldom rose above 65°F, even although it was only seven degrees north of the Equator. Tea bushes covered the hillsides and the mountain tops, apparently without end.[608] After this break at Ceylon's sanitorium he arrived back at Colombo

30.8.42 on Sunday 30th August.[1]

The two deck officers, as well as getting dengue fever, suffered from an exaggerated sense of duty; for days Scott was running a temperature of 104°, but would not go sick because his C.O. did not – although Hood was not so bad with it.[63] McKenzie got it last and worst.

It was a great moment for the Care and Maintenance Party

8.9.42 when, on 8th September, the main engines turned under their own power; the first time for seventeen months. Once started

1.10.42 they were kept running.[85] From 1st October a ship's company even further reduced in numbers victualled on board.[1] The two Aussie Leading Seamen had eventually got a ship bound for Australia, and both the extra engineers taken on at Aden had broken their leave and been dismissed the ship.[63] Of the two pi dogs picked up along the way, one had got rabies and been shot; the other had been run over by a train.[113]

On the 20th October *Glenearn* was alongside the dock wall ready for her steaming trials.[85] The Admiralty Overseer, Commander (E) A. E. Francis, RN, came to the gangway and said to the C.O. before everyone, that the credit was entirely due to the ship's own engineer and electrical officers. It was a difficult admission for him to make, and he was admired for it.[63] Messrs. Walker & Sons had, of course, helped the undertaking along with their admittedly limited equipment, and last but not least, much was due to *Glenearn*'s Commanding Officer for his handling of many very "sticky" situations, his patience, understanding and encouragement when times were bad.[85] Neither Lieut.-Com. Hood, nor Lieut. P. W. Scott had been away from the ship for more than twenty-four hours during the ten long weary months in Colombo.[63]

After the 24-hour trials, McKenzie had everything switched off for a day to see what would happen on re-starting. After switching on, only one or two minor switches failed, and they were very easily replaced.[85] Four passengers, two for Durban and two for the U.K. came on board, also a deck officer to work his passage, and on Thursday 22nd October, 1942, *HMS Glenearn* left Colombo for home,[1] and another war effort. She sailed without escort,[63] and after gradually working up speed to $17\frac{1}{2}$ knots arrived at Durban on 1st November.* The next day eight ships, it was said, were sunk outside the port.[85]

Sub-Lieut. (E) R. Price, RNR, who had served since October, 1941, left the ship, which stayed at Durban for more than a week waiting for a new Captain who had been appointed; time for the Second Engineer to visit a childhood friend at Port Shepstone, and for some of the ship's company to buy turkeys for their forthcoming Christmas Dinners with their families. Five passengers for home and two for Cape Town were embarked, and Captain E. C. L. Turner, RN, took

* Calculated date.

command on the 8th November,[1] after having served under the Flag Officer East Africa for a few months.[299] They sailed on the 10th.*

Captain Turner was not the type of RN officer likely to get the best out of RNR and RNVR men. He knew nothing about the engines of a Diesel ship; at Cape Town Lieut.-Com. Hood told him they could not leave until some electrical repairs had been done. Captain Turner replied, "We don't need to wait for them." Lieutenant (E) Aiken, with Scottish bluntness said, "My man, if the electrics don't go in this ship, the engines don't go."[63]

They left Cape Town on 16th November.[1] A day or two later a solitary friendly aircraft was sighted,[85] and further out on the South Atlantic course was changed to avoid a reported submarine. Captain Turner was all set to go into Freetown, and would hardly believe that *Glenearn* could easily reach the U.K. without refuelling.

The rest of the voyage was uneventful;[63] they were able to keep up a steady 18 knots and there were only two small stoppages.[113] *Glenearn* arrived at Greenock on Sunday, 6th December,[1] and as the anchor went down off the Tail of the Bank Tom Hood turned to Alex. Aiken and shook him by the hand, "Well, we got here after all."[63]

They had to wait a few days for an escort round the north of Scotland. At Sheerness McKenzie had everything switched off. When it was time to start up again to go up-river to Harland & Wolff's, the port sea-water pump was not working: it would start, but would not keep going. McKenzie recognized the signs of insulation breaking down, but reckoned the ship would not be sailing fast enough to need cooling water, so he left it. He turned round to find the port bilge pump looking like a catherine wheel, thus justifying the painstaking efforts of the engineers, and his own determination to have everything just right. He was able to shrug off these problems; what mattered was, they had made it – *Glenearn* was the shipyard's responsibility now.[85]

---

* Calculated date.

Postscript

THE LONDON GAZETTE

London Gazette 3rd June, 1941:

To be a Companion of the Distinguished Service Order (DSO)

  Lieutenant-Commander Julian William Best, RNR (retd.)

Distinguished Service Medal (DSM)

  Leading Seaman Lawrence Lamb, D/JX 145980

London Gazette 11th November, 1941:

To be a Companion of the Distinguished Service Order (DSO)

  Captain Lawrence Bernard Hill, OBE, RN (retd.)

Distinguished Service Medal (DSM)

  Shipwright First Class Charles Philip Menhenitt, D/M 6473

  Blacksmith Fourth Class John Charles Runnalls, D/M 60798

Mention in Despatches:

  Lieutenant-Commander Dennis Noel Venables, RN.

  Chief Petty Officer Reginald John Eddy, D/JX 163832

  Supply Chief Petty Officer Sydney Thomas Pegler, D/M 37541

  Assistant Steward Jack Gould, D/LX 25409

Distinguished Service Cross (DSC)

  Paymaster Lieutenant-Commander Arthur Roswell Jackson, RN.

London Gazette 2nd June, 1943:

Member of the Most Excellent Order of the British Empire (MBE)

  Lieutenant-Commander (E) Alexander Charles Lyons Aiken, RNR.

British Empire Medal (BEM)

  Stoker Petty Officer Joseph Hewett, D/K 62239

  Leading Stoker Ralph Sydney Burn, D/KX 82176

Mention in Despatches:

  Sub-Lieutenant (E) William McKenzie, RNVR.

BOOK TWO

CHAPTER 14

A POWERFUL CONTRIBUTION

HMS Glenearn was taken in hand by Harland & Wolff[286]   13.12.42
at North Woolwich and given Berth No. 3 King George V
Dock; the one previously occupied by *HMS Cheshire*, an ex-
Bibby liner converted to a Stores Ship.[151] The new arrival
was a mess on deck, there was extensive superstructural
damage, and the engine room a maze of timber shores,
planking and cement slabs.[3] Permanent repairs to the hull
were put in hand,[151] eight to ten plates being taken away and
either "faired" or replaced. Everyone was struck by the
tremendous strength of the ship, which was one of the heaviest
anyone had ever been on.[30]

Apart from battle and collision damage and the overhauling of her main and auxiliary machinery,[151] there remained to be settled the question of bringing her up to the
improved standard of what was now referred to as a Landing
Ship Infantry (Large). Whereas the Glen ships had every
advantage of construction and engineering, in terms of use-
fulness they had no superiority over many LSI(L)s flying the
Red Ensign. Compared with *Winchester Castle* or *Batory*, they
carried the same number of landing craft, about half the
number of troops, and were not so well fitted for the Senior
Naval Officer controlling a number of Landing Ships. In these
later conversions it had been possible to incorporate the
lessons of earlier work, but when the three Glen ships had
been first altered no one had had any experience. The low
trooping capacity in particular was due to an incomplete
conversion, rather than to lack of space.[218]

As far back as April 1942 Captain Petrie of *Glengyle* had
prepared a memorandum on the experience gained after
eighteen months of training exercises and operations. This
paper had contained a number of constructive criticisms of
the davit gear, the AA defence and the staffing – among a host
of other comments[235] – and had been well received by senior

officers of Combined Operations Command. Even before the return of *Glenearn* and *Glenroy* – the latter having stopped two torpedoes* on the way to Tobruk – it had been recognised that a decision would have to be made on the future of these two vessels.

16.12.42 On 16th December the Senior Officer, Assault Ships and Craft at Largs on the Clyde sent his thoughts on the subject to

29.12.42 the Chief of Combined Operations;† he in turn wrote to the Director of Plans at the Admiralty.[218] This was followed by a

3.1.43 meeting in the Admiralty on Sunday, 3rd January, 1943, to discuss the requirements for the White Ensign LSIs. It was decided that three 4-inch high angle/low angle twin gun mountings should be fitted, together with Fire Control.[219] Recent experience in North Africa suggested a definite requirement for long-range AA armament, to counter bombing attacks delivered from just outside 2-pounder and Oerlikon range.[218]

It was also considered desirable to double the number of "landing craft assault" – LCAs – at davits, but here the problem was that a satisfactory three-tier davit had not'even been designed, let alone produced, and would take months to fit.

Approval was therefore to be sought for installation of new davits during the period of the refit.[219]

Lastly, the accommodation should be increased as much as possible. Thus improved, *HMS Glenearn* would, in the words of the Senior Officer, Assault Ships and Craft, "be a powerful contribution to any assault force, suitable for the role of SNOL ship, well armed and able to carry a full battalion as well as a Brigade HQ".[218]

5.1.43 Two days after this meeting, another took place on board to decide which alterations could be effected whilst in dockyard hands. The previous decisions were confirmed, and furthermore it was agreed that whatever took place the ship should be ready to sail within six months – the period for which she could be spared, as far as the Chief of Combined Operations was concerned.[219]

---

* 23rd November, 1941.

† Vice-Admiral Lord Louis Mountbatten.

Meanwhile, the Care & Maintenance Party had drifted back from Christmas leave, with few cares on their minds other than the recent discovery that Durban turkeys came from the same tannery as Aden sheep.[1] The engineers were a great crowd, who could do anything.[113] The 2nd Engineer had worked well with the naval men and their routine; he and the Third Engineer got on all right.[63] Alex. Aiken was easy-going and always ready for a lark;[113] Willie Ramsay had a cheerful disposition and was quite a likeable bloke, although very young for his position.[63] Bill McKenzie had proved to be an awfully nice fellow.[106] All the Alfred Holt men were financially worse off than their mercantile equivalents, whose basic wages had been augmented by war bonuses.[113]

A pleasant duty which now fell to the erstwhile Commanding Officer was the composition of a short list – two engineers and two stokers – of recommendations for decorations. Hood's only regret was that he had done nothing to get some recognition for the Master of *Afghanistan*, who richly deserved it. OBEs had been given for less. Living in a wreck had left its mark on Thomas Hood; he felt bitter and depressed whenever he thought of the recent past.[63] Bill McKenzie for his part felt the efforts to save their ship would be justified if she could do one more good job.[85] *Glenearn* had stood up to so much; she was tougher than most of the people in her.[63]

Conversion work went on at high pressure. Normal working hours were from 8 a.m. until 7 p.m.,[146] but specific trades frequently worked until 11 o'clock at night, and on occasions all night.[134] Apart from the structural repairs, there was the familiar orgy of stripping out;[151] much of the timber of the port side boat decking was renewed where it had been destroyed by the fire.[34] Once the main and auxiliary machinery had been taken out for overhaul,[151] a temporary lighting system was supplied by Harland & Wolff, powered by a portable generator on the quayside.[134]

Morale of the restricted labour force was high;[151] partly due to the overtime earnings, but also because there had not been a serious air-raid on London since July 1941.[134] It cannot have been pleasant living through the "blitz": working all day and worrying about the wife and children all the while. Some of the shipyard workers were Air Raid Wardens at night[162] – still it made you feel a bit proud to put in these years of work, doing a good job for Old England.[134]

On the evening of the 17th there was an air-raid lasting two hours, and another between 0430 and 0600 later the same night. Few aircraft penetrated as far as central London, and each one was engaged by AA guns of every description, filling the sky with bursting shells.[452] A few days later, when most thoughts were on the mid-day break[453] and some on the gambling school in the bottom hold,[75] fast Focke-Wulf fighter-bombers came over just above the roof-tops; too fast for the anti-aircraft gunners, and much too fast for the barrage balloons – most of which were still on the ground, while several in the air were shot down in flames.[453] About twenty bombs were dropped; an unpleasant reminder that the war in the air was not confined to thousand-bomber raids on Berlin.[452]

No one was sleeping on board now. Most of the officers were living in "digs" within fairly easy reach[3] – that is, when they were not away on leave, which was coming round at the rate of ten days a month. When the Second Engineer went off the Chief gave him his air pistol for the former's son.[2] Tom Hood went on his foreign service leave and got married, only to be recalled from honeymoon to re-assume command; Captain Turner had wangled the appointment of Captain of *Glengyle*.[63] The sister-ship, having survived a Malta convoy, the Dieppe Raid and the North African landing, was back in Scottish waters.[610]

One by one the officers were posted; a process started in January with Surg.-Lieut. Johnson. Several of the junior engineers ended up in "Woolworth" carriers[299] – merchant ships converted to carry aircraft[R] – and the Second Engineer was notified of his forthcoming appointment as Chief Engineer to *HMS Prince Baudouin*, a Belgian cross-Channel ferry being converted to a Landing Ship Infantry (Small) at Tilbury.[1] The Ward Room Mess was closed down at the end of April,[A] and by the middle of May only Tom Hood and four engineers – Cahy, Ramsay, McKenzie and Sub.-Lieut. J. S. Taylor RNVR – remained of those officers who had "signed on" in 1940.[299]

Work went on apace. Four of the original gravity davits were removed, and after fixing the new heavy davits the riveting squad was ordered down to the hold to screw up and make tight the hefty big tanks that had been erected by the plater and his mates.[162] There were three of these petrol tanks, cylindrical and mounted on stools,[36] total capacity 10,000 gallons, located in the centre compartment of what had been the forward hold.[621]

From the storage tanks fuel was to be piped to points conveniently close to the stowage positions of the landing craft;[36] new petrol lines were required. Like everything else under Admiralty supervision this work was to the highest standards the plumbers had ever encountered: joints had to be arc-welded both in the collar and on the flange, faced in a machine at No. 10 Shop, then returned to the ship and hand-lapped by fitters. The pipes were supplied from Chatham and had to be free from improvised joints – no butt welds to make up a length. All the other plumbing – fresh water, sanitation, accommodation showers, baths and hand basins – was of course examined, but not by such a multitude: Admiralty Inspector, the Ship Manager, the Foreman Plumber and Line Superintendent – all concerned themselves with the petrol lines, and they would only accept perfection.[30]

Accommodation for the troops was completely altered; the after hold became a honeycomb of compartments, especially on the upper 'tween deck.[34] The fitting of armament involved the provision of considerable ancillary electrical gear; then there was the radar and general communications equipment.[151] Two replacement anchors were delivered in June after being tested at Sunderland.[296] Relations between the contractors and the Director of Naval Construction, and with the other Admiralty departments, were at all times extremely good. Occasionally there were shortages of materials, but the ship had considerable priority.[151] All trades speculated, as men do, why so much care was being taken – agreed, all work on ships should be good, because a breakdown at sea is always more serious than the same thing ashore, but such high class of workmanship ... it made one wonder.[30]

Lord Louis Mountbatten made regular visits; every section of the ship was inspected and progress discussed.[151] He impressed everybody with his appearance, the speed with which he moved about, and the rapidity with which he rapped out orders and questions. Furthermore, he was not surrounded by the usual high-ranking officer's entourage; one young officer, who could hardly keep up with him as he moved around on his tour of inspection, was enough. In one's humble opinion, a real man.[30]

Towards the end of May a few deck officers had arrived to replace the stand-by crew and join Sub-Lieut. W. C. Neill, RNR, who as *Glenearn*'s first new permanent deck officer had paced the lonely decks since the previous March. A few more were appointed in July, and several in August including a new Captain.[299] Colin Arthur George Hutchison, DSO and bar, RN (retd.), was no stranger to the *Glenearn*-class of ship, having commanded *HMS Breconshire*[85] which, still sailing as an Auxiliary Supply Ship (Commissioned), had survived many Malta convoys before being sunk just off the island on her eighth run in.[602] Lieutenant-Commander Hood handed over command and left for an anti-submarine course at Campbeltown.[63]

It was now the third week in August and the painting of the ship was far advanced.[A] Alleyways had been given two coats of red lead, two coats of white flat, and finished with gloss. The result was that everything below deck was gleaming white; the foreman painter probably expected the VC or at least the BEM. However, when Lord Louis saw it he went rigid, so to speak, and sent for the Ship Manager – an ex-foreman painter – and the Foreman Painter, and asked the reason. They pointed, quite rightly, to the indents. "Well", said Lord Louis, "If you think I am going to have my men wasting their time at sea washing down the lower half of this white paint in the alleyways which will obviously get dirty, you're mistaken. I want the lower half painted grey; that will save a lot of time and labour." When this story got around he went right to the top of the league as far as the shipyard workers were concerned.[30]

When later in the week it was reported in the newspaper that Vice-Admiral the Lord Louis Mountbatten, GCVO, DSO, ADC, had been appointed Supreme Allied Commander South-East Asia,[454] the reason for all the special care taken over the refit became clear – *Glenearn* was to be his head-quarters ship for S.E.A.C.;[30] an impression strengthened by the presentation (on loan) to the ward-room of two signed photographs, of King George VI and Queen Elizabeth respectively, during such time as *HMS Glenearn* remained a warship – but to be returned when and if she reverted to merchant service.[8]

26.8.43

Glenearn meanwhile dry-docked in King George V dry-dock, where all the underwater fittings and areas were dealt with.[151] When she came out it was time to balance the ship. All trades were ordered ashore, only those engaged in the balancing remaining on board. Large narrow barges filled with 56 lb. weights were raised and lowered on both port and starboard sides; it was presumed that the new davits were tested at the same time.

A week or so elapsed, then the new landing craft appeared around the ship,[30] and were embarked.[220] Eight of the original gravity davits had been retained after strengthening, and four gallows davits added; each of these fixtures hoisted one LCA. With the four big luffing davits handling three apiece *Glenearn* now carried no less than twenty-four LCAs, as well as the three LCMs carried as deck cargo[540] – and not forgetting the cutter and the dinghy.[621] Eight of the extra small craft had to be secured outboard because of insufficient deck space; this was bound to reduce the ship's sea-going capabilities if damage to these suspended boats were to be avoided.[540]

22.10.43

While the war at sea became ever closer, for the time being at least the war in the air seemed more real. By this time the Londoners thought they were immune from air raids;[30] they could see squadrons of British fighters flying south to carry the war to the enemy across the Channel.[2] And the Yanks too; sometimes returning of an afternoon pretty badly damaged, the four-engined bombers appearing to fly sideways on.[30]

Someone in *Glenearn* with a recent professional interest in the Americans was Surg.-Lieut. I. Payne-James who as a house surgeon in the Norfolk & Norwich Hospital had spent six strenuous months treating their casualties. On coming aboard the first person he had been taken to was the Captain. Payne-James noted "with dismay" the DSO and bar, and thought, "We've got a brave one here." Disclaiming any bravery himself, he nevertheless found the Captain a very nice little man – a "dug-out" who, having been axed at the time of cuts in spending on armaments, had been brought back when the war started.[106]

The ship's company poured in; officers and men from all parts of the country, but quite a few from the Woolwich area. One lad from Walthamstow, whose father was a docker, was caught by the Port of London Authority police, in civvies and trying to smuggle his accumulated rum ration ashore. Captain Hutchison was away at the time, so the wretched boy waited, under escort, from the Thursday until Saturday morning. He was sent away, and was to be seen no more.

10.11.43   By 10th November *HMS Glenearn*'s naval complement was something like complete, and she herself was something like shipshape; the same day she was inspected by Admiral Sir Martin Dunbar-Nasmith,[85] VC, KCB, CB, Flag Officer in Charge, London, and hero of submarine E-11's exploits at the Dardanelles in 1915.[302]

As with most wartime commissionings, there was considerable muddle due to stores not arriving as arranged; but worse was to come. While getting ready to sail as it were, an urgent message arrived from the Naval Constructors' Department at Bath saying that there had been a miscalculation, and the ship required 400 tons more ballast[85] – visions of *HMS Glenearn* proceeding to sea and toppling over.[106] The sand ballast was carried down through the naval mess decks until it formed a layer about six feet thick in the bottom of what had been No. 2 Hold and part of No. 3. To protect and retain the sand a crust of concrete 6 inches thick was also needed,[36] so stones and cement had to be taken below; by the time this had been done the ship was in a truly filthy state.[85]

A false deck was hurriedly welded into place[75] about fifteen feet below No. 2 Lower 'Tween Deck, leaving an air space over the ballast.[36] The additional weight of ballast and false deck together with that of the landing craft would have taken *Glenearn* down on to the dock mud, so the LCAs were sent away again.[75]

On 4th December *Glenearn* passed into the lock[85] – bows first as befitted a ship of the Royal Navy – and so out of King George V Dock.[30] She was a smart-looking ship to the watchers whose work was finished, as she headed down the Thames.[162] At Sheerness fuel and ammunition were taken in,[85] then it was on into the English Channel for sea trials; also tests and drills on all ancillary gear.[151] Practice ammunition was fired at an aircraft-towed sleeve target.[158] The new ship's company gave a good account of themselves, and the work was completed on the 9th;[286] at this point the dockyard men handed over the ship at the end of a very interesting job.[151] *Glenearn* returned up-river as far as Tilbury Docks; Harland & Wolff's men left her there and the landing craft with their Royal Marine crews were embarked. The LCAs were organised in two units – 535 and 536 Royal Marine Flotillas[85] – and had been ready for ten days.[221]

HMS Glenearn now represented the last word in the development of the Landing Ship, Infantry.[540] Well armed: six 4-inch Quick Firing Mk XVI guns, four 2-pdr Mk VIII on single mountings,[231] and absolutely festooned with 20 mm Oerlikons – eight of them, stuck everywhere that ingenuity could devise, including halfway up the funnel.[94] To complement this battery of guns she was well-supplied with Radar types 272P and 291, also a 285 Interrogator for I.F.F.* Mk III, P.P.I.† type B and a Q.H.R.F. unit type 25.‡ With all

4.12.43

9.12.43

10.12.43

* Identification Friend or Foe.
† Plan Position Indicator.
‡ Navigational aid also known as "the Decca Navigator".

this, and accommodation for 87 army officers and 1,002 other ranks,[232] there was no doubt she was admirably equipped for her purpose.[540] Indications of what that purpose was hung on every side for all to see: twenty-four LCAs bore silent but eloquent witness to that.[106] But, when all was said and done, she was still a bit of a Christmas tree.[63]

13.12.43   On the 13th December 1943, exactly one year from her arrival in the Thames, *Glenearn* sailed for Scotland, and after being delayed by fog anchored in the Cromarty Firth.[85]

CHAPTER 15

IN THE STEPS OF THE PROPHET

Glenearn had been allocated to Force "S", whatever that might be.[220] Headquarters of Force "S" were at Cameron Barracks, Inverness, with HQ 3rd British Infantry Division alongside.[205] Afloat, the Force consisted of nine Landing Ships Infantry and Headquarters Ships, more than twenty Landing Ships Tank, and upwards of two hundred major landing craft. All the ships were based on Invergordon, while the independent craft were divided between Invergordon and Inverness. Minor landing craft, most of them with their parent ships, numbered more than three hundred. For maintenance reasons, the Force had been divided into three groups, the idea being that each group could retire periodically to the Firth of Forth for repairs and leave.[194]

Ashore, starting from scratch in October, bases, accommodation and repair facilities had been developed throughout the Moray Firth area.[205] Marshalling camps had been established on the Black Isle between Munlochy and Rosemarkie.[562] All this preparation was for the purpose of training a naval assault force, able to lift, and land on an enemy-defended shore, one infantry division.[205] Presumably at other places around the British Isles similar Forces, differently lettered, were going about the same business of preparing for some majestic if awesome enterprise.[A]

HMS Glenearn approached the narrow entrance to the Cromarty Firth,[85] passed under the guns emplaced on the Sutors[123] and over the electrically-actuated minefield between them,[53] and anchored off Invergordon.[85]

Invergordon. Host to Admiral Beatty's battle-cruisers during the Great War,[123] scene of a naval mutiny over pay in the 'thirties,[R] and witness to a great naval battle earlier in the present conflict when an enemy submarine was sighted – or was said to have been sighted – in the Firth.[123] After the general engagement which ensued, a Highland sailor ap-

17.12.43

parently wrote to the Admiralty dockyard establishment asking when he might receive his "metal"* for having taken part in the action; only to be told that only one award was to be made, posthumously, to a cow on the Black Isle.[53]

22.12.43 On arrival it was learned that *Glenearn* would be required for a big combined exercise called "Burgher I". This took place in Burghead Bay. The weather was very bad and the Royal Marines not experienced in "hooking on" their craft in such conditions; having had no time to work up, the ship had a lot to learn about arranging boat ropes and handling davits. The exercise was completed and the ships were back in 24.12.43 harbour by the evening of the 24th.

Christmas Day was celebrated in the usual manner, but not without some restraint, as there was to be an early start on Boxing Day.[85] Two days after Christmas *Glenearn* berthed 27.12.43 alongside the jetty at Invergordon to take on 600 tons of fuel,[53] and troops for Exercise "Burgher II",[A] before sailing at 1100 on the 29th.[53] On the 30th No. 1 Mess Deck was flooded 30.12.43 with petrol fumes,[85] and Sub-Lieutenant (E) McKenzie, as Chief Electrical Officer, reported to the Captain that he was not satisfied with some of the fans that were used to extract fumes from the petrol tanks.[66]

The weather was continually bad, even between gales, and it was common knowledge that no invasion could take place in such weather – so why the insistence on carrying out exercises which were wrecking craft and davits? When the time came, equipment and gear would be worn out.[85]

14.1.44 At the end of the second 15-day period,[A] *Glenearn* sailed for Rosyth to have a few outstanding defects attended to, but nothing was done.[85] Captain Hutchison reported the petrol fumes to a Senior Naval Constructor, but was told that everything was quite satisfactory and he was not to make an unnecessary fuss about it.[66]

22.1.44 Three days' leave to each watch was given. During the second of these leave periods there was a full gale[408] in the Firth of Forth and the ship dragged her anchor.[85] There was no officer on the upper deck, only the AB of the watch who

* Medal.

was drinking cocoa in his little shack at the time; *Glenearn*'s hitting a coal barge on the way down river was the first intimation that anything was wrong.[112] She ended up on the mud[85] near the outer end of Rosyth breakwater, right opposite the depot ship occupied by the Wrens,*[112] but without otherwise coming to any harm.[85] The Captain's Secretary, Lieut. (S) Plunkett, RN, was sent ashore to Inverkeithing railway station to meet the "Old Man" back from leave and tell him that his ship was aground. Courts martial were planned, but never came to anything.[112] The second-in-command, Lieut.-Com. McLock,† RNR, was relieved of his job.[66]

536 RM Flotilla was transferred to *s.s. Empire Cutlass*, one of the recently constructed "Empire" Class of Landing Ships,[486] and 535 Flotilla was increased to eighteen landing craft.[487] This reduction in the number of LCAs secured outboard would, if nothing else, reduce the risks of storm damage.[A]

By the 4th February *Glenearn* was back in the Cromarty Firth, the Admiralty Pilot taking her alongside at 2030; a tricky job in the dark.[53] After the troops had been embarked[A] for exercise "Crown" there was a gale warning and as a result two 24-hour postponements; D-Day became the 9th.[563] The weather was still very bad; one of the Force's craft on its way from Cromarty to Inverness was caught in a strong blow and sank with the loss of several soldiers.[85]

4.2.44

9.2.44

A few days after Exercise "Crown", 706 RM Flotilla arrived at Invergordon having taken nearly a fortnight to sail from Aberdeen, including several days sheltering in the harbours of Fraserburgh and Buckie. The purpose of this flotilla with its LCP(L)‡ was to escort "swimming" tanks into shore and assist them when they broke down. "DD"§ tanks had two propellers, and the open turret was provided with a collapsible canvas screen intended to produce the necessary flotation. Each tank was provided with an aircraft inflatable

---

* Women's Royal Naval Service.
† Name changed.
‡ Landing Craft, Personnel (Large).
§ Duplex Drive.

dinghy,[205] and all the divers wore Davis escape apparatus; which was just as well, since the first two or three machines to be sent in just went, "Glug, glug, glug" and disappeared, thanks to the weather in the Moray Firth.[106] Those which sank usually left the crew to be picked up by the LCP(L)s; those which did not sink were sometimes kept afloat by the tank crew's attempts to hold up the canvas screen above the level of the water.[11]

After Exercise "Crown" the plan of attack had been changed; 3 Inf Div would make the assault on a single brigade front; 8 Bde landing first, followed two hours later by 185 Bde.[563] This was to be first tried out in Exercise "Anchor" later in the month. *Glenearn* was taken alongside Invergordon pier at 0830[53] and embarked two companies of the 1st Bn South Lancashire Regiment[251] and half of the 2nd East Yorkshires, including the latter's Battalion HQ.[252] Some amusement was apparent when the Commanding Officer of the East Yorks turned out to be a Colonel Hutchinson;[36] *Glenearn*'s C.O. pointed out that he spelt his name the Chinese way: "Hutch-i-son".[155]

The soldiers settled in to enjoy the change of food[159] and make the best of the rather cramped accommodation;[37] they spent two nights on board before the exercise was carried out.[563] Once again the weather was foul, so much so that Captain Hutchison had to assure the soldiers, and his Marine crews, that the weather could not possibly by anything like so bad on "The Day". As an experiment, sea-sickness tablets were issued along with the "bags, vomit", on the principle of belt and braces.[85]

The craft headed for a shore defended by an enemy provided by the Royal Engineers, Findhorn, and the invaders managed to capture most of Burghead before the firing of blank ammunition ceased and both sides adjourned to fill the three public houses in the village.[84] Meanwhile the LCAs had long since headed back towards their parent ships. Some of *Glenearn*'s davits were bent, and others badly strained by the heavy shocks received in recovering her craft from the heavy swell.[85] Having hooked them in and got them inboard the

20.2.44

22.2.44

effectiveness of the new sea-sickness pills became apparent; the craft were full of vomit. All the soldiers seemed to have been sick. And when the sailors went to clean up, one of the LCAs was found to contain an unconscious man – the poor fellow had been overlooked by his wretched companions as they staggered ashore. It was patently obvious that there was going to be a terrible problem if the sea were rough on D-Day.[106]

Glenearn left for Rosyth again. This time the petrol compartment was put right.[85] Four days' leave were granted to each watch, and Captain Hutchison went up to the Admiralty and argued that his ship required a Commander RN, as first executive officer.[36] Then north again for more exercises.[85]

27.2.44

In their absence "Pop Buzz", scheduled for the 9th March, had been planned to exercise naval units in support fire and practise the Force communications organization.[203] Live firing was carried out on the Tarbat Peninsula, with the direction of fire limited to avoid both the RAF airfield near Tain and the Fleet Air Arm's at Fearn. Some 900 inhabitants had been evacuated from the area under Defence Regulation 51[194] – at short notice, great inconvenience, and in the middle of an influenza epidemic.[129] Lord Rosebery, Regional Commissioner for Civil Defence for Scotland,[121] had addressed the local people in Fearn village hall to explain that it was due to vital wartime necessity that they were being ordered – asked – to leave their homes at such a bad time of year.

He had received not one complaint. Their attitude was exemplified by an old man, asked during the loading of an army truck with his essential belongings why he was bothering to take a fishing line, when he would get no fishing in Tain said, "*Cho cinnteach 's a tha mise 'ga thoirt air falbh, bidh mi 'ga thoirt air ais fada an deidh dhan au frusdair Hitler sin a bhith anns an naigh.*"*[129]

A Gunnery Officer, in the shape of Lieutenant Mayhew, RN, had joined on 15th February and soon established the

---

* "As sure as I am taking it with me I'll be taking it back; as this war will have only one ending and that is in the end of that trash Hitler."

fact that the ship was going to be able to look after herself, if gun drills and training could make it so.[94] Starting with untrained crews, a large amount of gun practice had been carried out, just as all the other departments were similarly being worked up.[85] A drill was thought out whereby a first flight of twelve fully loaded landing craft could be put in the water in twelve minutes.[152] The soldiers were practised in getting into the boats both in daylight and in the dark,[85] and an exercise was carried out on time only, in case of a breakdown in the telephone system.[293] While they were becoming accustomed to the procedure, *Glenearn*'s boat lowerers were turning into experts at handling davits.

The three other Landing Ships which would sail under the direction of Captain Hutchison were becoming efficient and skilful too, and a lot of experience had been gained in approaching an unlighted coast.[85] A new type of navigational aid called the Decca Navigator had been invented, and the first trials of it were carried out by *Glenearn* in the Moray Firth.[66] To fix the ship's position at any time it was only necessary to read off the numbers shown in an instrument called the Decometer, and plot the point on an Admiralty chart specially over-printed with sets of hyperbolic curves. The range of the system was about 300 miles from the master transmitting station ashore, and the accuracy very high: down to 150 yards, depending upon the angles of intersection of the position lines.[600]

So the weeks of March went past.[A] Richard Hardman-Jones, Commander, RN, was appointed Second-in-Command, and took up his duties.[299] All energies were concentrated on making ready for the last of the great rehearsals: Exercise "Leap Year".[564] As before, *Glenearn* had to embark her infantry direct from Invergordon Pier, and the question was raised whether she could come alongside with some of her LCAs slung outboard. D. S. Garson, the Admiralty Pilot went aboard, and after comparing measurements decided that the starboard outslung craft would, in fact, clear the top of the pier for a few hours, depending on the state of the tide.[53] *Glenearn* was very easy to handle – Captain

Hutchison could take her anywhere without tugs[66] – but as the pilot brought her in towards the pier an officer rushed out of the signalling tower gesticulating wildly; no one had considered the horizontal clearance between the projecting LCA and the tower. By this time, however, *Glenearn* was committed to coming alongside.*[53]

The Army arrived in craft loads, and Marine guides showed them down to their troop decks. Each soldier was given his craft number – which was also chalked up on a black square at the exit from his deck.[293] *Glenearn* was taken off again at 1330,[53] and soon afterwards a conference was held in the ward-room attended by all the officers on board, with the exception of the doctors and engineers. Details of the time-table were explained with the help of a sectional drawing through the troop decks, and a deck plan showing the positions of all the landing craft; also isometric projections for each half of the ship giving the troops' waiting positions in relation to their boat stations. Then the ship's officers acting as guides, took the army craft commanders along the respective routes from the troop decks to the embarkation positions.

27.3.44

Before night fell, the seamen had finished their preparations; removing the guys from the gravity davits, running special lines to keep turns out of the falls, and seeing that boat ropes were in position and to their marks.[293] Five miles away, on the far side of the Black Isle, work went on through the night as the Tank Landing Craft were loaded up from the flood-lit "hards" at Chanonry Point,[564] deathplace of *Coinneach Odhar*, the Brahan Seer.[550] By morning the entire Force was afloat, the flotillas formed up and in the late afternoon Force "S" set course north-east for the coast of Caithness.

28.3.44

Between Lybster and Wick the change of direction south for Burghead was made, and by the morning the "Lowering Position" was reached. But the weather was extremely rough and likely to deteriorate; it was decided to shelter in Cromarty Firth. The day was spent at anchor watching "Sunderland" flying boats, in the sunny spells between the

29.3.44

* The dating of this incident is uncertain.

snow showers, at bombing practice over Nigg Bay.

30.3.44   After a quiet night Force "S" sailed past the deserted Tarbat Peninsula, then south for Burghead Bay.[564] Burghead and its lighthouse were obscured by a smoke screen laid by aircraft flying past the eastern flank of the invasion area[84] as the landing craft began their run-in on a calm sea. Guns thundered,[564] their shells aimed at the Culbin Sands forming the western half of the invasion coast.[194] Touch-down, and the infantry were off up the beach, some carrying simulated demolition charges on their backs.[37] Amphibious tanks churned ashore, dropping their dripping flotation screens[574] as they passed between the old railway lines and poles sticking out of the sand above low water, before going on to attack the gun-emplacements built in 1940 to resist just such an invasion.

Tanks and troops found ways between the concrete blocks topped with coils of barbed wire, and disappeared over the sand dunes; some to consolidate the beach-head after capturing the telephone exchange and the Coast Guard Station at Burghead – a peace-time fishing village now inhabited by children, old age pensioners and women; the latter busy making cups of tea and preparing food for "the boys". Others charged off to capture the BBC wireless transmitter two miles away.[84] Exercise "Leap Year" was pronounced a success,[564] even if to a poor benighted infantryman it had seemed chaotic.[37] At least the sun had put in an appearance.[564]

At Cromarty waiting for the next move, *Glenearn* was camouflaged, or dazzle-painted, in stripes of different colours and varying widths, and a *GN* added in large letters on each side of the hull amidships.[155] At short notice a second Royal Marine flotilla had to be formed to restore the original outfit of two with twelve craft each.[487] 543 Flotilla was manned by some transfers – "chuckouts" was the unkind description[93] – from 535, together with some new appointments from Westcliff.[487] The additional LCAs arrived via the Caledonian Canal.[155]

From the middle of April convoys sailed for the south. The slow vessels left first, *Glenearn* in the seventh convoy along with an escort, an HQ ship and the three "Weapon" Class

Landing Ships *Empire Cutlass, Battleaxe* and *Broadsword*.[205] 25.4.44
They proceeded north-about through the Pentland Firth.[66]
Everyone knew what this move would mean, but where?
Norway? Hardly. The Pas de Calais – another Dieppe?[564] In
Exercise "Leap Year" the distance sailed from Cromarty to
Caithness then back to Burghead had been approximately 90
miles; there might be a clue here.[562] Most commonly held view
was that the Second Front would open with an assault on the
shores of France; somewhere, on a long coastline.[564]

Left behind in the Moray Firth were a few Tank Landing
Craft which, for one reason or another, had missed the earlier
sailings; they would be following on in a day or two.[205] 3rd
Infantry Division had left by road.[564] Already the south-west
wind had started the sands drifting over the debris of
rehearsal for battle:[161] the twisted steel remnants of mortar
bombs, the occasional unexploded naval shell. Shrapnel-
impregnated trees whose surface scars would heal, but
retaining a surprise or two for a later generation of tree fellers
and saw millers.[82] The Culbin Sands returned to their normal
state of desolation.[161] Burghead Bay could revert to an aerial
bombing range, and Burghead to being a point of departure
for secret agents returning to Norway.[84]

Across the Firth the inhabitants of Inver could return to the
peace and quietness of their thatched cottages after the
unaccustomed noise of their temporary stay in Tain. Having
never had a piped water supply, nor electricity, and with only
rough cart tracks for roads, they were not much worse off for
their unexpected contribution to England's war effort; apart
from the tracks of the tanks, the shell holes and some
unnecessary damage caused by local hooligans.[129]

All over the Black Isle the Nissen huts remained, a rusting
tribute to one who, in the manner of Highland prophecies,
had foreseen it all three hundred years previously:

> *Nuair a bhios da eaglais an Sgire na Toiseachd,*
> *A's lamh da ordaig an I-Stian',*
> *Da dhrochaid aig Sguideal nan geocaire,*
> *As fear da imleag an Dunean.*

Thig Miltearan a Carn a-chlarsair,
Air Carbad gun each gun srian,
A dh-fhagas am Blar-dubh na thasach.*[550]

All of which, in the manner of Highland prophecies, had come to pass.[A]

---

* When there shall be two churches in the Parish of Ferrintosh,
   And a hand with two thumbs in "I-Stiana",
   Two bridges at Conon of the gluttons,
   And a man with two navels at Dunean,
   Soldiers will come from Tarradale
   On a chariot without horse or bridle,
   Which will leave the Muir of Ord a wilderness.

CHAPTER 16

DELIVER OUR PUISSANCE

With a call at Milford Haven *en route*,[94] *Glenearn* eventually arrived at Spithead after dark on 29th April.[85] Daylight revealed Ryde on the Isle of Wight to the south and Stokes Bay to the north; the warm Spring-like weather contrasted markedly with the cold and bleakness of Scotland.[28] Captain R. C. Bateman, RM, arrived to take up his duties as flotilla officer;[9] from the first he insisted on referring to his command as "The Fighting 543rd".

Two half-battalions of infantry came aboard and the sailors were delighted to welcome back the troops of the East Yorks. and South Lancs. Regiments.[85] That night Force "S", together with Forces "J" and "G", sailed before a south-westerly breeze. Clear of the Isle of Wight area this armada turned to starboard towards the coast of France; most of those in *Glenearn* were unsure whether this might not be the heading for the invasion itself[564] – and a bombing attack by an enemy aircraft on a destroyer, and the explosions of mines were real enough – but D-Day for this operation found Force "S" off the beaches between Littlehampton and Bognor.[85]

The aims of Exercise "Fabius IV" were to practise the marshalling, embarkation and sailing of the assault force, the approach and the landings, and the setting up of the beach organization. Massive air cover was to be provided, in order to demonstrate the degree of support which might be expected; also to give the seaborne forces the opportunity of seeing the different types of Allied aircraft in the air.[201] However, in the event the freshening wind in the afternoon led to an early end to the proceedings to avoid damage to landing craft.[374]

As far as *Glenearn* herself was concerned all went well, and she was back at her anchorage by the evening.[85] The only untoward happening was that 543 Flotilla, landing their troops on a falling tide omitted to sound for depth, and

30.4.44

1.5.44

3.5.44

4.5.44

finished up gallantly arrayed, but stuck fast, "on the putty" until the tide came back in. This incident inspired Lieutenant R. Webber, RM, – of 535 Flotilla of course – to compose an epic poem along the lines of "After Blenheim," by Robert Southey.[155]

Glenearn was the repeating ship for all the signals that came off from Gilkicker Fort. Captain Hutchison had only one Yeoman of Signals, RN; all his other signalmen were "Hostilities Only" and not highly experienced, but they did their best.[66] Two most improper and very unfair messages were received from the signal station,[85] including one from someone in Portsmouth, telling him that he was not doing his job, and his men should be more attentive. The Captain was very angry, because they were doing the best they could…[66]

As it happened, the 2nd East Yorks. were aboard for a minor landing exercise code-named "Pas de Calais", a little way up the Solent.[152] That evening when Captain Hutchison went down into the ward-room he found a large gathering of army officers and their C.O. giving them a talk on the forthcoming operations. Colonel Hutchinson asked if they could first do one more landing that night and could Captain Hutchison suggest somewhere? "Yes, land at Gilkicker Fort and bring me back the Commanding Officer as a prisoner of war."

13.5.44*

To the Colonel this seemed like a good idea.[83] Lieutenant C. Waters, RM, was able to provide a sketch plan of the place, having spent several hours there during which Gilkicker had had to signal a number of times for a boat to bring him off, when he had joined *Glenearn* a few days before.[152] Accordingly on the Sunday morning an LCA of the Fighting 543rd was sent under cover of darkness to the Fort Gilkicker jetty, and about 0400 a platoon of tough Yorkshiremen with their faces blackened landed to test the security of the place.

14.5.44*

Needless to say they got in. Bypassing the WRNS on duty whom they found polishing their finger nails, they seized the Commanding Officer – a Lieutenant Commander RNVR – two other officers and two signalmen,† and brought them off.

* Assumed date.

† W. McKenzie thus. C. Waters and M. F. Mayhew say two WRNS were captured.

PREPARING FOR D-DAY.

19. During Exercise "Fabius" May, 1944.

20. Service on the fore well deck.

On their return one man was put on board a destroyer and the other on a tug which was just proceeding to sea. The three officers, still in their pyjamas, were told that they were prisoners and their parole demanded.[85] Thus when Captain Hutchison came on deck at 8 o'clock he found the Signal Station's C.O. in a dressing gown a prisoner-of-war, and said, "You can come and have breakfast with me." The "guest" was very angry and took some smoothing down, but it was pointed out, "Look here, you've been caught now; this is a defended area – how is it that we managed to get in?" He did not like this either,[66] but the three officers were given a much better breakfast than they would have had in the Fort, and then returned to the jetty.[152] No one was surprised when they did not complain to the Commander-in-Chief, for their C.O. would have got into serious trouble.[66] So ended, with a rumble rather than a clang, the Battle of Fort Gilkicker.[A] *Glenearn* then sailed for the "Pas de Calais", returning to her anchorage when that exercise was over.[152]

Experiences such as these were a factor in the tempering of the keen fighting weapon which the ship's company became under the influence of their leader. Captain Hutchison was a real four-ringed product of the Royal Navy,[94] and respected by the crew; he was known as "Clanking Irons" from the imposing array of medals he wore on Divisions.[28]

On that Sunday night there was an air raid warning but as an operation of war it was probably little more than an armed reconnaissance.[455] The following night, however, there was a more concentrated attack, and the bombing was fairly heavy.[456] Lieutenant Webber, RM, and the Padre, Rev. Janes were standing on the upper deck, starboard side. They could see nothing because of the smokescreen which had been put up; so intense and irritating was it that they even tried wearing their gas respirators to try and alleviate its effects. When a bomb exploded somewhere in the vicinity their thoughts and prayers respectively were, "Let's get out of this, these bloody things are far too close," and so they went below.[155]

Whether as a consequence of these night raids,[A] which if

15.5.44

they had been heavier and pushed home with determination might have dislocated the organization of the coming invasion,[85] or by a coincidence, Exercise "Cantab" on the 17th–18th May was a combined defence of an anchorage by Forces "J", "G" and "S".[205] A lot of gunnery practice was carried out. "Y" Gun turret was built on top of the Gunnery Lecture Room, part of which had been "pinched" by the Rev. Janes – known as "the Bish" – for a chapel. Lieutenant Mayhew, RN, – "Guns" – knew what happened to the lecture room when they fired the twin 4″ guns and told the Captain what would happen to the chapel, but Mayhew still had to take his films and apparatus elsewhere, and he was not pleased.[94]

A party was held in the ward-room and a number of WRNS were invited on board to a dance and supper. At the end of an enjoyable evening Captain Hutchison concluded his speech by saying, "This is the party before 'The Party' and when 'The Party' is over we'll have a party." There was a general feeling of expectancy and of "waiting for D-Day", but the time passed busily, with drills and routine preparations.[85]

There was another air attack on the 22nd. The raiders were over for some time and heavy gunfire was heard throughout; bombs were dropped ashore and there were fires in the Portsmouth area.[457] On the 24th, His Majesty the King inspected the invasion forces. He went on board the flagship *HMS Largs*, where Captain Hutchison was introduced to him. After this, all the landing craft from the squadron of LSIs carried out a "march past".[85]

Force briefing started on Saturday 27th, when the Naval Commander Force "S", Rear-Admiral A. G. Talbot, DSO, gave all Commanding Officers an outline of the operation. Force Headquarters had been established at Commercial Buildings, Portsmouth; one of the rooms there contained a large-scale model of the assault area mounted on a platform which allowed it to be viewed as from a distance at sea level, with simulated lighting such as would obtain at H-Hour. Air photographs and plans of the beach obstacles were also viewed and described.[295] Next day, the date of the assault was

22.5.44

24.5.44

27.5.44

28.5.44

given out as Monday, the 5th of June;[585] the ship was sealed and nobody was allowed ashore.[85]

During the next few days the Operation Orders were issued to senior officers for the detailed briefing of subordinates,[205] and Captain Hutchison, as Senior Officer Landing Ships Infantry wrote his orders for Convoy S.7 – Code-named "Abner" – giving route, anchoring plan and other instructions to the Landing Ships and their escort of destroyers and torpedo boats. Included in this information was the procedure to be adopted should *Glenearn* be damaged and unable to proceed...[293]

31.5.44 On the last day of the month the naval Commander-in-Chief of Operation "Neptune", the greatest amphibious operation in history, issued a special order of the day to each officer and man.[585] About the same time one of *Glenearn*'s medical officers gave a pep-talk, advising everyone to wear clean clothes on D-Day; explaining that when a bullet or other projectile carries bits of clean fabric into the wound there is less chance of infection.[155] Surgeon-Lieutenant Payne-James was a very keen young doctor who knew that if people were going to get hurt they were going to need blood. What seemed like the whole ship's company volunteered, and he got about 30 pints of blood off them.[106]

The tropical heat of May continued into the early days of June,[565] and the weather was fine when the infantry came 3.6.44 aboard at mid-day on the 3rd.[252] The 1st Bn. South Lancashire Regiment was represented by their *A* and *C* Companies,[251] and the 2nd East Yorkshire Regiment by Battalion HQ and *C* and *D* Companies.[252] This remarkable disposition of troops would ensure that if one ship were sunk the others could land sufficient forces to cover the frontage of attack, the follow-up companies having been trained in the tasks of the assault companies as well as their own.[576] In the afternoon Mr. Churchill and Field-Marshal Smuts reviewed the fleet from a launch;[252] many of the troops crowded the decks when they heard that Winston was passing.[37]

These particular Lancashire men had not previously sampled *Glenearn*'s hospitality,[105] but the East Yorkshires were thoroughly at home on board, and were greeted as old friends. Colonel Hutchinson presented Captain Hutchison with a silver bugle decorated with the regimental crest and inscribed with the words:

Presented to
Capt. C. A. G. Hutchison, D.S.O., R.N.
and the Ship's Company
H.M.S. "Glenearn"
by Lt. Col. C. F. Hutchinson
and all ranks
2nd Bn. East Yorkshire Regiment
May, 1944.[85]

Some ladies of Waterlooville in Hampshire had presented the Battalion with small command post flags – a black ground with the white rose of York embroidered in the centre.[115] The flag for Bn HQ had been attached to a pike provided by the Colonel,[252] and the ship's company added to this a pair of red foul anchors of the Navy; these were sewn on in the top quarter next the hoist, while the Royal Marines gave a brass cap badge to be sweated on to the pike head.[470]

For his personal contribution towards inter-service appreciation, Captain Hutchison, since he had troops of Yorkshire and Lancashire regiments on board – Yorks and Lancs – sent his steward ashore to buy as many roses of the white and red varieties as could be got in Portsmouth; then he decorated the ship with them.[66] At the other end of the scale 3rd Infantry Division had presented every ship with a mounted replica of the divisional sign, while *Glenearn* – like all the other vessels of the Force[205] – had the same red and black triangles in a red circle painted on the funnel.[153] As an additional mark of identification she had the Force "S" green band painted round her bridge and upper works.[205]

Every man had been briefed down to the last detail, with but two exceptions:[565] the next day's weather would dictate when the assault would take place, and only a select few knew where.[590] All the maps, models and photographs so far produced carried the same objective code-names as the exercises in the Moray Firth. The troops had been issued with currency in francs and a French phrase book, so there could be little doubt of a Channel crossing, but just whereabouts the irresistible Force "S" would meet the immovable German obstacle course would only become common knowledge at sea.[565] The salient points of the operation were that seven and a half minutes before H-Hour a line of swimming tanks would crawl ashore to take on the German defences before the arrival of the infantry, and simultaneously with the touchdown of the LCAs at H-Hour tank landing craft would be disgorging armoured fighting vehicles specially adapted for attacking and breaching permanent fortifications.[202]

4.6.44   Daylight on Sunday and the weather prospect was not at all good.[591] It was announced that D-Day had been put back 24 hours.[251] Rather more, in fact, since H-Hour was related to the state of the tide; Captain Hutchison's sailing order of 1st June for Convoy S.7, which had been framed round an unspecified H-Hour and subsequently given clock timings for a landing on the 5th, had now to be changed by a 40-minute addition to each and every figure.

Routine Orders for the next two days were drawn up.[293] The Captain had been asked by the Padre if he could broadcast on the tannoy a prayer before the ship went into action on D-Day. To this suggestion the Gunnery Officer had pointed out that if they were attacked, the defence of the ship would require the communications and the "Bish" would be better making his own arrangements. Padre Janes had complained to the Captain, who sent for Mayhew; he would just have to hope and pray that the enemy would resist the temptation to desecrate the religious formalities.[94]

It was a miserable day with lashing rain.[581] A postponement on account of bad weather was no new experience to those who had spent three months in the Moray Firth.[205] The troops had learned to look after themselves, and after getting used to the hammocks, [159] passed their time sleeping, reading and playing cards;[100] also checking their equipment.[37] Officers and sergeants were continually being called to briefing sessions.[105]

But for the ship's company the postponement was still a postponement; apart from writing letters to next to kin – and censoring others – there was little to do.[1] To keep people amused, one of the Royal Marine captains organised all sorts of games: "uckers", cards, dice – anything to keep the crew interested and not bored during the time of waiting. A Captain, RN, caught the fever and sent down a signal to the ward-room that he wanted three volunteers for bridge, at 2000. Commander Hardman-Jones found these by the method of, "You, you and you," and that was that.[94]

Monday, 5th June, and the invasion was definitely on.[85] It was a relief after the false start.[28] Colonel Hutchinson paid a last visit to his assault companies, and the soldiers' padre held a short religious service. The sealed bundles of maps were issued to junior army officers.[252] From 0945 the first small, slow ships set off from their assembly berths, each vessel keeping perfect station in the line as for a Royal Revue; each vessel wearing a huge battle ensign. As they went by, the troops crowded on deck or clambered over tanks and vehicles were in good spirits; especially the French commandos who sang rousing songs as they put to sea.[205]

The seemingly endless streams of tank landing craft sailed past; two, three, four abreast – it seemed as if they would never end. Some had small LCAs in tow – what an uncomfortable journey they were going to have![152] *HMS Largs* the Headquarters ship at the eastern end of the line of Landing Ships was flying the signal, "Good Luck: Drive On." Spithead, which had started the day a forest of shipping with every berth full, began to assume a more normal appearance as convoy after convoy slipped away;[205] the evident organisation behind it all was absolutely staggering.[106]

The weather was still quite unfavourable for landing craft, while the wind veered to the west; during the afternoon it was blowing force 5.[205] *Glenearn*'s ward-room bar closed at 1300, and the next few hours were spent trying to get some rest. At 1600 the mail box closed;[293] the mails were taken ashore, but it was believed that they would all be held up until after D-Day.[1] After tea the finishing touches were put to securing ship

5.6.44

0945

for action,[293] preparing the boats and checking over the troops' pre-loaded ammunition, bicycles and heavy gear.[155] Then before supper the change to clean into-action dress.[293]

The sky was still overcast but the sea was moderating.[581] Thoughts turned to the likely reception on the beach ... Hundreds of men on the troop decks heard a shot, then it was said that a private in the other battalion had blown off his right hand with his rifle, and would probably be court martialled...[159]

At 1945 the Mess Decks on *F*-Deck were closed up, and ship darkened. With engines ready, the cable was shortened in and then the anchor weighed. "Action Stations" was sounded by bugle. The last convoy of Force "S" passed the Northern Spithead gate in two sections: the destroyers *Verulam, Virago, Eglinton* and *Kelvin,* with four Motor Torpedo Boats of the 63rd Flotilla, then *Glenearn* leading *Cutlass, Battleaxe, Broadsword, Princess Astrid, Maid of Orleans, Largs,* two Landing Craft Infantry (Small), three U.S. Coastguard cutters and a high-speed launch. Passing the boom at 2145, guns were tested,* "Action Stations" relaxed, the destroyers took up their stations and speed increased to 12 knots.[293]

The sealed packages were broken open and the maps and photographs eagerly examined; here at last were the real place-names.[575] Force "S" was to land its troops in Normandy between Ouistreham and Lion sur Mer – the extreme left wing of the invasion front. The whole coastline had been divided into sections; that portion of *Q* for *Queen* Sector upon which the assault of 3rd Infantry Division had to fall was only 1,600 yards long and flanked by beaches unsuitable for landings. An error in landfall of only 2,000 yards eastwards would place the troops on the wrong side of the River Orne and cut off from land support – which would be disastrous. Closer in, the soft sandbanks at the mouth of the river extended about a mile out to sea, and were full of runnels. The western third of Queen Sector was backed by cliffs.[205]

535 Flotilla would land the assault companies[155] of the

* Electrical circuits and mechanical parts.[158]

South Lancs. on Queen White Beach, the middle third of the sector;[229] the Fighting 543rd would land the follow-up companies of the East Yorks. on Queen Red,[9] situated between the outskirts of Ouistreham and La Brèche. A major enemy strong point code-named *Cod* was situated near La Brèche at the junction of Red and White Beaches, and would have to be cleared by the assault.[229]

Aerial photographs of the objectives, dated as recently as 3rd June, showed obstacles on the sand below high water mark.[94] First hazard would be a double row of timber ramps eight to ten feet high, each armed with a Teller mine; then a double row of vertical wooden stakes of various heights.[205] Even more frightening were the "hedgehogs" made of seven-feet long angle irons joined at the mid-points to present sharp points in all directions; when struck they would either pierce the craft or turn over, to bring up another point to impale it from beneath.[227] There were also concrete tetrahedra. Nearly all the obstacles were armed with mines or shells intended to explode on impact, and there was, on average, one obstacle for each ten feet of beach frontage.[229] Ten feet; exactly the width of an LCA ...[238]

A photographic silhouette taken by an aircraft flying just above the waves gave a continuous panorama of the coast as seen from a distance of about 1,300 yards; it was low, dark and rather menacing. There were a few conspicuous buildings that might be used as guiding points,[615] but there was no guarantee they would not have been flattened by the preliminary bombardment, or at least obscured by dust and smoke.[205] But the wealth of information in itself was encouraging; everyone knew what they would be up against.[565] Objectives bore the same relationships to the landmarks, and had the same code-names, as in the Moray Firth – even the lighthouse at Burghead had its counterpart at Ouistreham. Soldiers, sailors and marines alike felt that here then would be no muddle; this time "they" had got it right.

Before sailing, Captain Hutchison had issued his sailing instructions to the other ships in sealed envelopes, together with one marked, "This envelope to be opened on passing the

NAB tower and the contents to be read over the loud speaker to the ship's company and all on board." Accordingly there boomed through the alleyways of *Glenearn* the words:

> *Shakespeare – Henry V Act 2.*
> *Now, Lords, for France; the enterprise whereof*
> *Shall be to you, as us, like glorious*
> *We doubt not of a fair and lucky war*
> *   – we doubt not now*
> *but every rub is smoothed on our way.*
> *Then, forth, dear countrymen; let us deliver*
> *Our puissance in to the hand of God.*
> *Putting it straight in expedition.*
> *Cheerily to sea; the signs of war advance.*[85]

to jostle for a place in the memory with Rear-Admiral Talbot's message:

TO ALL IN FORCE "S"

The great day for which we have all been training is at hand. The task allotted to us is a formidable one, and calls for all that is best in every one of us. The 3rd British Division has been entrusted to our care. They are old friends of ours; we have grown up together; we have come to look on them as our own. Let every officer and man in the Force feel a personal responsibility for the comfort, safety and maintenance of his "opposite number" in the 3rd Division.

> *And, above all FIGHT;*
> *FIGHT to help the Army;*
> *FIGHT to help yourselves;*
> *FIGHT to save your ship;*
> *FIGHT to the very end.*[612]

With so many exhortations from those in command of one's destiny the individual's memory has difficulty retaining even the most stirring call to arms.[A] General Eisenhower's leaflet:

Soldiers, Sailors and Airmen of the Allied Expeditionary Force! You are about to embark on the Great Crusade...[613]

That's true. D-Day is going to be the most exciting thing that is ever going to happen to any of us.[106] *The eyes of the world are upon you* ...[613] The eyes of the recipient are having difficulty concentrating on the written word.[A] *Your enemy is well trained* ...[613] we are going to be bombed ...[106] *well-equipped* ...[613] bombarded ...[106] *battle-hardened* ...[613] Germans attacking in submarines ...[106] *He will fight savagely* ...[613] and every other thing.[106] *But this is the year 1944!*[613] And how many of us will see 1945? ...[A] *overwhelming superiority in weapons and munitions of war* ...[613] the general opinion is that there will be more stuff going up and coming down tomorrow than has gone up and down so far in the entire war ...[85] *great reserves of trained fighting men* ...[613] Yes, life is cheap, and no one seems very worried about the risks ...[106] *The free men of the world are marching together to Victory!*...[613] Well, everyone wants to get on with it...[106] *The tide has turned!*...[613] And one hour into the next flood[583] tide it will be the the moment of truth for our lads...[A] *Good Luck!*[613] We'll need it, because the most experienced aboard does not think the ship will survive the morrow ...[85] *the blessing of Almighty God upon this great and noble undertaking* ...[613] Amen to that, anyway.[A]

Chapter 17

PTE. BENTON MAKES HISTORY

5.6.44   With *Glenearn's* leading and navigating, Convoy S.7 reached the first critical point* on the route on time at 2326. Here course was changed to $157\frac{1}{2}°$.[293] So far nothing had disturbed the even tenor of the voyage.[252] Captain Hutchison's previous venture into these waters had been almost exactly four years previously; then he had landed on the Cherbourg Peninsula, and had been in France at the time
6.6.44   of the capitulation.[377] About 0100 great spouts of flame leapt up above the horizon from the coast 70 miles ahead; the bombing had started.[85]

Thirty miles on, the northern entrance to the swept channel was supposed to be located by an FH830 Buoy giving out a characteristic underwater signal, and on the surface by HDML 1416 flashing "0" in the convoy's direction at 6-second intervals. It was found that the sonar buoy was correctly located at 50° 05′ 00″ N, 0° 28′ 30″ W, but the motor-launch was 1.7 miles to the eastward – possibly because the minesweepers, with a strong cross-wind and the tide to contend with, had found it impracticable to pass through the position of the beacon.[205] Be that as it may, the effect was that instead of entering the swept channel at 0200, the convoy was about 10 minutes late; as the destroyers *Verulam* and *Virago* took station ahead Captain Hutchison began to increase speed. After five miles it was obvious that the ships were still going to be late at the Lowering Position unless they made 13 knots; this change was made without signals, as previously arranged.

The passage was marked by flashing lights: white to port and red to starboard,[293] and as the convoy progressed, a series of Q.H. fixes proved that the danned channel gradually approached the true line, with agreement likely at the Lowering Position.[205] Accurate fixing with the Decca

* 50° 33′ 12″ N, 0° 46′ 42″ W.

apparatus was not, however, always possible – due perhaps to enemy interference – and the important component "latitude" was not easy to get.[293] But there had been no radar jamming, and no enemy reaction either by sea or air; the only aircraft showing up on the screens were on patrol away to the eastward over the Pas de Calais area. As the Landing Ships approached ever closer to the shore of France it became apparent that the invasion was achieving an increasing measure of tactical surprise.

At 0340 more signs of RAF bombing were seen ahead.[205] **0340** By this time the convoy had been steaming on a new course* of 170° for the best part of half an hour.[293] Hundreds of planes towing gliders flew over.[85] Very heavy "flak" went up from the direction of Le Havre, and the pyrotechnics soon spread westwards along the whole coast, lighting the sky with flares and the glow of explosions and fires.[205]

The troops, and those of the ship's company allowed some sleep, were wakened at 0425;[293] to be told that there had been no enemy interference on the way over,[252] and that the 4 to 5-feet swell of the previous day had decreased somewhat.[205] Breakfast was served.[37] Whilst the soldiers were eating, course was altered† to 190°; bringing the convoy of fast LSIs into convergence with the slow convoys in Channel 9.[293] Using the Plan Position Indicator it was easy to note the presence of each convoy, and assess its probable punctuality at the Lowering Position.[205] Whereas the forty or so Tank Landing Craft carrying the "DD" tanks were on time as far as could be judged, the AVRE‡ convoy was obviously late.[205] *Glenearn's* procession was going without a hitch;[85] a triumph for the organisers of this enormous armada on the enemy's very doorstep – and for *Glenearn's* Navigator, the careful and methodical R. D. Philpott, Lieut., RNR.[A]

At 0506 the order ... *MAKE READY*... went out through **0506** the loudspeakers to the soldiers on the troop decks. It had been explained that if the Lowering Position came under fire all LCAs would be loaded and lowered, then the ships would

---

* The change of course was made at 49° 52′ 00″ N, 0° 20′ 12″ W.

† This change of course was made at 49° 34′ 00″ N, 0° 15′ 00″ W.[293]

‡ Armoured Vehicle Royal Engineers.

slip their cables and follow *Glenearn* round to the north; the small craft would then have to wait for the major landing craft to arrive before forming up into their respective groups.

Minutes later *Glenearn* led the way into Channel 9, and altered course back to 170°. Less than three and a half miles ahead lay the Lowering Position,[293] in line with the flash and rumble of bursting bombs.[592] It was beginning to grow light. The convoy's escorts were pulling out to starboard; to port, seven more destroyers.[293] Two miles to the east *HMS Warspite* takes up her position, with the other battleship *Ramilles* a mile or two nearer the enemy.[588] ... *CABLE PARTY CLOSE UP* ...

0524   About 3,200 yards from the L.P. *Glenearn*'s telegraphs are put to 6 knots and the signal...*K6*...flashed back to *Empire Cutlass*; to be passed on along the line without acknowledgement, so that no light may be seen from the shore. 1,600 yards and the executive signal ... *XX* ... is made, and each ship's navigator starts counting the minutes before putting telegraphs to "*STOP*". ... *BOAT LOWERERS AND CREWS CLOSE UP* ...[293]

... *STAND BY* ... Flotilla officers head for the bridge for final instructions.[93] ... *SILENCE* ... The padre starts to read a short religious service over the loudspeakers to everyone on board. Reverend Janes says that today we will make history. After the troops have landed a fuel pipeline will be laid under the ocean to Normandy, and artificial harbours will be towed out from England. He offers a little prayer, saying that some on board this day will not see the sun set, and calling on everyone to repeat the Lord's Prayer with him. In some of the soldiers the padre's words strike a deep chord,[37] but the Royal Marines with action more imminent are a bit edgy, and on the boat decks the call to prayer does not get much response; still, the intention was good.[28] It had gone off fairly well, and the Gunnery Officer's fears that the ship might be attacked whilst the communications system was otherwise engaged have proved to be unfounded.[94]

Indeed, the whole operation is unfolding with unreal precision. Everything seems to be going according to plan; it might well be yet another exercise[85] – apart from the odd shell aimed at *Warspite*.[205] When the old veteran of Jutland opens fire with her 15-inch guns,[180] even these few shots cease. To port and starboard coastal minesweepers wait to lead in the bombarding destroyers when their time comes. Convoy S4 is to starboard while S3 is ahead at the Lowering Position. Aircraft come streaking in low, laying a thick smoke screen to mask the eastern flank of the invasion area from the long-range batteries at Le Havre.[205]

Glenearn's engines have stopped and she is losing way over the last 800 yards.[293] Suddenly, someone on *A* Deck shouts, "Look!"[106] About half a mile away off the port quarter a big Norwegian destroyer blows up with a great spout of smoke and steam.[85] Her funnel falls aft, and the whole ship seems to lift out of the water. She is the *Svenner*, and her ship's company fall in on the forecastle and quarter-deck, then as their vessel breaks in two amidships[268] – flames coming from both halves[155] – they commence jumping into the choppy sea, as the sinking ship bends like a pen-knife. Someone saw a torpedo track from *Glenearn*'s stern and someone else saw one over the other side,[106] before they* go on to create consternation among the starboard division of bombarding destroyers waiting stopped in a group.

This nasty experience was not allowed to interrupt the anchoring procedure.[205] It was important to know exactly when the ship had stopped; something that was very hard to tell, apparently. Surg.-Lieut. Payne-James had earlier been detailed for this job and told, "All you've got to do is stand out there on the Leadsman's Platform and drop bits of paper over the side, and when they stop moving past, you shout!" It had all seemed a bit archaic to the Doctor, and in the event the Navigator managed without his help.[106] *Glenearn* anchored at the Lowering Position† at 0533, just three minutes late;[293] thanks to her navigators – Philpott and Decca.[A] The other Landing Ships anchored shortly afterwards on the exact line of bearing 350°. *Glenearn*

0530

0533

---

* Launched from German torpedo boats under cover of the smoke screen.
† 49° 26′ 00″ N, 0° 15′ 30″ W.

switched on a single blue recognition light while the cable party broke the cable, ready to slip instantly; engines at 5-minutes' notice.

...*CRAFT NUMBERS 1, 2 AND 5, MOVE...CRAFT NUMBERS 7 AND 9, MOVE...*[293] Ten landing craft are lowered to embarkation stations and held against the ship's sides by bowsing-in wires. The ramps come down. Ten boat-loads of soldiers emerge on deck,[235] some of them to the sight of the two halves of *H Nor. MS Svenner*[255] protruding almost vertically from the water, like a "V for Victory" standing against the sky.[605] From all boat stations the sea looks very rough indeed,[37] with waves 3–4 feet high.[374]

Each platoon falls in opposite their boat, with the three sections of soldiers in the reverse order in which they will sit in it. The marine cox'n gives the senior army rank the order to man, and they enter in threes, filling up the craft from aft forwards.[235] It is a bit awkward for privates carrying Bangalore torpedoes and for platoon sergeants with flat boxes of "Fuse, Instantaneous Detonating" on their backs,[105] but, ignoring if you can the live ammunition and the real "beehive" charges, we might just as well be embarking on an exercise.[37]

Cox'n reports to the telephone operator that his craft is manned, and thence to the Control Room on the bridge. Tackles are unrigged, the ramp is recovered and the boat made ready for lowering.[235] Lieutenant Webber, RM, in charge of LCA 994 on the port side aft luffing davit, has something to say. "Listen chaps, look up as soon as we hit the water. Look up and keep looking up, because from the ends of the davits there are large steel balls hanging; when the boat rises on these pretty hefty waves, these steel things will crash down into it, and if one hits you on the head..."[155]

... *FIRST FLIGHT AWAY BOATS* ... with a rumble the
0545 loaded craft begin their descent towards the grey choppy sea and a brief but grim struggle, with one moment the wires singing at full stretch; the next – as she rises on the wave – the whole lot falling around you.[152] There is alarm, not to say panic, among the pioneers attached to *C* Company when only their forward end is unhooked,[153] and the boat assumes an

angle of about 45° in the rough sea, and in the dark.[159] After unhooking, the first boats pull away and circle round until the remainder of the flotilla is ready, then the divisional leaders Captain Richards and Lieutenant Jeffrey move off;[116] the two columns of craft taking up position forward and to starboard of *Glenearn* to await the arrival of the major landing craft.[202]

For about half an hour now there had been a steady stream of vessels steaming in two columns, one each side of the line of LSIs – landing craft carrying DD tanks, landing craft mounting naval guns, landing craft mounting anti-tank guns, landing craft and motor launches of all descriptions[205] – until the sea was simply covered with ships; each one with its exact position in the scheme of things and each with a specific job to do. It was enthralling to consider how anybody, even a committee – especially a committee – could have sat down and worked it all out.[106] Their deliberations had created a picture like nothing on earth or sea. One witness to it thought, "God, with all these ships, there can't be any more in the world."[159]

Ten LCAs of 536 Flotilla,[205] with the two assault companies of the East Yorks. got a cheer from their pals on *Glenearn*[578] as they sailed past to join up with 535 and the rest of Assault Group 2.[252] Marrying up between the LCAs and the LCTs carrying the Royal Engineer tanks was successfully carried out, but the craft carrying the self-propelled artillery were not to be seen.[205]

At 0605 the Group set off from the Lowering Position,[293] and shortly afterwards the tank landing craft deployed from two columns in line astern to one row line abreast,[205] ahead of the columns of LCAs. A *Hunt*-class destroyer marked each flank of the Force, and two craft mounting anti-aircraft guns brought up the rear.[202] They had eight miles to go,[9] and were due to touch down at H-Hour, 0725 Double British Summer Time.[202]

With one hell of a sea running, very soon there were signs of sea-sickness – and not just among the soldiers.[185] Once again the pills did not seem to be very effective,[205] and things became a bit grim in the boats. Only the simpler palliatives were left: at least one of the flotilla went to war with a large insulated container of tea sitting on the starboard bow, just abaft the armour plating. The marines dished it out to the chaps. Half of it got splashed with sea-water, but in the passing of it around some had to stand up, so they were all allowed to stand up – and smoke – and things got better then.[155]

After about forty minutes of misery,[205] in the course of which wireless communication was established with Battalion Headquarters,[251] it was light enough and the land near enough to be seen fairly clearly,[205] although only one or two large buildings – hotels, perhaps – stood out from the flat ground line.[615] Helped by the photographs issued with the final orders it could be seen that the flotilla was on course for the correct beaches, leading to the vital exits for the army's vehicles.[116]

The destroyers anchored out on the eastern flank opened fire, each in its own time, starting a steady sustained bombardment;[205] the thunder of the guns reverberating across the white-crested sea as the little landing craft struggled over and through wave after wave after wave.[A]

As the coastline inched ever nearer the deliberately-placed shells of the destroyers' guns were augmented by the covering fire of the specially-adapted landing craft, then by the self-propelled guns of the army's field artillery firing from LCTs. The greatest weight of explosive was concentrated on the strong point at La Brèche, on the left of the Lancashires' beach.[205] Shells screamed over, to land right on their targets – the concrete blockhouses. What a row.[159]

Aeroplanes joined in,[37] firing on the beaches and dropping bombs. Troops in the LCAs stood up to have a look at the pin-points of light made by the bombs bursting and the shells exploding,[105] although some soldiers who did so were told to keep down.[37] The air was full of bombers and fighters, and the smoke of the bombardment; the noise was deafening. What with the noise, smoke and dust it was difficult to tell whether the shell splashes near the water's edge were our own or the enemy's shots, and the beach was almost completely obscured.[116]

About half a mile from the shore,[205] and shells or mortar bombs were falling among the waves and the craft,[566] one small vessel was hit – a sheet of flame,[85] then blazing from stem to stern.[205] One of the flotilla was passing a massive rocket-firing LCT just as she fired:[37] sheet after sheet of flame, as salvo after salvo flew off – about a thousand rockets in just two or three minutes.[155] It was a most fantastic thing; hair-raising.[153] Red flashes as the rockets exploded ashore,[37] then the LCA was smothered in vile-smelling acrid smoke.[155] The shelling got more intense than ever.[37]

A few hundred yards from the beach the Flotilla Officer's craft hoisted two flags on its little signal mast and the two columns of boats deployed port and starboard to form a single line abreast for the final run-in.[116] Full speed; there was no point in hanging back now, when one direct hit could wipe out a whole platoon of infantry. Drifting smoke, flashes of flame and great clouds of dirt[566] obscured the beach until they were almost on it. The barrage was not due to stop for 5 minutes yet, but to wait would present the German gunners with a sitting target...[116]

...*STAND BY TO BEACH*...The bow-man casts off and overhauls the starboard door tackle, then returns to his position under cover on the port side. Using the port tackle he eases out the ramp door slightly to make sure it is running clear. The infantry platoon commander unbolts the armoured door, but holds it shut.[235] On LCA 994 Lieutenant Jones of the South Lancs. turns to his opposite number in the Royal Marines and says, "Lieutenant Webber, if I go out and disappear, for Christ's sake pull back and come in a bit further down the coast, because I shall probably have gone straight into a shell-hole under the water."[155]

...*DOWN KEDGE*... The sternsheetsman eases out the kedge.[235] One is dimly aware of passing stakes with mines on top sticking out of the water.[155] The boat touches bottom, the bow-man lets the ramp run out, the platoon commander opens the armoured door,[235] and the troops get what is for many their first sight of the beach. On the extreme left what they see is a strip of sand about 30 yards wide with wire

entanglements.[105] Further along *C* Company's front the eyes
are confronted by crossed steel girders with Teller mines on
them.[153] *HQ* Company's men see a very smoky beach with
scaffolding-like steel stuck in the sand and mines hanging
from it.[100] *A* Company had been told that a large white house
marked the centre of their front; when the doors of the LCAs
opened, there is their objective in front of them.[37] The beach
itself is flat and sandy, with sand-dunes beyond.[229]

After a rough run-in, for some a wet landing;[35] Lieutenant
Jones leads his men out. He does not disappear, and his men
follow him very, very gallantly – centre file first, followed by
port and starboard files together. They wade up to their
waists in water.[155] Other boat-loads are luckier; some getting
an almost dry landing, which made it better than any
exercise.[105] All the boats have touched down several minutes
too soon; fortunately, the shelling has stopped,[116] but leaving
an ominous silence in its stead.[229]

0720   Once the soldiers hit the beach it was as if they gave neither
the landing craft nor seasickness another thought; they just
wanted to get off the beaches as soon as possible.[37] By landing
on a low enough tide the assault craft had been able to avoid
the beach obstacles, most of which were still in front:[116] two
rows of ramp-type obstructions with shells on top,
"hedgehogs" with shells on the leg facing the sea.[229] The boats
were fairly well lined up all the way along. Lieutenant Webber
called out to Sub.-Lieut. Waghorn, RNVR, "Are you all right
over there?" and got the reply, "Yes."[155] Then the LCAs
pulled back off the beaches, the craft going astern and getting
clear just as the enemy's mortar fire started exploding along
the water's edge.[85] Corporal A. Williams, attached to *C*
Company, from his temporary resting place on the sand saw
his LCA reversing away; suddenly it seemed to him as if the
stern blew up, and he wondered whether they had detonated a
mine.[159]

The troops for their part had landed with very few
casualties and then run up the beach with no opposition from
the enemy.[205] 9 Platoon had grounded on the extreme left of
White Beach; there were no other boats to their left, but on

the right were two more of *C* Company's platoons. Almost opposite *9* Platoon was a German pillbox, but the bombing and shelling had been so good – and had stopped so recently – that the invaders were through the wire before the occupants had time to come out – too late. About 30 yards away was a concrete tower containing flame throwers, and every time the wire was touched they sprayed fire both ways.[105]

Further along White Beach, as soon as the assaulting infantry passed the high water mark they met the full fury of the German defence:[37] heavy mortar and machine gun fire,[251] while the rifles of snipers also began to take their toll.[205] Instead of exactly at H-Hour, the touch-down had been shortly before it, and for several long lonely minutes the infantry were on their own, unsupported.[229] But from 0730 a torrent of armoured vehicles poured ashore; most of them from tank landing craft, but a few sailing in under their own canvas.[205] "Scorpion" tanks flailed their way up and over the dunes in a whirl of thrashing chains,[153] with other tanks carrying huge bobbins of carpet attempting to lay them in some of the tracks so cleared. Armoured bulldozers, converted tanks carrying bridges, AVREs capable of firing "dustbins" full of explosives at concrete emplacements;[239] all with their specific jobs to do, criss-crossing the sand, trying to avoid each other,[617] and all under the enemy's guns – carefully sited to fire along the high water mark, while protected by thick concrete walls from seaward attack.[228]

0730

An AVRE is hit by a shell from an anti-tank gun and loses a track while still in the water, and the tide rising around it. A "bobbin" tank is likewise disabled in the same situation. An LCT coming in late grounds on top of a DD tank.[229] A mortar bomb strikes a flail in its landing craft, detonating the Bangalore torpedoes the tank is carrying and putting the two AVREs behind it out of action.[205] A German gun is silenced by a "Scorpion" flailing over it;[228] then has a girder bridge dropped on it.*[229]

Through this waking nightmare there lived and moved,[153] fought and fell, the infantry – unprotected, save when able to

---

* Lane 7, see Map F.

STRONG POINT "COD"

21. From the air 3rd June, 1944.
(Crown Copyright/RAF Photograph).

22. From the sea 6th June, 1944.

6th JUNE, 1944.

23. Queen Beaches from the air. Taken about 4 p.m.

24. Queen White Beach. Follow-up companies of 1st S. Lancs.

shelter behind some abandoned armoured vehicle for a few life-extending moments[616] – approaching the wire with 32 lb. of T.N.T. on the back and a 3-second fuse, blowing a gap for the flails,[153] placing a shaped charge against a concrete block containing Gerries.[159]

Later, there would be time for rational thought;[A] one to comment bitterly on the sergeant – none braver when blowing down trees and talking, back in England – with the small pieces of shrapnel in his toe, making enough of it to be evacuated along with the seriously wounded.*[159] Another to note that having been in the last party to leave Dunkirk he was now in the leading company on D-Day.[37] A third to contemplate the folly and the waste of war.[153]

Years of preparation, all those exercises, the dead-beat marches in damp battle-dress back to camp along the loch-side; all for what?[159] Another wet landing, a few minutes of hectic excitement, then a young life is snuffed out;[A] like pal Benton there, dead on the wire he tried to blow.[153] 14202503 William Benton, Private in the 1st. Bn. the South Lancashire Regiment, Prince of Wales' Volunteers.[284] You particularly disliked marching in wet clothes, and you did not have time to change after this last run up the beach.[159] You did not really have much time for anything; you were only 21.[284]

* Everyone else was an example to manhood.[159]

CHAPTER 18

THE FIGHTING 543rd

D-Day tasks of *Glenearn*'s junior flotilla were to land *C* and *D* Companies of the East Yorks. together with Battalion Headquarters, two detachments of the 246th Field Company RE for beach obstacle removal, one unit of Royal Navy Beach Commandos, and a Landing Craft Obstruction Clearance Unit. Two LCAs of 535 Flotilla were attached to 543 to carry the last two parties, and Lieutenant O. W. Jackson of 535 was in command of the L.C.O.C.U. Eight craft of 538 Flotilla from *Empire Broadsword* were to run in with them, to land various army units.[9]

Manning of the second flight of *Glenearn*'s boats was well advanced by the time the first flight left the Lowering Position at 0605.[293] However, one boat-load of soldiers was not piped to move at the correct time.[9] Then someone slipped on a ladder on the way to the embarkation station, dropping his sten-gun. It went off, and those higher up the ladder were in the line of fire;[65] three men were hit. Two of them were not too badly wounded – one in the calf – but the third was hit in the thigh; the bullet rupturing the right femoral artery. The Medical Officers did what they could for the boy* but they could not get out his artery to hold it, and when this artery is cut you have about two minutes to live.[106] A tragedy, but overshadowed by events; others were too preoccupied with weightier matters to spare much thought for the incident.[65]

As a result of months of training together, a bond of mutual respect had been formed, at every level between the ship's company and the 2nd East Yorks. which reached its strongest expression as the troops filed into the landing craft. Convention preventing any display of emotion, it took the form of witty remarks and instant repartee.[577] A final thoughtful gesture of concern for *Glenearn*'s departing guests was the packet of bacon sandwiches handed out to each

---

* Probably 4342710 Sgt. Eric Ibbetson.[284]

officer and man, to be tucked inside the battledress blouse against the moment when hunger would take priority over the other feelings, and there would not be time to cook up the dried food issued as the landing ration.[65]

The craft from 538 Flotilla were ahead of their places in the procession, and came plunging by before 543 was even lowered. With mixed feelings *Glenearn's* marines began their descent; a certain anxiety about touching down at the right spot on the coastline, together with suppressed excitement at taking even a small part in such a tremendous undertaking. Then more definite, if less historical, realities claim the attention: the hook of the davit falls fouls a chain and snaps it;[9] port 6 davit jams due to bad lowering,[293] and LCA 171 is left suspended.[204] Nine boats successfully lowered pull away from the ship's sides and make circles while the remaining four are lowered from the luffing davits.[116]

The Fighting 543rd quickly formed up ready for the run-in. Captain Bateman's LCA No. 1383 was carrying Lieutenant-Colonel Hutchinson, and as it pulled away his Battalion's bugler sounded off the "General Salute"; to be answered by a cheery wave from *Glenearn's* bridge[9] and the sound of their own presentation silver bugle.[577] Group 5 set off from the Lowering Position at 0650 – 5 minutes late.[293]

0650

HMS Largs had moved to the head of the line of Landing Ships and anchored a few cables south of the Lowering Position. Now, as the Fighting 543rd passed Divisional Headquarters Ship, the East Yorks' bugler sounded off again. Major-General Rennie and Rear-Admiral Talbot were seen on the bridge, returning the salute.[205] After this rather moving moment,[577] the LCAs proceeded in their two columns following Landing Craft (Flak) 573.[152] Beaching was supposed to be at H-Hour plus 20 minutes, that is, 0745.[202]

Having set course for the beach, after 15 minutes' running they picked up the navigational leader. The run-in was anything but comfortable; more than half the soldiers in Captain Bateman's craft were sick. Motor Launch 202 came flying by; she had a gramophone playing through her loud hailer and it was blaring, "Roll Out The Barrel". Our intrepid bugler replied with, "Cookhouse", then promptly deposited his breakfast over the side. His Battalion Commander was seasick; even the Marine coxswain Corporal Bicknell was sick, so some chewing gum was stuffed in his mouth.[9]

Wireless silence was broken at 0735: *A* and *B* Companies reported heavy opposition, but operation proceeding according to plan.[252] 535 Flotilla was passed on its way out; they appeared to have suffered no casualties.[116] About 500 yards off the beach the navigational leader, having identified the beaching spot gave the "thumbs-up" sign and turned away. Captain Bateman made the signal to deploy to port and starboard,[9] the division of leaders reduced speed to 750 revs on one engine while the boats behind turned in to line abreast at progressively higher speeds,[235] then the whole flotilla waited for instructions to proceed.[152]

0735

Lieut.-Col. Hutchinson in LCA 1383 asked Captain Bateman to go slow ahead as he wished to appreciate the situation. Beach landmarks were difficult to identify due to the smoke and dust, but standing up in the craft the Colonel scanned[9] through his binoculars an unnaturally familiar shore: on the left the little port and lighthouse of Burghead – correction, Ouistreham – then the houses tailing away into a featureless coastline that was Queen Red Beach,[566] terminating in a mismatched pair of houses, one with a pyramidal roof, the other lop-sided.[202] To Lieut. Waters in LCA 471 who could see the Colonel surveying the scene, the beach looked much shorter than expected from his study of the wave-top photographs; the craft would be beaching quite close to each other.[152]

After about 30 seconds, Colonel Hutchinson had satisfied himself that the assault was progressing and decided where he wished to be put ashore, his craft went full ahead and the whole flotilla as per orders went driving in at speed. At least, that was the theory.[205] Because of the rough weather, the going had been slower than expected,[9] with the result that the water which should have been just short of the beach obstructions was, helped by the inshore wind, well beyond;[205] so the boats would have to go through between them.[152] Only one channel had been cleared, and it was not as wide as expected.[X]

Captain Bateman's LCA 1383 and Lieut. Maton's LCA 1216, the latter carrying personnel of Battalion Headquarters including the Chaplain, the Medical Officer and Medical Orderlies, went through together; others queueing up astern and gingerly making their way through to the beach.[93] The Flotilla Officer's craft missed a Teller mine "by the skin of his teeth",[9] while Lieut. Maton's – none of whose occupants had been seasick – had difficulty beaching;[93] the assault troops had in consequence only a moderately dry landing.[9] Kedges were not used, and in the increasing swell LCA 1216 broached to, and her crew began the struggle to get her off.[93]

With the waves slopping about on the shallow beach the rest of the Flotilla only got through thanks to Lady Luck, Providence and some little assistance from the coxswains. Lieut. Waters was dimly aware of objects screwed to passing obstructions, but whether they were mines, shells or what, he was too preoccupied to notice; the one thing that mattered was his craft. That had to go in, do its job and come out again. LCA 471 got caught up in some wire strung between two of the obstructions, but he told his coxswain Marine Pyper to go full ahead and tear the craft out. This succeeded, and they beached. They always tried to give their troops as dry a landing as possible. This time the craft touched bottom, the ramp went down, and Major Barber,* Officer Commanding *D* Company, and his Sergeant-Major led the way out. They went in up to their waists – there must have been a shell hole just forward of the ramp – and the Marines got a very dirty look, as if it was their fault.[152]

543 Flotilla touched down between 0755[252] and 0805;[229] ten to twenty minutes late.[202] The assault troops appeared to have cleared the beach-head quickly, but not without casualties. The Germans were directing their attention to the numerous targets now on the beach, judging by the small arms fire and mortar bombs.[93] Impressions became a rapid succession of sensations: the tangle and turmoil of craft on the

---

* Killed in action 6 June 1944.

beach, a burning tank on the foreshore, the wham and crash of exploding bombs and shells,[9] the masts of the small ships like a fir forest after a fire, the extremely dirty water stirred up by the shelling and the rockets.[152] And ploughing into it all, like some gargantuan juggernaut, the unending streams of landing craft discharging – by some inverse simile, out from under its wheels – a steadily moving flood of khaki-clad figures.[9] You saw it all, yet it was as if you were somehow detached from it all; it was most peculiar.

A wounded soldier was helped on board LCA 471 and another with a nasty mouth wound climbed in himself; he was given a jab of "Omnipon" and went off to sleep. In the few minutes spent on the beach a small tank managed to sit on the rudderguards of the landing craft and bent them, so that the steering was impaired when it pulled off. They saw LCA 1383 still on the beach; Captain Bateman must have struck some snag, but he waved Lieut. Waters' craft away. The plan was to reform about 600 yards out. As 471 turned for the open sea, more barbed wire was seen, but the same tactics were adopted and at full speed they rode over it. Once clear of the land the feeling of detachment went, and the task of a long haul back to *Glenearn* began.[152]

In backing off the beach LCA 1383 had been rammed by a craft astern and her steering damaged. During the subsequent efforts to get off Captain Bateman noticed three other LCAs in difficulties, but could not make out their numbers. After going round in circles in futile attempts to get clear, he decided to beach in the lee of two LCTs which had been hit and had broached to. A wounded sailor was picked up and they all stayed under cover until such times as the shelling might moderate; enemy artillery had the range of the beaches and his fire was uncomfortably accurate.[9]

LCAs 900 and 664 were intended to stay on the beach under command of the Beach Master, and 352 was to be used in obstacle clearance.[152] The L.C.O.C.U. found only one channel from Red Beach ready to be buoyed out to seaward, instead of the two expected, and when this was done they attempted to carry on with work on submerged obstacles.

However, the surf was too heavy to control the LCA from which the divers worked, and they were in constant danger from flight after flight of landing craft bearing down upon them and driving in wherever a clear width of beach could be seen. After buoying a number of submerged wrecks Lieut. Jackson, RM, decided to land and assist the sappers working on the beach. Their tasks in turn were to assist the AVREs in clearing the landward continuation of the approach channels, and the beach obstacles generally.

0815   Obstacle clearance was proceeding painfully slowly, the heavy swell making the removal of mines almost impossible, except from the innermost row. Fortunately obstacles did not appear to be preventing the beaching or the unloading of craft, but more and more were being holed before going on to beach in a sinking condition,[205] while the congestion of armoured, and the infantry's priority, vehicles stopped the work of clearance immediately above the water line. The beach exits were not yet working properly. Shortly after 0830, because of the depth of water, obstacle clearance was suspended. The incoming craft would have to take their chances with the remaining Teller mines.

At the west end of Red Beach strong-point *Cod* was still holding out. Four flails had been put out of action by anti-tank gunfire before even reaching it, and a fifth had had a track blown off by a mine; however, another machine after doing good work knocking down pit props for the obstacle clearance team went on to flail two lanes* into *Cod*. With the East Yorks. attacking along these the flail started on a third lane, while

0840 self-propelled guns,† having landed and deployed in the shallow water fired at short range in support of the assaulting infantry. A Royal Marine Commando‡ touched down on Red

0845 Beach and crossed to White Beach, which was drawing less fire, before pushing inland.[229]

After an hour's effort Lieut. Maton and his men managed to get their LCA clear, only to find that with the rising tide the rows of mined obstacles were covered by water, and they

---

* Lanes 5 and 6.   † 76 Field Regiment RA.
‡ 41 Royal Marine Commando.

could not at first find the gap by which they had come in. At about 0900, after clearing the obstructions, mortar fire opened from the eastern extremity of the beach. The craft was hit near the cockpit; Lieut. Maton and Marine Precious the signaller. were both wounded. Water came pouring in, and another mortar bomb hit the port side forward; with the water right up to the gunwhales the order was given to abandon ship. Clear of the vessel Maton saw Marine Fox his stoker/driver still in it, and presumed him to be wounded; Marine Precious he had not seen since the second explosion. Coughlan the coxswain and Clifford drifted away to the east. LCA 1216 submerged bows first, with the stern still above water. Two LCMs from another unit were passing, and after beaching and unbeaching one of them picked up Maton, while the other went to the assistance of Coughlan and Clifford floating about 100 yards away.[93]

Above the embattled beaches barrage balloons were rising, while stores and motor vehicles poured ashore.[205] Two LCIs were hit by shell-fire as they approached, and the Commando troops* they carried had further losses on the congested beach, where only one exit appeared to be in use. The follow-up brigade† had already begun landing on a beach still under fairly heavy mortar and shell-fire.   0936 0955

With the clearance of strong-point *Cod*, there was a slackening of fire – at least over the western part of Queen Red – and the biggest problem on the beach became one of congestion. More self-propelled guns landed, but were held up there.[229] Craft continued to arrive until 1105, when Red Beach was closed because of the congestion of vehicles.[205] With all the beach exits blocked the disembarkation of two companies of 2nd Bn. Middlesex Regt., made matters worse, until one of the exits was re-opened and the transport got moving again.[229] The last of the Reserve Brigade‡ were being held to seaward in LCTs and Landing Craft Infantry (Large). Sporadic fire was still coming from the direction of Ouistreham, and the barrage balloons' wires were cut to stop the enemy ranging on them.[205]   1000 1045 1130

---

* 3 Commando.   † 185 Infantry Brigade.   ‡ 9 Infantry Brigade.

The sea had moderated. The turning of the tide left more than twenty major landing craft stranded; some deliberately, to unload stores, others because they were crippled or destroyed. Some fired their guns at snipers in the houses. By 1530 the tide had been falling for two hours, and the remaining beach obstructions were drying out again, but little or no effort was being made to clear them. Unloading of ammunition from the two LCTs on Red Beach appeared to have stopped; people were dazed, shaken and exhausted. The landing of Rear-Admiral Talbot to see the situation for himself coincided with an air-raid by seven Ju 88s.[205] One bomb dropped right in the middle of the welter of humanity that was Queen Red Beach on D-Day afternoon; amazingly, only a few men were killed.[229] Many of the stranded craft fired their guns at the individual 'planes sneaking in through the low clouds to bomb and strafe the beaches. LCTs bringing in the last of the reserve brigade, an armoured regiment and stores came inshore at 1550.

After Admiral Talbot had left, a Principal Beach Master was appointed, in the form of Commander T. I. S. Bell, DSC, RN;[205] Captain Bateman subsequently reported to him, then got his crew ashore where they dug in. The Flotilla Officer reconnoitred the beach and came up with the crew of LCA 171.[9]

After having had a temporary patch fitted,[204] LCA 171 had eventually left *Glenearn* at 0845.[293] The troops were landed successfully, but as the crew were trying to unbeach her, the engines had failed. As the marines were attempting to push the craft off, it had been hit in the ramp by a mortar bomb, although little damage had been done. Some of the men had then gone to seek assistance, as the seas were causing worse damage; whilst they were away another bomb near-missed the starboard quarter, after which she had filled up by the stern and sank.[204] Captain Bateman ordered Lance-Corporal Summerscales and his crew of four to come with him, and the little group of survivors were later joined by Lieutenant Weightman, RM, of 537 Flotilla, and the crews of two of his craft.[9]

By 1555 the beaches were being cleared, if slowly, and the stores from LCTs were once more being unloaded. The first of the ferry craft had arrived, and started the shuttle service between the merchant ships lying off-shore and the beaches. Removal of the beach obstacles as they were uncovered by the falling tide went on apace. Mines and shells were taken off, ramps, stakes and "hedgehogs" were towed away, concrete tetrehedra were run down by tanks. By nightfall the Royal Engineers and the L.C.O.C.U. had cleared away most of the obstructions.

Shortly after 2100, hundreds of aircraft towing gliders flew over; reinforcements for the 6th Airborne Division. Twenty minutes later another large contingent followed; altogether it was a most impressive and encouraging sight. At dusk a **2250** smoke screen was put up to cover the anchorage in case of air attack, which developed half an hour later; a stick of bombs fell across the beach and the anchorage. A third wave of airborne troops was overhead at the time, and light Ack-Ack guns ashore opened up on the transport planes. Merchant ships and LSTs in the anchorage joined in, and at least two British aircraft were shot down by the considerable volume of AA fire.[205]

During the forenoon of D + 1, more German fliers were **7.6.44** seen. Most of them were routed by the covering Spitfires,[373] but once *Glenearn*'s men were machine-gunned by enemy fighters. The bunch of survivors, which now included Sub.-Lieut. Hollick and the crew of Lieutenant Jackson's LCA 352, reported to *HMS Largs* and were put to work clearing up the beaches along with the Fleet working parties. A large number of disabled craft were hauled off after being suitably patched up. Marine Clifford rejoined; telling his comrades that he had been captured by Germans but had managed to escape.

Their second night on the beach was again disturbed by bombing raids,[9] and on D + 2 an enemy aircraft dropped a **8.6.44** single bomb on a dump close behind the beaches. A large fire was caused in which all the petrol landed to date, and half the ammunition, went up in smoke.

The same afternoon *s.s. Cap Tourane*, a depot ship

arrived,[205] and at the end of the day the *Glenearn* group embarked in her.[9] From her accommodation, beach working parties were being organized from survivors and spare crews;[205] one of the latter stemming from 535 Flotilla and consisting of Marines Townsend, McGraw, Legg and Cockerell. On D-Day, they had been sent to *HMS Largs*, but as no LCA returned to that ship they had been ordered to take an LCP and lay smoke parallel to the beach to screen fresh craft arriving. After about an hour of this they had struck, and been holed by, an underwater obstacle. They had been just able to reach the HQ Ship. *Glenearn*'s contingent of survivors joined up with RN Beach Party 166A.[28]

That day too, four merchant ships were scuttled off-shore to form the centre-section of a breakwater of blockships, and two more were added to the line in the evening. A French battleship *Courbet*, the Dutch cruiser *Sumatra* and *HMS*

9.6.44   *Durban* went down on June the 9th.

The working parties, with the assistance of large numbers of prisoners of war soon got the beaches tidied up.[205] *Glenearn*'s men managed to get two of their own craft off with the aid of bulldozers.[9] One of them, LCA 352, was damaged in the process and then her engines failed. She was towed by the other to a repair barge, but as no spares were available the

10.6.44   craft was sunk.[204] Now the beach organization could handle all that the Ferry Service could deliver, and more. Daily figures improved until the 13th, when over 3,000 tons of stores, more than 400 vehicles and 2,200 personnel were landed; then the weather started to deteriorate.

13.6.44   D + 7 was also the first without a daylight air attack, but every night without exception the enemy were over. Smoke screens were laid at dusk and dawn by landing craft and motor launches, and Radar gave plenty of warning of air attack.[205] The standard procedure was for a German reconnaissance machine to drop a line of flares to guide the bombers. As soon as the lights appeared patrol craft tried to shoot them out one by one while all the vessels in the anchorage made smoke.[582] The attackers were met by controlled barrages fired blind; merchant ships were forbidden to fire with close range weapons under any conditions whatsoever. As a result, when the enemy began to lay parachute mines he flew over the anchorage with impunity.

Six LSTs beached on the 15th and when dried out came under very accurate fire from mobile mortar batteries in the neighbourhood of Franceville Plage, just across the River Orne. Five of the ships were hit and several casualties caused. *(15.6.44)*

Visibility was low next day with rain, but not much wind, and the weather report for the next day was promising: "... becoming fair, good visibility and light wind". Instead, the wind went round to the north-east and by the afternoon of the 18th was blowing force 6. DUKWs* were able to continue unloading, but unwieldy "Rhino" ferries broke adrift and were driven ashore; then they charged about in the heavy surf demolishing everything that got in their way. The gale freshened to force 8 and all the minor vessels took refuge inside the "Gooseberry" breakwater. At high water the seas were coming green over the blockships and many craft were damaged by the swell, while pressure-activated mines exploded spontaneously all around.[205] *(16.6.44 / 18.6.44 / 19.6.44)*

When the gale had finished on the morning of the 23rd June appalling wreckage was piled high along the shore; Queen Red and Queen White Beaches were completely cluttered up, with craft piled on top of each other and left aground by the retreat of the neap tides. Large working parties were once more organized, some of them from the cruisers of the bombarding force.[205] *(23.6.44)*

Captain Bateman and most of his men left Normandy on 26th June in the light cruiser *HMS Sirius*, which took them to Portsmouth.[9] Sub.-Lieut. Hollick remained on the beach, together with Marine Boulton of LCA 171 and the four others of the spare crew.[204] By the 28th the worst of the mess had been cleared up, and the following day *HMS Largs* withdrew from "Sword" Area.[205] *(26.6.44 / 29.6.44)*

Mobile batteries firing from east of the Orne had become

---

* Amphibious lorries.

increasingly dangerous. Their fire was extremely accurate.* During the last week of June smoke screens had been laid almost continuously throughout the day, but the enemy knew the range exactly and fired through the smoke. Casualties mounted fast. As "Gold" and "Juno" Areas could handle all the shipping that would have been "Sword's", the ships and coasters were transferred westwards and on 1st July the naval beach organization was closed down and the use of the beaches discontinued.[587]

1.7.44

The last of *Glenearn*'s men reached *HMS Westcliffe*, the minor landing craft holding base at Westcliffe-on-Sea, on 11th July 1944.[204] There they were sorted out, interrogated and sent on leave,[9] only to be recalled a few days later.[28]

11.7.44

* On 3rd July a German officer was found concealed in a wrecked house on Queen White Beach. He was in uniform and well supplied with food, drink and cigars.[205]

CHAPTER 19

CROSS-CHANNEL FERRY

At 0720 the first lot of survivors from *Svenner* were brought alongside in two U.S. Coastguard cutters and an LCI (L). There was a bad sea running. Captain Hutchison used his engines to make a lee, but *Glenearn* did not hold it for long enough, and he thought it neither safe, nor wise, to get under way. Because of the conditions, the sally ports could not be opened to aid the operation, and it was extremely difficult to get the badly-wounded out.[293] Altogether, 73 men were taken on board,[85] which was seventy-three more than one would have thought could have survived the explosion of the torpedo.[106]

As soon as 543 Flotilla had pulled away from *Glenearn* the two LCMs 433 and 471 were got ready to be put in the water;[293] a slow process. They were to be used as ferry craft for the unloading of merchant ships lying off-shore,[205] and were not expected to come back to "Mother".[94]

One of 535 Flotilla's spare crews, consisting of Marines Townsend, McGraw, Legg and Cockerell were told that they had to go to the HQ Ship *Largs*. Their job would be to take over the first assault craft to return from the beaches and to try and rescue any wounded men they would find there. The Marines were to be taken off *Glenearn* by an MTB and there was not much time. The heavy sea was still running and the four men were in fighting order, which weighed them down; they had to jump from the ship to the torpedo boat when it came close enough on the crest of a wave. It was all very unpleasant, but they made it at the second attempt. They expected to return to *Glenearn* the next day.[28]

It had been estimated that the returning LCAs should be seen about 1910, but more than forty additional anxious minutes were to pass[293] before Captain Richards was sighted with his whole flotilla in good order.[85] All ten of his craft were hoisted by 1030.[293] There were plenty of tales to tell; when asked what things were like, one of the Marine coxswains replied, "The beach looked bloody big, and the soldiers running up it looked bloody small."[85]

There had been no casualties among the flotilla, but a few of the lads had bumps or bruises; some had been seasick and were sent to the Sick Bay for a reviver. Lieutenant Mayhew, whose guns so far had had nothing to do, remarked uncharitably that once word had got round, it was amazing how many of the Royal Marines discovered that they too were suffering from *mal der mer*.[94]

Captain Hutchison had intended leaving for the Isle of Wight area about 1040, but as 543 Flotilla had not returned, and it was apparent that a Landing Ship could still be of use embarking wounded, he remained. Some LCAs from Force "J" were about, asking to be hoisted; these were sent on to *Battleaxe*.

1100   By 1100 543 Flotilla were returning. Seven craft had been hoisted by 1130; seven had failed to return. Of the latter, three – 337, 900 and 1216 – were known to have been lost or damaged. Three were missing: Captain Bateman's 1383 was believed to be out of action, Fleet No. 664 carried RE details and might not get off the beach until much later, and 171 had left the ship late. 535 Flotilla's LCA 352 with the L.C.O.C.U. was not expected back. Two complete crews out of the three known to be lost were safe and back on board.[293]

Among the last to reach *Glenearn* had been LCA 471. Soon after pulling off the beach and negotiating the obstacles again, Lieutenant Waters' craft had come across 337 in trouble. She was secured alongside for the tow back, but filled with water to such an extent that, after her crew and stores had been transferred, she was abandoned. This gave Lieutenant Waters three coxswains: Marine Pyper, Corporal Macintosh and Marine Bartlett of 337.

It was a hard lonely trip back against the tide, with the boat making water and hogging. As she met each incoming wave, the flat bottom tended to send a lot of water in over the bows, and they had had enough of that already; the coxswains were instructed to meet each wave bow-on, and then steer to starboard in the direction of *Glenearn* down the rear slope. Finally, Corporal Macintosh was put in charge of the baling party – the pump had packed up – and Marine Bartlett took over most of the duty at the wheel. It had been a great joy to see the pyramid-like shape of *Glenearn* eventually show up on the skyline. After the craft had been hoisted, the wounded went to the Sick Bay and the others to get out of their wet clothes and into some food.[152]

When some shells fell near the LSI Squadron, Captain Hutchison ordered the ships to weigh but remain in the vicinity of the Lowering Position; *Glenearn* still embarking casualties.[293] An LCM from another unit brought back the wounded Lieutenant Maton as he had requested to be returned to his own ship;[93] he was given emergency treatment for a pneumo-thorax.[106] *Glenearn*'s doctors and sick berth attendants were hard-pressed, but assisted by *Svenner*'s Norwegian surgeon-lieutenant they were more than adequate for the tasks they were called upon to perform.[93] Throughout the forenoon, landing craft and the US Coastguard vessels had been coming alongside with survivors and wounded;[293] some of *Svenner*'s men ended up in *Glenearn*'s ward-room,[155] while the Medical Officers cleaned up most of the casualties, and gave blood transfusions to four of the more seriously wounded.

One case was quite extraordinary; an old boy with the right frontal bone of his cranium blown away. You could see his brain, yet he was quite *compos mentis*; the doctors just covered it up until they got back and someone else could stick in another bone and sew him up properly. Another soldier had half his foot blown off by a landmine; happy as a lark, he was.[106] Lieutenant Webber, RM, was sitting on *A*-deck stuffing himself with a monstrous great "tiddy-oggy"* when a Sick Berth Artificer came out of the Sick Bay. The "Tiffy" crossed to the rail and dumped over the side what appeared to be a number of bits of limbs, particularly feet. Being an ex-policeman and inured to blood and guts, the witness to this scene was callous enough to continue eating his "Action Stations" fodder.[155]

* Cornish Pasty.

On inspection, LCA 471 was found to have six neat holes under her water line – no wonder her crew had had to bale all the way back! Many of the Royals felt that they should have gone up the beach with the soldiers and fought alongside them, instead of pulling off and leaving them to go on alone. Very commendable sentiments, but as their officer pointed out they had done their job, and their duty was to get their craft clear to make room for others to come in and land more troops; and more in similar vein. They were very good chaps, some of them; quite young to be in charge of landing craft

1300 laden with troops.[152] By 1300 it was apparent that all the landing craft that could get back had returned,[85] and the Captain ordered the other LSIs to follow *Glenearn*; the six ships re-tracing the course up Channel 10 at 13 knots, escorted by the frigate *Torrington*.[293] Many in *Glenearn* were tired after the excitement of the landing or having been at action stations all the while,[94] but the day had cleared up

1345 beautifully; there were now no clouds in their sky.[106] At 1345 *Glenearn* had reached the position 49° 34′ N, 0° 14′ W.[293]

The explosion was so close that splinters of steel clattered on the bridge.[94] Everyone thought they were being bombed, but there were no 'planes in the sky.[106] It was found that they were being shelled by the medium calibre guns sited at Cape de la Hève near Havre, where a battery was indicated on the secret maps from photographs taken by the RAF.[94] Captain Hutchison ordered his ship to engage the enemy, but was persuaded to leave well alone;[93] the range, both by finder and from Lieutenant Mayhew's charts, was 27,000 yards[94] – about 6,000 more than *Glenearn*'s 4-inch guns in Low Angle.[158] The first shot had been a plus, the second was a minus, they must have got the range and everyone became a bit "jumpy".[116] Captain Hutchison ordered ...*MAKE SMOKE*... which was much more sensible and practicable.

Every now and then in the past the Officer of the Watch had been obliged to tell the Engine Room, "You are making smoke," a most heinous offence. Now to be told, "Make smoke"...the Engine Room surpassed itself. Phew! In addition, *Glenearn* set off smoke canisters,[94] as did her flock, and *HMS Torrington* laid a screen.[293] Out of the pall of smoke came a lovely sight: *HMS Warspite* with her great guns, steaming at a good speed between *Glenearn* and the Germans, and pointing the latter's way. The shelling stopped and no one blamed Gerry for doing so;[94] the LSI Squadron, escaping behind the smoke screen made at best speed[85] for "Piccadilly Circus", as the buoy at the Nab Tower was called.[36]

Lieutenant Mayhew had the watch coming back, and was on the bridge with Lieut.-Com. Philpott, the navigator. They were all alone at sea when the Isle of Wight came over the horizon, but suddenly every ship in the invasion fleet seemed to appear from nowhere. *Glenearn*, doing about 13 knots, was bearing down upon a flock of small craft. Mayhew was very, very nervous... the Captain was required on the bridge. The O.O.W. pressed the bell for the Captain, but got no reply... he tried again, with the same result. By this time there were a lot of ships about so he pressed the voice pipe bell and asked, "Captain on the bridge, please, Sir." "What is it, Guns?" Mayhew explains, although the Captain can see the situation from the stateroom windows. The answer came up the voice pipe, "Carry on through 'em. I'm going six no trumps and I'm vulnerable... you get on with it, Jack!"

Otherwise they returned to the Solent with little excitement, but with a feeling of a job well done.[94] The incredible fact was that you could get all these ships, this absolute armada, only six or seven miles off the French coast, and the Germans could do little or nothing about it, and no one had seemed worried at all about anything – except when they had had occasion to put up the smoke screen.[106]

On passing the Nab Tower about 1930, Captain Hutchison hoisted the special signal to indicate that they had serious casualties on board and received an acknowledgment.[293] "Ossie" Maton was visited by his fellow officers; Richard Webber,[155] and Cyril Waters who lent him a khaki shirt to wear as his own were either blood-stained or dirty. Lieutenant Maton was a nice fellow, quite popular down below and had often spent an evening talking with the chaps; a good-living young man.[152]

The squadron anchored in Area 18, off Cowes, at 2100. No medical assistance for the serious casualties was offered, and during the resulting delay three men died.[293] At 0400 an order was received to proceed up to Southampton to the Ocean Terminal[85] where the surviving wounded – including fifteen from *Svenner*[605] – were eventually carried off the ship and on to a hospital train.[93]

7.6.44

Copies of the daily papers were obtained, and eagerly scanned, to see what the operation had all been about. There was quite a screed about the Americans, say five column-inches on the Canadians and an inch and a half about the British – still, it was nice to know that they had been there.[152] Loads of letters which had been held up since before D-Day arrived on board.[1] Captain Hutchison wrote a report to Rear-Admiral Talbot on the delay in receiving medical assistance for the casualties and a message was received from Colonel Hutchinson saying, "We captured all objectives by evening and suffered rather severely. Self slightly wounded."[293]

8.6.44

While still at Southampton, reserves* of the 51st (Highland) Division were embarked, but sailing was delayed due to some muddle over destroyer escorts.[85] The organization supposed to be controlling the build-up forces for Normandy had virtually broken down. Congestion in the Solent anchorage was acute, since apart from warships returning to refuel, store and ammunition, landing ships – even follow-up convoys – had arrived back before some of the vessels loaded prior to D-Day had left for France.[586]

9.6.44

Glenearn finally sailed at 0400 on the 9th,[85] in company with her sister-ship *Glenroy* and escorted by the sloop *Crane*.[206] This was the first time the two Glen ships had been together since the old days of Force "Z" in the Mediterranean. Almost immediately the ships ran into fog, but in spite of this the Channel crossing was quiet and uneventful.

Glenearn anchored off "Juno" Beach at 0920.[85] Among the mass of shipping lying off-shore were several battleships, and hundreds of landing craft shuttled between ship and shore in complete safety;[250] and in complete contrast to the imagined

---

* Possibly administrative elements.

scene when, three days previously, the 3rd Canadian Division and their supporting units had assaulted.[R] *Glenearn*'s soldiers were landed, and she was back off Cowes at 2100.[85]

A few days passed at anchor. Several LCAs had had trouble with bent rudder guards obstructing free movement of the rudders, so all the rudder guards were cut off. A spot of shore leave and a number of *Glenearn*'s officers were in "The Bugle", Newport, Isle of Wight. An Engineer called for a round of drinks, and felt for his money. He, like many others, had anticipated the possibility of *Glenearn*'s being sunk, but forgotten that he had stowed his notes in a "french letter" to keep them dry. Result, one red-faced "plumber".[152]

There was an indication that they might be sailing again with *Glenroy* and *Empire Arquebus* for the British Sector at midnight on 13th/14th, but as it transpired *Glenearn* went up to Southampton to embark 1,500 American troops.[85] They were all lined up on the quay, with quite a few coloured chaps among them.[106] To some of the U.S. infantry the studied pace of quayside activity seemed inconsistent with a war being fought on the other side of the same water,[560] but for one negro soldier its imminence was too much to bear; he cut his throat rather than go over there. It was really nasty, even for those who did not actually see it.[106]

Glenearn sailed in the early hours of 16th June, unescorted, but with two other transports: *City of Canterbury* and *Macklenburg*. The last-named had as its destination "Utah" Beach on the Cherbourg Peninsula; *Glenearn* and the other ship were bound for "Omaha".[207] There a complete port was already functioning with breakwaters, piers and runways on a stretch of coast where the Americans had met the most effective resistance of all the Normandy landings.[R] On D + 10 the excitement was in watching the departure of the American nurses; one of them left a cabin littered with hair pins, and that caused quite a stir.

Glenearn was almost back at Portsmouth when a flying machine of some sort passed on the port side. It was going "like stink" and was so low that officers on *Glenearn*'s bridge felt as if they were looking down on it. They were left

15.6.44

16.6.44

AT "OMAHA"

25. U.S. Nurses 16th June, 1944.

ON THE BRIDGE

26. Lieut. A. M. Hart, RNR on watch.

wondering what it was. Very disconcerting indeed.[94] Later on, anchored in Cowes Roads, one or two more flying bombs went over, but none dropped too close for comfort.[36]

Another trip was made on the 18th,[85] with men of Canadian infantry regiments. As *Glenearn* was creeping in at very low speed they passed *Glenroy* lying unusually deep in the water;[36] Lieutenant (E) McKenzie recognized the appearance of a Glen ship with her engine room flooded, and sure enough she had set off a pressure-operated mine in the "Utah" area,[85] and was just leaving under tow by a United States tug.[208]

18.6.44

An unexpected north-easterly gale began on the 19th, and it was the 22nd before it subsided.[205] There was little to do but wait for mail from home and think of leave. Lieut.-Com. (E) Cahy had lunch with his opposite number on *HMS Prince Baudouin*; Lieut.-Com. (E) Aiken's ship had landed U.S. Rangers on "Omaha" on D-Day, and had made a comparable number of ferry trips since.[1]

19.6.44

On the 23rd there was intimation of yet another Channel crossing,[209] and by the forenoon of the next day *Glenearn* was at Southampton embarking personnel. About lunchtime she pulled away from the quay, and in the early afternoon anchored in the Solent. The whole area was alive with every sort of landing craft, many of them still sporting the red and black triangles of 3rd Inf. Div. After the storms of the previous week the weather was lovely and at least one of *Glenearn*'s first-class passengers had difficulty thinking himself into part of the greatest invasion in history, what with the whitest of bread on the tables and deck chairs on the boat deck. With the lines of ships it looked like the Spithead Review, but stripped of its bunting; only the white hull of a Union Castle hospital ship relieved the ubiquitous battleship grey.[115]

24.6.44

Passengers included officers and men of 48 RM Commando; reinforcements and most of one troop that had been unable to land on D-Day[222] – they had already received one mauling before even stepping ashore.[152] There was also a contingent of nurses: Q.A.I.M.N.S.,* much decorated with

* Queen Alexandra's Imperial Military Nursing Service.

Africa Stars; battle-hardened, and physically attractive into the bargain.[115] And Naafi personnel – even sightseers from the Government in Whitehall; the shooting war must be over, over there![94]

The usual Navy hospitality was provided, an apology having to be given only for not opening the ward-room bar because of the numbers of officers on board. A casual word by a Captain Renison to one of *Glenearn*'s Royal Marine Officers to the effect that he was going out to join the 2nd Bn. East Yorkshire Regiment resulted in his getting the story of the months of training together culminating in the D-Day landing, and his being bidden to take messages from several of the ship's officers to the Battalion.

25.6.44 The ship sailed in the early hours, destination "Gold" Sector. The voyage itself was uneventful – blue sky and a flat calm – but an almost continuous stream of vessels of all sorts and sizes heading in all directions was a sight for some never to be forgotten. It seemed incredible that all this traffic was generated by the invasion of a coast still largely in the hands of the enemy, bar a short stretch of 30–40 miles; one would have deemed it impossible for the Navy and the Air Force to protect such a concentration of shipping whilst all the war material for two great armies poured ashore over open beaches.

Something that looked like an upturned kitchen table was the most noteworthy of the craft crossing, and one was at a loss to know what it was. Then the excitement of seeing the coastline gradually appear, quite low and very quiet. Near at hand the swept channel seemed very narrow, while afar off barrage balloons were tethered to many of the ships. Nearer to the coast again the artificial harbour at Arromanches with its breakwater of sunken ships and many other mysteriously-shaped components. With so many quite large vessels lying close inshore once again the thought: could the Luftwaffe let such a concentration exist unchallenged save by the most occasional sneak raid? Then the bows of a sunken vessel pointing towards the skies gave some inkling of the perils of an earlier crossing; wrecked craft on the beaches seemed to tell the same story.[115]

The approach had been very slow and difficult because the enemy had mined the shallow water,[85] and *Glenearn* went in very close before dropping anchor. It was said that on one of the other trips the escorting warship had ordered Captain Hutchison not to go any further. To this he had replied, "Who is the senior officer here?"[115]

It was a beautiful day, with only the mutter of guns in the distance. A signal had been received: "Anything flying is enemy", but the only thing seen on the wing was a butterfly. The nurses refused to be carried ashore and cheerfully waded in the last few yards, but some of the males – not front-line troops – had to be urged to get their feet wet.[152] *Glenearn* returned to Cowes about midnight.

There followed a period of inactivity[85] which gave time for reflection. Since D-Day the ship had been employed as a ferry boat, and although her spirit remained high the excitement was over. It had been a placid life taking reinforcements to the various beach-heads,[94] even if the long hours at "Action Stations" had been a bit trying. We appeared to be doing alright across the way; very soon they should have the Hun on the run – how could they stand up to the material resources at the Allies' disposal? Hopefully it would soon all be over and everyone could get back to their normal way of living.[1]

And time for recreation. A dance was held on shore, a concert was given on board by an ENSA Party,[85] and an invitation issued to several members of the women's forces to come aboard as guests of the lower deck. The galley set to work. In due course landing craft were bringing off WRNS, ATS and WAAFs. The ship's side being perforated with outlets from heads and the like, a "pipe" had been made that no heads or bathrooms on the port side were to be flushed. Alas, the inevitable happened; just as one LCA was discharging its load of ladies at the foot of the gangway, someone in the Petty Officers' flat ignored the order. The poor girl was in a mess. A very irate Officer of the Watch dashed down hoping to find the culprit, but no one could be seen.[152]

On the last day of the month Lieut.-Com. (E) Aiken had   30.6.44

lunch on his old ship, and about nine of *Glenearn*'s officers accepted the invitation to dinner followed by a picture show aboard *Prince Baudouin*. There was little left to do except wait hopefully for letters from home and take the odd trip ashore.[1] Commander Hardman-Jones was a bachelor, and one of his pastimes was to have his very tall bycicle put ashore, then ride around to some little pub and there have a pint of beer. If any of his ship's crew happened to be there he would be delighted to buy them a pint as well; halves were not permitted. Pedalling back to Cowes one evening he overtook two sailors from *Glenearn*. He suggested that they would be rather late aboard and why not run? But one said that he had bad feet, so Hardman-Jones gave him the bike, took off his jacket and stowed it on the back, then ran with the other sailor all the way; as a result the two *matelots* were only half an hour overdue and not stranded ashore until the next morning.[152]

Morale of the ship's company – which rose or fell depending upon whether they were active or swinging uselessly round a buoy[160] – took a dive when both 535 and 543 Flotillas were ordered to *HMS Cricket* on the River Hamble. All the gear was loaded into the craft, and with very long faces they sailed away. They were met at the landing stage by a signal to return at once to *Glenearn*, so it was with joyful speed back to their ship and willing hands to hoist them aboard.[152]

5.7.44 On the 5th of July, 1944, *HMS Glenearn* left Cowes to carry out a redistribution of LCAs. This involved sailing to Milford Haven where the Flotillas were put ashore for two days; *Glenearn* went on to Swansea, then Liverpool, before going back to pick up her Royal Marines and their craft again.[85] Then north to Greenock and a short refit in the floating dock there.[152] Everyone had a few days' leave.[85]

* * *

Extract from Admiralty War Diary for 10 July 1944: "Early decision is expected that LOTHIAN, GLENEARN, PAMPAS, EMPIRE BATTLEAXE, EMPIRE ARQUEBUS, EMPIRE MACE, and EMPIRE SPEARHEAD will form

Force X and will be required to proceed to the SW Pacific about 1 August under command of a British Naval Force Commander for duty under American higher command concerned. Last 5 ships will be commissioned in HM Service not later than 25 July."[287]

CHAPTER 20

FIRST INTO YOKOHAMA

Several of *Glenearn*'s men with homes in the south of England had their leave disturbed by "doodle-bugs",[85] as the flying-bombs had come to be called. But if the risks occasionally shared with the civilian population had risen again, the prospect of an untimely death off an enemy-held shore had receded; there was even the possibility of surviving the war. Hope was rekindled; the idea of living to a ripe old age was intoxicating.[A]

One watch had returned from leave and the Captain was about to go on his, but wanted to see the Warrant Shipwright first. This worthy – a West Countryman – was also the rum bosun, and, as it happened, was "plastered". Absolutely "plastered", and the Captain wanted to see him. Surgeon-Lieutenant Payne-James tried to get him round, but failed; Commander Hardman-Jones tried too. The Medical Officer even gave the patient an injection to try and waken him up a bit, but no, he was absolutely plastered, so Payne-James had to go and report to the Captain.

"Colin Arthur George" liked Payne-James quite a bit, as evinced by the latter's "flimsy":* "...socially unreliable, but in an emergency, very good." That and the fact that he had recommended him for the Distinguished Service Cross. Having been informed of the condition of the shipwright Hutchison said, "Well, I want you to write a note saying that he is drunk." "I can't do that, Sir" – because at an early stage in his naval career they had been told quite definitely that doctors were not allowed to say that anyone was drunk – to make sure that no one was chucked in a cell and maybe died overnight – they could only say, "Suffering from no organic disease". Old Hutchison was absolutely furious. He jumped up and down like a little monkey and said, "You civilians, you come into the Navy and tell us what to do..." "Well, Sir,

---

* Confidential report.

228

speaking as a civilian –" "You're not a civilian!" Poor Payne-James did not know where or what he was, and because he had been so obstinate, Captain Hutchison went down to the Admiralty and arranged it that Payne-James did not get the DSC.[106]

543 Flotilla had to be made up to strength. Lieutenant Maton was in hospital and Lieutenant O. W. Jackson had been left on the beach;[152] Lieutenant Whitworth went off with tummy trouble.[155] Replacements were Lieutenants F. G. Bell, C. Ince and H. Wolstencroft. Bell arrived on 14th July, none too pleased at being posted 2 i/c; he and "Loftie" Wolstencroft were from 706 LCP(L) Flotilla and had spent a hectic month on the coast of Normandy.[11] A Sub.-Lieut. (E) Steel,* RNVR, was appointed Flotilla Engineer Officer.[215] Captain Bateman himself rejoined on the 17th July.[85]

The landing craft were repaired and the missing numbers made up; LCA 471 was replaced. Lieut. Waters had found Marine Bartlett to be such a good coxswain that he had him transferred to his own craft.[152] Coxswains of 535 Flotilla checked over their equipment and made good any shortages from the Flotilla stores during the forenoon of the 18th.[155]

Refitting and regrouping went ahead. Force "X" was to consist of *Glenearn* and the *Empires Arquebus, Battleaxe, Spearhead* and *Mace* – all now flying the White Ensign.[215] The place in the D-Day LSI Squadron of *s.s. Empire Broadsword*,[85] sunk by a mine on 2nd July,†[561] had been taken by *HMS Lamont*, formerly *s.s. Clan Lamont*. It was said that her Captain Angus Campbell had flown the Scottish Standard from her masthead going in to Normandy; now, however, a completely new crew – even engineers – had been put aboard at the last minute.[152] Force "X" would be under Rear-Admiral Talbot, flying his flag in *HMS Lothian*, formerly *s.s. City of Edinburgh*.[35]

The Force's CRM‡ accompanied by his Deputy and his Assistant visited all the flotillas on 27th July, to hear questions

14.7.44

17.7.44

27.7.44

---

* Name changed.
† *Maid of Orleans* had also been sunk, on 28th June.[214]
‡ Commandant Royal Marines.

about personnel and equipment, and next day a meeting of all the Royal Marine officers was held in *HMS Empire Battleaxe* to discuss *A* and *Q** matters. In the afternoon a Major Messer-Bennetts left for the Royal Marine Office with a list of queries, returning two days later with the answer that reserves of clothing for the Force would not reach it before sailing, but that some of the tropical gear required would be supplied by *HMS Monck*† and placed in bulk aboard *Glenearn*.[215] A few of the latter's RM officers bought tropical tunics in Glasgow.[11] There was much to-ing and fro-ing of drifters with personnel.

30.7.44

Squadron staff were appointed, one corporal and five marines joining *Lothian* as orderlies without having had leave for nine months.[215] Lieutenant Ives was drafted to 535 Flotilla, and the spare crew rejoined on 2nd August – recalled from leave.[28] A Royal Marine Sergeant PTI joined the Force, was posted to *Lamont*, only to be relieved next day as unfit for foreign service; the Squadron's Company Sergeant Major was discharged to *HMS Monck* as unfit for his appointment,[215] and *Glenearn*'s officers were banned from the Bay Hotel on the Pier Head at Gourock.[94]

1.8.44

Admiral Talbot came aboard on the Thursday afternoon to speak to the ship's company mustered on the fo'c'sle. He told them how proud he was of their efforts in Normandy. On D-Day Force "S" had lost approximately 250 killed, so the casualties had been very light. He then said that Force "X" was going to New York – an announcement greeted with loud cheers. They would be the first Royal Naval Force to be attached to the U.S. Navy.

3.8.44

Glenearn sailed at 1900. The gramophone had to take the place of a band, but it was a thrilling experience nonetheless. Force "X" picked up a large convoy bound for the United States and then headed round the north coast of Ireland.

Both ward-room and mess deck conjectured on the reception the Force might get, and how long they would stay in New York. Some felt that three months would be about

---

* Administration and Quartermastering.

† Shore Establishment, Greenock.

right; Panama after that, then across the Pacific to the Far
East. They would be used for training American troops at
first, but of course that would depend on the U.S. Navy.
Having sorted out *Glenearn*'s future, one could sit back, relax
and listen to the music on the radio – until some tune with
associations brought back all the emotions of recent parting,
and one's thoughts dwelt miserably on the happy home life
that was every moment receding further and further.

The smooth sea lasted all day Friday, but it began blowing   4.8.44
hard at night. Rough weather was promised by the First
Lieutenant; he also threatened to turn off the fresh water.
Both promise and threat were fulfilled with *Glenearn* rolling
badly – waves breaking over the fo'c'sle – and water reduced
from 30 tons to 15 tons per day. Individuals became aware of   5.8.44
the existence of their tummies, and began to hope that
somehow seasickness might be avoided. Possibly because of
these factors, one Royal Marine officer downed only three
lemon squash all day, while another was drunk on the bridge
and nearly court-martialled in consequence.[11]

Captain Hutchison had insisted that flotilla officers took
their turns as Assistant Officer of the Watch, walking around
the decks during the night checking that the landing craft
were all secure. Of course the Marines moaned like hell when
it meant getting up for the middle watch,[155] and they did not
care for it when the ship was sailing through fog,[152] but the
new regime opened up possibilities for learning a tremendous
amount about the purely naval side of things,[155] and
incidentally for expanding the mind, if not quite to an
understanding of Man's place in the cosmos, then at least to
an awareness of his relative importance. Long hours were
spent spell-bound by the inexorable progress of the convoy
plunging on and on, by the big yellow moon glistening on a
thousand miles of sea, by the seas rushing at a constant rate
past a stationary ship – stationary except for the rolling!

After heading south-west for two days, about 180 miles
north of the Azores course was changed to almost due west
for the long straight run of over two thousand miles across the
Atlantic. New escort vessels appeared, for U-boats could be

expected now; the hidden menace of the submarine being added to the constant uncertainties of weather and sea. Shipboard life settled down and individuals settled in;[11] flotillas were employed cleaning, repairing and maintaining the craft, and the sailors in making everything shipshape after the spell in the floating dock.[215] At the request of the Captain, Lieutenant (E) McKenzie began writing an account of *Glenearn*'s First Commission, and the Second up to the start of the present voyage.[85] A ship's magazine was started with Lieutenant Mayhew RN as Editor,[94] and Lieutenant Webber, RM, continued his occasional poetry writing with "Little Ships", a rhyming record of the D-Day landing.[155] In the evenings there were successive entertainments: a Quiz Competition between the Navy and the Marines which the "Royals" won, and cinema shows which when scheduled for projection in the ward-room created a fever of excitement as if some officers had never seen a film before; even the "Old Man" attended one of them. And there was always music on records.[11]

7.8.44

On the radio they heard, "Already units of the Royal Navy are on their way to the Pacific to support the Americans in their fight against the Japanese".[106] When the officers were having dinner at 2000 that night it came as something of a shock when the BBC announcer said that the time was 11 p.m. and "Goodnight" – the unexpected manifestation of a thousand-mile separation triggered off individual miseries of home thoughts from aboard – wondering, hoping, wanting. Homesickness went on for days; everything conspiring to re-open the wound; tropical inoculations reminding one of a small child so recently similarly safeguarded against diphtheria, a school of porpoises – great sleek playful things – moving along in families just like one's own...

7.8.44

But time passed quickly as the convoy steamed steadily westwards; 348 miles from noon till noon winning *Glenearn*'s sweepstake one day, 345 the next. That day's clear blue skies gave place to an awful night; pouring with rain and as black as pitch.[11] Of the rest of the convoy nothing could be seen except the spout of water from the marker towed astern of the

8.8.44
9.8.44

ship ahead.[152] It would be terrible to go overboard on such a night; nobody would know.

Throughout some days of mixed weather *Glenearn* was rolling badly, but those who had found their sea legs did not feel it at all. On Friday afternoon two emergency turns to port were made in consequence of responses picked up by the escort and believed to be submarines, but there was no panic and the report may have been incorrect. With the weather much warmer, legs which had hitherto been decently covered suddenly sprouted from beneath short trousers; not a pretty sight. Everybody – almost everybody – started getting sunburnt. Salt water tanks were rigged up on the decks for swimming. It was swelteringly hot. A school of flying fish followed the ship for a while, one of them landing on the deck.

11.8.44

After church on Sunday morning "the Skipper" spoke a few words. The convoy was on the last lap of the Atlantic crossing, and should arrive at New York about noon on the Monday, but Force "X" would probably finish up going all round the world. What the Captain did not say, and what everyone wanted to know was *when* would they be finishing up!

13.8.44

Arrangements were made for entering harbour. Everyone was keyed up, eager to see the Statue of Liberty and the New York skyline; everybody had been well warned about stoppage of leave if anyone misbehaved on shore. Last-minute letters were written ready for posting on the morrow; this activity bringing on another attack of vehement emotion.

Monday 14th August 1944; the Royal Navy in the form of Force "X" sailed up the Hudson River in boiling heat with records playing. Of the ship's company lining *Glenearn*'s sides many were shaken by the enormity of the Statue of Liberty Enlightening the World, and astounded by the New York skyline; it was like something from Walt Disney – great towering pinnacles showing through the mist, like the spires of a fairy castle. It was simply fantastic.

14.8.44

On docking at 51st Pier exactly at noon they were met by several members of the U.S. and Royal Navies bringing details of places to go for food and entertainment; also many invitations to parties and the like. Liberty men went ashore with the usual intention of walking the streets and calling in at a few bars and returned raving about this most American city. They now understood why the Yanks were so proud of it; Grand Central Station – made famous in films – was like an enormous hotel, spotlessly clean, quiet and not a train to be seen. Everyone in New York seemed to eat six meals a day, each running to about eight courses; such quantities of food as had never been seen before, even pre-war, every food shop and every store stacked out with great roasted joints of every meat; the Officers' Services Club offering a list of amenities "ten yards long".

And after dark the amazing sight of a myriad of tiny lights and snakish neon signs, seen from the roof of the Rockefeller Institute sixty-five stories high; air-conditioned throughout.[11]

15.8.44   At 2 o'clock in the morning the Captain could have been seen in "The World-Famous Leon and Eddie's" on West 52nd Street, accompanied by "Guns", "Doc" and the "Bishop".[66]

16.8.44   Tuesday was terribly hot; nearly 100° in the shade. Another day and night on the town, returning at 0500. All those candy shops would have been a child's delight, but most of the items were too expensive with the exchange rate only $4 to the £. After an evening in the Hotel Delmonica, on to The Gay Nineties: old-fashioned songs and performers, with everybody singing; a few English ditties introduced for the benefit of the Limey visitors.[11]

Rear-Admiral Talbot had flown up to Washington to tell Admiral King, USN, how to beat the Japanese;[36] something the Americans seemed to be doing quite well without British help.[106] Captain Hutchison for his part had many staff talks in New York[66] while American troops embarked for passage to the Far East; all the Landing Ships, with the exception of *Lamont*, were loading to capacity.[215] The American Transportation Corps Major wanted his ship to go "dry", but Captain Hutchison replied that the Royal Navy had always been "wet" and would continue to be so. The hospitality of *Glenearn*'s ward-room was offered, but refused; there was then the spectacle of two American colonels wandering about the ship, both looking very unhappy.[152]

Glenearn's flotillas were employed stowing ship and receiving embarking troops; no training could be carried out as all the landing craft were hoisted. A conference was held in *HMS Lothian*; all the flotilla officers attended. With the U.S. troops embarked there would be no space available; training would have to concentrate on the individual – promotion exams for coxswains, reports on potential flotilla officers to be forwarded, training programmes to be sent to the CRM by the Sunday of each week, and so on. Flotillas would be organised into divisions of six craft each, and ship's companies would be trained in lowering drill.[215]

A last run ashore and Royal Marine officers returning in the ubiquitous taxi before tottering back on board on ankles swollen by the heat. This time they had been in Jack Dempsey's Bar, looked inside Madison Square Gardens and had a roast beef sandwich containing the equivalent of a full week's ration of meat back home. Shore leave ended at midnight and Force "X" sailed next morning at 0830, bound, it was believed, for Australia. 17.8.44 18.8.44

Two days later found them running south down the coast. A warning had been received of two strong hurricanes on the route ahead, and the ships were sailing close inshore in the hope of avoiding them. A sudden turn to starboard had everybody guessing; the hurricanes were imminent and the Force was heading towards Charleston, South Carolina. What luck! 20.8.44

Charleston looked very pretty from the harbour; the whole scene was fringed with green bushes and woods, like a bit of Southampton Water. A great spidery bridge over the channel was said to be the longest in the world. A few lucky officers got ashore to sample chicken "fried the Charleston way" while the flotillas exercised in the harbour. The hurricanes having blown themselves out, or gone a different way, the Force sailed at 1100 next morning – although around 1800 they turned about and sailed back in the direction of Charleston for half an hour before resuming the course for Colon at the north end of the Panama Canal. 21.8.44 22.8.44

And so along the unseen coast of Florida, half-expecting the 23.8.44

tail end of a hurricane, then past San Salvador, Columbus' landfall in 1492. They were into the tropics now; it was very hot and there were quite a lot of flying fish about. One officer said that a wild canary had flown into his cabin.[11] A warning order was received that flotillas would have to go through the Canal under their own power.[215]

25.8.44 After sailing between Cuba and Santo Domingo during the night of 25/26th, Force "X" passed Jamaica, where *Glenearn's* Navigator's wife and two daughters were living, and headed for the Isthmus of Panama.[11] After passing a two-mile long

27.8.44 breakwater, Colon was reached at 1600 on the 27th August.[606] There would be no shore leave, which was a disappointment to those keyed up to see the sights; in other words the ill-famed night clubs.[11]

The Authorities required all davits to be turned in before entering the Canal,[215] so the eight outboard craft were lowered; each in charge of an officer. *Glenearn* set off, followed by her brood, along the buoyed channel. It proved to be a very interesting little run. The banks were one long stretch of bright green vegetation: towering palm trees complete with coconuts, immense thickly-wooded hills in the background and swampy-looking hollows hazy in the mist hanging heavily over them. There was very little civilization after leaving Colon Harbour – just occasional wooden shacks with American servicemen standing outside them watching the vessels go by.[11]

At the end of the seven-mile long entrance channel a bend in the channel opened to view the gigantic structure at Gatun; a colossal double three-step flight of locks. Electrically-powered locomotives took hold of *Glenearn*; two pulling on hawsers at the stem and two more at the stern to check her speed. Behind the parent ship, and dwarfed by the towering walls,[606] the brood of steel cygnets huddled together in groups of four[11] as the great double mitre gates closed behind them.[606] It had been said that, provided the small craft were stationary, the filling of the lock would create no difficulties,[215] but it was quite exciting enough when the water boiled up from below.[152]

And similarly into the second and third locks, before reaching the surface of Gatun Lake, 85 feet above sea level.[606] All this time it had been pouring with rain and the air thick with midges. Fortunately no mosquitoes. Back on board, the flotillas' personnel found a large heap of air mail and telegrams ready to be distributed.[11]

This passage through the locks had taken about an hour, and left *Glenearn* on a broad smooth expanse of artificial lake inviting full speed,[606] but there was a delay caused by *HMS Lamont*. At Colon there had been some indecision aboard, leading to a signal to the flagship; this had been answered by placing *Lamont* under orders of *Glenearn*, which by this time had moved off and was out of sight. Then the Canal pilot had arrived expecting to sail at once, and demanding to know why the landing craft were still in the davits. Lowering was commenced, in slow time; since it was their first experience of operating the winches for some of the ship's company. On arrival at the locks there had been considerable confusion due, at first, to the absence of orders, then to too many... Once on the lake, *Lothian*'s craft could have been hoisted, but it was decided they should make the complete passage under their own power; as a result *Glenearn* had to go slowly to keep an eye on them.[215]

Twenty miles on, the mountains closed in and the width of the channel reduced to about 300 feet. This was the beginning of the great Cut; a nine-mile excavation through ground rising to twice the height of *Glenearn*'s masthead.[606] By the time the next set of locks was reached it was dark;[11] the darkness of tropical night, if relieved locally by the blaze of electric lighting.[606] The landing craft were lowered again at 2200*[11] and passed through the set of single locks at Pedro Miguel, then along about two thousand yards of lake to a double set and so down to sea level again;[606] finally trailing after *Glenearn* the eight miles to Balboa before the crews got back aboard at 0230.[215] Torrential rain; in a few minutes about six inches fell, and visibility was practically nil.[11] The other LSIs passed through without difficulty; LCAs from

28.8.44

* Clocks had been put back one hour.

Lothian making the complete journey under their own power at night and without charts.[215]

Flotillas from *Glenearn* were landed for drill, and later given canteen leave until 1900; this meant they could go ashore to the U.S. Naval Base, but with Balboa and Panama out of reach on the opposite side of the Bay. Craft were hoisted and at midnight *Glenearn* sailed[11] with the four "Empire" ships under Captain Hutchison as senior officer[66] – *Lothian* and *Lamont* remained behind for refitting.[215] *Glenearn*'s Marines had been praised by the Admiral for the way they had handled their craft through the Gatun Locks.

Next stop, Bora Bora, one of the Society Islands; French territory and five thousand miles away across the Pacific. A terrific gale blew for two days;[11] through it all the American escort vessels were rolling, rolling, rolling[152] – and *Glenearn* likewise. But at least the atmosphere was cool and pleasant, and quite a good concert was given in the ward-room by the Americans.

Friday 1st September 1944 was a memorable date in nautical history. Nothing to do with Culpepper Island – a big lump of brownish rock standing out alone on a great ocean – which was passed in the afternoon,[11] but because a signal was received warning that King Neptune was coming aboard that night for the Crossing the Line Ceremony on the morrow. The preliminaries duly took place promptly at 1800 when a bugler appeared on the fo'c'slehead and sounded a fanfare. He then descended the starboard ladder to the platform on the fore well deck, followed by King Neptune – not looking anything like CPO Kilkins – and his retinue. Captain Hutchison stands on the Oerlikon-gun platform before his quarters. The bugler sounds off another fanfare. Then:

Neptune: "Are you the Captain of this ship?"
Captain H: "This is His Britannic Majesty's Ship *Glenearn*, and I am its Captain."
Neptune: "Have you on board any landlubbers, dry-ilders,* or others who have never before entered my domain, Sir?"
Captain H: "There are such, Your Majesty."

* Dry-ilder: Etymology uncertain, poss. corr. *dry idler*: teetotal non-watchkeeper.

(margin notes)
30.8.44
31.8.44

1.9.44

And so on, for several more exchanges.

At 0930 to fanfares and, "Hear Ye, Hear Ye, Hear Ye", the   2.9.44
Court sat and passed judgment on those summoned by
warrant; a list that included Surg.-Lieut. Payne-James and
SBPO Rostron... "did inflict grave indignity and discomfort
upon many of Your Majesty's Subjects"... the Reverend
Leonard George Janes... "the craven, knock-kneed rabbit-
chested runt you see before you"... and even two officers of
the United States Army Air Force... "did try to feed Your
Majesty's Subjects with baloney and sauerkraut"... These
and others did suffer directly at the hands of barbers and
bears, after which King Neptune and Queen Aphrodite –
whatever became of SBCPO Dewey? – seated themselves
while the policemen dashed off to arrest victims for
initiation.[155] After all this excitement it was almost an anti-
climax to hear that British ground forces were almost across
the Belgian frontier.[11]

Glenearn was very crowded, with all available deck space
being used by the passengers, but some individual training
was carried out: navigation for coxswains, elementary
engineering, small arms and signals;[215] the last subject being
practised with the U.S. signal-book, since they were to be
under the Americans.[66]

All the while Force "X" sailed steadily onwards, covering
four hundred miles each day.[94] And if every day's mileage was
much the same, so was every day. Everybody was either
homesick or "browned off"; some were both at once. The   5.9.44
water had been turned off for a week. There was rather a lot of
illness on board, including two cases of scarlet fever, and
many with colds.

Second typhoid inoculations did nothing to improve   6.9.44
matters, although the news that the "blackout" back home
was to end cheered everybody up for a while. That and the
fact that the fresh water was turned on all day made the 7th   7.9.44
September a gala day; everybody, it seemed, had a bath, and
great piles of washed clothes appeared all over the ship. Then
it was back to worrying about losing weight – due possibly to
the poor food or the lack of exercise – and not sleeping, and

the terrible effort of writing letters home.

With the sun now blisteringly hot there was much bathing, and with the campaign in Europe looking as if it would soon be over there was a great deal of discussion on the subject of retention in the service after the war. Rumour had it that they would all be kept in uniform for seven years after the cease-fire; more gloom, followed by a relapse into extreme boredom. They would all be glad when this boring trip was over. Monotony grew every day. The occasional film, or quiz between U.S. and ship's officers was a welcome change.

12.9.44   *HMS Lothian* caught up with the Force and *Glenearn* performed a brilliant maneouvre to bring her into station and the Admiral complimented "Father" on it. Preparations were

13.9.44   made for Bora Bora, where it was hoped to land and stretch the legs, American and British. After that they would be proceeding to New Guinea, not to Australia as commonly believed; apparently Force "X" was urgently required. No one was very pleased at the prospect of New Guinea.

14.9.44   They arrived at Bora Bora at 0800 on the 14th; it was a wonderful sight. A typical South Sea Island: palm trees, coral reefs, thick green vegetation and beautiful placid waters of varying hues of blue and green. As the ships entered the harbour dozens of small outrigger canoes came out to meet them. The native craft were not allowed to come alongside so they paddled round and round the ship; each canoe was filled with bananas, coloured cloth and strings of beads made from seashells, and contained two or three natives. The women were a bit of disappointment; not a bit like the grass-skirted hula girls of the films.[11]

While the ships refuelled the landing craft were employed in putting the Americans ashore and in exercising the Royal Marine signallers.[215] The flotillas landed for drill ashore; there was no shore leave – it was a case of route marches only. The place was another disappointment: hot and dusty, native villages absolute hovels – dirty and smelly – and the American Army Officers' Club was short of supplies and would not serve drinks to Britishers. The fortnightly air mail had left just

15.9.44   two days before. Seaman Whetton received a telegram telling him that his mother was dying. He could only reply that he could not get home.

No one was allowed to mix with the natives, because of the prevalence of vile diseases – possibly brought by earlier voyagers – to which the inhabitants had become almost immune. Captain Bligh had visited these Islands for bread fruit shortly before the mutiny on *HMS Bounty*.[11] It transpired that there had been a mutiny on *HMS Lothian* on 1st September, when some men had walked ashore at 6 o'clock in the morning singing "The Red Flag" and refused to take the flagship to sea.[66] The ringleaders were under armed guard,[215] and someone had written the initials of Rear-Admiral Talbot on his door.[106]

The Landing Ships sailed at 1100 on Sunday 17th September. There were those on board *Glenearn* who were not sorry to leave this delectable – from a distance – island. New Guinea was going to take approximately fourteen days. With nearly four thousand miles to go, it looked like being another boring trip.

The Admiral seemed to be in a hurry, as the Force put on speed. They crossed the Date Line at midnight on Thursday the 21st zone time + 10, missed out Friday and it became Saturday the 23rd zone time – 14. That day a signal was received from the Commander Seventh American Fleet saying that Force "X", if operationally fit, would on arrival at Finschhaven be required for active operations. Admiral Talbot in turn passed on the message that if they hurried they should be in time for the next operation which was just about to commence.[11] Flotillas were ordered to bring all LCAs to A1 condition, all operational stores to a state of readiness, and to organise into divisions of three or four craft.[215] The Squadron was running at the top speed of the slowest ship[11] and making good about 440 miles every 24 hours.[94] It looked as if a spot of British naval history was about to be made, especially if they got there in time for this operation, whatever it was. "Action Stations" became a regular practice.

After the mail had been passed to them at sea,[11] *Empires Mace* and *Arquebus* were detached in order to land their

17.9.44

19.9.44
21.9.44

23.9.44

25.9.44

passengers at Espiritu Santo in the New Hebrides.[215] The
remainder of the Force pressed on, passing the Solomons on
26.9.44   the 26th; they did not see Guadalcanal in the darkness, but
during this night contact was made, and depth charges
dropped, by the escort on a presumed submarine. On the eve
of arrival at their destination Captain Hutchison inspected
28.9.44   the boats, and letters were hurriedly written. The days were
simply whizzing by.

29.9.44   Finschhaven was reached at 0700, *Glenearn*'s anchor going
down in 65 fathoms only about 100 yards from the shore.
From there New Guinea seemed to be one big forest, and so
dense that how the Australians had ever cleared these hills of
Japanese beggared understanding.[11] An Australian officer of
1st Australian Corps had flown up to see the Force and he
visited all the ships to assess their accommodation.[215]

Courts martial took place on *Lothian* to try the mutineers.
Captain Hutchison was the President,[66] and Lieutenant
Waters, RM, an officer of the Court; both complete with
swords.[152] The mass insubordination had involved thirty-four
seamen who had refused duty on sailing;[215] mainly because of
the severe restrictions on their meagre water supplies. It was
claimed that these restrictions would not have been necessary
if the Flag Officer Commanding had not demanded "whites"
as dress of the day on all occasions.[32] After being addressed
by their Captain seventeen of the mutineers had returned
aboard to duty, whereupon the three chief ring-leaders and
fourteen other ratings had been placed under arrest by Royal
Marines. The seamen had tried to seize the Marines' rifles, but
had been unsuccessful; fourteen armed sentries had then been
posted.[215]

When the Court had heard the whole story they came to
the conclusion that the accused had been very severely
provoked, and they were all "hostilities only", and not
accustomed to naval discipline;[66] this of course had to be
preserved, and they were duly found guilty.[32]

30.9.44   *Glenearn*, *Lothian* and *Empire Spearhead* sailed next day at
1700. It was pouring with rain and great clouds of steam rose
from the forests to hang, still and lifeless, as if preparing to

sink down again and smother every living thing beneath. Even without having set foot on it, it was a relief to get away from this dark and forbidding place. They were sailing north-west; Captain Hutchison was FOC for the occasion, as Admiral Talbot had gone ahead by air. "Father" seemed to know what the job was going to be, and was quite excited; he said that *Glenearn* was the luckiest ship in the British Navy, and would be the first to enter Yokohama. Lucky?

As they sailed onwards it was a change to be always within sight of land – on previous runs the sighting of any shore brought almost everybody up on deck. As they passed the still-active volcano of Bam, brick-red smoke and billowing steam formed a pall around its cone. 1.10.44

Hollandia looked just the same as Finschhaven – or any other part of New Guinea, that hilly tree-covered green land – when they arrived there at 0730.[11] The American troops were disembarked and Captain Hutchison reported to Admiral Dan Barbey, USN – known as "Dan, Dan the Amphibious Man" – the American Vice Admiral in charge of the 7th Amphibious Force in his flagship *USS Blue Ridge*. This Force was busy preparing for the invasion of the Philippines.[66] 2.10.44

An American landing craft, known as an LCVP,* was tried in one of *Glenearn*'s davits, but it did not fit. The British ship's capacity of 800 troops and her cargo space were both extremely limited by American standards, and her speed was nothing to boast about; the future of Force "X" hung in the balance.[11]

The Americans wanted to run their own show and Admiral Talbot had upset Admiral Barbey. Captain Hutchison invited the American Admiral aboard for dinner and tried to smooth him down; he was successful up to a point, but it was no use.[36] The Landing Ships were to be split up: *Lamont* and *Empire Arquebus* were to be sent to Cape Gloucester in New Britain, *Empire Mace* and *Empire Battleaxe* to Noumea in New Caledonia, *Glenearn* and *Empire Spearhead* to Cairns, Australia.[215] Force "X" had been "sacked".[94]

---

* Landing Craft Vehicle, Personnel.

CHAPTER 21

DOWN UNDER

5.10.44   *Glenearn, Spearhead* and *Lothian* sailed at 1400 on 5th October. *Glenearn* had some seventy casualties on board; she and the "Empire" ship were bound for Milne Bay at the eastern end of the island, in Papua. *Lothian* would be leaving them to go for a refit of refrigerators, possibly at Sydney. They passed the volcano of Bam, again, and Wewak on the New Guinea coast. Wewak had been bombed by the Yanks only the previous week; there were quite a lot of Japs there.[11]

On board *Glenearn* there were those who professed to be delighted at the latest turn of events,[106] and some who felt that if the Americans wanted to run the show themselves, let them get on with it.[11] But others held to the opinion that their ship could have done the job – whatever it was – just as well with her LCAs, and certainly much more quietly.[152] As far as fighting was concerned it seemed to be much easier than in Europe: an Australian LSI at Hollandia, *HMAS Westralia*, had been in four operations without a shot having been fired at her.[11]

8.10.44   Milne Bay was a big base, nice and peaceful now, but two years before the scene of a Japanese defeat when an attempted landing had been repulsed by the Australians.[R] Here *Glenearn* picked up her LCMs and received a few guests from *Empire Spearhead* before dinner. Also the information that a Japanese submarine had surfaced on their course somewhere along the way just two hours before they had appeared.

9.10.44   Having discharged the sick and wounded, and taken on a few Australian passengers, the two ships sailed next day for Cairns, Queensland. After a while the course became very tricky, with many rocks and shoals, and dozens of islands on both sides. Distant colourful native huts brightened the views as the ships twisted through the lovely China Straits before sailing out into the open sea.

Two days of steaming brought them to the Grafton

Channel by which they passed through the Great Barrier
Reef. First glimpses of Australia were impressive – in the
distance great mountains, with the low-lying town of Cairns
nestling in the Bay. The off-lying islands of the Reef looked
almost tropical; the sun was warm and pleasant. *Glenearn*
anchored about nine miles out as the water was too shallow
for the ships to get in. Liberty men were put ashore by tender
at 1300.

Cairns proved to be a nice place. No Americans. Everybody
seemed pleased to see the Britishers, and welcomes were
showered from all quarters. Shore leave was due to end at
1700[11] by which time everyone was very happy, so when they
boarded the destroyer that was to take them out to *Glenearn*
and found a party of about forty Australian soldiers of the
2/27th Infantry Battalion, they proceeded to entertain them
with bawdy songs. To the Australians the sailors' broad
Pommy accents made delightful music and harmony, and
when they found themselves alongside with a scrambling net
to climb, the new-found friends helped each other aboard. The
guests were taken below decks to a meal of steak and eggs,
and given sleeping accommodation,[79] while *Glenearn* sailed
for Townsville; hoping to be in time for the morning tide.

While many aboard still slept,[11] *Glenearn* went alongside
the jetty. There the infantry working party had their duties
explained to them; namely the cleaning up of the ship while
she took on stores. Their implements were the traditional
mop and bucket, but no concerted effort was possible because
of the frequent calls to, " 'Ave a coop a' tea, chum." Both sets
of individuals had mixed feelings about the Americans and by
comparison this was like the rediscovery of long-lost members
of the same family.[79]

A lecture on American landing technique was delivered by
the CRM to both of *Glenearn's* flotillas. The objects of the
forthcoming training were to accustom the troops to living on
board and to practise them in all types of boat work and
landings, to exercise Brigade and Battalion staffs in the
preparation of orders and landing tables, and at the same time
experience the craft crews in the modified methods of landing

observed in this theatre of war – because during the outward voyage there had been virtually no collective training.[215]

Each watch also got 24-hours leave; the first for over seven weeks, so they reckoned it had been well-earned. They returned impressed by the way everyone had said how pleased they were to see British sailors and marines – and by the way the "Aussies" drank.[11] For their part, after imbibing the local beer the Pommy sailors became liable to "do over" any luckless U.S. serviceman they got in their sights; fortunately there were very few Americans left in Townsville.[79] At the Officers' Club there Lieutenant Ives, RM, for breakfast had four eggs at one sitting – and could have had six if he had wished – compared to the one a month back home. On his return from leave Lieutenant Bell received a letter; his first since Panama.

14.10.44   *Glenearn* sailed for the training ground and arrived early
15.10.44   the following morning at Trinity Bay.[11] This was about ten miles north of Cairns, fairly big, discovered and named by Captain Cook on Trinity Sunday 1770. Before the war it had been a popular place for picnics. From the sea the beach sloped up gently, a wide strip of clean white sand leading to low scrub; the only buildings were occasional weekend shacks.[18] Here the fatigue party was put ashore – infantrymen of 21 years made to feel old by the youthfulness of sailors and marines[79] – and the equivalent of a battalion of 21st Brigade of 7 Australian Infantry Division[215] taken on, but made up of groups of about 300 men from 2/27th Battalion[18] and brigade-attached troops.

While the mess decks were being checked and landing craft being allocated, a meeting of officers was held. A United States Officer from No. 3 Amphibious Training Unit had embarked with the troops and he considered himself in charge of the training, but it became clear that in practice it would be the responsibility of *Glenearn's* Captain, with the American holding a "watching brief". Neither the local naval nor the military authorities had been aware that the landing craft crews were unfamiliar with the American method of amphibious warfare; and although a lecture had been given, and a *précis* issued, arrangements would have to be made that allowed time to practise the new methods with troops embarked. To add to the difficulties *HMS Empire Spearhead* had run aground and the troops which should have embarked in her would be unable to do so; the training could still be carried out from the beaches but would necessitate a daily run of about 30 miles by the LCAs of 539 Flotilla.

At 1000 the first embarkation exercise, in slow time, took place,[215] with the troops moving from the 'tween decks up the narrow companion ways, along the decks and into the boats swinging from the davits;[18] before returning to their mess decks. This was repeated in quick time at 1100, when the craft were lowered to circle in the rendezvous area, before being hoisted again.[215]

Morale of the Australians was very high, for reasons that were not far to seek. For them it was at once a change of scenery, a change of diet, a change of company, a change of routine and a break in the monotony of camp life on the Tablelands which had become very irksome; six months of jungle training not being really necessary after two years in action against the Japanese in Papua and New Guinea. A spell on board ship with no fatigues, no duties, no guards and a lot of spare time to lie about the decks sun-baking was as good as a holiday.[18]

At 1630 they were all summoned on deck for the Captain's introductory address.[215] He made a magnificent figure in crisp starched white uniform and "miles of gold braid"; his appearance drawing a few derogatory remarks from Australians in faded jungle green.[18] Captain Hutchison's first point was that he would not tolerate anyone referring to his ship as a boat, and his second that there was no crew in *HMS Glenearn*, but she did have a ship's company.[109] Then, without any warning he said, "I must tell you now that I don't like Australian soldiers." There was a visible stiffening in the ranks before he went on, "The last time I was on leave in London I was waiting for my wife outside a cinema when this Australian came up to me and said, 'What time's the next show, sport?'" It was a very old joke, but it must have been new to a lot of them because it brought the house down.

Having got the audience on his side, the Captain then went on to give the history of the ship, saying she had been used in Scotland for training English soldiers for the Normandy landing. He looked round from the ship to the still blue sea, to the palm trees, and back to the Australians stripped to the waist soaking in the sunshine, then said with some asperity in his voice, "If you think you've got any complaints, just think of the poor bastards who had to do their training in the middle of a Scottish winter; sea-sick, shivering, and jumping into ice-cold water. It was no holiday for them." The Australian soldiers, tough and to some eyes undisciplined, reckoned that the Captain had got his message across.[18]

Colin Hutchison had a short temper to match his height. He wore a monocle, which made memorable his Captain's Defaulters. The accused matelot, after hearing the charge and listening to the Divisional Officer's saying his piece, knew he was "for it" if the Captain let the monocle fall from his eye. He would look up from the charge sheet, open his eye – down went the monocle – "10 days' cells!" and a baleful glare.[112]

The Australians for their part soon learned that the "brig" consisted of three small cells at the after end of the centrecastle, and that one of them had an occupant. They immediately started passing cigarettes and food to him through the barred hole in the door. Within 24 hours they were assembled and spoken to by one of their own officers. He told them that the ship's officers knew what was going on, but none of them wanted to make a big thing of it, with courts martial and so on, but would the troop lay off; otherwise the first man to suffer would be the prisoner himself, so would they please not make it so obvious what they were doing. The hint was taken, and henceforth the feeding of the prisoner was done very surreptitiously.[18]

A change of eating habits, from three to four meals a day, had the Australians mystified although it was generally welcomed,[27] but the whole navy routine was so different that it was a continuous source of merriment. They were highly amused at the ...*WAKEY, WAKEY, WAKEY!*... in the morning, and found something highly ludicrous in the peremptory call ...*COOKS TO THE GALLEY...* which was heard so often. For some reason it sounded rather offensive. Once when it came through, a soldier jumped to his feet and shouted back at the loud speaker, "And officers to the shithouse!" Something about this exchange caught the collective imagination, and within minutes it was being echoed round the ship. Thereafter, whenever ... *COOKS TO THE GALLEY* ... was sounded, the soldiers would shout their reply. It was a wonder to the sailors that the perpetrators were not all clapped in irons, but no official notice was taken of it – either the Australian accent was not understood, or the two set of officers had come to an understanding about the best way to deal with such situations.[18]

After a night embarkation on the first evening of their training, at 0700 the next day there was another exercise[215] with the troops landing in waist-deep water. It was all very easy, and the whole operation was treated more as a lark than as hard work, especially when they leapt out of the boats; in the tropical climate it was cooler in the water, and their clothes dried in half an hour.[18]

After this the troops were re-embarked. As one craft carrying members of a Tank-Attack Regiment was being hoisted, a waste pipe higher up discharged some decidedly evil-smelling liquid. The slight swell of the sea ensured that all the passengers had a turn of swaying through the stream, and the remarks of the Australian soldiers directed at His Majesty's Royal Navy did not bear recording. Once on board, enquiry led to a rather grudging short session under the salt water showers; which was about all that a ship unsuited to tropical service could provide, anyway.[27]

Before the next night embarkation exercise there was a lecture on naval terms, which may have helped to clear up some of the mystery surrounding the calls and orders that floated round the ship through the loud-speakers. The English accents – some of the thick provincial ones could not be understood at all – combined with the distortion of the Public Address System and the unusual words and phrases made a lot

11.10.44

of them unintelligible; so much so that translations had to be sought from passing sailors. One call that remained a mystery for a long time sounded like ... *NO LEAVE TO MOSCOW...* but turned out to be ... *NO LEAVE TO MUSTER* ...[18]

17.10.44   At 0430 embarkation in the craft began, leading to a landing exercise at first light.[212] On return the troops boarded *Glenearn* by scrambling net, having been taught by the ship's instructors in the art; both hands on the one vertical rope and **18.10.44**   the feet left to their own devices.[27] On the fourth day of training the landing at first light was a battalion operation, with the troops landing in their proper sequence behind imaginary assault troops.[212]

Four craft of 40 tons carrying capacity from the 41st Australian Landing Craft Company were operating out of Cairns and helping with the amphibious training. They were manned by Royal Australian Engineers who regarded *Glenearn* anchored a few miles out as a grand old sentinel who would help them out should the need arise, and were grateful for the way her navy speed merchants were always very considerate whenever communication was by signal flags. The ALC40 in the charge of Sgt. E. J. Lodge was returning to Cairns when in the distance, and well away from *Glenearn*, they saw one of her LCAs frantically calling them up with semaphore flags. After the usual response had been made, a message was slowly spelled out to them, "*W-E A-R-E S-T-I-N-K-I-N-G.*" Having asked for and received a repeat which still claimed the senders were stinking, the recipients guessed otherwise and made full speed to their aid. On reaching the scene they found some very relieved and thankful Royal Marines in a craft with stern gland trouble, and a quarter full of water with no engines operable. It was touch and go, but the rescue vessel managed to tow the distressed craft back to her parent ship, ending with a very bumpy "alongside" in the heavy swell.*[78]

With the sea running the hoisting of the LCA was obviously a tricky operation, but the business-like manner in which the task was carried out without any fuss drew

---

* The exact date of this incident is uncertain.

admiring remarks from the soldiers leaning over the ship's rail. Subconsciously the Australians seemed to give credit to the "English" sailors for having seen much more concentrated and fierce warfare – either at sea or in the blitz – than they themselves had.[18] Nevertheless the 7th Australian Division had seen a fair old amount of fighting in the Western Desert, Crete and Syria before being ordered back to Papua and New Guinea, where they had fought on the Kokoda Trail in September 1942, and later at Gona; both extremely bitter campaigns.[150]

For the second four days of the training period the two other battalions of 21st Brigade were embarked in *Glenearn* and *Empire Spearhead* for individual training, culminating in a Brigade landing exercise[109] on 22nd October. For this the shipping available consisted of the two LSIs, two LSTs, four LCIs and the four Australian ALC40s; the remainder of tonnage required was imaginary. All the orders and landing tables had been prepared by the Brigade Staff for the assault battalions to land at first light from the LSIs with the follow-up troops embarked in the imaginary ships – or in other words, on the coast about two miles from the beaches ready to be uplifted by a ferry service of landing craft.[212]

At sunrise that clear morning, *Glenearn* lowered her LCAs for the mock assault. An Australian officer had just been brought out in an ALC40 which had to return to the shore. To lend colour to the scene *Glenearn* let go a broadside from her 4-inch guns, just as the visiting craft was easing away, with the result that her crew were showered with blazing cardboard. After returning this compliment with a few favourite Aussie expressions they christened *Glenearn* "the flaming old cardboard chucker" and boasted about having sailed, not only with the landing craft of *Glenearn*, but actually under her guns.[78]

22.10.44

The landing took place on Unity Beach and 21st Australian Infantry Brigade successfully established a beach head.[109] When it was all over the rank and file peeled off their wet clothes and hung them on tree branches to dry, while the owners swam or sun-baked. Shipboard life had been a novelty and a welcome change, while between Australian soldiers and "English" sailors a mutual respect had developed. No lasting friendships had been made; there had not been time for that, but there had been time for friction and antagonism, and there had been none. While there had been differences in so many things – accents, customs, attitudes to the service, and so on – there had never been any sign of bad relations. The only criticism ever voiced was that the Australians had not been summoned to ... *UP SPIRITS* ... although they had been able to buy duty-free tobacco from the sailors.

Yes, mutual respect; the Australians certainly admired an efficiently run ship, and the cool down-to-earth manner in which the ratings went about their duties. The Royal Navy, and the Royal Marines with their distinctive headgear,[27] had brought recent experience of a hotly-opposed landing; something that had been lacking in the earlier American instructors.[109] As *Glenearn* turned and headed south for Townsville the Australians sorrowfully returned to the old routine on the Tablelands. None of them knew what the future held for them.[18] Admiral Barbey's assault convoys, after a 1300-mile voyage from Hollandia, had descended on Leyte in the Philippines on the 20th,[R] so one could guess that some day the Australians would be making a landing on some tropical shore;[18] whether their recent training would be of any use to them was another question, with possibly more than one answer.[A]

CHAPTER 22

ALWAYS IN A HURRY

Glenearn had returned to Townsville for water and 23.10.44
provisions. The exertions of the ship's company during the
preceding spell had been considerable, and everyone was
ready for a break. In port the Royal Marine Officers, much to
their annoyance, reverted to watch-keeping duties, which
meant they had only 24 hours in which to have leave.
Needless to say they made the most of such time as they had –
it was a pleasure to get away from the ship, and a luxury to
sleep in a bedroom again with all the windows open[11] – then
away to Trinity Bay again and the training of 25th Australian 25.10.44
Brigade.

The routine was eight days of exercises, then back to
Townsville for two days to recover.[35] Almost continual use of
the LCAs meant that little time was available for maintenance
– something that became very necessary. Rough weather for
four or five days made hoisting very hazardous,[215] and it was
fortunate that there were not many serious accidents; as it
was, one man got a broken thigh when a chain hit him.
Another cut his jaw very badly, and there were many other
minor hurts. A lot more were avoided by the skill of the boats'
crews.[11] *Empire Spearhead* lost two craft in the same exercise;
one sank while under tow and the other broke up on the
beach after filling up. Because of the damage being sustained
by the craft, and to the falls and davits of the ships, Captain
Hutchison requested that embarkation of troops from the
beaches be carried out by LCI; this saved his LCAs, but took
considerably longer.[215]

Training of 18th Brigade ended with Exercise "Octopus" at 13.11.44
Unity Point,[618] and with it that of 7 Australian Division. It
was a great day when it was announced that *Glenearn* was
going to spend the next 8-day period at Townsville, even
though a training programme would have to be followed
during it. There was plenty of time off. The population of

Townsville – mainly service personnel – made a great fuss of the whole ship's company; it being generally assumed that they were the fore-runners of a big British fleet on its way out with a sizeable part of the Army.

On nights off, everyone enjoyed themselves thoroughly, having met a number of very decent chaps in the AIF; much time was spent at the Officers' Club and in army messes.[11] Lieutenant Waters, RM, became an honorary member of the Bowling Club. Bowling was secondary; the beer was good.[152] The Aussies were terrific drinkers and jolly good fellows;[11] after half a bottle of potent white wine with a name like "Porphyry" it was claimed that one's progress was after the manner of zag-zigging, rather than the more usual zig-zagging.[152] Lieutenent (E) McKenzie met an Australian colonel who described in graphic detail the sinking of *HMS Glenearn* in the Mediterranean; he took some convincing that she was still afloat.[85] The band of the Australian Imperial Force, which on an earlier occasion had played *Glenearn* out of the harbour, gave a concert on board.

A few Marine officers went on a kangaroo shoot, returning with a baby 'roo whose mother they had killed. He was a nice little fellow who,[11] if you bent down, would jump inside your shirt.[45] They called him Bambi and wondered vaguely what they would do with him when he grew up.[11]

The Brigade Commander and the Battalion Commanders of 21st Brigade entertained Captain Hutchison to dinner at the Atherton Officers' Club, the evening confirming the soldiers' suspicions that beneath the grim exterior of an old sea-dog who did not suffer fools gladly – among his superiors as well as his subordinates – there did nevertheless beat a human heart.[109]

A most uncomfortable experience for the Captain's Secretary, Michael Plunkett. He and Mark Waghorn the young RNVR boats' engineer borrowed an LCA from 535 Flotilla to take a party of WRANS and Army girls on a trip to Magnetic Island.[112] Waghorn was the only officer with landing craft experience and he would have been in the engine room; had one of the others looked at the chart they would have seen that the breakwater extended a short distance beyond the breakwater marker.[152] The craft hit a submerged post, was holed and sank; the passengers had to swim for it, surrounded by floating sandwiches and gramophone records. Someone said they had seen a shark fin circling them, so they swam ashore fast. It was very embarrassing to report all this to "Hutch"; landing craft were at a premium. *HMS Lothian* was arriving soon and Captain Hutchison did not get on too well with Rear-Admiral Talbot. But Lieutenant-Commander Cutler was put in charge of salvage operations, the craft was raised and handed over to "Chippy" Gloyn for repair; all would yet be well.[112]

Glenearn sailed for Trinity Beach and a continuation of the seemingly endless series of dawn landings.[487] *HMS Lamont* had joined for the amphibious indoctrination of 9 Australian Division,[215] and the training of the second brigade of this formation culminated in a full landing exercise at Red Cliff Bay, 9 miles north of Trinity Bay.[179] U.S. Navy procedure regarded going in to a beach as the equivalent of an approach march rather than as a military assault; under this system landing waves were supposed to be led in by the Flotilla Officer in a "Landing Craft Control", and the lack of these LCCs – fitted with range-finders and loud-hailers – was a handicap. In the battalion and brigade schemes it was not possible to fix accurately the line of departure; timings of successive waves were in consequence not accurate – but from the mistakes made the appropriate lessons were learned.[215]

By 0740 *Glenearn* was back at Trinity Bay where one party of soldiers was landed and another embarked, the latter being officers who were to control a practice bombardment of Dido Rock. The ship then sailed 140 miles to the south before anchoring for the night. After 4-inch gun drill the WT*-controlled bombardment took place.

Later in the forenoon they sailed 6 miles to Juno Bay where they were joined by *HMS Lothian*. Courtesy and service visits were exchanged before darkness descended and sentries were posted. *Lothian* sailed early; *Glenearn* followed at 0830,

24.11.44

2.12.44

3.12.44

4.12.44

* Wireless Telegraphy.

joining her at the anchorage off Acheron Island 20 miles away. *Glenearn* fired at targets on Herald Island before the two ships sailed together, carrying out another shore bombardment whilst under way. Stops were made to embark troops from *Lothian* and to pick up the spotting party from Rattlesnake Island; then on to the anchorage off Townsville.

5.12.44   With the ship tied up at No. 1 Pier East Side[179] and the training of the Australians completed, everyone expected to stay for at least a week to replenish and overhaul. A shore training programme lasting four days had been prepared for the Royal Marines, and every effort was to be made to include as many officers and men in it as possible.[11] For the information of the Commanding Officers of the other ships in Force "X" a memorandum on the embarkation and training of troops was being prepared;[293] when, if ever, this summary of hard-won experience would be utilised was a matter for conjecture.[A] Likewise, the next destination was a source of many "buzzes"; Sydney was the popular choice.[11]

6.12.44   Deck hands cleaned ship, worked stores and ammunition, and overhauled derrick gear; 535 Flotilla went on a route march. 543 Flotilla carried out field training. The latter unit
7.12.44   returned from their route march at the same time as two stokers returned from the Police Court.[179] 535 were on the range firing Lewis guns.[215] At 1600, much to everybody's surprise,[11] *Glenearn* slipped from the wharf, turned round with the assistance of a tug and sailed. Four ratings missed the ship.

8.12.44   Stopping at Trinity Bay just long enough to put ashore the remaining army personnel, *Glenearn* passed through the Grafton Passage in the Reef and pressed on towards Milne Bay. The ship went to "Action Stations" for several hours during which the guns' crews were at 1st Degree of Readiness, and breakdowns were exercised. With the onset of evening, look-outs closed up, ship was darkened except for dimmed side lights,[179] and the 272 Radar scanned the surface of the sea.[36]

9.12.44   At Milne Bay two LCAs of 535 Flotilla – 223 and 994 – left the ship and were replaced by Nos. 1268 and 1296; during the

midnight hours another craft patrolled the water line against
sabotage. At 0300 *Glenearn* sailed for Finschhaven to pick up
Americans[179] – or so it was believed[11] – and anchored in
Langemak Bay just south of there the following morning. U.S.
Army staff officers were followed by the C.O. of *Spearhead*.[179]
Glenearn's engines were beginning to give a lot of trouble;
Spearhead and *Lamont* would have to do a job for which it
was believed the Glen ship had been intended, but her engines
– her engineers – had let everybody down.[11] But by this time
the necessary decision had already been taken.[1] And the
young kangaroo died; he had just wasted away.

In the absence of the other two ships, *Glenearn* stagnated.[11]
Three of the absent ABs – Kenny, Earley and Bignall –
returned, were duly sentenced to three weeks' "chokey" and
left under escort for Lae. Then on the evening of the 17th
December the ship sailed for Hollandia[179] and, it was
supposed, more stagnation.[A]

At Hollandia, the C.O. was at a convoy conference when
three U.S. Naval Staff Officers came aboard.[179] The first
rumour was that *HMS Glenearn* was going to take on a
number of news reporters and cameramen, with a couple of
United States Senators thrown in, and take them all round the
battle areas. This sounded too good to be true. It was.
Obviously the Americans did not want to use a British ship if
it could possibly be avoided, so she went on swinging round
her buoy in Humboldt Bay[11] – scene of some very fierce
action earlier in the war.[R]

Christmas Day went down very well. Starting with a
Midnight Mass, then Holy Communion at 0600 followed by a
service of carols at 0900. Afterwards the officers received the
petty officers and the sergeants in the ward-room for a drink
before visiting the mess decks to join the boys. In the
afternoon many slept it off, then in the evening the Captain
came down for dinner in the ward-room. The food was not
bad. Not good, but not bad. The chicken, or turkey, or
whatever it was must have been the highest and toughest that
anyone had ever tried to eat[11] – and tasted strongly of the
sacking it must have been wrapped in[152] – but a few real

10.12.44

11.12.44

12.12.44
14.12.44
17.12.44

19.12.44

25.12.44

"spuds" had been dug up, and the wine was fair. After dinner a concert was given by the ship's company.[11] For the ship's magazine Lieutenant Webber, RM, had written "Christmas 1944", a poem looking forward to the next Christmas which would be spent at home in a world at peace.[155]

Two days earlier Captain Hutchison had been to *USS Blue Ridge*. On Christmas Eve mail for transport had been received on board, and just after noon on Christmas Day an American draft of 5 officers and 42 enlisted men had joined ship.[179] In consequence a new "buzz" had circulated faster than any of the others; they were going to Sydney.[11] Strange to relate, this one was true, and *Glenearn* together with *Lamont* and *Empire Spearhead* sailed early on Boxing Day.[179]

26.12.44
27.12.44

Those on afternoon watch on the 27th saw the beginning of a waterspout. It reached down to the sea, making quite an impression on it, then gradually drew back into the clouds. Preceding the spout were two great schools of black fish, looking like sharks with only their fins and part of their backs showing; they went down like a flotilla of submarines as the ship sailed past. Then came the rain, in one black sheet; the bridge, and those on it, were simply swamped.[11] Captain Hutchison did not like waterspouts, and had some theory that if you put a high-explosive shell into one, it stopped.[106]

28.12.44

Langemak Bay was reached and left again on the same day; Milne Bay was similarly visited on the 28th. The fact that little time was being wasted in port suited everyone. There were several submarine scares on the way down, but none near enough to be a nuisance. Signals intercepted from very far north gave the impression that Japanese naval forces had shelled the beaches at Leyte.

From Milne Bay the ships sailed almost due south, outside the Great Barrier Reef down the east coast of Australia. There were many squalls and strong winds, with no sight of land until well past Brisbane. It was learned that instead of spending only two days in Sydney they might stay for eight.

2.1.45

Outside Port Jackson they stopped zig-zagging. Passing between the Heads at the entrance to Sydney Harbour was very much like passing Dover, because of the high cliffs. The harbour itself was smooth and quiet, with Sydney spread out on all three sides; the city looking like a miniature of New York – the skyscrapers were not so tall, but impressive enough all the same.[11] By 0700 there was a line out to No. 3 Buoy; later in the forenoon Captain Hutchison went ashore and the U.S. Navy men left the ship. In the afternoon, when the liberty men had gone, an Engineer Commander and dockyard personnel came aboard.

Next morning Lieutenant-Commander (E) Aiken, MBE, RNR, joined;[181] or rather rejoined. The new Chief Engineer had been appointed as far back as the last week of October, and ever since the beginning of November had been on the way out to Australia in a "Blue Funnel" ship, leaving her at Adelaide and coming up by train to Sydney a few days previously.[1]

3.1.45

The port LCAs were lowered to clear that side, then with a tug standing by *Glenearn* slipped from the buoy, then passed under Sydney Harbour Bridge on the way to the Dockyard at Cockatoo Island, where she secured up to Sutherland Wharf. The Dockyard people commenced repair work next day, the officials holding a conference in the C.O.'s quarters, and the floating crane *Titan* coming alongside to lift out the armature crankshaft.[181]

4.1.45

Glenearn's C of E padre, the Rev. Janes, was usually referred to as "the Bishop" or more often as "the Bish". On this particular Friday he had the Assistant Bishop of Sydney to lunch; the venerable gentleman spending some time in the anteroom where the atmosphere was friendly, indeed cheerful, before eating.[11] Bishop Pilcher[181] was half-way through his meal when the Captain's Secretary burst in on the scene. In a loud voice Plunkett called out, "Where's the bloody Bishop?" Both the real "Bish" and the honorary "Bish" looked at "Scratch", who looked at them, then realising the reason for the sudden chill in the air waited neither for a reply nor for lunch. The holy pair looked round the room, then without a word turned back to their food, while everyone else breathed a sigh of relief and had a silent giggle.[11]

5.1.45

7.1.45   There was no dockyard work done on the 7th so on board
it was Sunday routine: Divisions followed by Church.[181] The
new Chief Engineer got the job of playing the hymns on the
8.1.45   small pedal organ. His predecessor left the next day to await
passage back to England. One thing that the newcomer had
noticed already was that the prestige of the engineers had
sunk considerably, and it would be an uphill struggle to get it
back to what it had been during the First Commission.[1]
Captain Hutchison this day formally admonished two of the
junior engineers for having left the ship improperly on the
Saturday.[181]

While the Royal Marines in their blues were "cutting a
dash" ashore the refit went ahead.[11] *Titan* hoisted in the
repaired machinery, then *Glenearn* slipped from the wharf
and, with the assistance of a tug, entered drydock. Within 15
minutes of the commencement of pumping she took the
blocks and as the water level lowered, dockyard labourers
started scraping the ship's side. Direct magazine flooders and
the ship's fire mains were connected to the shore lines;[181]
there was to be no repetition of the disastrous fire in drydock
at Colombo.[A]

Painting of the ship's bottom began. Anchors and cables
9.1.45   were lowered into the dock and the chain lockers cleaned out.
New wires were reeved in the LCA davits. The ship's bottom
10.1.45   was inspected by executive and engineer officers, and the
steering tested, before flooding of the dock began. All fire
connections were taken over by the ship, and a fire party
exercised in the evening.

12.1.45   At 0650 on the 12th January 1945 the dock gate was
opened and *Glenearn* floated out. Once the tugs were slipped
and her LCAs hoisted she moved the 4 miles to Kurraba
Wharf; there mails, fuel and water were taken on board. Also
some 400 passengers: Royal Australian Navy and U.S. Army
personnel.[181] On the other hand, one of *Glenearn's* seamen
had deserted. His name was Kingnape;* a very good worker,
and intelligent, but always in trouble and at the time of this
refit confined to the ship. To effect his escape, he had first

* Name changed.

obtained a suit of civilian clothes from somewhere, then shaved off his beard but leaving on the moustache. Thereafter all he had had to do was to walk around the ship making notes in a little book, looking exactly like one of the dockyard technicians, and so off and away.[11]

Glenearn slipped from the wharf at 1650, let go tugs and hoisted her remaining LCAs. Across the De-gaussing Range and through the Gate speed was increased, and past the Outer Head course was set for Brisbane.[181] Then? Probably New Guinea again and more sweat. In Europe things were beginning to look brighter, with Gerry going back again; in the Philippines a landing had just been made on the island of Luzon. Heaven alone knew when *His Majesty's Ship Glenearn* would be used again as an LSI; all she seemed to be now was a passenger ship.[11]

CHAPTER 23

OMEGA OF "X"

The only incident on the 583-mile voyage from Sydney to Brisbane was on the evening of the 13th when a suspicious radar contact was made; evasive action was taken for 15 minutes before things returned to normal. Early the following morning *Glenearn* stopped to take on the river pilot.[181]

The entrance to Brisbane was long and winding, with wharves on each side. On her way up the ship ran for some time past one of the sprawling residential districts, and all the way people waved from their windows; many of them holding Union "Jacks".[11] In the Bulimba reach *Glenearn* had to be turned to the flood tide. With the aid of one tug, and by going ahead on one engine and astern on the other,[181] Captain Hutchison turned the ship in her own length without touching the sides. With only "18 inches" to spare at each end it was a fine piece of seamanship.[28]

By 1010 the ship was secured up at No. 2 Newstead Wharf.[181] Being Sunday, Brisbane was dead. *Glenearn*'s officers had an invitation to the U.S. Naval mess, but it was little better than staying in the ward-room.[11] A party of Marines also went ashore in the afternoon. There was a beer shortage, so they had to drink fast before moving on to the next "pub"; then they went into the Botanical Gardens to sleep it off. When they awoke, the cloudy sky had gone pitch dark – although their watches said the time was about 4.30 p.m.[28] They hurried back into the town, to learn that there had been a partial eclipse of the sun.[316]

After taking on water, oil and stores, and embarking U.S. personnel, *Glenearn* sailed for Milne Bay.[181] The weather was much warmer than at Sydney, and the ship's company had changed into tropical rig.[11] One John Chatterton, Roman Catholic padre of Force "X", had found *Glenearn*'s company preferable to that of the Flagship's, so the "Bish" had been joined by the "Pope".[36] The two chaplains got on very well together,[1] the "Pope" proving to be an excellent shipmate and a hard worker, even if only a mediocre bridge player. When a steward upset the soup over his white tropical shirt he merely looked up and, beaming around the assembled company, asked, "Would some layman kindly say something appropriate?"[36]

Mainly because too few members cared about what they ate, the standard of feeding in the ward-room was poor. At the time when liver had appeared frequently on the dinner table – as hard as boot-leather, and stuck in a pile of dehydrated potato – Lieutenant Waters, RM, had suggested to the PO cook that the liver might be done in a casserole – thus making it softer – and served with some nice gravy. When this was duly done, one rather lowly Scots engineer had looked at it and said, "What the bloody hell's this?"[152] However at a Mess Meeting, Lieutenant Bell, RM, was appointed Mess Secretary – a job he did not particularly relish[11] – and Lieutenant-Commander (E) Aiken was voted Mess Treasurer; a post he had held before.[1] 18.1.45

At Milne Bay a Royal Australian Naval draft was put ashore, four Able Seamen returned from their jungle detention, and the Commanding Officers of *Empires Mace* and *Battleaxe* paid a visit.[181] *Mace*, *Arquebus* and *Battleaxe* had just finished training the U.S. Army's Americal Division at Bougainville Island; while there some of the landing craft had actually taken part in an operation, in support of a Brigade of II Australian Corps.[215] *Glenearn*'s Lieutenant Curling, RM, was informed that he had been promoted Captain,[35] and he left to take over 541 Flotilla in *Empire Mace*. 19.1.45

At Ora Bay U.S. personnel were disembarked.[181] It was just the same as any other part of New Guinea; hills and red coral. Continuous heavy rain made sleeping on the upper deck impossible, and it was extremely hot, especially at night when the ship was blacked out;[11] one just lay on the bed with practically nothing on and sweated.[1] But it was a lovely clear morning when they arrived at Lae. 20.1.45

Lieutenant Bell took in four boat-loads, and by 0600 *Glenearn* was going full speed for Langemak Bay. This trip 21.1.45

was turning into a Southern Railway passenger train service; picking up and dropping people all along the line.

At the second port of call in the one day[11] they went alongside No. 9 Wharf to embark U.S. Hospital Staff, a U.S. Army draft disembarked, and Royal Australian Navy and RAAF men came aboard; also one hundred bags of mail.[181] Sailing through the night brought them to Madang, another little coral harbour. It was mainly an Australian base, and they felt more at home there; the Aussies made a great fuss of them, and gave both troops and seamen a good time for the few hours that they were there. Plenty of Japs were still around, and it was known that their submarines were always sneaking in to replenish the survivors – said to be turning cannibal – of those driven out of Madang. In the early evening *Glenearn* sailed, this time for Manus in the Admiralty Islands.[11]

The anchorage at Manus was called Seeadler Harbour, after Count von Luckner's privateer; wrecked there by a tidal wave during the First World War.[91] There was little to see, and *Glenearn* sailed in company with *HMS Lothian* for Humboldt Bay, Hollandia.[11]

Mr. Wheeler, the commissioned gunner, was officer of the afternoon watch when at 1400 he sighted smoke coming out of the sea,[158] bearing 170°, range 2,000 yards.[181] He reported to the Captain, who came on the bridge. Captain Hutchison's only remark was, "Schnorkell – we will drop two depth charges." These were of the 25 lb. variety which could be picked up and thrown over the side. The Captain conned the ship towards the smoke, which promptly disappeared. Judging the distance very nicely, he signalled with his hand to let go, and Mr. Wheeler in turn waved to the two ratings on the poop deck. Minutes later pieces of wood, like bits of packing cases were seen; Captain Hutchison remarked that it probably had been a Japanese supply submarine, and the explosions had disturbed its deck cargo.[158]

Approaching Hollandia they ceased zig-zagging, and after dropping anchor started disembarking the troops.[181] This business of passenger carrying was causing many adverse

23.1.45

24.1.45

comments; it was being said that the ship's signature tune should be "Ferryboat Serenade". One of the American officers had announced over the tannoy, "All passengers getting off at the next stop are to be ready . . ." He was not very popular after that.[11] After *Glenearn* had moved to the anchorage off Hollandia a Captain King, USN, and the Port Director came aboard;[181] someone asked for the "first mate", saying that there was some cargo to be taken to Manus. He was quickly disillusioned, and his cargo not accepted, but all this displeased everybody on board; especially the Captain.

25.1.45

One bright spot on the canvas was the receipt of the first mail since early in December. There were piles of it; the sorting took almost 24 hours.[11] Awards for D-Day had been published in the London Gazette of 14th November 1944. *Glenearn* had picked up a few mentions in despatches for her Captain and the Navigator, and in 535 Flotilla Captain Richards and Sub-Lieutenant Waghorn, RNVR, Sergeant Dickens, Corporal Harvey and one Marine;*[370] in other words the O.C. and one "gong" per section.[152] Sick Berth Chief Petty Officer Dewey had been awarded the Distinguished Service Medal[370] and Surgeon-Lieutenant Payne-James had not been awarded the Distinguished Service Cross.[106] For some reason 543 Flotilla also got nothing,[152] but Rear-Admiral Talbot had been given a bar to his DSO[370] for his part in the escapade. When Captain Hutchison heard of this – he already had a bar to his own DSO – he sent one of those witty messages that naval signallers spent much of their time making, "Congratulations on your bar, when does it open?"[106]

Glenearn continued to swing round her hook, waiting for her next job; everyone hoping that it would be something a little more interesting. With nothing to go ashore for, the film shows – different every night – were much appreciated; even the poor ones.[11] The days passed in the mundane jobs of harbour routine, the occasional little emergency, and in exercises of various kinds; particularly the fire party.[181] From the outset of the Commission some fifteen months before, the

---

* The marines had drawn lots to decide who was to get their award.[102]

smell of petrol had sometimes been noticed on the forward mess decks.[36] Lieutenant (E) Ramsay and Sub-Lieutenant (E) J. H. Dubois had complained of the dangerous fumes given off whenever they discharged the gas from the petrol tanks after refuelling the landing craft.[39] Repeated research by experts had failed to locate the cause, and as a natural precaution ratings were forbidden to smoke on the mess deck,[36] while Ramsay and Dubois took very elaborate precautions during refuelling to avoid the explosion which might happen anytime.[39]

Glenearn's Chief Engineer had inherited something of a hornet's nest – not the job, but the atmosphere in the department. He and the Captain were getting on quite well; the former knew that he was being watched very closely, but had no fears on that score,[1] but within the engine room it was a different matter. Before the advent of the new regime life had been very pleasant for the junior engineers. The Chief had not interfered in any way with the running of the ship, and the Second had been a very pleasant taskmaster, but the discipline had been very slack. Willie Ramsay was a good engineer[39] – he had once made for Dr. Payne-James' camera a threaded fitting, turning it out on a large lathe about three feet long[106] – and most people liked him, but he could be very annoying and he was too friendly with the junior officers.

Ramsay had been brought up on the West Australian run, where promotion was relatively quick;[85] Aiken had started as 9th Engineer in *s.s. Ascanius*, and had held his "Chief's Ticket" for twenty years before getting the appointment. Also the older man's Board of Trade Certificate was for steam with motor endorsement, which meant he could sail as Chief in any ship;[1] Ramsay's "Ticket" was for diesel which could not be endorsed for steam. He could serve only on motor ships.[63] It appeared that Willie Ramsay had been more than willing to take over complete control of the engine room, so when Aiken arrived and insisted on doing the duties the Chief was supposed to do, but which the Second had more or less been doing, Ramsay suddenly had his job cut in half and resentment was aroused.[39] Aiken for his part remarked privately that when he was Second the Chief Engineer never had to go round wakening officers to get them on watch on time.[1] So inevitably changes had taken place and discipline had been improved; none of it to the liking of the junior engineers.[39]

Glenearn's Ward-room Mess Committee too was having a busy time; holding a meeting, preparing a new set of Mess Rules and preparing for the Mess Dinner in honour of the Captain's Birthday. Everything went off very well indeed. The meal was good, and the ship's concert after it especially so.[11] One turn was a sailor dressed up as Carmen Miranda, another was a sketch with "Will Hay" as the schoolmaster; the schoolmaster's part being taken by the Captain's Secretary, Lieutenant Plunkett.[1] After the show the officers entertained the artistes in the ward-room.

It had been confidently predicted that *Glenearn* was going north to Luzon, scene of the most recent landing by the Americans, but one convoy had already left without her. *Empires Mace* and *Battleaxe* had arrived to swell the mass of shipping in Humboldt Bay, and now on Sunday 4th February a lot of U.S. troops and a small amount of stores were taken on in the morning; the ship sailed in the afternoon.[11] Clear of Cape Soeadjar she joined a merchant convoy[182] bound, it was believed, for Leyte which had been taken a couple of months before.

First day out they went to "Action Stations". Quite like the old Normandy days, except of course nothing happened; but the same feeling was there all right. It was a very slow convoy, taking all day to pass the island of Biak; although they did manage to cross the equator. *Glenearn* spent most of her time astern of the convoy acting as anti-aircraft cruiser.[11] On their third morning the ship was stopped and LCA 895 sent to torpedo-boat PT45 to take off a seaman with eye trouble.[182] Soon after the landing craft had been hoisted, the Australian frigate *Gascoyne* reported an Asdic contact. She dropped a number of depth charges, damaging her stern in the process. The sub. scare continued all day; during the night a periscope was sighted and more depth charges were dropped, but no hit reported.

3.2.45

4.2.45

5.2.45

6.2.45

7.2.45

This convoy was "deadly"; just a long series of ships slow and silent, pushing a way through the sea.[11] *Glenearn* was acting as vice-commodore; although Captain Hutchison was the senior officer in rank, he had to take second place to the American convoy leader. One of *Glenearn*'s engines was a little suspect, so she ran on her starboard engine only, at the same time executing a form of zig-zag to keep her speed down to 6 knots.

The American troops were a different crowd from those brought out across the Pacific; their Colonel accepted the offered ward-room hospitality, but rationed his officers so as not to swamp their hosts.[152] When the censoring of letters became oppressive,[106] with each British officer having to check twelve to fourteen a day,[1] the American officers lent a hand. They were very impressed by the literacy of the ordinary British matelot: "Jeese! Are these all High School boys?"[106]

8.2.45   "Father" Hutchison announced that this would be their last trip for the Americans. The 1st of February should have been their last day but General McArthur had cried out for more shipping and stopped their going. C-in-C British Pacific Fleet had yelled even louder, and the finishing date was now 1st March. Many were the rumours as to their next destination: Canada, New Zealand, Bombay?

10.2.45   Approaching the Japanese-held island of Mindanao, trouble from the air was expected.[11] Anti-flash gear was checked and there was a dusk 'stand-to'.[182] Most of the

11.2.45   Sunday was spent at "Action Stations" during which time the convoy passed over the greatest known depth of water in the world, the Emden Deep; 5,703 fathoms, or over 34,000 feet.* Later in the day an LST was torpedoed in *Glenearn*'s 0800 position – not one of the convoy's vessels, but going the other way – probably hit by the submarine that had followed them so far.

There was a terrific swell, with the ship rolling badly, but at least it was a lot cooler. During the night one of the convoy,
12.2.45   an LCT, lost its tow.[11] Land was sighted at 0630; Suluan

---

* Now regarded as erroneous.[R]

Island bearing 319°. At 1013 the convoy was formed into three columns, and shortly after this *Glenearn* streamed paravanes.[182] As they entered Leyte Gulf the convoy commodore gave the signal to the rear commodore and to *Glenearn* to proceed independently. A race started. *Glenearn*'s other engine was put in, the revolutions increased and clouds of black soot – unconsumed fuel oil – belched from the funnel. With her American troops cheering wildly, and the engines doing 110 revolutions, the British ship drew ahead and, off Dulag, dropped her hook first.[152]

Arrangements made for disembarking the troops were very much like an operation, but the troops did not leave after all; no one seemed interested in them. It seemed likely that they would have to be taken further north, but in the meantime *Glenearn* swung around her anchor in sizzling heat. From where she was Leyte looked a most uninteresting place, with a lot of flat ground. On board, there was more conjecture about their next job; there was a strong feeling that the Marines would be leaving the ship. It was learned that the convoy from Hollandia that they should have sailed with had lost three of their vessels, including one that foundered after losing her tow.

The water situation was becoming very acute, with only about one gallon per man per week, which included cooking, and the people ashore were not at all helpful. Eventually, after great tension between ship and shore orders were received to proceed to Leyte, so Captain Hutchison moved the ship fifteen miles into San Pedro Bay. As they were about to drop anchor off the *USS Wildcat*, lots of natives came along in canoes. All the women were gaily dressed, while the men wore odd scraps of American uniforms. The water boat came alongside and *Glenearn* picked up 350 tons, which was a help. Landing craft took parties to U.S. store ships;[11] LCA 1491 was damaged by the forward derrick before *Glenearn* weighed and moved back to the anchorage off Tolosa.[182] In the interval, a number of American fighting ships had arrived from the invasion area; these were the first the ship's company had encountered in this area. They looked very formidable.

16.2.45

17.2.45

Lots of rain fell; the hands with buckets and cans catching it as best they could. It was reported that there was mail ashore for the ship, so the postman was sent 18 miles to the base for it. He came back with four letters. This Sunday afternoon the ship moved to San Pedro to allow the hands to bathe, then back again to Tolosa. Two days later after U.S. stores had been brought aboard the trip was repeated, for more water; they were due to sail next day for Lingayen Gulf.[11]

18.2.45
20.2.45

At 0825 the hands fell in and secured for sea. Lines to *USS Wildcat* were cast off, all the LCAs hoisted, and *Glenearn* proceeded. At 1035 a destroyer came alongside to say that *Glenearn* had been appointed convoy commodore.[182] Pretty late; and showing a lack of organisation, or contempt for the British. At the least, very unfair.[11] Captain Hutchison quickly made his presence felt by charging down the middle of one space between the columns of ships and up the other displaying all flag signals in duplicate. To the few British vessels present she made rather a brave sight, with the occasional bugle call sounding forth; a change from the normal sloppy job made of convoy commodore.[54]

21.2.45

The convoy consisted of forty ships[272] carrying men, stores, fuel and munitions,[11] guarded by four escorts; *USS Woodson* Senior Officer of the Escort.[272] Course was set almost due south through the Surigao Strait,[182] this taking them over the wrecks of Japanese battleships, cruisers and destroyers sunk in the Battle of Leyte Gulf the previous October.[R] At 1230, as the watch-keepers were coming off duty, a report came through that a destroyer had just been torpedoed in the position the convoy would reach the following morning.[11]

In the Mindanao Sea all watertight doors below *E*-Deck were closed for passing the Japanese-held island of Negros. *Glenearn* circled the convoy before resuming her post as guide of the fleet.[182] The sun was very hot; those on afternoon watch were scorched badly, as no cover was permitted that might obstruct the sighting of enemy aircraft.

22.2.45

This was not a bad convoy for speed: 9 knots.[11] Their course led through the Mindoro Strait, and four ships left the

23.2.45

convoy for San Jose on Mindoro Island;[182] later three ships
joined from the same place.[272] Manila, capital of the
Philippines, was passed on the morning of the 24th, but too
far away to see anything of the fighting still going on there.[11]
A section of four ships left for Subic Bay.[272]

24.2.45

Air cover was provided all the way.[11] One interesting
development was the USS *Thomas Le Valley*, a converted
"Liberty" ship which carried helicopters. One of these
machines was regularly flown off at dawn, and again at dusk,
to carry out an anti-submarine patrol ahead of the convoy.[272]
From the decks of *Glenearn* a most wonderful sunset was seen,
full of glorious colours which changed continuously. There
was a green flash as the sun set.

On their last night before leaving the ship a pretty hectic
party was given by the Americans on passage.[11] Some of the
ship's company, including the Chief Engineer, were made
"short snorters". This was a craze involving a dollar bill
signed by several individuals; it had to be produced on
demand on pain of a presumably alcoholic penalty.[1] The
function was well set off by an excellent dinner, which
included chicken and ice cream – the last decent meal both
guests and hosts would receive for some time, as the latter
were running short of provisions.[11]

Once the convoy had rounded Cape Bolinao Captain
Hutchison took his ship to the head of one of the columns and
so led the convoy into Lingayen Gulf, scene of the American
landing. Then at 0715 she left the convoy, increased speed and
entered the anchorage. After her Captain had been to USS
Foote for orders *Glenearn* weighed and moved to the inner
anchorage.

25.2.45

At 1425 it was . . . *AWAY BOATS* . . . and a proper
technical landing.[182] But not very pleasant. The swell made
the landing craft range under the heavy hoisting blocks;
one Marine was knocked into the water, but rescued
unharmed.[152] Ferrying continued throughout the afternoon
in the worst seas yet encountered. There were ten casualties;
one a bad one, and it was a relief when all were back on board
again.[11] Just as well there had been no opposition.[152] And the

luck of the day held; it was learned that they would be catching a convoy south on the morrow.[11]

That evening, courtesy of the American Naval Film Service, they watched a film on the after deck starring Monty Woolley and Gracie Fields.[28] Ashore an artillery bombardment was in progress some few miles inland; the gun flashes could be seen quite distinctly – all highly incongruous.

26.2.45 There was quite a lot of shipping in Lingayen Gulf, including several Australian ships.[11] Captain Hutchison went to the cruiser *HMAS Shropshire*, flagship of the Australian Squadron; a visit returned later in the forenoon by Commodore Farncomb, RAN. The Commanding Officer of *HMS Empire Spearhead* was also on board.

After the LCAs had been shuffled and then secured for sea, by 1258 *Glenearn*'s anchor was aweigh and she set about forming convoy, for she was again commodore.[182] They played martial music as she left the Gulf, and gave a brilliant and very impressive salute to *Shropshire* as they passed.[11] Convoy IG 101 for Hollandia consisted originally of twenty-two ships with six escorts, but as they moved down the coast of Luzon odd ships were dropped off and others joined.[272]

27.2.45 There was a sub. scare the second night out when those off watch were wakened by the rattle of depth charges resounding off the ship's bottom.[11] They had been dropped by *USS Johnnie Hutchins*.[272]

28.2.45 A very strong wind, about Force 6 or 7, was blowing with heavy seas, but the old ship rode very well. The wind was still
1.3.45 blowing as they rounded the corner past Mindoro and Negros, and continued on their way between smaller
2.3.45 islands.[11] *HMAS Burdekin* sank a floating mine, then left the convoy with some ships bound for Leyte.[272] At the north end of the Surigao Strait another Leyte section was seen converging;[183] it consisted of about forty ships. *Glenearn* was commodore of a convoy now about seventy strong. *Battleaxe* and *Mace* were among these ships from Leyte, while *Empire Spearhead* had been with them all the way.[11]

At first light one morning Captain Hutchison looked out over his flock and seeing two merchant ships trailing far behind sent them a signal to the effect that if they were thinking of joining his convoy they should make formal application; if they were part of it would they please keep stations for God's sake if not for the Commodore's.[28] *Battleaxe* was sent to round up the stragglers.[183]

5.3.45

Captain Hutchison demanded that all ships kept station. Apart from neatness, they could all be seen and were a safe distance from each other; thus avoiding collisions. Yet it was strange that about 20 minutes before the end of each watch every ship was out of position except *Glenearn*. On her bridge it was suspected that someone in the engine room was too lazy to keep the revs. steady; instead they were making a quick calculation at the end of the watch then slowing down or speeding up as required to make the figure right for the full four hours. When Lieutenant Waters, RM, went down and stood on top of the fiddley* to try and count the "beats" of the engine, Ramsay found out and threatened to "do" him. Waters replied that he was letting the ship down – the commodore ship at that – the vessel astern could have rammed them – had often had to take avoiding action because of this – and did he wish the Captain to know of these suspicions . . .

Later in the forenoon the same Marine officer was sent[152] in an LCA to a Dutch ship the *Van Heutsz* with a doctor to give medical aid.[183] The injured man had been squatting on the "throne" when it had cracked under him; he was brought off on a stretcher lying face downwards,[152] through pouring rain and in a heavy sea. He was Javanese and could speak no English.

After crossing the equator again, *Battleaxe* was sent on ahead to arrange water for them; apparently no time was going to be wasted in getting away to their next destination. Hollandia was approached at 1300 on 8th March.[11] After the convoy had stopped, *Glenearn* acting independently moved to the inner anchorage, and a United States oiler came alongside. That evening Lieutenant-Commander Turner, USN, Senior Officer of the Escort, called on the C.O. to take

7.3.45

8.3.45

* Deck hatch leading down to stokehold.

his leave, and that of the United States Navy.[183] *Glenearn* was being turned over to the British Pacific Fleet for trooping duties between Australia and the forward bases. *HMS Lamont* and *Spearhead* were to be used as accommodation ships, while the other three *Empire* ships were to return to the U.K.[215]

Force "X" had always been an abortive expedition. The U.S. "top brass" considered the Pacific to be theirs, and had resented the arrival of the White Ensign. This attitude, however, had not been reflected down the line, and many officers of the Force had made very good friends among the Americans. And the British had always been made very welcome ashore.[35] *HMS Glenearn*, at least, had shown some of their Admirals how a warship should be run.[94] But to send out ships to the tropical heat of New Guinea without additional distilling equipment could only be blamed on someone in the Admiralty;[32] that particular albatross could not be hung round any American neck.[A]

CHAPTER 24

THE EYE OF THE CYCLONE

Shortly before the sailing from Hollandia, three British 9.3.45 seamen were taken on board for passage. They had been prisoners of the Japs, but had been rescued near Manila in a daring feat 25 miles behind the lines by an American raiding party. The stories these ex-POWs had to tell made most unpleasant listening.[11]

Glenearn had now been away from civilization for over two months, and all this time working near the equator; her company was just "about melted" and nearly all were suffering from prickly heat. Everyone was looking forward to a spell, however short, in the more temperate climate of Sydney.[1] The latest "buzz" was that 543 Flotilla would leave the ship there to take the longer way back home; but of those likely to be affected, some were past caring what happened to them.[11]

After dinner in the ward-room there was an impromptu party. Naval officers were in whites, and the Marines in khaki. Someone noticed a large tin of red floor polish, and started hurling the stuff around. Others joined in, until the ward-room and everything in it – including the white uniforms – were liberally besplattered with bright red. Next day all those who had taken part were brought before Commander Hardman-Jones and given a sharp ticking-off, for not behaving like officers and gentlemen.*[155]

Madang this time seemed quite the prettiest spot in New 10.3.45 Guinea.[11] They picked up some water there; also more water and fuel at Finschhaven.[183] Then running down the coast 11.3.45 even the background seemed wonderful, with the Owen Stanley Range standing out, forbidding and imposing. A stop was made off Lae to send a rating to the detention barracks there; also to pick up four offenders who had served their sentences.[11] Back in September, after *Lothian*'s mutineers had

---

* The dating of this incident is conjectural.

275

been found guilty, orders had, it seems, been given to march the prisoners from Finschhaven to the detention camp. However, the tropical heat, the dense jungle and the numerous quagmires along the way had caused this scheme to be abandoned before Cape Cretin had been reached. The subsequent notoriety had outlived the existence of Force "X".[32]

12.3.45 After an exceptionally good film – "Cover Girl", starring Rita Hayworth – had been screened on the upper deck, the ship sailed.[11] Next morning *Empire Battleaxe* was sighted, and *Glenearn* stopped in order to return a leading seaman to his own ship. Later in the day some depth charges were dropped in the vicinity of Cape Nelson.[183]

13.3.45 Crossing Milne Bay a tidal race kept swinging the ship round, and approaching the China Strait visibility was extremely poor – barely as far as the fo'c'sle head. Fortunately the radar showed no other vessels in the offing. The wardroom stewards had laid the tables for breakfast, so when she met the seas and gave one especially large lurch – what a mess! When breakfast time came, there were very few items of crockery left intact.[152]

By noon the wind, which had been from the north-west Force 2, was blowing west by north Force 6. Two hours later the indications and the reports both were of a cyclone in the vicinity.[183] Lifelines were placed on the decks, and everything possible was battened down.[28] *Glenearn's* bridge on top of the wheel-house was open to the elements, and as she pitched and sprayed the watchkeepers got the lot, with spindrift coming right over. Despite a towel round the neck, the water ran down inside the oilskins.[152]

At 1800 the centre of the storm passed over the ship, and the wind dropped to a light air.[183] Hundreds of frightened birds were fluttering about in this the "eye" of the cyclone. They perched on the rigging for a rest, but were all swept off again as the storm area was re-entered.[28] The wind, which had been over the starboard quarter, was now over the port bow from the direction east by south. There were some very hard squalls, with wind to Force 9 at times,[183] and great billows of sea broke over the forecastle in the worst weather many of the ship's company had ever seen. The lifelines saved a watch-keeping officer* from being washed overboard while doing the rounds of the boats.[11]

Glenearn's whaler, stowed on the fore well deck, was smashed to matchwood,[28] and the LCA at No. 1 port side came adrift. A party was sent forward to the unenviable, risky job of securing this landing craft,[152] and the ship turned into the wind; the pitching and rolling went on, rain poured down in torrents and the lightning was almost continuous, but the work was completed without accident.

Although the gale lessened a little,[11] it continued blowing hard, with heavy seas and *Glenearn* shipping water over all; but she kept to her course of 159°, and made a speed of 15 to 16 knots through the water.[183] After two inoperative days the galley functioned again.[28] Paravanes were streamed, although by the time they were due to be taken in the port one, together with its recovery wire, had carried away.[183] 14.3.45 16.3.45

Sydney was reached at 0730. It was a lovely morning; cool yet sunny, with a faint mist – just like the beginning of an English summer's day. For once it really felt good to be alive. Everyone seemed so cheery, as they picked out familiar sights: the Bridge, the skyline, the beaches.[11] Once his ship was shackled to the buoy Captain Hutchison went ashore;[183] while he was away a signal was received saying that each watch was to get four days' leave.[11] 17.3.45

After a quiet day, *Glenearn* moved to dolphins at Clark Island, and from there the first of the long leave men left the ship. The remainder of the company was variously employed scaling and painting overside, working stores and exercising fire parties; it was very quiet on board. Captain Hutchison paid a visit to *HMS Activity*,[183] an escort carrier with a distinguished record of protecting Atlantic and Arctic convoys, but which had started life on the stocks as one of the *Glenearn* Class.[291] 19.3.45 21.3.45

The Chief Engineer did not take any leave, as there was a job to be done below; in port all thoughts of work seemed to

---

* Lieutenant Bell, RM.

TWO CAPTAINS

27. J. A. Grindle
28. C. A. G. Hutchison

SIX ABLE SEAMEN

29. Special painting party, March, 1945.
Back row (l. to r.): Dodd, Nuttall, Pearson.
Middle row (l. to r.): Unknown, Jackson.
Front: Earley.

be forgotten, and supervision "went haywire". He managed ashore on only two occasions; both on ship's business. Since becoming Mess Treasurer he had also been asked to take over the catering for the mess with its 44 permanent members, and its 40 to 50 occasional paying guests. He spent £300 on food and stores, in many cases buying at 20% less than had been paid before. But some people are never satisfied; they got the riposte, "If you think you can do better, have a crack at it".[1]

535 had been told that they, and not as expected 543 Flotilla, would be leaving.[11] The senior Marine unit was to be transferred to *Empire Battleaxe* and *Battleaxe* was believed to be going home. Some of the individuals concerned were happy about the idea;[155] others did not seem very pleased.[11] Ammunition in the charge of the Landing Craft Obstruction Clearance Unit was disembarked and 535's kit transferred. To replace the flotilla Marines a draft of 30 Patrol Service ratings was received from the shore establishment *HMS Golden Hind*;[183] these men had done a good job at home mine sweeping and so on, but had only minimal ideas about drill and discipline.[152]

26.3.45
27.3.45

With the tug *Hero* standing by, *Glenearn* cast off and turned in the fairway. After passing Garden Island the LCAs were dropped before going alongside No. 7 Berth, Woolloomooloo. There 535 Landing Craft Flotilla Royal Marines, the spare crews of 543 Flotilla, and the L.C.O.C.U. went ashore.[183] They may not exactly have had tears in their eyes,[94] but there were very mixed feelings among those who were leaving;[152] 543, now reduced to 493 Ancillary Flotilla, were simply "browned off".[11]

28.3.45

Loading of cargo and the working of stores went on until less than an hour before midnight. At 0800 on the 29th March the hands fell in and started preparing ship for sea.[183] A naval draft, which included about 25 New Zealand radar ratings, arrived for passage; their destination was given as "Forward Drafting Party" – a replenishment pool for the British Pacific Fleet.[91] Petty Officer Streeter and Leading Seaman Downs left, and Lieutenant-Commander (S) Fulljames went off to hospital.

29.3.45

After an early dinner all the navigation equipment was

tested in the usual manner. Lines forward and aft were let go, and *Glenearn* backed clear of the wharf; the LCAs were hoisted and so the voyage to Milne Bay began.[183] Everyone felt better for the ten days in cooler weather; some claimed never to have felt fitter, and many had put on weight. After a few more jobs they would probably be joining 535 Flotilla in the UK.[11]

Even Captain Hutchison seemed affected by the general euphoria. About ten men of the naval draft had gone ashore from the barracks in Sydney the previous night, in defiance of orders to remain on board. After they had returned they had been told they would be punished later, and when the draft boarded his ship Captain Hutchison had been instructed to sentence the offenders to the cells. The ship's company were duly summoned on deck to hear him read out these orders, but when he had finished he added, "The cells in this ship are not fit for a dog, let alone a man, so consider your sentence served." Everybody cheered, and the Skipper was reckoned to be an absolute gentleman.[122]

31.3.45   Saturday morning's Captain's requestmen[183] included some of the New Zealand ratings complaining that they had not had a cup of tea since arriving on board. Apparently they did not take sugar in their tea, and the custom in *Glenearn* was for the brew to be issued from the galley in a large fanny with the milk and sugar already added. Captain Hutchison was taken aback: why had they not spoken up earlier? His reaction was impressive; the whole ship's routine was altered just for the New Zealanders taking passage – tea-making in the galley would be discontinued, and instead each mess would be issued with separate tea, sugar and milk, and boiling water collected from the galley as and when required.

The "kiwis" had other difficulties with the Navy. Being used to the fresh air way of life, they found their mess deck unpleasantly hot, and considered the adjacent latrines very unhygienic, so once the heavy weather had subsided they tried sleeping on the wooden deck. However, at 0630 the following
1.4.45   morning they were rudely awakened by the crew's hosing down of the decks, so they did not try that one again; instead

some slept in the landing craft, while others found good quarters in the backs of the canvas-canopied army lorries being carried as deck cargo.[91] Other deck cargo included two aeroplane engines, which came in handy at Milne Bay as a source of nuts and bolts to be used as weights on the fishing lines of some of the "passengers".[122]

2.4.45

The main purpose of the call at Milne Bay was to take on water, which was still one of the main problems of life on board *HMS Glenearn*. In such a hot climate it was natural to feel like taking a shower frequently[91] – except perhaps "Granny" Philpott the "pilot" who did not believe in having too frequent baths because the natural oils of the body were washed off; he used the bath tub to do his own dhobi work,[106] and not infrequently that of junior officers who had slipped theirs in too. Commander Hardman-Jones avoided the problem of laundering his outsize shorts by drawing from "slops" a new set of tropical rig whenever he needed it.[112] Thus the idiosyncrasies of the officers – but in the men's ablution blocks the fresh water was turned on for a short period only in the morning and another in the evening.[91]

Before leaving Sydney some old pontoons which had been lying in the Harbour for some time had been loaded on *Glenearn's* hatches. From their prolonged immersion the pontoons had developed a fair covering of barnacles and other marine growth, which reacted adversely to the weather as they were carried northwards.[152]

Between Milne Bay and Manus their next port of call, it got very hot;[11] prickly heat and other skin complaints reappeared. Manus after dark was a blaze of lights with the appearance of some big city.[91] That night the film on the upper deck was accompanied by one of those tropical downpours, but the one was sat through and the other enjoyed.[11] Seeadler Harbour was very large and could have provided anchorage for just about every ship there was in the world – not that there were many there just at present,[91] although part of the British Fleet under Rear Admiral J. H. Edelston was;[66] also *HMS Lothian*, now flagship of the Royal Navy Fleet Train.[11]

3.4.45
4.4.45

Eleven maintenance personnel joined from *HMS Lamont*,
and early on the Friday LCA 601 went to *Lamont* with
Glenearn's padre; later a U.S. Navy chaplain came on board
to say Mass for the Roman Catholics.[184]
At night, as well as a film show, there was a mess meeting.[11]
The most interesting item on the agenda was a share-out of
profits.[152] Surgeon-Lieutenant-Commander Morrison the
wine steward had made a lot of money selling Australian gin
to U.S. Army officers at 15 shillings a bottle, having bought it
at Sydney out of bond for 2s. 6d. Everyone was happy with
this arrangement; the Americans particularly had been
delighted to go ashore with a bottle apiece of drinkable
alcohol, on an island where none was to be got at all, except
the "jungle juice" stuff.[106]

7.4.45   There was quite a lot of flotilla work going on. *Glenearn*'s
LCAs were offloaded and placed under the guard of a
sergeant, one corporal and eight Marines. Then the ship
moved, to anchor close to *Lamont* and took on landing craft
ex-*Arquebus*; at the same time half of *Lamont*'s flotilla joined
as working passengers. *Glenearn* was almost ready to
move.[184] Captain Hutchison had received orders to sail for
Leyte again.[66]

In the afternoon a team left to play football; while they
were away the cutter went inshore with the postman, and a
draft of 25 Royal Australian Navy ratings came aboard.

8.4.45   At 0540 the hands were called and the ship secured for
sea. A boat from *Lamont* took off despatches and the
Commanding Officers of the anti-submarine escort[184] – the
Australian destroyers *Nizam* and *Norman*[276] – came aboard.
Shortly after the destroyer Captains left *Glenearn* weighed
anchor and at 0900 the voyage began. Outside the gate course
was set, zig-zagging begun and the escort took up their
stations; the weather was very heavy, with the ship pitching
badly.[184]

Elsewhere in the world it was set fair. In Europe the Rhine
had been crossed, the Ruhr surrounded and German
resistance on the Western Front had collapsed; the Russians
were less than 50 miles from Berlin and also at the gates of

Vienna. In Burma Mandalay had fallen to the 14th Army,[460] and in the Pacific things appeared to be moving at a good pace:[1] the cities of Japan were being attacked by long-range bombers,[459] and the Americans had assaulted Okinawa, only 360 miles from the main island of Kyushu. Britain's Pacific Fleet was protecting the left flank of this amphibious operation.[458]

In London arrangements were being made to ring the bells of St. Paul's and other churches to celebrate victory over the Germans,[460] and the Admiralty had already published details of the gratuities to be paid on "demob". A Lieutenant-Commander would get two months' leave on full pay and £2 for each month of service; *Glenearn*'s Chief Engineer reckoned he would get over £100, but wondered what it would be worth when he got it. He, like everyone else, was getting very tired of this war;[1] but, since rejoining the ship in January he had at least gained the respect of his fellow officers – that was something.[66] To his subordinates he had proved to be a thoughtful man and a good engineer, and as for Ramsay's resentment – there had been nothing personal in that.[39]

Of course, they had all had their ups and downs, their terrible to-does; all sorts of things had gone on. And everyone had their worries. It was just like a family.[106] Despite what one said about the "plumbers" turning off the water at the crucial moment of soaping ... about the pursers' staff who kept everybody "starving" ... about the "Royals" ... They had all been profanely classified at one time or another ... despite all that, it was a fine crew.[94] Morale, on the whole ... jolly good;[106] and when fully operational, *HMS Glenearn* ... a fine ship.[66]

About 2200 on 8th April 1945, they crossed the Line again.[11]   8.4.45

CHAPTER 25

AN UNEVENTFUL TRIP

9.4.45 Monday the 9th of April dawned. It was a beautiful morning, with the Pacific Ocean living up to its name: very peaceful, very quiet, very calm.[91] Such wind as there was blew from the west north west,[184] as *HMS Glenearn* with her escort of two Australian destroyers[85] zig-zagged into it at $16\frac{1}{2}$ knots.[184] Open-air sleepers uncoiled themselves from rafts 0530 and spars,[91] and by 0530 the hands were employed cleaning ship;[184] in accordance with tropical routine they only worked mornings, when it was cooler – provided, of course, no one required them in the afternoon.[11]

Having no work to do was perhaps the most tedious occupation,[A] except for the Australian naval ratings taking passage who spent their time playing cards. Their one commissioned officer was just as great a gambler as his men, and was indistinguishable from them in shorts with no insignia or badges of rank whatsoever.[91] On the equator even just a pair of short trousers were too much for comfort.

With the departure of 535 Flotilla the ship had lost her Royal Marine Quartermaster, and this was a job Lieutenant Waters, RM, had inherited. The overall tally of the Paymaster's Department had taken a bit of understanding, but the various documents had eventually been checked and now, with the help of two Marines, he was down in the storeroom aft of the engine room getting the actual stores straightened out.[152]

While 543 – correction, 493 Ancillary – Flotilla continued to work the landing craft on the port side, the Patrol Service ratings taken on at Sydney were required to look after the starboard LCAs. These naval personnel did not yet regard themselves as "ship's company", since their duties were confined to the servicing, painting and general upkeep of their craft.[101] They were accommodated on the starboard side of No. 1 Mess Deck, which was also known as "the Marines'

Mess Deck";[160] in mercantile marine days it had been No. 2 Upper 'Tween Deck.[36]

Although the port-side landing craft had been fuelled two days previously, the LCAs taken on at Manus needed petrol.[39] The normal procedure was for the boats' engineer, Sub.-Lieut. (E) Steel* to approach the ship's engineer of the day,[132] but on this occasion it was Captain Bateman, RM, who asked Lieutenant (E) Ramsay to take the necessary action. Ramsay refused, as he was going off watch at 0800.[113] However, the watches changed,[39] and in due course ... *NO SMOKING UNTIL FURTHER ORDERS* ... was broadcast,[122] and the fuelling operation began.[39]

0800

The rest of the ship's company went about their business.[A] Those who had come off watch went to their quarters,[39] while others had their individual jobs to do.[A] A young Marine Lieutenant started conducting a kit inspection,[36] Lieutenant-Commander (S) Maclean the Paymaster worked in his cabin,[86] while Stoker Petty Officer Roy was in the upper part of the engine room. Able Seaman John Williamson was in the wheelhouse – that being part of his off-watch duties – and his fellow Seaman John Hennessey was employed near the Kelvin sounder.[160] Behind them Lieutenant A. M. Hart, RNR, was in the Chart Room; he was due to take defaulters at 1000 with Commander Hardman-Jones.[58]

At 0950 ... *STAND EASY* ... was piped,[184] and there was a concerted dash down to the mess decks for a cool drink, if not the usual cigarette, as smoking was still banned.[122] Able Seaman John Earley was one of the first in the rush, and was soon down in No. 27 Mess on the starboard side below the Marines' Mess Deck. He was sitting there with his leading hand and three or four other ratings, chatting and drinking lime juice when there was a strong smell of petrol.[40] But there had been trouble with petrol fumes, off and on, for a long time.[36]

0950

Able Seaman Williamson left the wheelhouse to go below. On *A*-Deck he passed Stoker PO Roy. On *B*-Deck he was stopped by John Hennessey who had already been down, and

* Name changed.

was now bringing his tea up top, "Don't hang about below, you can cut the air with a knife." Williamson carried on down. As he reached the ladder from the *D*-Deck canteen flat leading to the Marines' Mess Deck he was joined by Able Seaman Leslie Rowe. They exchanged a few words as they descended the ladder, then at the bottom they split up; Rowe going straight down the mess deck past the right hand side of the lockers and Williamson along the left side, intending to cut across – but found his way blocked by a pile of hammocks. He turned about to go the other way...[160]

Patrol Service Stoker John Tait was at the top of the starboard gangway down to the Marines' Mess Deck.[135] Using the same set of stairs was another stoker Leslie Milverton; he was about three feet above the deck,[96] whereas First Class Stoker David Walker[147] and Seaman Malcolm Morrison had already found seats.[101] Duncan MacLennan who was mess man for the day had just filled the last mug with ice-cold lime juice...[87]

One of the ship's butchers, Kevin Lamble, was half-way down the corresponding staircase on the port side,[74] while on the *D*-Deck he had just left New Zealand AB Stan Martin was standing in line for the canteen; Martin was a few feet away from the top of the companion way, and about third in the queue. In another twenty or thirty seconds he would be served. He was there to buy a packet of biscuits for his tiffin, and had no intention of going below; he was going up on deck forward, to sit in the sun and eat his biscuits...[91]

Opposite the Naafi on the starboard side, radar mechanic A. H. Thompson was in the Petty Officers' Mess.[141] Above him in his *C*-Deck port side cabin 2nd Engineer Willie Ramsay was drinking tea,[113] while Sub-Lieut. (E) Dubois was asleep in his.[39] Electrical Engineer Bill McKenzie was talking to Rex Bateman in the Marine Captain's cabin aft.[9] Dr. Payne-James was in the ward-room drinking coffee,[106] and Lieutenant-Commander Cutler was squatting in the "heads".[36] Lieutenant Mayhew, as Officer of the Watch, was on the bridge[94] with Captain Hutchison not far away. It was exactly 5 minutes past 10 a.m....[184]

1005

...Even well aft on the troop deck below No. 5 Hatch the explosion sounded tremendous. A wit remarked, "You always get a bang when you cross the equator." Another replied, "Not that loud, though," and they all dashed up on deck – to see a large cloud of smoke rising into the sky from somewhere forward of the centrecastle, and the Australian destroyers flashing to ask what was the matter. Everyone thought they had been hit by a torpedo.[122]

...the explosion had shaken the ship like a depth charge,[11] so both McKenzie and Bateman ignored it, thinking that a mine had been detonated by one of the escorting destroyers.[9] From the ward-room windows, although nothing could be seen, it was pretty obvious that something had gone wrong, so the two medical officers went straight down to the Sick Bay.[106] Willie Ramsay did not know what it was, but went below to look for torpedoes;[113] James Dubois knew straight away what it was.[39]

...Paymaster Maclean assumed the ship had struck a mine, so collected his codes and cyphers before heading for the bridge.[86] Ken Cutler's first impression was that this was nothing affecting *Glenearn*; more probably one of the destroyers had got in the way of a torpedo, or had dropped depth charges, but when ...*ACTION STATIONS*... went seconds afterwards he reached the bridge in record time, to find the Captain and the O.O.W. peering over the front end.[36] There had been this big explosion forward, and all sorts of things had been flung up into the air; tables and other fittings from the men's mess. Captain Hutchison thought he had been torpedoed and waited for his ship to take a plunge, going down by the bows. But she did not; instead, flames came up.[66] Obviously there had been an explosion within the ship, and this had been vented through a small section of armoured hatch kept open when not in dangerous waters.[36]

...New Zealander Martin had picked himself up several yards away from where he had been standing in the canteen queue; his first assumption being that they had struck a mine.[91] Kevin Lamble had been blown down the steps of the port gangway by a blast that had come along the passageway,[74] although having its origin in the vicinity of the ladders leading to 27 and 28 Seamen's Messes below the Marines' Deck.[160]

...Torpedo! Mine! Bomb! These had been the thoughts that had flashed through the mind of Able Seaman Earley, still sitting at his table in No. 27 Mess.[40] The explosion had started as a low rumble somewhere underneath them. The ship had shuddered, then as they looked towards the stairs, something like the sun, a ball of fire, came down the staircase towards them.[125] His head felt squashed in from the sides; he was deafened. Nobody moved. He thought, "This is what happens when you are dead." Now he could hear screaming and moaning from the mess deck above, yet still nobody moved.[40] The ball of flame went back to the top of the stairs and dispersed.[125] Suddenly their "killick" – Leading Seaman Heywood was a long-serving man who had been recalled – shouted, "Come on lads, you're not dead yet!" With that they all sprang to life, glad to be so, and made for the ladder. Just as they got to it the lights went out.

When they got up to the main deck, the smell was vile; paint was alight, towels on locker doors were burning – even cases on top of lockers. And the police lights were not working. Everyone was trying to climb on the lockers to get out through the small hatchway overhead, but as often as one or two got half-way up, they were clawed down again by those below. There were port and starboard staircases further aft, but nobody wanted to take a chance through the flames and smoke.

Then the cockney kid saw a way out. Running towards the ship's side Earley climbed onto the lockers, then ran back along them to the small hatch. As he was heaving himself through he had to kick out with his feet, otherwise he would have been dragged down again. On the well deck he found very few ratings about and reckoned he must have been one of the first out.[40]

First person to gain the forward well deck had been Duncan MacLennan. In the dark there had been some panic, but he had soon got a hold of himself again. As he had been furthest from the stairway he had gone for the half-opened starboard hatch.[87] David Walker for his part had recognized immediately a petrol explosion, but before clearing the mess deck he went over to the hatchway leading down to the lower deck and shouted down in case anyone was there. As there was no answer and no one was coming up the ladder, he assumed that everyone was clear, and then went out on deck.[147]

When AB Leslie Seymour had come up from No. 27 Mess he had heard somebody calling, and recognized the voice of an old friend Bert Barnard. Seaman Barnard was somewhere on the Marines' deck, and Seymour went down the mess to look for him. When he found him, Bert had been terribly burned. Leslie did all he could to reassure him saying, "You'll be back in England before I am," then carried him to the stairs and mounted them with the injured man over one shoulder. In this way he got him out, and took him to the Sick Bay. Bert asked Leslie to look him up when they all got home, and to visit his wife and family.[125]

...Malcolm Morrison had been momentarily stunned. He could not think at first, then went for the nearest stairway. Finding it crowded, he crossed to the one on the port side. He had been injured, as had many, many others.[101] They emerged on the canteen flat; dozens of them. "Shorts" had been their downfall; flames had seared skin, burnt hair and singed eyelashes[91] – but all the casualties walked to the Sick Bay,[132] helped by some of the uninjured.[160] Marine Lieutenant Waters at "Stand Easy" having shut the door of the Store Room came up on deck for a breather; as he entered the starboard alleyway he saw men walking past with skin hanging off their arms and hands, and in pain.[152]

On the forward well deck it was a matter of trying to get hoses rigged, but all the coils were tied up, and only Seaman Earley had a knife. When the first hose was ready he ran with it along the top of No. 2 Hatch and played it down the vent; those still below must have been glad of it, because everyone who had got out had blisters on their hands from holding onto almost red-hot hammock bars.[40]

1006
1007

The call had gone out for damage control parties to close up, the ship's speed reduced and course altered to 90° in order to put the wind astern and facilitate the fire-fighting.[184] Some survivors with only minor burns and bruises spent a few minutes checking on who had got out alright; for by this time the damage control team was making its way to the scene.[160]

At the first announcement of disaster Lieutenant (E) McKenzie and Captain Bateman, RM, had dashed forward;[9] Lieutenant Hart, RNR, had also gone to the point of explosion and found the 'tween decks an inferno of flames, with men trying to escape.[58] The Chief Engineer went straight to the petrol control chamber[66] – which was a very nasty place to get in and out of, and the valves very complicated[39] – to shut off the petrol, and climbed up the ladder again unharmed.[36]

Some of the men taking passage, having no duties, were told to keep aft,[91] as were some of the ship's company involved in the explosion but not seriously injured;[96] there they would all be out of the road,[91] as there could be another blast any time. Others, including some of the officers, although anxious to help kept clear to let the proper chaps get on with the job – but stayed ready at hand in case they were needed.[152] Able Seamen Seymour was detailed to go down to the bilges with the Fire Party and pump out petrol with a hand pump, but after four or five minutes was brought out unconscious from the fumes.[125]

Two damage control parties, led by the Chief Engineer and Commander Hardman-Jones, went into action.[152] Some poured water and foam into the 'tween decks;[36] others ripped off hatch covers, then by leaning over the coaming hooked and hauled out burning hammocks and the like.[152] Sub-Lieutenant (E) Dubois was ordered to take his party down to the Marines' mess deck just above the petrol tanks.[39] Commander Hardman-Jones said he was going in with the others to investigate, telling Lieutenant Hart to telephone from the fo'c'sle to the Captain on the bridge and inform him of what was happening.[58] The damage control party, wearing anti-flash hoods, overalls and carrying face-masks, went below.[39]

The fire-fighters had asked for volunteers to go back in and look for survivors. Able Seaman Earley volunteered, and was given one of the two asbestos suits to wear, but it had split open, so that stopped him. Leading Seaman Heywood went down wearing only a hat, shorts and slippers;[40] so did one or two others, including a young seaman who just wanted to see what was going on.[141]

Captain Hutchison had already sent forward Lieutenant Mayhew to find out what he could; the gunnery officer had ascertained that the Marines' mess had been blown about a bit, and that there was a fire in No. 28 Seamen's Mess. He tried to get down into the fire, but the steel ladder had gone, so he came back up again, getting his hands trodden on by the Chief Engineer who had had the same intention. At the top of the ladder were the leaders of the damage control parties; Hardman-Jones told Mayhew to report an explosion of unknown origin, that he was investigating and would report later. The fire was recurring. Lieutenant Mayhew left the scene and as he was getting clear by way of the stairs...[94]

Marine Lieutenants Ince and Bell had been ordered to assist the Captain in the absence of the Officer of the Watch. Ince was sent away somewhere, and Bell was told to snoop around to see how things were going; he went down to find the Commander. First he went to the starboard gangway, but no one there had seen him, so Bell moved over to the port side. Then the Chief Bosun's Mate told him that Commander Hardman-Jones was down below. While these enquiries were being made and answered another Royal Marine, Lieutenant Trickett, went past on his way down. It was difficult to negotiate the gangway because of a hose which left little room, but "Dinger" Bell reached the bottom and had moved about three paces across the deck...[11]

When Sub-Lieut. (E) Dubois' party had arrived they were told that people were trapped in the lower mess deck. He gave the order to put on Salvus face-masks, and had just put on his own and was about to descend the ladder...[39]

Aiken, McKenzie and Hardman-Jones were standing at the hatchway, looking down at the fire raging below. From where he was it was not possible to see the whole of 28 Mess Deck, so McKenzie decided to walk round a locker to get a better view...[85]

Most of the lights were out, and the smoke was quite thick[39] as a Leading Seaman went over and opened a scuttle to let in some fresh air...[4]

1021   ...It was more of a flame than an explosion,[11] but to the damage control party as they were hurled off their feet it was as if the main deck had indeed exploded under them.[39] Lieutenant-Commander Aiken and Commander Hardman-Jones, looking down into the mess deck hatch, both caught the blast full in the face.[36] Lieutenant McKenzie saw the flame roaring towards him and was able to dodge into a locker, which fortunately was standing open, but was burned on the back of his legs and up one arm.[85]

...Lieutenant Bell was spun round, but managed to crouch low with his back to the force and to cover his face with his hands. The blast started as a hot wind, then increased to terrific pressure which almost lifted him off the deck; the heat was searing. The tail end of the flame wasted itself just as it reached him, with some sparks flying beyond.[11]

...Lieutenant Mayhew was blown up his ladder and head first into the "heads".[94]

...Men leaning over the hatch coaming, most of them stripped to the waist in the tropic heat, were caught without much protection.[152] Lieutenant Hart, having telephoned his report had just returned to this hatchway. Looking down into the flames and smoke of what had been a tidy forecastle mess deck, he had been able to notice only that the damage was extensive and everything wrecked, when the flames shot up, singeing his face and head, and blowing his hat right off.[58] A blue flame roared up into the sky.[132]

To an onlooker on *A*-Deck, this second explosion did not seem as heavy as the first,[158] but down below – although the whole thing had lasted only a few seconds – it had seemed to take an eternity to pass. Lieutenant Bell was sure another enormous explosion would finish off all of them, but for a long, long fraction of a second no one moved; then there was a concerted dash for the ladder. He was pretty close to it and moved quickly, but he was still well to the rear as the gangway choked with scrambling men, all trying to get up the very narrow opening. All were fast, yet none were moving. The officer called to the men not to crowd, to take it easy; the press of bodies eased off gradually – taking years it seemed – finally leaving room for Corporal Worrall and Lieutenant Bell. They were the last up, apart from the injured, who were further forward and could not find their way back because of the smoke.

From the top of the ladder the Corporal shouted to these men. Guided by his voice they came up one by one. He assisted them, and as they emerged, the officer helped them over the step and turned them in the direction they had to go. Little guidance was, in fact, needed, as once they were up they seemed to know by instinct the way to the Sick Bay.[11] The whole of the damage control party had been trapped.[4] Commander Hardman-Jones and other casualties with terrible burns came out at this main exit.[58] Bell recognized no one, although Lieutenant "Lofty" Wolstencroft his closest associate was one of them; they were all black and burning. One who had been screaming in the mess deck went off down the alleyway, hysterically laughing and leaping, towards the Sick Bay. Lieutenant Trickett came up the port side stairway apparently unconcerned, although all his skin had gone; he was unrecognisable, even when he spoke.

Then all was quiet. Bell and Corporal Worrall went forward to the hatch covering the mess.[11] There they found a group which included Lieutenant Hart and the fo'c'sle Petty Officer Richardson, pulling two or three badly burned men out over the coaming.[58] Last one out was the Chief Engineer who had been helping the others[39] although in a terrible mess himself;[11] he had lost most of his clothes and all of his hair.[58] They got him up, and began tearing the burning pieces of clothing from his body, but his only concern was for his glasses, which he said they were to be careful not to break. There were no glasses.[11] In spite of pain and shock he controlled himself and walked to the Sick Bay.[58]

All the injured had made their way there;[132] some with assistance, some with their clothes still burning.[141] The Commander had run back on fire; Payne-James grabbed a blanket and put the flames out, but by this time Hardman-Jones was terribly burned. *Glenearn's* postman, a Leading Seaman,* had also run the length of the centrecastle on fire. The anti-flash gear of the damage control party had not burned, but their overalls had; it was an awful business. Young Lieutenant Trickett came staggering back; when caught by the blast he had been wearing only shorts. He just sat there, not seemingly too badly affected. Dr. Payne-James said, "Hello, how are you, old chap?" Then the patient's skin just fell off him. He was not in pain or anything, but obviously there was nothing effective the doctors could do for him. Nor for Lieutenant-Commander Aiken; the moment the Surgeon-Lieutenant saw him he knew very well that the Chief Engineer could not possibly survive.[106]

There were now about seventy casualties;[A] many of them very serious. The small Sick Bay was full, as were most of the spare transit cabins; the officers' anteroom was cleared to accommodate the overflow of stretcher cases. Five officers had been injured, all, including James Dubois, seriously. Four of the Flotilla had been burned; one badly. Lots of fellows were walking about slightly hurt[11] and stained with the doctors' gentian violet.[152] Lieutenant Bell had escaped with a few scorched hairs; Corporal Worrall had come through both explosions without a scratch.[11] Stoker MacLennan went to get treatment, but when he saw the state some were in he just walked out again, as he was not really bad.[87] The two doctors and their staff were doing a marvellous job of work.[11]

When Lieutenant Mayhew had come round, he had gone back to the bridge. There they had stood down from "Action Stations" and were concentrating on getting the fire out.[94] At 1030 there was a third explosion, and a new damage control party attempted to extinguish the fires using foam.[184] After being revived, Able Seaman Seymour was detailed off for deck duties by Lieutenant Hart.[125] A check had revealed that two

* Frederick Heywood.

men were missing: Able Seamen Jackson and Pearson, both of the No. 28 Mess. Repeated efforts were made to reach them, but all were unsuccessful due to the fire, the thick smoke,[160] and the fact that the first explosion had blown the false deck out so that it had dropped, hingeing about its fore end.[36] Captain Hutchison came down, but saw that there was nothing he could do – in fact he was only in the road – so he went back up.[91]

The lower deck was flooded to try and quench the fire, and to ascertain the extent of the damage.[160] Finally the fire party got down into the Marines' mess deck, and there in the darkness battened down the small hatches covering the two lower mess decks; thus the main conflagration was contained, and then the other burning material could be dealt with.[152] By 1055 the fire was under control, and course was altered to 130°[184] to let the wind clear the smoke from the ship. The two escorting destroyers kept close all the time, in case they could help.[11]

1055

The results of the accident were distressing.[66] Poor "Lofty" Wolstencroft: all that was visible was his nose, mouth, part of his shoulders, a little of his stomach and the top of his legs. Lieutenant Trickett, supposed to be working his passage to Leyte, was in a very bad way.[11] Leading Seaman Heywood also had terrible burns; he told John Earley that there was no feeling left in his body nor his face.[40] Men were lying about the anteroom on stretchers. As Lieutenant Waters entered, one of the casualties with singed hair and smothered from head to waist in gentian violet, waved. The officer did not know who it was. "Chief Petty Officer Dunstan," he was told. Waters went over. "Didn't recognize you, Chief." "No, I didn't expect you did; I haven't got my teeth in."[152]

Glenearn increased speed then resumed her original course,[184] but the fire had still not been completely extinguished;[276] damping down of 28 Mess continued.[184] First move towards clearing up the shambles was to ditch petrol from the sound tanks[36] – about 20 tons of it – which was too close to the forward magazines for comfort.[11] This operation was not too difficult, and pumping of the fuel

1130

1200   overboard commenced;[184] petrol fumes swarmed all over the
ship and mixed with the water on the decks.[11]

Meanwhile the ship's doctors were able to assess the
situation. One of the factors operating against their patients
was the climate, which made everybody sweat freely all the
time;[106] so, as well as the plasma leaking from damaged
capillaries,[614] all the casualties were losing fluid through what
was left of their skins – a combined loss which had to be made
up if heart output and blood pressure were to be maintained.
Some were being transfused with glucose just to try and keep
up their fluid volumes,[106] but it leaked out of circulation
again within a few minutes.[614] Some got rectal drips, but with
all the cells in a body calling out for fluid, fluid and more fluid,
still it was not enough.

After giving first aid to all, and doing what they could
without outside help,[106] Surg.-Lieut.-Commander Morrison
reported to the Captain that many of the injured were very
serious[66] and the Sick Bay had not the facilities to deal with
1524   them.[106] Captain Hutchison decided at once to alter course
190° for Hollandia,[184] where there were excellent hospital
arrangements.[66] A cypher message was sent to the Port Director, RAN, spelling out what had happened, and giving the
expected time of arrival as 0800 the following morning;[4] and
another signal made to CTF 112* saying that *Glenearn* was
putting into Hollandia "to land 34 repeat 34 casualties."†[209]

Some of the worst cases were recovering from the initial
shock.[611] Sub-Lieutenant Dubois regained consciousness
briefly, long enough to recognize Lieut.-Com. Aiken near him
in the Sick Bay.[39] The Chief Engineer did not appreciate the
gravity of his injuries – when McKenzie visited him he said
they were to call and collect him on the way back; not to leave
him in hospital.[85] Dubois passed out again and was later
moved to his own cabin.[39]

Elsewhere in the ship things were settling down to some
1630   extent.[11] Pumping of petrol was completed,[184] but smoking
was still forbidden.[11] All the forward power systems,

---

* Commander Task Force 112: Rear-Admiral Fisher, Flag Officer Fleet Train.
† The timing of this latter signal is uncertain.

including the degaussing gear, had been shut down,[184] but temporary repairs were made so that the navigation lights on the foremast could be brought into use; also the machinery on the forecastle deck.[152]

Re-appearance of smoke suggested that,[184] although the mess deck was sealed, something was at least smouldering down there. Lieutenant Bell had to go periodically to check how hot the deck was. He was a bundle of nerves, and jumped at the least unusual sound, while the lightning playing round the ship throughout his watch did nothing to improve matters. At 2200* the equator was crossed again.

It was still impossible to get down to the two missing men on the lower mess deck where the explosion had taken place. Any chance of their surviving had now gone, and it was decided to damp down the fire by steaming the mess deck head. To do this would mean letting in a certain amount of oxygen while the steam hose was being attached to the valve inlet. Lieutenant (E) Wilson was down there waiting when Lieutenant Bell and his Marines did the rounds, and he asked the officer to help him. "Tug" Wilson stood over the cover ready to fit the hose, with Bell about four feet away holding two special spark-proof torches, and hoping he did not look as scared as he felt. It was dreadfully quiet, with only the occasional swish of water underneath. The patrol had disappeared, and the smell of burning deck head was sufficient reminder of the probable consequence of air's getting in once the valve cover were removed.

Suddenly from the hosepipe came an angry splutter, as if annoyed at having to come so far, and "Dinger" nearly dropped his torches. The steam came through and the engineer did not flinch; with a quick movement he changed the valve over and inserted the hose...and it was as if the whole ship sighed with relief. Not having had a smoke since the early forenoon, at least one commissioned member of the ship's company could have done with a cigarette just then. But back on the bridge it was still like sitting on a gunpowder barrel.[11]

1815

2200

2215

* Clocks had been retarded 30 minutes at 1930.

The survivors from 27* and 28* Messes had been found accommodation down aft on one of the troop decks. Some of them were formed into watches and every half hour they went, in twos, round the deserted mess deck over the seat of the explosion: feeling the hatches and listening to hear if any more fires had started. It was very eerie in the night watches,[40] and for Petty Officer Thompson who had to visit – somewhat apprehensively – the 272 Radar Cabin at the far end of the Marines' Mess Deck.[141]

* Thus in all contemporary accounts. Ship drawings refer to Nos. 3 and 4 Mess Decks respectively.

CHAPTER 26

NOTHING WRONG WITH OUR SHIPS

It was another fine morning as *Glenearn*,[91] with two 10.4.45 damage control parties closed up,[184] a cable party on the fo'c'sle and a patient on the operating table[101] approached Hollandia in Dutch New Guinea.[175] Out in the harbour one of the ships had lots of what looked like women's underclothing hanging from lines rigged on deck.[91] *Glenearn* was directed past the destroyer repair base to No. 1 Navy Pier; as she swung towards the wharf two RAN officers took the lines. Eventually – because of the lack of normal power forward – the ship was berthed;[4] still in very deep water, although only 0823 twenty or thirty feet from the shore[91] where the Americans had a fleet of ambulances drawn up.[66]

As the gangway was so difficult to negotiate with stretchers, an LCA was lowered to deck level – like a lift – and the injured carried off on to it.[152] All of them looked very bad;[11] covered in gentian violet,[122] and many with bottles of blood plasma dripping into their veins. It was impossible for the onlookers to tell whether the men going past were dead or alive.[91] Commander Hardman-Jones went ashore wrapped in a blanket.[96] Lieutenant Mayhew was with Lieutenant-Commander Aiken before he went over the side,[94] and to him both the Chief Engineer and Lieutenant Trickett looked almost gone. Lieutenant Wolstencroft was expected to live; Lieutenant Bell saw him before he went ashore and promised to write to his mother. As the last of the thirty-two were lowered to the dock-side and loaded into the cars,[11] a very fat 1100 American military policeman drew the revolver from his belt and told the drivers, "Go like hell; anyone who gets in the way will be shot."[91]

The RAN Port Director had come aboard as the first casualties went ashore;[184] he had previously arranged for his secretary, Sub-Lieut. Allison, RANR, to contact the U.S. Navy Base Stores Department about kitting out all the

299

occupants of the forward mess decks who had lost clothing and other items. *Glenearn*'s Executive Officer was taken up to the Base Store to draw the kit required, against the Sub-Lieutenant's signature.[4] With all the casualties unloaded, the Port Director left.[184]

Word was received from United States Hospital No. 17 that all the injured had been put into one ward,[66] and that Lieutenant Trickett, RM, was being returned for burial at sea. As Colour Sgt. Mouel was extremely busy with the rehousing of the Marines and the salvaging of their belongings, Lieutenant Waters set about arranging a Royal Marine Firing Party.[152] Captain Hutchison asked Lieutenant Kevin Kelly, RANVR, an Intelligence Officer whom they had met before, to do all that he could for the remainder of *Glenearn*'s men ashore.[66] The hatch to No. 28 Mess had been opened briefly and one of the two bodies seen,[11] but nothing could be done yet;[122] *Glenearn* was urgently required at Leyte for "important operations".[66]

1130   At 1130 the body of Leading Seaman Heywood[184] – not Lieutenant Trickett as expected[152] – was brought on board, and received by a Marine Guard.[11] Seven minutes later

1137   *Glenearn* had slipped from the wharf.[184] Passing the ship used by the American nurses as safe off-shore accommodation,[91] *Glenearn* picked up *Nizam* and *Norman* from their anchorage in Humboldt Bay and all three vessels departed, bound for Leyte.[276]

The ship's doctors, having been relieved of only half their patients, worked on.[106] Lieutenant Waters rehearsed the firing party through a very hot and stifling afternoon.[152] The body had been placed on the Captain's Quarter Deck with Royal Marines standing guard. Apparently a number of other casualties were not expected to live.[11]

1645   ...*CLEAR LOWER DECKS*... and the ship's company
1700   mustered. Speed was reduced to 60 revolutions and course altered to bring the wind over the port beam. The ship's
1714   colours were half-masted. *Glenearn*'s engines were stopped for the funeral service held on the fore well deck,[184] with the firing party on top one of the "Sydney" pontoons.[152] It was a

very sad occasion;[91] "Jazz" Heywood had been a regular
RN[74] and a good seaman, with service going back to the days
of Egypt and the tow to Colombo.[63] In the heavy seas
Glenearn was rolling all the time. At the appropriate moment
the order was given to fire, then as the Marines reloaded, the
hot empty cartridge cases fell on the balding head of the
Captain and on the open book of the Chaplain.[152] At 1715   1715
the body of D/J 115424 Leading Seaman Frederick Heywood,
RN, was committed to the deep* over the starboard side.

The brief ceremony was soon over; the engines went to half
ahead, then course 331° was resumed and 110 revolutions   1719
telegraphed down to the engine room.[184] At 1730 the colours 1730
were rehoisted over a very subdued ship. If anything, the
fumes seemed to be getting worse – this was probably
imagination – and with things still on the verge of explosion,
one jumped at any strong breeze or sudden noise. Smoking
was still not allowed in any part of the ship. Everyone would
be jolly glad when this awful trip was over.[11]

The hatches were not going to be opened until Leyte was
reached, so the steaming of the lower mess decks was
continued. At night it was decided to transfer the steam from
the port to the starboard lower mess deck. It was suggested to
Lieutenant (E) Wilson that he shut off the steam first, but this
would have entailed going back to the engine room, so he just
yanked the pipe out of the plughole. Then he had to do a bit
of chamfering before he could get it into the corresponding
hole in the starboard hatch cover; it made for some
excitement, while it lasted, with live steam flying around.[152]
No. 1 Mess Deck was visited every half-hour throughout the
night[184] – a job for the RM Assistant Officer of the Watch
and the Duty Engineer Officer.[152] Towards the end of the
morning watch the steam was transferred from No. 27 back to   11.4.45
No. 28 Mess.[184]

It was a quiet, almost peaceful day, with a smooth sea and a
lovely sun; the ship's company began to pull itself together

---

* 01° 21′ S, 140° 20′ E. Ship's log (Ref. 184) gives latitude as 02° 21′ S, but this is
inconsistent with the positions at 1758 (01° 12′ S, 140° 12′ E) and 2000 (00° 47′ S, 139°
57′ E); also with the ship's course (331°) and speed (16 knots).

and lose some of its despondency.[11] The problem of ditching flood water from around the undamaged petrol compartments had now to be solved. Pumping lines led to pumps in the engine room where the temperature was 120°F and there was the possibility of a spark, while the presence of free petrol on the surface of the water had to be assumed. By overflooding then pressurising, the surface water was forced up through the air vents, and the suspicion about petrol confirmed; but after repeating the process many times until the overflow was clear, it was deemed safe to ditch the bulk of the water through the normal channels.

The damaged section was even more difficult; with the suction valves closed and the extended spindles intertwined like knitting. There was no suitable portable pump on board, so a unique brand of pneumatic submersible was built, with an old 2-inch centrifugal unit driven by what had been a pneumatic drill. Air pressure was no problem, as there was a 1,000 lb./sq. in. air line running along the deck to the forward gun mounting for partly recharging the recuperators.

It was a slow process, but eventually the water level was lowered sufficiently to get at the extended spindles. Cutting through these below the damage was a job for an engineer officer suspended in a bosun's chair, armed with a hacksaw and clad only in a pair of swimming trunks. In case he produced any spark, Lieutenant-Commander Cutler, sitting above, kept the operator well dowsed from a large hose fitted with a spray nozzle; all good clean fun.[36] In the late afternoon jettisoning of the remaining petrol was commenced, and by 1900 just under two hours' pumping had seen 5,500 gallons go overboard.

At 1229 on the 12th the starboard engine was stopped for repairs.[184] Speed fell from $17\frac{1}{2}$ to 13 knots until 1353.[276] That night a Telex message[106] came through which, when decoded, said that six of the injured had died: the Chief Engineer, Lieutenant Trickett, RM,[11] Stoker Petty Officer Roy and Able Seamen Barnard, Rowe and Schorfield.[284] With Leading Seaman Heywood and the two men still below, this made a total of nine.[11] Captain Hutchison got down to the task of

1900

12.4.45
1353

writing to the next of kin.[66] The following morning it was
learned that another man had died:[11] Petty Officer Jones.[284]
There was also the announcement of the death of President
Roosevelt. This was another great blow. The ship's flag was to
fly at half mast in harbour for thirty days. Lieutenant Ince,
RM, was heard to remark that it would be nice to hear of a
birth somewhere.

Land was sighted – a more comforting experience than
ever before[11] – and at 1300 *Norman* closed to receive
correspondence before the two escorting destroyers went on
ahead.[277] Leyte Gulf was entered and at 1557 *Glenearn's*
anchor went down in 10 fathoms of San Pedro Bay[184] after
what the Commanding Officer of *HMAS Norman* described
officially as "an uneventful trip".[277]

Within minutes a Captain (S) and a Captain (E) came
aboard, within the hour the hospital ship cases had left, and
Captain Hutchison had gone to *Lothian*, anchored 600 yards
away. *Empire Spearhead's* Captain arrived, and stayed several
hours.[184] Among the many ships in Leyte Gulf – nearly
all British[11] – was the River-Class frigate *HMS Parret*,
commanded by Lieutenant-Commander Thomas Hood,
RNR. Invited to dinner in the ward-room, he had been
looking forward to meeting his old friends again and so got a
terrible shock when he heard about the recent deaths;
especially as he had not known about the change in Chief
Engineers.*[63]

Shortly after noon on the Saturday one of the Chief Staff
Officers to the Rear-Admiral Fleet Train boarded
Glenearn;[184] he was Captain E. M. C. Barraclough, RN, and
an old friend of Colin Hutchison from their submarine flotilla
days.[7] The British Pacific Fleet had just finished bombarding
the island of Formosa, and would soon be arriving at Leyte
Gulf.[R] *HMS Glenearn for* for the immediate future would have
the mundane job of an accommodation ship; at the same
time her landing craft were badly needed to assist with
harbour transportation work.[7] So much for the "important
operations".[A]

---

* The dating of this incident is uncertain.

Meanwhile exhaust fans had been brought on board and preparations made for degassing No. 28 Mess.[184] The hatch was opened and the fumes cleared as much as possible[11] while two men – one a real "bad boy" by normal standards – were selected and well dosed with rum before they were sent

1750 down.[141] The two bodies were floating on the water[121] at the foot of the ladder;[40] they had died instantly and were unmarked,[94] but after five days' immersion in warm water, together with the tropic heat and the steaming, they were in a pretty bad state. It looked as if one was being helped up the ladder by the other – who had been a strong lad, and might have saved himself – when they met their end.[40] After being brought up, the dead seamen were sewn up in canvas, ready for their committal on the morrow.[11]

15.4.45 On Sunday 15th April, after the LCAs had left with working parties, *Glenearn* moved out to sea. In Leyte Gulf due east of Dulag.*[184] Able Seamen Dunstan Austin Pearson, D/JX 418600, and Lawrence Milner Jackson, D/JX 554628, RN,[284] were with full ceremonial and a seamen's firing party sent to their rest.[184] One of them had been engaged to be married on the next visit to Sydney.[40] All the dead were now buried, as those ashore were to remain there. Of the surviving injured, there had been no further news.[11]

After the funeral *Glenearn*, with all ports and doors open, steamed up and down[122] for an hour and a half[184] to force air through the ship and get rid of the various smells,[152] while the

1214 mess decks were pumped out. By 1214 the ship was back at anchor.

Whereas on the previous Monday the entire ship's company and the passengers had been involved in the petrol explosion and its immediate aftermath, one week later selected witnesses would be called upon to recount their experiences for the benefit of a Board of Enquiry.[184] But for the remainder not cited there was nothing to prevent anyone pronouncing an individual judgement, however incompletely informed, and sticking to it.[A]

That part of the ship that would concern the enquiries

* 10° 58′ N, 125° 16′ E.

mainly was the original No. 2 Hatch, which had one through shelter deck and a deep hold. This shelter was used as an open mess deck, with only lightly-partitioned areas in the port and starboard forward corners and midway between, while the hold was divided into six compartments[36] – relics of *Glenearn*'s spell as a fleet supply ship[620] – by an amidship fore and aft bulkhead and two transverse bulkheads. Forward and aft pairs of compartments were used as mess decks with a false deck about fifteen feet down;[36] the remaining two compartments contained light diesel oil, and a naval bulk store respectively.[621] Beneath were three 10,000-gallon petrol tanks. All were circular and mounted on stools;[36] one dated from 1940, the others from 1943.[113]

Delivery was controlled from a watertight chamber inset between the fuel oil and the naval bulk store, and the method was by air displacement;[36] that is to say, air was blown into the tank until it became pressurised and the pressure forced the petrol out. When the fuelling operation was finished the pressure was released.[39]

The compartments containing the tanks were always maintained 95% flooded with water, with the 5% air space allowing for surge. Various pipes led into and from the tanks through this water jacket.[85] Exhaust fans sucked any foul air off the free surface of the flood water,[36] through a breather tube $2\frac{1}{2}$ inches in diameter, which led out on deck between the chocks of an LCM* on the fore well deck. Doors had been fitted to the chocks to form a locker, in which ropes and other odd bits and pieces were stowed. Also in this space, only a foot or so away from the breather tube outlet was a ventilator to the mess deck.[85] The Marines' mess deck had always smelled of petrol, but when craft were being fuelled, it reeked.[40]

The most likely explanation was that a flange or other fitting on the high pressure air inlet had cracked[36] – due to rough weather, perhaps back in the Moray Firth – where it passed through the water jacket.[71] Between fuelling operations the relative pressures would, if anything, have tended to cause contamination of the petrol by water getting

* The LCMs had been replaced by "Sydney" (or "Tobruk") pontoons.

in, then the other way about. Once the system was pressurised, leakage into the water jacket would have been mainly air and, it must be supposed, any loss of pressure would have been indistinguishable from the normal fluctuations created by the opening and closing of valves at the delivery points. After the completion of fuelling, however, the air inlet valve would be closed, prior to releasing the pressure through the exhaust system. During the few moments that all valves remained closed[A] high-pressure gas and petrol would be forced out on to the surface of the flood water, with vapour filling the air space.[36] These petrol-laden fumes, after being discharged within the well deck locker, were then carried back down to the mess deck by the air-conditioning fans[39] – hence the fumes experienced in the forward mess decks from time to time. All that was needed for a catastrophe was a spark.[A]

Several commentators, with accommodation well away from the Marines' mess deck, filled this gap by stating categorically that at "Stand Easy" someone had lit a cigarette; it was obvious.[36,91,152] But mess deck opinion was that only a maniac would have attempted such an act in the remarkably volatile atmosphere, and no one had come forward to say they had seen this.[160] To this last point of course the immediate answer was that any witness was now dead, along with the presumed culprit.[152]

There was also the question of whether all possible safety precautions had been taken. Engineers Ramsay and Dubois had complained of the dangerous fumes many times, and the facts had been recorded in the defect book. Under the old regime only these two officers had had access to the petrol control room. They could not have prevented the Chief Engineer from drawing the keys, but Lieutenant-Commander Cahy never did, and it had become the practice for either Ramsay or Dubois to fuel the craft. Whenever they did so they had taken very elaborate precautions to avoid an explosion; even clearing the mess deck and mounting sentries to keep it clear. Also stopping all the fans running.[39] Captain Hutchison had been told, of course, and had concurred in the arrangements for closing down power forward of the bridge and forbidding smoking in the forward mess decks.[74]

Lieutenant-Commander Aiken, as Chief Engineer, naturally had learned the controls of the petrol tanks.[39] On the fateful morning the 2nd Engineer had refused to do the job[113] and Dubois, after coming off watch, had gone to sleep on his settee without knowing anything about it. Later on Aiken had looked into his cabin, but gone away again without disturbing him;[39] similarly checking on Ramsay.[113] The boats' engineer had been responsible for having the "No Smoking" order broadcast,[132] and it was said that he had turned on the petrol[39] – a pretty simple job as he understood it[132] – and started pumping without the Chief Engineer's knowledge.[39] Ventilation fans were not turned off, sentries not posted, and the mess deck was crowded with men drinking tea and only too ready for a smoke . . .[A]

The sudden flooding of the mess deck with fumes – corresponding in time to the release of pressure within the petrol tank – had been reported to the Captain, who was believed to be going to inspect the area after "Stand Easy".[152] When the first explosion occurred, there were two people in the petrol compartment: the engineer officer and a stoker; both got out unharmed.[147] The Chief Engineer's first action had been to go down there,[66] and later – much later – it had been found that everything was as it should have been, as far as the settings of the valves were concerned.[131]

A theory that fitted most of the known facts was that two seamen had rushed down to have a smoke in No. 28 Mess as soon as "Stand Easy" was announced; before anyone else got there, and before the Marines' mess deck was flooded with fumes. Apart from the presence of other people, the smell alone on the upper mess deck would have been sufficient reminder to anyone also tempted to disobey orders; but in the confines of the lower accommodation any petroleum vapour wafted in through the small hatchway high above could have spread into a layer between the beams of the deck head – a layer of potentially explosive gas/air mixture which could have accumulated into a considerable volume before the final fatal eddy carried a wisp of hydrocarbon towards the glowing tobacco below.[A]

However initiated, the explosion caused the collapse of the false deck, which in falling tore away the after bulkhead, allowing petrol-laden flood water to pour in.[36] This additional inflammable material had caught fire and burned, but relatively inefficiently due to shortage of oxygen in the confined space, until the scuttle was opened and fresh air admitted. The deadly flame of the second "explosion" had been the result,[A] while the third could have been fuelled by exhaust gas and petrol leaking out of a tank cracked by the first.[113]

16.4.45   Monday 16th April was the date of the Enquiry. A Commodore Larne was President of the Board.[184] He was to be assisted by a Constructor Captain; to Captain Hutchison's astonishment this was the very man who had been on the staff of the Senior Naval Officer in the Firth of Forth, and had told him he was making a fuss about nothing. Both Hutchison and Lieutenant (E) McKenzie were witnesses. In the enquiry it came out that one of the ventilation fans, which normally ran 24 hours a day, had an armature which was sparking and the sparks from the brushes could have had the effect of a cigarette lighter. Now this was exactly what the Captain had reported when they were in the Firth of Forth, and here was the Electrical Engineer saying that this was the trouble again.[66]

The Constructor Captain left; followed by the Commodore.[184] No one knew what their conclusions might be, although it was a pretty safe bet they would not find that there was much wrong with the ship – but in Captain Hutchison's opinion, McKenzie had been right all the same.[66]

CHAPTER 27

HOTEL GLENEARN

Glenearn's arrival at Leyte had found many ships of the Royal Navy's Fleet Train already there. In that part of the huge San Pedro harbour allotted to the British there were, in addition to the not unfamiliar escort carriers, destroyer depot ships, tugs and a netlayer, a bewildering variety of vessels specially equipped for the servicing of a fleet at sea:[91] repair ships, store issuing ships, ammunition ships, oil tankers; a distilling ship, a water tanker – even a demagnetising ship.[589] All of these, and more, were essential for this new venture of a British Fleet serving so far from established shore bases.[91]

Several drafts had already left for other ships,[184] while the remaining "passengers" were sent out to work on transferring supplies to those vessels needing them. The working parties went out in the early morning with a box of bully beef sandwiches for their mid-day meal, but by noon the meat had gone off in the heat, and the workers made no show of eating it. Whether it was this lack of food, or the temperature that made them lethargic,[91] the men were most unenthusiastic,[122] and there was not much work done. For a couple of days they were sent to a collier. They had these big coolie baskets with which they were supposed to unload coal into the landing craft, which then peddled it round the various ships, but *Glenearn*'s coolies did not unload much coal. The civilian crew of the collier were appalled at the idea of servicemen being sent out to do a day's work on inedible bully beef, so at night the ratings were presented with several bags of Kellogg's Cornflakes and some tins of jam which were greatly appreciated.[91] On the morning of the Board of Enquiry the Slop Room,[184] which housed the minor necessities – tobacco, toothpaste[36] – of life was found broken into.[184]

16.4.45

That afternoon a report arrived saying that Commander Hardman-Jones had died on the 15th and had been buried in Hollandia. In *Glenearn* they had begun to think that in

Hollandia the remaining injured stood a good chance of recovery, but now they were not so sure, and there was more than a little worry over Lieutenant Wolstencroft, whose burns had compared with the Commander's. Still, "Lofty" was younger.

17.4.45 Next morning there was another scare.[11] Just before noon smoke appeared on the starboard side of C-Deck forward,[184] abaft the Marines' mess deck.[11] Lieutenant-Commander Cutler was passing the Wireless Room and saw the smoke issuing from a vent, so promptly stuck a hose down it. Lieutenant Mayhew was inside wearing a clean white suit and got a ducking; he had already put the fire out with an extinguisher. An amplifier had overheated, that was all;[36] the damage was negligible and soon put right, but for everyone it had been an uncomfortable twenty minutes.

The once-proud Landing Ship, Infantry (Large) was now being used temporarily as an officers' accommodation ship, and in the evening Captain Anthony Kimmins, RN, well-known BBC and War Correspondent, came on board with his staff. The ward-room resounded with bitter jokes about "Hotel Glenearn", the PMO* with his wine list, Joe Simons the new Mess Treasurer as Mrs. Simons a boarding-house keeper with prices for Bed-and-Breakfast, a Royal Marine officer in blues standing on the gangway with an umbrella, the boats lined up like taxis . . . it was a pretty grim come-down after *HMS Glenearn's* operational standing. And there was very depressing news of the future; they stood a good chance of staying in this theatre of war for a long, long time. Another fifteen months or so . . . a jail sentence.[11]

A death ashore. Leading Stoker Austin Phillips, RN,[284] another veteran of the tow to Colombo,[63] bringing the toll to twelve. That night the film show was a relief for everyone aboard, still keyed up after the explosion; one could sense the emotions of the men.[11]

18.4.45 Two sections of "Tobruk" pontoons were towed to *HMS Illustrious*,[184] which had returned to Leyte with structural defects,[R] before the next day's working parties left for *m.v.*

* Principal Medical Officer.

Denbighshire.[184] *Glenearn*'s sister-ship had survived several Malta convoys almost unscathed, and was now doing duty as a "Victualling Store Issue Ship".[291]

Portable pumps having been brought on board two days previously, while the working parties were away the remaining hands were employed cleaning 27 and 28 Messes.[184] There was still some petrol on the flood water from the petrol compartments which repeated flooding and pumping failed to shift. The ballast beneath the false deck absorbed the petrol like blotting paper as the water was pumped out and exuded it again when next the flooding was repeated. Heat to break down the volatile portion of the spirit was the real answer, but *Glenearn*'s little donkey boiler could not produce a sufficient volume of steam to get the temperature up enough – but they did try.[36]

Another death. Seaman James McIlhargey, RN Patrol Service, had joined at Sydney and died on the 16th.[284] The deaths of so many officers and men where recovery might have been expected brought a message of sympathy from the Commander-in-Chief, Admiral Sir Bruce Fraser.[211] Yet another death was reported.[11] Ordinary Seaman Cyril Arnold, on the 18th April,[284] bringing the trail of fatalities to fourteen; would it never end? 19.4.45 20.4.45

The C-in-C's 'plane was on Tacloban Airstrip, about 20 miles along the coast, with the crew residing in "Hotel Glenearn". Squadron Leader Baker, the pilot, offered to take some of the ship's officers for a "flip" when he went for a trial run. Accordingly, on Monday morning the "Bish", the PMO,* "Tug" Wilson, "Dinger" Bell and Johnny Rushton a "plumber" got ready to leave.[11] Before they did so, however, the British Pacific Fleet started arriving, with the cruisers *Uganda*, *Gambia*, *Euryalus* and *Newfoundland* entering harbour.[184] After the fliers had left[11] for the shore *HMS King George V* and the carriers *Formidable*, *Victorious* and *Indefatigable* with destroyer escort came to anchor[184] reasonably close to the ships of the Fleet Train.[376] When the four-engined "Liberator" aircraft appeared about 1400, it circled 23.4.45

---

* Surgeon-Lieutenant-Commander Morrison.

over the bay for a while before moving off inland.[11]

Fuelling, ammunitioning and storing of the Fleet commenced at once;[376] two sections of Tobruk pontoons were towed to *HMS Formidable*.[184] Some of the fighting ships had been damaged in action; others needed crew members to replace seamen gone sick,[91] so from 1700 drafts left *Glenearn* for the escort carrier *Speaker*, the "*K.G.V*", *Indomitable* and *Victorious*, the *Swiftsure*, *Whirlwind* and *Wessex*.[184] The ranks of the passengers thinned considerably.[91]

The intrepid flying party returned at 2000, having had to hitch hike a lift back, but it had been a thrilling day for them all, especially those for whom it had been their first flight. From the air the battleship *King George V* had looked quite small, but the old *Glenearn* had looked good.[11]

Another guest to arrive by air from Sydney was Lieutenant G. I. Finkel, RNVR. As he walked into the ward-room the Petty Officer Steward recognised him from the voyage round the Cape in 1941 and had his usual drink poured and ready: lime juice, soda and a dash of bitters.[46]

Although *Glenearn* was anchored quite a long way from land, the sea around was floating with thousands of coconuts. Through them came natives in their little outrigger canoes with bananas and fresh coconuts to barter for bread and cans of food; money did not interest them at all. With the menfolk were some Philippino women, bare from the waist up. It was their natural way of life, but to lonely sailors lining the rails they seemed very, very attractive women.[91]

With so many ships in harbour, water transport was a major problem.[376] For *Glenearn*'s landing craft it was a matter of "Boats for Hire", with the LCAs in the Boat Pool doing jobs whenever and wherever required. It was hard work; away early and back late. What with dirt and the shortage of water encouraging the spread of ringworm, many of the crewmen became colourful characters after the Sick Bay's treatment first of gentian violet, followed by a green variety.[152]

One casualty of the transport shortage was shore leave for the Fleet. As the libertymen could not be landed to get their rightful beer, Vice-Admiral Rawlings authorised the delivery of the beer to them. The allowance was to be one bottle per man per day,[376] and working parties were sent from *Glenearn* to unload it; for once they were the envy of all their mates.[122] It was Australian bottled beer "Toohey's" and "Tooth's" and when it came time to return to the ship some of the lads had – while the Petty Officer's back was turned – imbibed too much of it.

Coming back that night many were very happy with the day's efforts,[91] but one rating was fighting fit, and thumped his non-drinking pal. The workers returned to their mess decks where their mates had kept a meal for them – all the while warding off the abundantly numerous cockroaches – and the aggressive beer-shifter started eating part of his, which consisted of a large bone with some meat on it. Everyone else was sitting about playing cards when . . . *ATTENTION ON THE LOWER DECK* . . . heralded the arrival of the Master at Arms and the Lieutenant-Commander to sort out the disciplinary trouble. Everyone leapt to their feet except the inebriated culprit who stood, without a stitch of clothing on except for his boots, nonchalantly chewing on the bone. In his free hand he held a cigarette. The Master at Arms started to read the riot act about striking a shipmate, but could make no impression at all on the drunken seaman, who just continued munching away, alternating with deep drags on his fag. The Executive Officer could not keep his face straight and turned away, but catching sight of the messmates with big grins on their faces, he just exploded with laughter.

The outcome was that the Master at Arms asked the troublemaker if he would agree to a "grudge fight" – to which the drunken reply was that he would agree to anything, anywhere, at any time! . . . *CLEAR LOWER DECKS* . . . was broadcast and everyone, officers and men, went to No. 4 Hatch to watch. A rope had been placed across the centre and the principle of the "grudge fight" was that if you backed away from the rope the other fellow could not hit you.[122] Boxing gloves came out.[91] Half a dozen times the drunk approached the rope only to be struck down by his opponent. Each time he staggered to his feet and the Master at Arms asked him if he wanted to carry on; each time he said he would. Then suddenly he had had enough and shook hands with the winner; both of them the best of friends again.[122]

24.4.45   Two sections of Tobruk pontoons were towed to *Formidable*.[184] Around the Fleet generally precautions were being taken against attacks by midget submarine, explosive motor boats and suicide swimmers, but security in other

28.4.45   respects seemed to be very lax. It was heard that there was to be a landing in Borneo by the Australian 7th and 9th Divisions about Wednesday 2nd May. Another "buzz" was that Japan was to be invaded in ten days' time ... They were just living on "buzzes" now. *Glenearn*'s relief ship was supposed to be on its way out; the 3rd of May was the date to watch ...[11]

29.4.45   After divisions on Sunday a church service was held on the fore well deck.[184] The Australian ratings had always refused to dress up for divisions, which made Captain Hutchison very angry,[91] but his patience in that respect was not to be tried

30.4.45   much longer. Next day naval drafts left for *Victorious*, *Indomitable* and *Indefatigable*;[184] the latter carrier getting the six remaining New Zealand ratings to replace crew members killed by a Japanese suicide aircraft on 1st April.[91] Single ratings were sent to the cruiser *Black Prince* and to *HMS Undaunted*.[184] All the War Correspondents who had been staying on board and whose despatches had come through *Glenearn* for onward routing moved out also, presumably to cover the "do" on Borneo. When the Fleet sailed next

1.5.45   morning,[11] with the recent passengers now on the decks of the aircraft carriers,[91] went the wishes of their late hosts that *Glenearn* might go with them.[11]

During the week just passed there had been no air raids – although there had been a few nights when the Fleet had been alerted by a "Flash Red" from shore stations – nor enemy activity of any kind.[376] A petrol tester confirmed that the mess deck was still 100% explosive; it was like living on a mine.[11] For the immediate future it was a matter of observing the spirit of that sentence used in signal training, "With the hill behind us, and the road before us, and the determination in our hearts we will go on". In other words, continuing with the training of the Patrol Service ratings who, under Lieutenant Waters' Marine tuition, were becoming a credit to their ship;[152] and waiting for the return of the less seriously injured of the 9th April.[A]

On the 2nd May the Japs reported a landing on the island of Tarakan a few miles off the east coast of Borneo.[11] Perhaps *Glenearn*'s frustrated efforts in the Pacific had borne fruit at last. Or maybe it had all been a waste. A waste of time. A waste of effort. And a waste of fourteen good men.[A]

2.5.45

CHAPTER 28

THE OLD ROUTINE

Glenearn's future, always a favourite topic of discussion in ward-room and on mess-deck alike, had already been the subject of correspondence at considerably higher levels.[A] As

12.2.45 far back as February the Vice Chief of Naval Staff had approved the retention of *Lothian*, *Glenearn* and one "Empire" Class Landing Ship – but only as a temporary measure and not as a permanent part of the Fleet Train; the U.S. C-in-C had released Force "X" to prepare for landing operations elsewhere, and it would invite criticism if many of the ships were to remain in the Pacific acting in a role for which they had not been designed.[287]

29.3.45 On the 29th March the Admiralty had sent a message to the Commander-in-Chief BPF saying that the ship must be sailed to arrive in the UK by mid-June,[211] as she was to be fitted out for SEAC.* His reply was that Sea Transport *Glenearn* was required for embarkation and disembarkation of drafts.[210] "Sea Transport" in this context covered two functions: on the one hand a barrack ship with accommodation for 133 officers and 1,455 men; on the other a fast ship for shuttling pool ratings, reliefs and drafts between Australia and the forward anchorage.[212]

10.4.45 The day after the explosion the Admiralty had made the rejoinder that *Lamont* could be retained for temporary service, in which case *Glenearn* must sail as directed, since one or other had to be refitted for service at the end of the year with an assault force. A personnel transport to replace *Glenearn* was being considered, but none should be expected immediately and in the meantime the Fleet Train would have to rely on its own resources. Seizing on the implied choice between

11.4.45 the two ships, Admiral Frazer replied next day that he would prefer to release *Lamont* and keep *Glenearn*.[211] That day too, *Empire Arquebus*, *Empire Mace* and *Empire Battleaxe* left

---

* South East Asia Command: Ceylon, Burma, Malaya, Sumatra.

Sydney for Fiji on the first leg of the voyage home, with Flag Officer Force "X" flying his flag in *Arquebus*.[215]

The disposal of Force "X" coincided in time with the dissolution of the Third Reich.[R] By the early days of May the news was absolutely splendid: Berlin had fallen to the Russians, Hitler and Goebbels were reported to have committed suicide, and enemy divisions throughout Germany were capitulating. In Italy they had asked for unconditional surrender, while in not so far away Burma the British were making great strides against the Japanese. In *HMS Glenearn* some of the ship's company were in a fever, waiting for the declaration of Peace in a Europe containing only a few pockets of last resistance.

A concert on board was a great success. At the end of the show the Captain brought on to the stage a bag, out of which was tipped a dazed cat, blinking in the glare of the lights. Captain Hutchison: "Well, the cat's out of the bag. What's its name?" Everybody yelled, "Sydney!" to which he replied, "Sydney it is."[11]   *3.5.45*

Officers and men of 539 Flotilla ex-*Spearhead* joined ship bound for Sydney and the route home.[185] Everyone seemed bright and cheerful preparing ship for sea;[11] by 0500 on the 6th May the anchor was aweigh[182] and they were all set for Hollandia, Manus and Sydney.   *6.5.45*

At 0725 next morning smoke was seen billowing out of the hatch over No. 1 Mess Deck, the scene of the explosion – everybody thought there was a fire, but apparently one of the fans used to clear fumes had burnt out. Everything was soon under control, but it had come as a shock; if the ship had decided at this point to blow herself up they were quite a few miles from land.   *7.5.45*

Very little news from home was coming through, but enough to understand that everyone at home seemed to be going crazy celebrating Peace before the war in Europe was in fact over. Then Churchill's speech was broadcast over the new British Pacific Service at 2200 on the 8th. Hostilities against Germany would end officially at one minute past midnight Double British Summer Time – 0701 *Glenearn* time – but the   *8.5.45*

"Cease Fire" had already taken effect. The Prime Minister reminded his listeners that Japan remained unsubdued, and some had difficulty in getting excited; partly due to the distance separating them from the events, and partly to the lack of anything with which to celebrate.[11]

9.5.45 The ship anchored in Humboldt Bay before orders were received to go alongside No. 2 Navy Wharf.[185] Captain Hutchison then went ashore and visited United States Navy Hospital No. 17; there he heard how much had been done to try and save the lives of his men. Captain E. S. Kelley, Medical Corps USN, had cleared a ward, and had eight doctors ready to attend the injured. Large quantities of blood and plasma and penicillin had been used, and more had been flown in at short notice. Lieutenant-Commander J. W. Griffin, Medical Corps USN, had never left the ward for seven days.[66]

By the time the casualties had arrived at the hospital, "burn shock" – caused by the reduction in the volume of circulating fluid in the vascular system – had already set in.[611] The Chief Engineer had died at 7 p.m. on the 10th of April,[66] three blood transfusions having proved futile.[131] Those who had survived the first two days hovered on the brink while a grim spectre waited, biding its time, raising false hopes; then beckoning to one here, another there, claimed its rightful, frightful due.[A] Commander Hardman-Jones had been in a coma some of the time, but had fought for life tenaciously; and every day he had asked after his fellow-patients. The day before his death his voice had been as resonant as ever, and he had even asked to have his regards sent to Captain Hutchison and his ship.[66] In his final delirium he had been dictating daily orders.[152]

Lieutenant K. T. Kelly, RANVR, had visited all the patients from the day of their admission, and was with quite a few as they passed away.[66] Sub-Lieutenant K. J. Allison, RANR, lived at the hospital during the critical days, writing letters on behalf of those with burnt hands, and helping generally; he had become very attached to Commander Hardman-Jones during the last five days.

But the real job at the Hospital had been done by the staff:[4] the doctors, the nurses, the plastic surgeons, and a group of girls from the American Red Cross who had been extra-ordinarily helpful. Lieutenant Scott Field Bailey, USNR, the Episcopalian Chaplain had done excellent work and been in constant attendance. There were in Hollandia insufficient ratings to furnish an RAN firing party, but Captain A. L. King, USN, Commander of Naval Base, Navy 3115, had done all that had been requested and more. Full military honours, with firing parties of U.S. sailors, had been accorded the dead. Captain Hutchison had asked the U.S. Authorities to re-inter them at Finschhaven, so the bodies had been embalmed and placed in steel caskets before being placed in coffins. After the funerals the bodies had been retained temporarily in a vault, and on the 28th April interred at the Royal Australian Air Force Cemetery No. 2 at Finschhaven, which was under the control of the Imperial War Graves Commission.

The twenty survivors had embarked on the escort carrier *HMS Fencer* on 29th April. With three exceptions they had all been in pretty good shape, but nearly all were in need of a prolonged period of convalescence.[66] Sub-Lieutenant (E) Dubois, after two weeks of semi-consciousness,[39] was out of danger, as was Seaman* Kelly, but Seaman* Hughes had still been far from well. Several months were expected to elapse before some of the patients – especially Corporal Bryant and Sub-Lieutenant Dubois – regained the full use of their hands. The Americans had done everything within their power to save as many of the injured as possible.[66]

Lieutenant Kelly and Sub-Lieutenant Allison were invited to Captain Hutchison's quarters and there he expressed his gratitude on behalf of the ship's company for the work of the two Australians.[4] Kevin Kelly had provided copies of photo-graphs taken at the funeral services, together with a letter describing the efforts made by everyone, and giving the names and addresses of the officers who might be thanked in writing.[66]

At 1500 *Glenearn* prepared for sea, then slipped from the wharf and backed clear. After turning, course was set for

---

* Presumed rank.

Manus. Two hours out ... *CLEAR LOWER DECKS* ... time to "Splice the Main-brace";[185] every man and officer was issued with $\frac{1}{8}$th of a pint of rum to celebrate Peace.[152]

10.5.45   At Manus it was raining, as usual. After less than 24 hours
11.5.45   at that insalubrious place *Glenearn* sailed for Finschhaven, amidst lots of "buzzes" that they were going home, arriving
12.5.45   early on the 12th. It was pouring with rain there too.[11] At 0850 the Captain and as many of the ship's company as could be spared[185] – about eighty – landed to attend a memorial service for those who had died ashore.

The cemetery lay in a valley. It was a beautiful setting: wooded hills beyond, green grass underfoot, flowering shrubs – and many white wooden crosses to mark the resting places of men from far-separated parts of the world brought together by Fate's varied ironies. The Reverend Janes conducted the service, with the worshippers gathered around the memorial column; then, standing at the bare ridges of recently-disturbed earth, they took last leave of their shipmates.[66]

By 0950 the Captain and his company had returned.[185] In the early afternoon they left Finschhaven, all set for Sydney, de-gassing and repair. A number of "Aussies" watched them go, and there were cries of, "Good old England". It was very touching, especially the sight of one old grey-haired man who waved and waved, until they were well past. It must have meant something.[11]

One last formality was observed regarding the deceased. At
14.5.45   1700 on the 14th there was the sale of the personal effects of the late Leading Stoker Phillips;[185] as was the custom on British ships. And as was the custom unrealistic prices were paid.[91] The money realised from this was added to that already raised by the earlier auctions and other means, including the concert of 3rd May, bringing the total in the trust fund* for the next of kin to something like £500.

16.5.45   Between 0400 and 0800 on the 16th the temperature dropped 10 Fahrenheit degrees. Late in the afternoon the ship

---

* Possibly intended for the dependants of lower-deck casualties only. At this time the widow of the Chief Engineer was also having to come to terms with the information that she was not considered eligible for a naval pension, on the grounds that her husband had not been killed "in action".

ran into a gale far worse than the one experienced the last time they had come this way, with wind Force 10 at times, and waves breaking over the 60-feet high bridge.[11] From *A*-Deck one could look up towards the crest of each huge wave.[106] There was very little abatement, and *Glenearn* arrived at Sydney five hours adrift. There it was cold and wet and miserable, but good compared to the weather outside the harbour.[11]

Tied up at 2B Dolphins, Bradley Head, stores were brought aboard, ammunition was taken ashore, and the four surviving sections of "Tobruk" pontoons were towed away.[185] "Lofty" Wolstencroft came from the hospital in Sydney to see his shipmates. He looked very well, considering the short time he had been away. After an initial disappointment, a great pile of mail arrived;[11] some of it addressed to the deceased.[2] It was very quiet in the mess in the evenings. Everyone was to get four days' leave; this caused some excitement – a break from the ship would do everybody good.[11]

18.5.45

Fire parties were exercised almost daily. The hulk *Meda* was secured alongside;[185] the Scotch boiler it contained was capable of delivering a sufficient volume of steam to break down the petrol absorbed by the ballast.[36] This solved one problem, but Cockatoo Dockyard did not seem to like the idea of dealing with the petrol gas that was still about.[94] It was decided that *Glenearn* would go to Melbourne to be de-gassed; there the oil companies had experience of, and facilities for, dealing with petrol in comparable situations, such as empty fuel tanks.[66]

25.5.45

The first long-leave men returned – very despondent at having to come back to the ship and unable to face the food aboard after the magnificent eating ashore – and the second party left. Lieutenant Wolstencroft, RM, came aboard to say goodbye before sailing for home in *s.s. Nieuw Amsterdam*; 539 Flotilla left to catch the same ship.[11] At 1600 on the Sunday *Glenearn* slipped and backed clear.[186] Everybody seemed sorry to leave.

29.5.45

1.6.45

3.6.45

Port Phillip was entered at 0700 on the 5th. Melbourne lay in the north-east corner of this enormous basin; from the bay

5.6.45

the city looked much like an English Midland town, with many factory chimneys all puffing out industrial smoke.[11] The ship moored alongside the Inner East Nelson Pier at Williamstown and the repairs to the explosion damage were commenced by Williamstown Naval Dockyard first thing

6.6.45 next day.[186] The anniversary of D-Day provided a considerable contrast with the situation a year before. Then one had been grateful just to be alive; now all was eagerness to enjoy life after a long spell at sea.

Lieutenant Bell, RM, had prepared a training programme to fitten up the Marines – including himself. They were all pretty soft after such a long spell without exercise, and after

7.6.45 the first route march there were many pairs of sore feet. Not that the programme was really rough; just a gradual hardening, with lots of drill and cross-country running.[11] There was always a fog in the early mornings, so when 493 Flotilla went to the rifle range the targets could not be seen at all.[487]

Captain Hutchison had taken up motorcycling and he insisted that the first thing put ashore was his motor bike.[139]

8.6.45 When representatives of the Press arrived to interview "Father" for the local papers,[11] this made good "copy", to go with impressions of D-Day and his claim to have been the youngest Commanding Officer in the last war and the oldest, at 57, in this one. His name had been given to Hutchison Island, North Queensland, and to Hutchison Shoal off Guadalcanal in the Solomons, when serving in the survey ship *Sealark* a few years before the outbreak of war in 1914.[377] Once, approaching the coast somewhere off New Guinea, the Navigator Lieut.-Commander Philpott had remarked that they had better be careful, because the charts might not be too accurate. "Not accurate bedamned," said Captain Hutchison, "I surveyed them myself."[152]

Williamstown was some eight miles out of the city. The rail route to Melbourne was very dreary, with dilapidated wooden bungalows and soot-grimed patches of countryside, but the centre was well-planned and totally different from the suburbs. The people of Melbourne were extremely proud of their city and even more friendly than the inhabitants of Sydney. Many invitations to people's homes were received, and several cocktail parties given on board by way of return. When weekend leave was granted many spent it on the town; some going up into the hills to enjoy the lovely scenery, to return not at all willingly and disliking the thought of going to sea more and more with each trip ashore.[11]

Commander R. M. T. Peacock, RN, joined as Executive Officer and Padre Janes left. The new Chief Engineer was Lieut.-Commander (E) A. N. Chisholm, RNR,[186] another "Blue Funnel" man.[71] Captain Hutchison wrote again to the next of kin of those who had died ashore, giving information about the burials, and enclosing photographs of the funerals at Hollandia and the memorial service at Finschhaven.[66] *12.6.45* *13.6.45*

Able Seaman Kingnape, who had deserted back in January, had been under close arrest on board since the 28th May.[11] His court martial took place on the 27th June and lasted an hour.[186] Seaman Kingnape, who was said to have worked as a barker at a showground before giving himself up to the authorities,[106] received one year's civil punishment and was discharged to prison.[11] *27.6.45*

Repairs were nearing completion. Alterations had been made to part of the ventilation trunking,[66] and a new pipe fitted to the petrol tank which was then tested with jacks, to see if any relative movement took place between the tank and its container, but none had been observed.[85] Petrol was embarked. Engine trials were carried out before the ship moved $3\frac{1}{2}$ miles to Prince's Pier, Port Melbourne, and sailed from there for Sydney.[186] The ship's company had enjoyed their stay.[11] Too much, in the cases of those – including a junior engineer – who had misbehaved ashore.[186] Everyone was sorry to go. *29.6.45* *30.6.45*

Sydney looked just as fresh and clean as ever, and the warm sun was a pleasant change after the cold of Melbourne. The scene was exactly as it had been a month before, and *Glenearn* had the same berth; it was just as if they had never been away. There seemed to be a lot of secrecy about their date of sailing, but with stores and drafts arriving every day, it could not be *2.7.45*

far away. An argument had been going on over the future of
the Flotilla; a Colonel Brockman, RM, wanted to take them
off the ship, whereas "Father" wanted to keep them. Captain
Hutchison seemed to have won – this time.[11]

10.7.45   They sailed at 1100 on Tuesday 10th July for
Finschhaven;[187] it was a case of back to the old soul-
destroying routine,[94] obviously. From the start the seas were
rough, with a heavy swell. Thursday was a terrible day, with
blinding rain, a gale wind blowing and visibility nil. The ship
rolling, tossing and pitching all at the same time, or so it
13.7.45   seemed. Friday the 13th was indeed a Black Day.[11] At 0900
strong petrol fumes were reported in No. 1 Mess Deck.
Captain Hutchison gave orders to clear the whole fore end of
the ship.[187] Lieutenant (E) McKenzie found him on the
bridge and was told to shut off all power forward; McKenzie
did this dangerous job in the full knowledge of the April
explosion.[66] Then a quick inspection of the tanks was carried
out; no leakage could be traced, but it must have been
considerable, as the pumps could get no pressure on the
fuel.[11] Sub-Lieutenant (E) Winstanley had been overcome by
petrol fumes, and was treated by Dr. Payne-James.*[97]

It was decided to discharge the contents of the tanks over
the side; a matter of 5,000 gallons. Hand-pumps were used
and, of course, no smoking was allowed. The Marines who
had only just returned to their mess deck after the long spell
away, were moved to another part of the ship. At intervals the
empty deck had to be visited by the Assistant Officer of the
Watch to see that everything was in order; it was all very
reminiscent of the last time.[11]

* The dating of Winstanley's experience is uncertain.

CHAPTER 29

MARKING TIME AT MANUS

They arrived at Finschhaven on the morning of the 15th, 15.7.45 and sailed again in the afternoon for Manus; still pumping out petrol from the mess deck tank. To a passer-by the southern islands of the Admiralties looked very picturesque, with each one a thickly-packed mass of trees and dense foliage. Some hours after anchoring in Seeadler Harbour, 16.7.45 *Empire Spearhead* sailed bound for the UK, and saluted as she passed. *Glenearn* was now the last of Force "X" in the area, and it looked as if she would be staying for a long time.[11]

In spite of being poorly fitted out for troop service, *HMS Glenearn* was regarded as indispensable on account of her ability to transport and maintain landing craft,[212] but while the British Pacific Fleet was busy "softening up" Japan,[7] there was little to do. Thus while carrier-borne aircraft cratered runways,[R] landing craft crews exercised "Away Boats";[187] while battleships bombarded Tokyo,[R] the officers played "fender ball".[11] Always the ship was ready for action, but never did the enemy appear.[36]

The island of Pityolu was available for recreational leave. Liberty men in the charge of an officer were taken ashore at 1330; on the island there was swimming, tennis, football, cricket, baseball, handball – and each man before leaving got a ticket entitling him to a bottle of beer. It did not add up to much really, but it helped to break the monotony of the ship's routine.[11] Shore leave ended at 1630[187] and sometimes it had deluged with rain the whole time.[11] The cooks found a crew for the whaler and started a rowing team.[139] When Sub-Lieutenant (E) Duncan Kennedy, RNVR, joined after having served throughout the war in *Glengyle* the first question he was asked was, "Do you play football?"[71]

One Saturday, the "buzz" had them moving very shortly; 28.7.45 probably early the following week. And so a flurry of excitement was created when a defect list was circulated to all 30.7.45

departments.[11] This tally came to 59 hull and miscellaneous items, 28 electrical faults, 18 machinery and boiler defects and 6 radar;[211] clearly a six to eight-week refit somewhere was indicated – perhaps Australia.[11] After the near-explosion of 13th July, the pipe which passed through the water jacket[85] and had fractured again at the top flange,[36] had been replaced by a copper one.[85]

1.8.45   Another "buzz". This time it would seem that they were going north to meet the Fleet.[11] A generally discounted rumour, although in fact *Glenearn* was being considered for Operation "Coronet"[225] as part of the British contribution to the provisionally-planned assault on the main Japanese Island of Honshu. This was supposed to take place towards 4.8.45 the end of the year,[7] but some Americans ashore were saying that the war would end within a month.

    The Commander-in-Chief was expected, so a Royal Marine guard of honour stood by, but when *HMS Duke of York* 5.8.45 entered harbour Admiral Fraser was not in her.[11] This business of just swinging round the anchor was absolutely killing.[106] Manus; two degrees off the equator and one of the worst climates in the world, yet some individuals tried to rise above their physical discomforts.[A] Lying on deck at night* one of the cooks on stand-by tried to imagine *Glenearn* in peacetime. Filling up with tea, perhaps, and the planters coming aboard to sip gin slings with the Master; or loading down to the mark with great teak tree trunks, while excited coolies padded along the decks...[139]

6.8.45   ... sleep was disturbed by a call from the hospital ship *HMS Gerusalemme*; the signal said they had fire on board and assistance was requested. Later all available smoke appliances were wanted, and a boat left with them, returning at 0645.[188]

    Later in the day news of the new Atomic Bomb came through. It had been tried out on a Japanese city with a name that sounded like "Iwoshima". Apparently it was a small bomb, but its effects were equal to a conventional two-thousand bomber raid; windows were rattled two hundred miles away, a column of smoke and flame had risen to a

---

* Date conjectural.

height of 40,000 feet and was still there four hours later, when a reconnaissance 'plane went over, casualties had been estimated at one hundred and fifty thousand.

Another Atomic Bomb had been dropped; this time on the Isle of Kyushu. It was followed by the signal: Japan was willing to surrender provided they could keep their Emperor. This was stupendous news; *Glenearn* became a ship full of life and interest, with much speculation over the future. There was the possibility of carrying released prisoners of war, probably from China or Japan to Australia; a thousand at a time, as on operations. *10.8.45*

The Captain and the Commander were playing "fender ball" with Marine Lieutenants Ince and Bell when the small ships in the harbour began sounding off on their sirens. First reaction to this was the thought that Victory had been announced, but it was only an unofficial report that had come through of an acceptance of the Allied terms, so the officers went back to their game. *14.8.45*

Wednesday the 15th of August 1945 was VJ Day. In the morning news from Washington, London and Moscow that the Japanese had offered unconditional surrender and their offer had been accepted. All the little American ships started blowing their sirens and a wave of excitement passed through the Fleet Train. All the national anthems of the Allies were played on the radio and speeches were made by many personalities, including Admiral Fisher and the U.S. Commander of the base at Manus. Fisher said that there were still humanitarian duties to perform, the British Commonwealth and the United States must move together in the future to ensure peace, etcetera.[11] *15.8.45*

"Splice the Main-brace" time again,[188] and after dark the ships began a firework display of flares, rockets and star shells, the sky lit with signalling lamps and searchlights; as if to relieve the dark tension of apprehension which had become part of one's nature. It was hard to realise that this meant peace of mind after six such frightful years. Some of the officers indulged themselves in a celebration, but quite a number lacked the necessary high spirits; feeling that the occasion deserved serious thought rather than jollifications, but without in any way detracting from their gratitude for the event.[11] Upper deck sentries were posted as usual.[188]

16.8.45

17.8.45

Next day there were reports of fighting in Manchuria between the Russians and the Japs; also of air attacks on the Fleet – presumably by fanatics.[11] At 0530 on the 17th, however, *Glenearn's* sentries secured for the last time.[188]

Three Royal Marine officers were warned that they would be required for special service in Shanghai or Formosa as liaison officers with POWs. Captain Bateman, Lieutenants Bell and Ince were the lucky ones, together with three NCOs and six Marines; they were expected to be away from the ship for about a month, but one at least of the chosen officers doubted if he would see *Glenearn* again. All three were the envy of the Mess. They were all inoculated against typhus and

18.8.45

cholera; also vaccinated for good measure.[11]

Captain Hutchison had been in command of *HMS Bee*, flagship of the Yangtse Flotilla 1922-1929,[409] so after

19.8.45

divisions he spoke to the three officers in his cabin about Shanghai, giving a very good description of it, and producing a plan of the place. He also warned them against the three W's: Water, Women and the Wangpoo.* Lieutenant Bell was informed that he was bound for Formosa via Hong Kong, at 5-minutes' notice to leave – having packed nothing he had to leave half his gear behind – he and Rex Bateman got a great send-off from their fellow officers when the Royal Marine party left for *HMS Indomitable*, flagship of Admiral Harcourt;

20.8.45

the big fleet-carrier sailed at 1830, passing *Glenearn* on the way. Lieutenant Ince left the following morning for the light fleet-carrier *Colossus*; destination Shanghai.[11]

Finally *Glenearn* herself was ordered to Hong Kong,[66] but first she had to go to Brisbane for medical and other

27.8.45

31.8.45

supplies.[160] Fully fuelled with oil and petrol, the ship weighed anchor and proceeded.[188] By 1900 on the 31st August they were in Moreton Bay[94] approaching the mouth of the Brisbane River,[66] and about to pick up the pilot.[188] The landing craft were being fuelled.[85]

* Hwang P'u or Woosung River.

Down in No. 1 Mess Deck an overhead pipe started leaking petrol.[147] Lieutenant (E) McKenzie* was somewhere below decks and had time to remark that he could smell petrol fumes,[85] before an electrical short circuit ignited the fuel and flames spewed out of the ventilator trunking all over the row of Royal Marine lockers.[152]

When the fire was reported, damage control parties closed up, speed was reduced and the ship turned stern to wind.[188] Leaving the Navigator in charge, Captain Hutchison went down to the fore deck and sent for special breathing masks and long flexible tubes,† before supervising the rescue of the injured. All the would-be helpers remembered the previous explosion and its horrors; no one would go down to rescue the trapped men, so the Captain seeing it as his duty, put on a mask himself before being lowered through the hatch into smoke-filled darkness. He managed to get two men out on ropes and then had to come up for air, as he could not breathe.[66]

There were still some injured down on the burning mess deck, and it seemed quite on the cards that the thing would go off again . . .[106] Stoker Francis O'Toole and Able Seaman John Kenny volunteered to go down.[372] Kenny was a real old "stripey";[106] a "clipped" Petty Officer[40] and a bad character in his Captain's opinion, but there must have been some good in him since he cared less for his own safety than for his shipmates'.[66] Kenny and O'Toole between them brought up two more,[372] then there was a count.[66] A Patrol Service rating, Seaman Gowing,[284] was still missing. Captain Hutchison went down again and found him right forward. With the unconscious man on his shoulders he carried him down a passage-way right aft, and handed him over to the Doctor – then went back to the bridge and took his ship into Brisbane.[66]

The fire took two hours to put out. Thereafter the mess deck was inspected at hourly intervals;[188] on one such visit some smouldering rags were extinguished.[189] Surgeon-

1.9.45

---

* McKenzie had been awarded the MBE as announced in the London Gazette of 14th June 1945;[371] this came from a recommendation of the C-in-C's following the April board of enquiry.[A] Captain Hutchison never recommended anyone for decorations, except in battle.[66]

† Presumably to supply fresh air to the point of rescue.

Lieutenant Payne-James, working single-handed, asked for help – which appeared in the form of his old friend Kenneth McRae.[106] Most of the thirteen casualties were very badly gassed, and all were taken ashore by Dr. McRae.

Various craft came alongside with stores, motor cars and passengers. Also forty-four ship's company to replace a draft of ratings discharged to *Golden Hind* for demobilisation[189] in accordance with the Commander-in-Chief's message anticipating the difficulty of returning ratings from China with the priority being given to the evacuation of released prisoners.[213] At 1303 the anchor was aweigh.[189]

There was nearly a mutiny then, because one side of the ship had been flooded and she was listing appreciably. Instead of going into Brisbane for repairs the Captain had said, in effect, "Right, we're off", and they were going back up to the islands again, and the ship's company just did not want to go. They were getting fed up with this ship and its petrol going up every time the bell struck.[106] Morale was very bad,[94] and the "buzz" was that the Marines were going to mutiny, unless repairs were done properly.[141]

But the damage had not been serious, and the Marines had not suffered any casualties; only the loss of kit and lots of "rabbits".* Marines and Patrol Service ratings were evacuated yet again to the after part of the ship. When the "Royals" got down to rescuing their gear and transferring it to their new quarters in the poop, some of their stuff could be salvaged, but some had to be dumped. It was a hard and dirty job. Here the "skates" came into their own; those chaps with records of minor disciplinary offences, but when it came to a job in hand they really could work – better, in fact, than most of the "good" boys.

Admittedly there did seem to be a jinx on the Marines' Mess Deck, but after a reasoned chat with their only remaining officer,† and with a job to be done they were soon back in the arms of discipline.[152] Eventually the talk of mutiny just . . .[106]

---

* Gifts for people back home.
† Lieutenant Cyril Waters, RM.

CHAPTER 30

PICKING UP R.A.P.W.I.

Seaman Kenneth Gowing died in hospital of pneumonia,[106] while *Glenearn* was crossing the Coral Sea.[189] 3.9.45 As the Peace Treaty had been signed in Tokyo the day before and the war was over, Captain Hutchison ordered the emptying of the petrol tanks.[85] The fault lay in the original design of the system.[36]

After a two-day stop at Manus for fuel, stores,[189] motor transport and some rusty drinking water,[152] course was set 7.9.45 for Hong Kong. Three days' steaming found *Glenearn* midway between Morotai and Mindanao when at 1620 course was 10.9.45 changed to close what seemed to be a ship in distress. Off the island of Talaud* Commander Peacock took in two LCAs manned by Patrol Service ratings to investigate signal lights coming from the shore. The boats returned having found nothing[189] – the lights must have been natives moving round a bonfire[71] – but the Royals were amused to learn that the landing craft had been told to go in stern first,[487] presumably to make a fast getaway in case of trouble; the point being that the stern was the unarmoured end of the craft.[152]

To see the countries of Asia pop out of the horizon, seen from the deck of a ship, is a sight never to be forgotten.[139] While still some 40 miles out, orders had been received from 14.9.45 *HMS Parret*, and *Glenearn* was following *HMS Enchantress* through the swept channel to Hong Kong,[189] past barren hills on each side dotted with gun emplacements like scars on the face of the ground. To port what looked like country mansions; to starboard, bunches of squalid little square buildings. Beyond the Lymun Pass the city rose up in a mass of grey unlovely buildings frowned over by the mountain on which they were built.[11]

Among the warships in the harbour was *HMS Glengyle*. As *Glenearn*'s anchor went down,[189] swarms of frail sampans

* 04° 21′ N, 126° 42′ E.

approached. They were in almost every case crewed by old women or extremely young children; all begging for food, and eagerly scrambling for pieces of bread thrown to them by matelots. The sampans hung around the "gash" chutes; while careful sailors sorted the rubbish first so that edible scraps were free from dirty waste.[11]

Captain Bateman, Lieutenant Bell and two Marines rejoined.[189] Everyone was pleased to see them and they were glad to be back. After entering Hong Kong with Admiral Harcourt's liberation force they had sailed for Formosa aboard the destroyers *Tuscan* and *Tyrean*.[11] On arrival at the shambles of Keelung they had joined three heavy cruisers of the British Pacific Fleet and the New Zealand Hospital Ship *Wanganui*. Nearly all the POWs had already been removed by the Americans, and only the sick were left; they were in pretty bad shape, having been forced to work waist deep in water down a copper mine at temperatures of over $100°$F.[9] After five days there the duties of the Royal Marines had finished, and they had returned to Hong Kong in the destroyer *Quadrant*.[11]

15.9.45   After the motor transport and a draft of men had been taken off in a lighter, *Glenearn* left for Hainan.[189] They sailed south through the night with all lights on; no blackout now.

16.9.45   The island was sighted early next morning,[11] and at 1300 *Glenearn* was joined by a destroyer *HMS Kempenfelt*. A floating mine was seen off the southern extremity of land, but the port of Sama was reached safely.[189]

Japanese landing craft – showing marks of sampan parentage in their design[152] – full of released prisoners of war came alongside.[11] In half an hour a total of 334 POWs were embarked:[189] Australians, Dutch and Indians, including Moslems and Sikhs. No attempt was made to segregate the other ranks on the mess decks where the ship's company took them under their wing[94] and made them feel at home;[11] they were so grateful for the hospitality offered.[94] A few of the Dutch prisoners were in a bad way[66] and were brought on board on stretchers;[106] poor souls so starved that they were in an advanced stage of beri-beri.[71] Dr. Payne-James had to be very careful not to feed them too much, and gave them just tiny bits of food and drops of milk.[106]

Most of the guests, however, were fairly fit[11] – the majority of the sick having gone to the hospital ship *Gerusalemme*[158] – and surprisingly enough could eat a normal meal. A very good film show was put on for them, including about six news reels and comic strips.* All the officers had a drink in the ward-room,[11] but next morning they said that the hospitality had been just a little too generous.[152] 17.9.45.

Back at Hong Kong one or two of the ship's officers went ashore. It was not a very pleasant experience: streets full of hawking coolies, little girls begging or selling newspapers, hundreds of bicycles and rickshaws. Several thoroughfares deserved the title "Street of a Thousand Smells", and the prices were fantastic. But some of the women were indeed beautiful. 18.9.45

When the POWs were disembarked, all the Australians went to the escort carrier *Vindex* bound for Sydney. The 159 Sikhs who had been the Hong Kong Police were said to be going back to take over their old jobs.[11] *Glenearn* prepared to sail for Shanghai. Twelve LCAs went on loan to the dockyard,[189] and three Marines were left behind awaiting transport to the UK and eventual release from the service.[11] 19.9.45

21.9.45

Formosa was sighted on the 22nd September;[189] Formosa with its sheer cliffs going straight down into the sea.[152] *Glenearn*'s course led round the eastern side of the island[11] as the Formosa Channel was still mined.[36] The main-brace was spliced again to celebrate V-Day; an observance held over from the correct date of the 2nd September.[11] 22.9.45

While still miles out from land there was a sudden change from the blue water of the open sea to the sluggish yellow of the Yangtse River.[152] Between the small bare islands sweepers were still busy searching for mines,[11] and a Japanese gunboat led the way through the minefield[71] to an anchorage near *HMS Colossus*. 24.9.45

Next morning a pilot took the ship up the Yangtse into the Hwang P'u and so to Shanghai, finally turning and tying up at Holt's Wharf.[189] Few natives came alongside, and those that did had no trinkets to sell. All the Chinese looked fairly well- 25.9.45

---

* The film officer was Sub-Lieutenant (E) E. L. Holden, RNVR.

fed and cared for; much more so than their compatriots in
Hong Kong,[11] although one sampan woman was seen to grab
a piece of bread from the yellow water, squeeze it out and pop
it into her baby's mouth.[152] On shore, only one person was
observed walking in that peculiar stilted manner, resulting
from having had her feet bound in infancy, usually attributed
to the whole race by ignorant Occidentals.

Just before midnight a drunken sailor was carried, like a
sack of flour on his mate's shoulder, up to the Officer of the
Watch. Against strict orders some of the ratings had traded
with the sampan women for Shanghai beer. In more normal
times this had had a good reputation, but the sailors who had
drunk it had gone out like lights – apparently the beer had
been doctored by the Japs before they left.[11] Surgeon-
Lieutenant Payne-James was sent for, and he ordered that one
man in a very serious condition was to be wakened every ten
minutes throughout the night.[152] Two other men had also
been affected but they were not so ill. None of them would be
tempted to imbibe "hooch" again.

The city of Shanghai lay further up the river, and from
Glenearn's berth many tall skyscrapers could be seen. When
shore leave was granted the liberty men found the usual terrific
prices; one became a millionaire in Republic of China Bank
dollars, then had to pay fifty thousand for a rickshaw ride.
The Hwang P'u seemed to be living up to its dangerous
reputation, with three Americans and two English women
said to have been drowned in the preceding week; the water
was thick and soupy, with a fast underwater current.
Glenearn's crews were ordered to wear lifebelts on duty.[11]

Captain Hutchison had been told that there were many
women and children, and one or two old men, who had been
behind barbed wire for more than three years; could his ship
take some of them away?[66] After their luggage had been
loaded,[189] some 350 British, Australian, Dutch and Canadian
nationals, including missionaries and nuns, arrived on
board.[409] Thirty-two were allocated to cabins and the
remainder to the troop decks, which had been designed to
accommodate assault troops on an overnight trip to France.

26.9.45

29.9.45

As the voyage to Hong Kong could be expected to take a little over two days the conditions would not be too bad,[36] but some of the late prisoners of the Japs did not quite appreciate the conditions. One female passenger complained to Lieutenant Waters about the spartan troop decks. With some restraint he pointed out that *HMS Glenearn* was primarily intended for carrying troops, also she was the first ship out of Shanghai and the next one was *HMS Guardian* a net-layer and even less comfortable. That shut her up. Others were most grateful for anything that was done for them.[152]

When some of the officers returned from shore leave at 1830 they found a lot of children sitting down to a meal in the ward-room with their mothers waiting on them. It was going to be strange having women and children aboard, and being wakened by childish voices and pattering feet early in the morning. Strange, but good.

The body of a native woman was seen floating past; no notice was taken of this common occurrence. Meantime the children were keeping the Sick Bay busy.

Lieutenant Ince, RM, who had been staying in a camp on the other side of the river since flying up from Formosa, rejoined. Also pressmen and photographers from the *Shanghai Herald* came on board to do their stuff. This resulted in two big articles on the ship and her Captain. *Glenearn*'s sailing had been postponed 24 hours, and then another 24 hours, because of a typhoon in the Yellow Sea.

30.9.45
1.10.45

Four LCAs were to be left in Shanghai.[11] Some of the remainder had to be stowed stern forward, as the current was too strong to turn before hoisting.[152] At 0800 *Glenearn* cast off. On the jetty the Royal Marine Band from *HMS Belfast* struck up "Will Ye No' Come Back Again?" followed by "Auld Lang Syne". *HMS Glenearn* meanwhile had moved away about 10 yards and stopped. The band played the two tunes again. The ship tried hard, but the wind was preventing further movement,[11] even when emergency power was used.[152] While the struggle continued, the band played "Will Ye No' Come Back Again?" and "Auld Lang Syne" about four times each, then they went away, probably quite

2.10.45

exhausted.[11] By 0838 *Glenearn* was secured alongside again until the wind direction changed from north to west.

The ship eventually sailed at 1400 and anchored in the Yangtse for the night, detained by the weather.[190] Already throughout the ship swings and see-saws had been fitted up and had been in full use, with officers, Marines and matelots pushing, steadying and generally enjoying themselves as much as the children.

Some of the passengers talked about going home, having leave and then returning. It appeared that these were internees who, because of their money, had had an easier time under the Japs.[152] All the ex-prisoners were in very good condition; there was nothing wrong with them, although one was pregnant. One woman, frightfully smart, complained bitterly, "Do you know we even had to peel potatoes?"[106] Another, the wife of an insurance company's representative – a big blonde woman with a child – apparently had been taken out of the internment camp by a Japanese officer and set up in a flat in Shanghai. At any rate, none of the others would speak to her.[71]

One fine old lady was Mrs. E. Spence.*[409] The film show one evening included some recent newsreels, one of which showed the sinking of *HMS Barham* in the Mediterranean; a sequence which had been censored until the war was over. When the battleship blew up in a cloud of smoke with tremendous loss of life, Mrs. Spence was very upset and her hosts were horrified to discover that her son-in-law had been *Barham*'s Commander. She had known that he had been killed, but had not known how.[36]

6.10.45   After a rather rough time Hong Kong was reached with the kiddies still swinging and see-sawing. The passengers had now been on board for six days but they did not leave; there was chaos ashore, no accommodation for new arrivals and the only passenger ship in port was already full.[11] Captain Hutchison went to *Montclare*, saw the Commander-in-Chief and told him he did not think these people should remain in China.[66]

---

* Referred to by contributors as Lady Spens.

Sunday's Divisions were attended by the passengers.[11]
Liberty men were landed[190] and Dr. Payne-James received an
invitation to meet his friend Kenneth McRae again.*[106]
About 75 repatriates disembarked to await shipment to
Australia, South Africa and elsewhere,[412] and Lady Louis
Mountbatten looked around the ship.[190] Having shaken
hands with everyone on the well deck including the cooks,[139]
she shook hands with all the senior officers and, at the end of
the line, the Royal Marine O.O.W.[152] A few more POWs
were brought alongside in *HMT Empire Saw* shortly before
Glenearn sailed for Colombo.[190]

The approach to Singapore was between innumerable little
islands. There was quite a lot of merchant shipping in the
port, also the County-Class cruisers *Cumberland* and *Sussex*
with a few destroyers and other craft. One passenger was
dropped;[11] Mr. Dickson a policeman. Within minutes the
anchor had been weighed and within the hour *Glenearn* was
travelling at full speed. Late in the evening *HMS Glasgow* was
passed.[190]

Through the Malacca Straits, with Sumatra on one side
and the Malay Peninsula on the other, and so past Pulo Weh
into the Indian Ocean.[11] During the night they ran into some
very bad weather which upset all but the most hardened
sailors.[36] The pronounced rolling of the ship was attributed
by some to the reduction in the number of boats now carried.

A liner, the *Tacwina*, which had left Singapore ahead of
Glenearn, was reported aground on one of the Nicobar
Islands. Her 800 repratriated prisoners of war and internees –
RAPWI for short – were taken off by *Empire Crossbow*, one of
the landing ships of the Normandy campaign. Through
running at reduced speed *Glenearn* lost at least a day, and was
still rolling and pitching badly. For the time of year this
weather was unusual; the most popular explanation being
that the Atomic Bomb had affected the elements.[11]

After passing the Mount Lavinia Hotel at a distance of $4\frac{1}{2}$
miles and then picking up a pilot, *Glenearn* approached
Colombo Breakwater by the south-west entrance.[190] The

* The dating of this incident is conjectural.

harbour was simply packed with shipping of all kinds, and there seemed hardly room to move.[11] After letting go both anchors Glenearn's port quarter struck the s.s. Port Fairey and one of the propellers carried away the ammunition ship's cable, which flew up into the air in a shower of rust.[152] Captain Hutchison must have thought he was in a destroyer. He blamed the engine room for not going astern when ordered, but while some of the engineers at this time were not very good, on this occasion a stoker had been noting the orders and the times.[71] In the afternoon a diver went down to inspect the damage[190] and reported that one of the propellers was dented on the stern side; proof that the engines had been going astern at the moment of impact.[71]

19.10.45   Next morning the RAPWI left ship after an unsuccessful attempt by some of the passengers to get Glenearn to carry them all the way home;[152] a hope shared by many of the ship's company.[11] The reception organisation was first class, and in a very short space of time they were all away to more comfortable quarters;[36] some to the Highland Monarch and some to shore to await another ship. As they left Glenearn they sang "Auld Lang Syne".[11] Highland Monarch sailed at 1730.

21.10.45   Workmen came on board and then the ship moved into dry-dock for repairs to the damaged propeller.[190] It needed a new blade; also the ship's bottom was to get a scraping and a touch of paint.[11] Whilst there the Board of Enquiry into the
22.10.45   collision with s.s. Port Fairey was held on board.
23.10.45   After her two days in drydock the flooding was commenced and one hour and a quarter after floating, Glenearn had cleared the breakwater and was working up to full speed;[190] heading for Madras to embark troops and take them to Java because of trouble there. The ship was on loan to SEAC for the moment, but would be going back to Hong Kong eventually with the garrison for the colony.[11]

Lieutenant Hart, RNR, and nearly fifty ratings had left at Colombo bound for civvy street, and there had been a number of arrivals;[190] the ship's company was largely new.[11] While in dockyard hands a brass plaque had been engraved with an account of the ship's wartime service.[A]

At Madras they anchored outside the harbour which looked as crowded as Colombo. The natives paddled queer craft – which looked like half tree trunks and were for the most part waterlogged in the heavy swell – and dived for coins. Safely hove alongside, the 2nd Battalion 13th Frontier Force Rifles, Indian Army, was embarked and *Glenearn* sailed for Belawan in Sumatra.[190]

They were a very decent crowd these army people.[11] Being one of the regular battalions of the Indian Army it was frequently referred to as the 56th Rifles, its original title. In March, 1942, it had arrived in Rangoon just in time to take part in the retreat through Burma. It had gone to the Arakan early in 1944 as part of the 26th Indian Division and had finished up back in Rangoon in the May of 1945. As a unit it consisted of the usual four rifle companies but with each drawn from a different race: *A* Coy were Sikhs, *B* Coy Dogras – both Hindus. *C* and *D* Companies were respectively Pathans and Punjabi Mussalmans; both Mohammedans. Battalion HQ was mixed and the officers were British and Indian; all worked together very well.[118] One of the English officers gave a lecture on the various types of Indian soldiers, why they wore bangles, and carried knives...it was all most interesting.[106]

It was a nice smooth crossing, although the troops did not get much of a trip because of the overcrowding and the fact that they all came from areas many hundreds of miles from the sea, and in consequence they were not "natural" sailors.[118] The main galley was split into two sections with Indian cooks preparing their own highly aromatic national dishes.[139]

Passing the Nicobar Islands the *Tacwina* was seen high and dry. In the evening the Drum and Fife Band of the Battalion played on the well deck for the ship's company. After moving south along Sumatra's east coast,[11] *Glenearn* passed through the swept channel and anchored off Belawan.[190] That night in the ward-room there was a farewell session with the Indian Army officers.

Next morning the troops were up and about early; the other ranks chattering like ten forests of monkeys,[11] and their

25.10.45

26.10.45

28.10.45

29.10.45

30.10.45

officers feeling a trifle delicate after the night before.[118] Three
LCTs came alongside and by lunch time they were all away.*
Glenearn sailed and set course for Madras.[190] Some forty
miles out a mine was sighted close on the port side;[11] Captain
Hutchison reduced speed, put about and sank it with a single-
barrelled Oerlikon[190] – *HMS Glenearn*'s first angry shot of
the Second Commission.[158]

31.10.45   They were a little past the Nicobar Islands heading for the
Bay of Bengal when a signal came through to proceed with all
speed to Singapore. This was assumed to be in connection
with the Indonesian trouble in Sumatra where a British
2.11.45   Brigadier had been murdered. On entering port the first sight
was that of the body of a woman floating swiftly downstream,
and the second that of the French battleship *Richelieu*.

Two days passed; so much for the hurry in getting there.
4.11.45   Shore leave was granted but being Sunday, only a few shops
were open and the prices prohibitive. The Raffles Hotel was
also closed; although frequented in the past by British officers,
it had been used by the Japs for a less seemly purpose. The
major buildings of Singapore were impressive examples of a
more eastern and artistic form of architecture than either
Hong Kong or Shanghai.[11]

5.11.45   Using the LCAs the embarkation of an Indian Artillery
Regiment commenced.[158] These troops came from different
tribes, and were not such a good crowd as the previous unit,
which had a long record as a regiment. But they were tough
eggs just the same; one fellow wished to confirm that they
were going to Soerabaya as he wanted to kill Japs – or Dutch,
he did not seem to care which. The trouble in Java was getting
out of hand with the Indonesians attacking an aerodrome and
taking sixty-two 'planes, guns and ammunition. *Glenearn*
sailed at 1800 and four hours later crossed the equator.

6.11.45   Next day was beautiful, with the sea like glass. *Glenroy*
7.11.45   passed. On arrival at Soerabaya the troops were taken off by
LCT; a total of 1,026 being disembarked.[191] The shore people
wanted to embark RAPWI, including women and children

---

* The Japanese ashore, although classified as "surrendered personnel" were not
completely disarmed until the second half of 1946, after having fought as allies of the
British against the Indonesian insurgents/nationalists.[R]

that day, but 24-hours were requested in which to clean up the ship.

When the ship sailed the following afternoon, it was with 8.11.45 478 women and children, also some men, most of them Dutch nationals who had been prisoners of war for a long time. They had some pretty bad stories to tell. Apparently the convoy of vehicles carrying them to Soerabaya had been attacked; nearly all the men had been killed and many of the women and children bore knife, bayonet or bullet wounds. Many of the children were orphaned and cared for communally by the surviving adults. Whole families had been lined up and shot; one woman had lost four of her five children and had no idea where they were. Few of the people spoke English and quite a number had beri-beri in varying degrees.

Among the passengers there was a petty thief with a liking for fountain pens and cigarette lighters. The Captain, the Commander and three other officers all lost articles before a little Indian boy was caught red-handed; he and his father 9.11.45 were put in the cells.

After crossing the Line for the tenth time in this commission,[11] *Glenearn* anchored at Singapore and seventeen 10.11.45 RAPWI were sent to hospital.[191] Next morning after going 11.11.45 alongside the remainder disembarked. At 1100 there was a two-minute silence for Armistice Day. A crowd from *Glenroy* came over for gins, and some of *Glenearn*'s people repaid the visit in the evening.

Eleven hours out of Singapore and bound for Madras 12.11.45 orders were received to go to Penang and drop stores for the 7th Minesweeping Flotilla.[11] After passing through two minefields and skirting a third in the dark, *Glenearn* anchored 13.11.45 off Penang and two minesweepers came alongside to collect their stores.

At anchor in Madras Roads Captain Hutchison went 16.11.45 ashore and Lieutenant Mayhew, RN, rejoined;[191] the latter had left to have an operation in the U.S. Hospital Ship *Repose*, and had been chasing *Glenearn* for weeks and covering 7,000 miles in the process. He arrived back only to find that the Commander had put all his kit ashore.[94]

21.11.45   After some delay the ship went alongside and embarked troops. They were a mixed crowd of Army, RAF, Salvation Army, adults of the Boy Scout Movement, public relations people and Red Cross, including six women; two of them nurses. These passengers were a quiet lot compared to the Indians. To add to the variety on board, the Marines had a small menagerie of animals: monkeys, parrots, canaries, cats – to say nothing of the cockroaches which were rapidly infesting the ship. The monkeys had coloured coats with "Royal Marines" embroidered on the fronts.[11]

25.11.45   On Sunday morning a horned mine was sighted, so the ship was put about and the mine exploded by gunfire.[191] Half an hour later while the hands were at prayers another,[11] hornless variety, was spotted and duly sunk.[191]

About one third of the officers of *Glenearn* were now due for release. Lieutenant Bell, RM, for one had been told by the Admiralty that he must be returned to the UK by 23rd February, 1946.[11] Captain Hutchison had received a signal to transfer to the *Orsonia*, a repair ship.[66] A Captain Conway, RN, was to take over, and *Glenearn* was to drop in at Singapore to change captains, and leave some more men due

26.11.45   for release.[191] At Singapore Captain Conway joined and Captain Hutchison made his farewell speech.[152]

During the preceding two years of very active service[66] this small and pugnacious man had impressed his character on everybody. He was a good navigator and a good shipmaster,[7] and did not know what it was to be afraid; all his officers would have gone anywhere to sea or into battle with him.[152] But on the other side of the coin, opinions varied from Mayhew's, "the finest Captain in the Royal Navy"[94] through Payne-James', "a very good little man"[106] to Waters', "bombastic, intolerant and egotistical." When he left there was hardly a cheer.[152]

CHAPTER 31

UNDER CONWAY'S COMMAND

Captain H. R. Conway, RN, was quite a different type of man from Captain Hutchison; much more friendly, although by no means sloppy.[152] He had been Flag Captain to the Admiral Commanding Force "W" in *HM Ships Largs* and *Bulolo* for the Burma campaign, and the subsequent Japanese surrender at Singapore.

On appointment to *Glenearn* he had been informed of the accidents and the lethal explosions which had taken place, and on taking over he had been given to understand that all tanked petrol had been removed from under the mess decks, except for a very small amount required for ready use. It therefore came as a surprise when Commander R. M. T. Peacock, RN, asked him to inspect the mess decks during a pronounced swell in the South China Sea; it was clear that there was still a large amount of petrol remaining in the tanks – and moving ominously, by the sounds coming from them. There and then work commenced on emptying the tanks completely, "casing" the petrol and storing the containers on the upper deck for discharging at Hong Kong.[29]

29.11.45

Meanwhile a letter from British Pacific Fleet had said that all Royal Marine personnel in *Glenearn* were to be sent to the United Kingdom forthwith. Those concerned were busy packing and clearing up their affairs. A Mess Meeting had been held to change office-holders, and all the Royal Marine officers had given up their various duties.

Hong Kong was bright, sunny and cold; reminiscent of Sydney. The Chinese in their sampans seemed smarter, cleaner and more cheerful than on the previous visits.[11] While the army prepared to disembark, Captain Conway went to *HMS Montclare*.[191] Now that *Glenearn* had rejoined the BPF there were, it seems, two possible moves for the ship. The first: Shanghai, then home, was considered very unlikely. The other was Shanghai, Colombo, Madras, Singapore, Tokyo then

30.11.45

Sydney and home. What was certain was that the Royals would move out on the 5th December and be accommodated in *m.v. Aorangi*;[11] a ship of one of the New Zealand lines.[152]

2.12.45   Lieutenant-Commander (E) Chisholm left, and next day
3.12.45   Captain Conway went off in the motor cutter across the harbour. It broke down, and when he arrived back after two and three-quarter hours[192] he sent for the ship's "boat" officer, who found him a not very friendly Captain then.[152]

Twenty-nine RN Patrol Service ratings who had been operating LCAs for Hong Kong's Naval Dockyard since 20th
4.12.45   September rejoined and,[192] after a terrific party in the ward-room[11] – during which an old piano was buried with full
5.12.45   naval honours[86] – 493 Flotilla's Royal Marines departed; as did a draft of eleven ratings.[192]

6.12.45   A notice in the South China Morning Post listed over twenty adults and children to be repatriated to Singapore and India via Shanghai, and leaving in *Glenearn* "on or about 10th December."[413] The day before this sailing date Lieutenant
9.12.45   Bell, RM, came back aboard for lunch. With Rex Bateman's release coming through, "Dinger" would be taking over the Flotilla which had been warned that they might have to go ashore to work with the RM Commando Brigade. In the evening a few officers went to *Aorangi*.[11] Surgeon-Lieutenant Dickson had joined ship,[192] releasing the PMO Surg.-Lieut.-Commander Morrison for passage home.[106]

10.12.45   The 10th of December dawned, and a number of passengers[192] – some less eager than others[29] – assembled at Kowloon Godown Wharves No. 1 Pier.[414] First to be embarked were about thirty Indians;*[192] renegades who had collaborated with the Japanese as part of Subhas Chandra Bose's Indian National Army, and had spent the latter part of the war in Japan. Captain Conway's orders were to return them to India, but they had their own views about that; one of them evaded the guards and jumped into the harbour. He was fished out of the water by a sampan-man and placed under arrest.[29]

At 1500 *Glenearn* cleared the wharf, hoisted her boats and

* Referred to in the ship's log as "students".

set course for Shanghai;[192] her first sailing for over two years without Royal Marines on board.[A] In that period there had been many happy times, and some at least of the individuals left behind would gladly have gone on with her.[152] Two hours out the ship exercised "Fire and Collision in No. 1 Mess Deck".

After sailing through the Formosa Channel, Shanghai was reached on the 14th December.[192] As they came alongside Hongkew Wharf they were given a tremendous welcome, for news had preceded them that the ship was carrying a large consignment of Christmas and New Year refreshment for the Shanghai Club. Captain Conway was convinced that if it had been possible, he would have been made a Freeman of the City.

14.12.45

However, the main purpose of the visit was to uplift a number of Sikh policemen and their Chinese wives and take them to India; also some loyal Sikhs who had been imprisoned in Japan. On embarkation it was given to understand that the latter half-dozen were estimable and somewhat elderly gentlemen with the desire only to be returned to the bosoms of their families. Because of the shortage of passenger accommodation the military officers' cabins immediately forward of the Captain's day cabin were used to house the senior Sikh policemen and their wives.[29]

15.12.45

After two days in Shanghai, *Glenearn* slipped from the wharf, then dropped anchor in Garden Reach to swing to the flood tide before going on.[192] It was clear from the moment of leaving that the cabin class policemen had no wish to import their Chinese consorts into India. Whether this was because of "caste" with all its ramifications or some other reason, the wretched ladies were subject to the most fearful beatings by their husbands at all hours of the day and night. It was as if the men were determined that their wives should be in no two minds about returning to China by the first available means; the resulting bedlam was a menace to the sanity of Captain Conway in his nearby quarters.

16.12.45

It had transpired that the Formosan Channel was still extensively mined, so on this return passage *Glenearn* had been re-routed outside the island. Most forenoons and afternoons the venerable Sikh gentlemen – untroubled by marital problems – reclined in deck-chairs on the promenade deck enjoying the warm sunshine. All the more astonishment, for the Captain, therefore, when the Commander arrived in haste to report that one of the old men had seized a fire-axe, crept up behind one of his unsuspecting compatriots recumbent on a deck-chair, and dealt him a fearful blow with the weapon. It turned out that the would-be murderer had – quite unjustly – borne some grudge against his victim from the days of their incarceration in Japan. And in the event, he had hit the wrong man; fortunately the latter's turban had saved his life. His attacker was led away.

One evening *Glenearn*'s harassed Captain was sitting at dinner in the "cuddy" when there was a knock on the door and Commander Peacock asked if he could have a word with him. Two passengers, a Pole and his Macaoese wife, had approached the Chief Bosun's Mate and intimated that they had something of the utmost importance to ask the Captain. They had refused to say what the question was; nor, when taken to the Commander had they been prepared to tell him either. They had assured him, however, that it had to be answered immediately and had requested – because of the vital nature of their business – to be taken to the Captain without delay. Solely because of the obvious gravity of their request the Commander had come to report at this incon-venient hour; the couple were outside at that very moment, under the protective presence of the Chief Bosun's Mate.

The steward hurriedly cleared the table; the Captain took up a good tactical position at his desk, and the Chief Buffer was instructed to usher in the two passengers. A most presentable couple entered and came over to the desk where the Commander, reading from a slip of paper, introduced them as Mr. and Mrs. Demussa Emanhsilop.* Commander Peacock then explained that they had asked to be seen on a matter that was clearly as secret as it was urgent. Thinking it best to get to the heart of the matter, without beating about the bush Captain Conway asked, "How can I help you?" At

18.12.45

---

* Assumed Polish name.

that the wife burst into tears, whereupon the husband, striking an attitude that could have encompassed the liberation of Poland, cried in broken English, "Where can we hang our baby's nappies?"

Dead silence for several seconds. Then Captain to the aggrieved parents, "This will be arranged. Good evening," and nodded to the Chief Bosun's Mate to take them out. The Commander began to apologise, but was cut short, "Not a bit of it. No doubt you will see that the Mate of the Upper Deck takes the necessary action, so that honour will be satisfied. No doubt too, you would like a little sustenance to ease the pain of this exacting world . . ." so saying, the Captain pointed towards the decanter.[29]

About four in the morning[106] Lieutenant Mayhew was on duty when he was approached by one of the junior officers who said that the "Jaunty"* had found trouble on the mess deck aft. There, surrounded by a crowd of other passengers,[94] they found Sukhdev Kaur, pregnant wife of Sohan Singh.[192] Mayew sent for the Medical Officer.[94]

Payne-James was wakened by a Petty Officer, "Sir, there's a Chinese woman in labour." He said, "Well, there's an Indian doctor on board, you'd better get him." So the Petty Officer banged on the cabin door of the Indian doctor taking passage, only to be told, "I am very sorry, but I do not do midwifery." Back to Dr. Payne-James. "You'll have to do it." It was obvious the woman was very early in labour. They got her up to the Sick Bay, examined her, and Payne-James said, "Oh well, as far as I can ascertain it will be quite some time before she has her baby."

After breakfast the Captain called the Surgeon-Lieutenant to the bridge and said, "I understand there's a woman in labour in the ship, Doctor." Payne-James, "Yes, Sir. There's nothing to worry about; plenty of time, plenty of time." At that moment a white-faced Petty Officer Rostron rushed up to him. "Sir! Sir! Something's happening." When they got there, the girl had just had the baby; as easy as anything.[106] Just like that, at 0840.†[192]

20.12.45

* Master at Arms.   † Lat. 16° 42′ N, Long. 116° 08′ E.

Where could they put the mother and child? It was suggested that the best cabin was the one next door to the Doctor's; one previously occupied by Padre Janes. Both Medical Officers were full of glee over the event,[94] and had their legs pulled for at last using the maternity bed in the Sick Bay for its designed purpose.[36] Three days later a floating

23.12.45

mine was sighted; Glenearn reduced speed and turned, to blow it up by gunfire.[192] Payne-James went down to the cabin and tried to convey to the mother that there was going to be, "Big bang, big bang!" Just then the mine was hit and went off. The Medical Officer got a terrible fright, or so he claimed, but the girl just sat there without turning a hair.[106]

Later the same day Glenearn anchored in Singapore Roads. Some of the passengers disembarked and a few ratings joined,

24.12.45

before the ship sailed for Madras.[192] Throughout the voyage all sorts of religious occasions had been celebrated above the well deck; some of these functions going on all night.[139] The wife-beatings had gone on too, and the renegades had proved to be difficult customers – attacks on the guards had become so prevalent that it had become necessary to handcuff the prisoners together during their periods of exercise on the upper deck.

29.12.45

On arrival in Madras Harbour HMS Glenearn was greeted with a fanfare of sirens from all the ships there; ships which were dressed over-all as for an occasion. There was a large welcoming party of distinguished Indians on the jetty, apparently under the impression that the prisoners were war heroes captured in Burma by the Japanese. The dismay on the faces when some twenty-eight wretches, handcuffed in pairs, shuffled down the gangway was understandable, but worth watching.

Down the gangway too, strode the Sikh arms of the law, followed by each suitably chastened wife; to what future one could only surmise.[29] And of course the little stowaway, Glenda Kaur, was carried ashore. All Sikh boys are called Singh and the girls Kaur; this baby had been named Glenda after the ship in which she had been born.[106]

CHAPTER 32

CHAPTER 32

ONCE A GOOD SHIP ...

At Madras, fuelling had started even before the passengers had commenced disembarking. After they had all gone, ship's stores were landed alongside the North Quay and electrical stores for Trincomalee taken on. At No. 11 Berth Trincomalee stores arrived for Naval Party 2504, and the afternoon was spent embarking wireless equipment ex-*Lothian*. Then *Glenearn* sailed for Colombo. There, secured to buoys bow and stern, stores were received for both the ship and NP 2504.[192]

Naval Party 2504 was forming at Colombo to carry out the occupation of the Japanese naval base at Kure, which was to be the main supply port of the British Commonwealth Occupation Force (BCOF). Since there would be nowhere to live until they had built their own accommodation ashore, the plan was for NP 2504 to use *Glenearn* as their headquarters ship. First priority was to get the port of Kure working again; the main piece of planning information produced was "complete devastation and semi-Arctic conditions". In recognition of the great pressure to release *Glenearn* for return to her normal trading function, the intention was to take, in other ships, material for building both a Nissen-hutted camp and a barracks, so that the Naval Party could leap-frog from the ship to the hutted camp, and thence to a proper barracks built using Japanese labour.[57]

During the first few days of the New Year *HMS Glenearn* paid off and recommissioned[107] with a new and mainly volunteer ship's company.[56] All the executive officers except Mr. Wheeler the Gunner and the Navigator left the ship,[158] to await passages home as opportunity afforded. Surgeon-Lieutenant Payne-James and Paymaster MacLean stayed on,[106] as did nearly all the Merchant Navy officers and stokers;[57] also Sub-Lieutenant (E) Steel, RNVR.[132] Volunteering for further service in the Far East when everyone was thinking of demobilisation required a certain type of dedication, although others not having been abroad very long, were drafted. Obviously no one who was entitled to go home within a month or two was going to be sent out to Japan at a time when passages home were at a premium, but some hoped to get the best of both worlds and accepted the risk of having their demobilisation delayed.

2.1.46   Commander J. Hamilton, RN, joined, having been appointed Commander of *Glenearn*, and Executive Officer of Naval Party 2504, after handing over Pulo Weh with its port of Sabang to the Dutch authorities.[57] Captain J. A. Grindle, CBE, RN, flew in from Malaya where he had been NOIC Port

3.1.46   Swettenham, and came aboard next day.[56] Captain Conway turned over the ship to Captain Grindle, with whom he had worked quite recently in the reopening and operating of Malayan ports, and left for home.[29] Staff Officer to the new Captain was Lieutenant-Commander R. F. G. Elseworth, DSC, RN, who had volunteered to join this party as his job as Staff Torpedo Officer to the Commodore Destroyers Eastern Fleet had become unnecessary with the ending of the war; while not particularly anxious to return to the UK, he was keen to visit Japan.[42]

A tremendous amount of work had to be done to get the ship ready for service very different from her wartime function of Landing Ship, Infantry. There were personnel to be released, new men to join, the Port Party to embark and a great quantity of stores and special equipment to load and stow. After her years of war service *Glenearn* was in a terrible state both above and below decks, and the mess decks – possibly suitable for temporarily-embarked troops – had to be made smart and habitable as a home for several months. In the aftermath of war, with everyone's thoughts on home, there had been an inevitable relaxation of standards; Captain Grindle and his Commander realised it was essential to run a taut ship and re-establish proper naval discipline and smartness. So they "got cracking".[57] To glorified-civilian Payne-James it was like sailing with Captain Bligh of the

Bounty.[106] However, the prospect of going to Japan was a stimulating one, and all hands worked very hard.

At first there were four virtually "private navies" on board: the sailors who worked the ship, the RN Patrol Service who manned the boats, the small Royal Marine detachment, and the T 124X engineers. Each appeared to run an independent existence. With the exception of the engineers, who had their statutory position, Commander Hamilton made the whole lot subject to the ship's routine, administered in the normal way, by himself.

With the Port Party embarked, they were ready to sail on the 9th January.[57] It was a mixed force or squadron, of Royal and Royal Indian Navy vessels including a flotilla of eight minesweepers, a minesweeper depot ship, an oil and water tanker and a store ship; the latter carrying the prefabricated materials and the plant – including a steam road-roller – for building a naval depot and signal station in the completely destroyed Japanese naval base.[56] A ten-day passage to Hong Kong would be the ideal opportunity to shake everybody down and then get the ship worked up to a degree of seamanlike competence.[57] It was a very young ship's company; mostly wartime entry, with less than half-a-dozen regular RN officers and not many long-service Petty Officers.[56] However, Commander Hamilton was well served by Master-at-Arms Dermondy and Chief Bosun's Mate CPO Kettle,[57] and relations between naval personnel and engine room staff were excellent.[42]

9.1.46

Soon after leaving Colombo, Hamilton was doing Commander's mess deck rounds and came to a door in one of the big flats on the main deck. He tried it, but it was locked. "What's in here?" he asked. "That's not usually on the rounds route," he was told. "Well it is now, get it opened." "Don't know who keeps the key," said the rating standing the rounds in the flat. "Well, I'm standing here, and so are all of you, until the key is found and this door is opened." A sheepish look on the face of the sailor, who produced the key from his pocket and opened up. Inside was the "caboosh" to end all cabooshes: in effect a beautifully fitted cabin, with an officer's bunk, bedding, chair, desk, carpet, table lamp, masses of green baize and bunting.[57]

14.1.46 After a brief call at Singapore,[160] Hong Kong was reached
19.1.46 on the 19th. There they started painting the ship overall and
24.1.46 embarking more stores.[57] Lieutenant Bell, RM, came aboard for lunch, but with only a few of the old crowd left it was not the same. He found the new boys quite pleasant, however, and had some of them up at Murray Barracks for a drink. 493 Flotilla's marines were patrolling the streets of the city to protect the Hong Kong Police, a few of whom had been shot at whilst searching armed criminals.

Lieutenant Bell had been told by Admiral Lord Fraser that Captain Hutchison had been awarded the OBE[11] for his courage and leadership of the rescue work on 31st August, 1945;*[372] he was also informed during his visit that *Glenearn* had been offered the Philippine Liberation Medal by the Americans, but the Admiralty had turned it down. Only three British ships would have qualified for this award, which was supposed to have carried a bonus of two hundred dollars.[11]

26.1.46 A rejuvenated *Glenearn* was inspected by the Commander-in-Chief BPF and the Australian Lieutenant-General Northcott, Commander-in-Chief BCOF Japan.[56] On being piped aboard they were met by Captain Grindle backed by a Marine guard of honour. During his course of inspection Lord Fraser spoke to several individuals, then in a short address to the ship's company he told them they were going to Japan to carry out an important task; part of the allied plans for keeping peace in the world.[415] It was a great occasion after
27.1.46 a week of unremitting work. Next day the Force sailed for Japan.[57]

Bad weather affected progress, and more time was lost when *Glenearn* made a search for survivors from an American aeroplane which had fallen into the sea. Nothing was found, and it was believed that the twenty passengers were picked up
30.1.46 by other ships.[461] A message was despatched to *HMAS*

---

* Stoker O'Toole and Able Seaman Kenny were to get the British Empire Medal.[372]

Hobart reporting a 24-hour delay in landing the occupation forces; the cruiser sent the Australian destroyer *Warramungo* to meet them, and shortly before midnight *Glenearn* anchored at the southern end of the searched channel.[274] General MacArthur had broadcast a welcome, "The presence of British Commonwealth troops materially broadens the base along international lines of the burden which up to this time has, of necessity, been carried to a large extent unilaterally by United States forces."[461]

31.1.46

The tricky passage through the Inland Sea was a memorable experience.[57] Escorted by *Warramungo*, *Glenearn* led the flotilla;[274] it was bitterly cold and blowing half a gale off the snow-covered mountains. After the fascination of winding through narrow channels between the islands, as they approached Kure itself there were on each side the wrecks of Japanese warships, battleships and an aircraft carrier lying on their sides. The great dockyard and arsenal was a scene of indescribable destruction; a tangle of twisted metal, crumpled buildings and rubble. Huge machine shops totally wrecked, a big graving dock filled with midget submarines looking for all the world as though some giant's hand had picked them up and tossed them into it. The town itself was flat. "Complete devastation" had been a good planning assumption. It was all a remarkable tribute to the effectiveness of American seaborne air power.[57]

1.2.46

Only a handful of British and American officers were present on the dockside when *Glenearn* berthed. That afternoon 300 bluejackets and marines comprising the advance party landed; the job of the Port Party was to clear the harbour and sweep the approaches. Having done that they were to establish an operational base for ships of both the Royal and United States Navies. *Glenearn* was to serve as Headquarters Ship for the Port Directorate, also as a wireless signal station and responsible for local operations and movements.[56]

Naval Party 2504 took over from the small American Port Directorate who, understandably, had done little to rehabilitate the facilities since their arrival the previous September.

Because the area had been completely devastated by the bombing – there was no fuel, little water and electricity, a dispersed labour force and a harbour littered with wreckage and rubbish – there was a great deal to be done before the port was ready to accept the ships bringing the main body of the Occupation Force.[42]

The port of Kure was formally under U.S. Control, Captain Grindle being the Port Director, responsible to Admiral Griffin, USN, Commander Naval Forces Japan, who was based on Tokyo and therefore under General MacArthur. At the same time Glenearn's Commanding Officer was the Senior British Naval Officer of the British Commonwealth Occupation Force and the Senior Naval Officer in the British-Indian element of that Force. As he also had a responsibility to, and a direct link with, the Commander-in-Chief of the British Pacific Fleet based on Hong Kong, Captain Grindle's loyalties were nicely balanced; a situation not without advantages at times.[56]

Surgeon-Lieutenant Payne-James in his additional capacity as Port Medical Officer received a signal saying that there was a freighter coming up from Hainan with returning Japanese and it was believed that there was smallpox on board. When it arrived it had about 4,000 people in it, in the holds and so forth, and they nearly all had smallpox. Payne-James had never seen anything like it. Five or six hundred dead bodies were just lying about; others had been slung over the side. The Japanese had no penicillin nor drugs of any sort, but they did have a big smallpox hospital in Kure.[106]

Thirteen miles away from Kure was another devastated. city: Hiroshima. The atomic bomb had destroyed more than four square miles of it and killed eighty thousand people. Everything wooden had been burnt to the ground leaving only a few tall chimneys standing and the skeleton of the occasional concrete-framed building. The place was full of objects of macabre interest to visitors, such as the asphalt roads which had retained the "shadows" of those who had been walking on them at the instant of explosion. Surfaces of polished granite had been roughened by the heat of the fire

KURE

30. At the quayside.

31. Beating retreat. 1st Bn. Queen's Own Cameron Highlanders.

ball except where someone had evidently been sitting on the stone...[609]

Glenearn, secured alongside at Kure and looking spick and span, was a fine sight. Within, a haven of orderliness, comfort and warmth.[57] Looked upon by some as simply a hotel providing a cabin and a ward-room Mess; but much appreciated in the bitter weather of the Japanese winter, nevertheless.[42] She was however also the centre of a ceaseless round of every imaginable activity; a kind of universal aunt, her workshop and her men, her boats and her landing craft, fulfilling all the tasks necessary to get the shore base going and providing the services needed by visiting British, American and Australian warships and supply vessels.[57]

Towards the end of February, *HMS Glengyle* arrived with about nine hundred British Army and Royal Australian Air Force personnel.[610] The British Commonwealth Occupation Force was the first attempt at unified Commonwealth command; the Royal Navy had the job of running the naval side of the base, but the army was made up of Australian, British, Indian and New Zealand troops, while the British Brigade consisted of the 2nd Dorsetshire Regiment, the 2nd Royal Welch Fusiliers and the 1st Bn. the Queen's Own Cameron Highlanders.[57] By the time *Glengyle* returned with more RAAF men, the amenities at Kure included a concert party, a cafeteria and a brewery – all contained within the converted Blue Funnel ship *Menestheus*.[610]

1.4.46

Glenearn came to be greatly appreciated by the soldiers, who seemed to wallow in discomfort and have little ability to spruce up their quarters. There was great football rivalry, *Glenearn* and the Camerons striking up a particularly close comradeship. On more than one occasion the band of the Highlanders played for the entertainment of the Navy.

There were many visits by senior officers.[57] General Northcott inspected the Naval Party and took the salute at the march past on Australia Day.[56] Lord Fraser came again to see how they were getting on; Admiral Sherman, Commanding the U.S. 5th Fleet paid a visit. And many others. Captain Grindle, as Naval Officer in Charge, was immensely

25.4.46

busy, and Commander Hamilton made sure everybody else was too. Warships of many nations came and went; all were accommodated.[57]

Glenearn's ship's company was steadily being reduced in numbers as discharge groups came up.[141] Dr. Payne-James left in an LCT for Hong Kong,[106] and several ratings were transferred to the cruiser *Cumberland* for their voyage home. Some of these chaps had served in *Glenearn* from start to finish and were very upset; it was so different from what they had thought it would be like. It was a great emotional upsurge;[139] a case of the pride one felt in a ship not being fully realised until the moment came to leave it.[610] The time had gone so quickly, never again to be recaptured.[139]

Glenearn was taken to sea for steaming trials.[57] Berthing gave her Captain – used to steam propulsion – some anxious moments as he waited for his engines to go into reverse. After a couple of false starts, the end of the dock looked very close under the bows.[56]

14.5.46

By the end of May the hutted camp was nearly completed and the administrative officers for running the base were fully established ashore with their own communication facilities.[57] To commemorate the Glorious First of June the pipes and drums of the Camerons beat retreat alongside,[56] to the huge delight of the sailors. Two days later the Port Party disembarked and commissioned the newly-built base as *HMS Commonwealth*, an old and in this case appropriate naval name which had come to Commander Hamilton in his bath. He and Captain Grindle transferred ashore with the Port Party.[57] *HMS Glenearn* had not played a very spectacular part in the postwar Far East, but she had proved to be an adequate depot and headquarters ship, and had enabled the Port Party to move ashore as a "ship's company", which meant a great deal.[56] They had all grown very fond and very proud of a fine ship.[57]

1.6.46

3.6.46

Numbers in *Glenearn* were reduced to a Steaming Party consisting mainly of officers and men of the engine room and catering staffs on T 124X engagements, supplemented by naval officers and men due for demobilisation.[56] Captain

J. W. Grant, DSO, RN, joined and took command. Royal Marine Commandos and other passengers for the UK were embarked,[158] then, trailing her immensely long ribbon-like paying-off pennant from the after masthead, at 0600 *HMS Glenearn* sailed for home.[56]

5.6.46

9.6.46

Hong Kong was rapidly becoming a clean neat-looking town, with renovations being made everywhere.[11] Stoker Maclennan put his suit ashore for cleaning, but when the ship sailed sooner than expected, he had to leave it there.

11.6.46

Apart from having to explode a floating mine,[87] there was a peacetime atmosphere about the trip. Smooth sailing. Slow merchantmen passing on silky seas under the hot lazy sun,, then flashing . . . *BON VOYAGE* . . . before disappearing below the horizon astern.[11] It was an uneventful voyage by way of Singapore and Colombo[158] – Colombo with its smells and its sunsets – and Aden. Aden – a beautiful bay surrounded by hills like slag heaps; Suez and almost the last chance to see the Pole Star and the Southern Cross in the same night sky. Port Said, then on past Pantellaria;[11] *Glenearn* ploughing her course without fuss . . . as always, in fine weather and foul, good times and bad . . .[94] the sickening thud as the ship dropped onto the sea after rising high on the wave . . . the drenching cold after one had broken over the fo'c'sle, pouring itself through the ship before plunging over the stern . . . the danger from falling spars . . . pitiful attempts to secure deck cargo while clinging on with both hands . . .[11]

Glenearn was a fine ship, unlucky with her deaths, injuries and not being allowed to make her number in the Pacific.[94] But she had played her part. Looking back on these war years there had been something great about them;[87] like in the Mediterranean in 1941 – *Glenearn* trying to keep a low profile, but once the Italian bombers appeared, putting up every White Ensign to really show them who was British.[106]

Sometimes one is inclined to credit a mechanical artefact such as a ship with a life and will of its own, quite distinct from the corporate humanity without which that life and will could never be expressed – if it exists. A moot point to be sure,[A] but it has been observed that if a ship's initial trials –

using the word in its widest sense – are very successful she starts "life" on a high note, and often lives up to it. What does seem undeniable is that a ship retains the features of the first ship's company, so it must be a case of "Once a good ship, always a good ship."[29]

This particular specimen is rolling badly now, but the air is sweet and clean; so much better than the humid suffocating heat of the tropics. One more day. Feel terribly excited. England tomorrow ... it seems such a long time ...[11]

MEMORIAL

CHANCE ENCOUNTER

"Ahem, I say, but isn't it . . . ?
Thought so! You haven't changed a bit.
Me? Oh, tum too large, funds too small
Civvy street complaints, that's all;
It's the stress that goes for one, you know
Knotting the gut, clenching the jaw . . ."

Beyond the pane a trim vessel hoves
Stirs the silt of youth-left loves.
She's well-armed: torpedo breast,
Armour: denim, knicker-stressed
Across that starboard quarter wild –
Could be the elder daughter's child.

". . . Cheers, old man, down the hatch!
Must be off . . . train to catch.
Yes, nice to meet you . . . Yes, very soon
A gin or two some afternoon."
Strange meeting that . . . has done you good
Raking old bones in nostalgic mood.

'Been the same had we survived
Dry-eyed the tale to tell contrived
How old Smith – or was it Brown?
Died of wounds – or did he drown?
You're getting old, lest you forget
But we are dead, and yet . . . not yet . . .

Stanley Thomas Fox, Royal Marines   6.6.44
Geoffrey Alan Precious, Royal Marines   6.6.44
Dunstan Austin Pearson, Royal Navy   9.4.45
Lawrence Milner Jackson, Royal Navy   9.4.45

360

Frederick Heywood, Royal Navy — 10.4.45
Thomas M. Roy, Royal Navy — 10.4.45
Alexander Aiken, Royal Naval Reserve — 10.4.45
Donald Frederick Schorfield, Royal Navy — 11.4.45
Norman Leonard Trickett, Royal Marines — 11.4.45
Albert W. Barnard, Royal Navy — 11.4.45
Leslie D. Rowe, Royal Navy — 11.4.45
Henry E. Jones, Royal Naval Reserve — 11.4.45
Austin Phillips, Royal Navy — 15.4.45
Richard E. Hardman-Jones, Royal Navy — 15.4.45
James McIlhargey, RN Patrol Service — 16.4.45
Cyril E. W. Arnold, Royal Navy — 18.4.45
Kenneth Gowing, RN Patrol Service — 3.9.45

EPILOGUE

CHAPTER 33

BORDERLINE SECOND SIGHT

The Devonport-manned *Glenearn* arrived at Plymouth in the early afternoon, and tied up at Millbay Docks. There the passengers were put ashore; also 130 Royal Marines and 22 ratings due for "demob". About one hundred of the ship's company were expecting to be met by relatives and friends given to believe that the ship would be remaining at Plymouth for some time. Great had been the dismay on board when it had been learned that *Glenearn* was bound for the Clyde, stopping only long enough to disembark men due for release through the depot, and that no shore leave would be granted.[468] However, once the problem had been appreciated,[469] a signal to the Commander-in-Chief, Plymouth Command,* and permission was received to stay for 24 hours.[468]

9.7.46

Before leaving, the Captain sent a message of welcome to the incoming *Duke of York*, a ship that had been abroad for only fifteen months, and mainly flag-waving at that. *Glenearn*'s C.O. for his part was displeased when on the way to the Clyde the radar packed up; he gave PO Radar Mechanic Thompson a right "telling-off".[141]

10.7.46

At Greenock the circumnavigation of the globe foreseen by Captain Hutchison was at last completed;[11] a round trip – if all the adventures since leaving Woolwich were included – of 94,454 miles.[158] Ammunition and gunnery stores were disembarked, and a cargo of Australian jam – picked up in Hong Kong from the aircraft-carrier *Indefatigable* and a gift from the people of Australia – was unloaded. Most of the already much-reduced company were then paid off,[160] and at Plantation Quay, Glasgow, the remainder went on foreign leave; other formalities were lost in the general concern to get home and be free men again.[87] Only a steaming party was left

12.7.46

---

* Admiral Sir Henry Pridham-Wippell (Vice-Admiral Light Forces, Mediterranean 1941).

to get on with de-storing.[160] A lot of gear was put ashore,[87] and all the guns were dismounted.[524]

1.8.46 Lieutenant-Commander Philpott, RNR, the navigator, became *HMS Glenearn's* next and last Commanding Officer.[111] On arrival at North Shields on the Tyne more men were paid off,[141] and only a small party based ashore under PO Fee was left to remove the remaining navigational equipment.[160] Finally the T 124X Engineers went their various ways, Willie Ramsay taking with him the big battle-ensign borne to France on D-Day,[113] and the ship handed 8.8.46 over for reconversion by Smith's Dock Company.[290]

The ship had been delivered to her refitting port in first-class condition, her' cleanliness between decks and her state generally being the subject of many favourable comments;[56] all this was soon changed once the dockyard men got to work ripping off temporary bulkheads and store decks in the holds. There were redundant deck erections to suppress, while the naval personnel cabins and crew spaces had all to be stripped and fitted out for passengers and peacetime ship's officers.[524]

Although the Liner Requisition Scheme had ended on 2nd March, *Glenearn's* return from naval operations had been achieved only after prolonged argument;[291] now she was all but submerged by a deluge of Ministry of War Transport inspectors. From their discussions with Holt's men the contractors assembled work lists for all departments, and there were frequent progress meetings which were chaired by the Principal Officer, M.O.W.T. *Glenearn* was Smith's Dock Company's first reconversion to peacetime trade.

Mr. Dickie, Chief Superintendent for Alfred Holt's, was a character of the times; Mr. Souchotte was Engineer Superintendent in Chief and Arthur Howard local Engineer Superintendent. Shipwright in charge of the refit was Mr. Bob Kay; a very knowledgeable person with tremendous energy and also extremely conscientious. The aim was to put *Glenearn* back to the original layout, with everything as near to new condition as possible; this included even slightly scrubbed rivet tails and plate edges. One hold and 'tween decks were reinsulated, and all new cargo gear – derricks, samson posts and electric winches – supplied and fitted. Tabernacles and deck houses containing the contactor equipment for the winches were rebuilt. Electrically the ship was almost completely restored to the original drawings, as was the plumbing. Electrical sub-contractors were the firm of Sunderland Forge; their manager was Mr. Penny, and the foreman electrician a Mr. MacDonald who had been foreman in charge of electrics when the vessel had been building in Caledon Yard.

Glenearn's funnel was raised to its original height. Wood decking, which was under licence and impossible to acquire for any other refits was produced by Holt's – teak of all things[149] – for the $5'' \times 2\frac{1}{2}''$ sheathing.[619] Teak, which often outlasted the steel structure,[541] when others had to make do with deck "compo" or jarrah.[149]

New refrigerating machinery was fitted and the whole of the main engines overhauled and repaired.[524] Worn liners were renewed, pistons cleaned and new rings fitted, bearings re-metalled as necessary and adjusted; the fuel ignition equipment was serviced by Wilson & Kyle of Brentford.[149] Experience had proved the 2-stroke auxiliary engines unreliable, and the consumption of lubricating oil much too high;[538] as part of this refit therefore, the after Burmeister and Wain engines were replaced by two 4-stroke units[70] of 330 BHP each, manufactured by W. H. Allen, Sons & Co. Ltd., and driving 220 kilowatt generators made by the same company.[297] To effect these engine replacements the crankcase gear in the Nos. 4, 5 and 6 units of each main engine was removed, the auxiliary engine shipped in pieces between the main engines and then out-board through them.[70]

Glenearn lay alongside what was known as the fitting shop quay, served by a static 50-ton crane and a travelling one of 25 tons; it was the only quay with the necessary depth of water at low tide: 25 feet.[149] On 25th October the ship was drydocked in No. 4 Dock;[289] so neatly that the Production Manager could touch both the stern and the dock gate by inserting the four fingers of his right hand into the space between. In accordance with Alfred Holt practice the anchors were lowered to the dock bottom as soon as the water had been

25.10.46

pumped out. Tail-shafts and the rudder were put back to as-new condition, all the propeller blades were removed and the blade pitch reset using the shaped gun metal stopper-pieces in the elongated flange holes.[149] Part of *Glenearn's* bottom was coated with "bitumastic" composition.[297]

About three hundred men were employed in the refitting. The joinery work was enormous, and the foreman joiner visited Liverpool on several occasions to discuss room mock-ups, the modern furnishing of the Master's cabin, and veneers. This was the first time the firm's joiners had come across the bonding of veneer to prepared structures; the staircase to the main rooms became something of a showpiece.[149] The plaque commemorating *HMS Glenearn's* wartime service was mounted on the forward bulkhead of the cross alleyway at the passengers' bar – known as "The Pig and Whistle" according to the sign.[70]

As the year 1947 drew on towards Autumn the small nucleus of ship's officers standing by – Mr. Coslett, Chief Officer, Mr. Owen, 2nd Officer, Mr. Stephenson, Chief Engineer, and a few others – were joined by Albert Brown, Acting Radio Officer. He had been a prisoner of war after the sinking of *Glenorchy* in 1942, and now joined *Glenearn* for Purser's duties as the paperwork was becoming time-consuming. More officers arrived as the refit neared completion and finally the rest of the crew, before they all moved on board. Apart from the officers, the Chief and 2nd Stewards, a carpenter, Mr. McGowan, a Chief Cook and a Linen Keeper, the remainder were Chinese. Captain J. A. Russell was Master.[19]

11.11.47   *Glenearn* entered drydock again on 11th November to be surveyed, which took until the 16th.[289] Her trials were memorable; she was balloon-light, and in some very nasty weather pitched and rolled frightfully.[19] Only a handful of the trials party, which included various company and dockyard officials, were not seasick; but she performed well and there were only minor jobs to readjust afterwards.[149] *Glenearn* was

6.12.47   discharged from His Majesty's Service at 1800 on 6th December 1947, and sailed next day.[289] She looked very regal and impressive with her red and black funnel;[149] the refit had been an outstanding job for Smith's Dock Company,[524] and the biggest so far in the career of their fairly junior production manager, who was correspondingly proud to have taken part. The price of the conversion was said to have been seven hundred and fifty thousand pounds[149] – considerably more than her first cost – but to have replaced a ship of *Glenearn*'s class would have resulted in a bill of well over a million pounds.[291]

At No. 3 Berth King George V Dock, Glasgow, *m.v.* *Glenearn* commenced loading for Australia.[19] Just returned from there at No. 2 Berth lay *s.s. Eurymedon*[362] a smaller American-built "Liberty" ship, thus setting the scene for a strange little echo of the quite-recent past. Chief Engineer of the Blue Funnel* boat was Jim Cahy, all set apparently to spend Christmas aboard, alone. His wife contacted the widow† of his late colleague and asked her to invite Mr. Cahy to the Aiken home. The 18-year-old son was sent to deliver the invitation, and from the dockside saw *Glenearn* towering over both himself and *Eurymedon*, looking very different from the last time he had seen her, early in the war.[2] Mr. Cahy received him politely, but never turned up. $\qquad$ 11.12.47

Voyage 13‡ began from Liverpool at 5.36 a.m. on 6th January 1948, presumably on charter to Ocean Steamship Company. Fremantle was reached by way of Suez and Aden, subsequently calling at Adelaide, Melbourne and Sydney.[290] At one of these she was recognised by Commander G. I. Finkel, RN (retd.), but with no opportunity to go aboard.[46] On return Hull was the last port of call before the voyage ended at London's King George V Dock. $\qquad$ 6.1.48 / 22.5.48

The second post-war trip took *Glenearn* to the Far East ports of Shanghai and Kobe, and on the return passage to

---

* The writer is convinced that on this occasion *Glenearn* had a blue funnel too.

† Thanks to the efforts of the British Legion, Mrs. Aiken was now in receipt of a naval pension; however the Widows', Orphans' and Old Age Pension, to which voluntary contributions had been made since January 1938, had been disallowed because "no one can receive two pensions from the government". The contributions were of course not returnable. Cf. the story of the man who raffled the dead horse; even he gave the winner his money back.

‡ Voyages 6–12 appear to correspond to the years 1941–47 respectively.

Tangier and Rotterdam. Voyage 15 missed out China but took in Macassar in Celebes and went all round the Dutch East Indies: Soerabaya, Batavia and Belawan, returning by Colombo; also Amsterdam and Middlesbro'.[290] This three-part tour of the Alfred Holt trading areas seems to have been intended to give agents and shippers an idea of what future tonnage would be like.[19]

June 1949, saw the completion of the programme of ship construction initiated in 1936. Two of the original eight vessels of the *Glenearn*-class had been sunk during the war, but with the transfer of the new Blue Funnel *Achilles* to the Glen Line as *Radnorshire* the company was at last able to operate a regular twice-monthly service entirely with fast ships; albeit requiring nine instead of the eight considered sufficient pre-war when port operations had been more efficient.[291]

Thus began for *Glenearn* a succession of hopefully unremarkable and profitable voyages, ploughing essentially the same route to Port Said, Malaya, Hong Kong, China and Japan, returning to Continental ports and starting and finishing at London.[290] Useful but unexciting voyages, with only isolated incidents that might be called remarkable, such as that in Kruisschaus Lock, Antwerp when *Glenearn* was struck by *s.s. Rattray Head*. In this collision two plates were fractured and four frames bent inwards.[285]

27.5.50

15.7.50

On 15th July 1950, *Glenearn* was 60 miles north of Keelung, Formosa, bound for Tsingtao. This was Voyage 19,[289] and the Korean War had broken out less than three weeks previously.[R] It was a warm evening and all the port holes were open. Mr. Sydney Cowan, the Chief Steward, was in his cabin on the starboard side forward, and the Captain's Chinese steward who was on watch, had his head inside the port hole listening to a tune called "Sons of the Desert" that was playing on the radio. He said something about, "Shooting . . . too much shooting," but had scarcely got the words out when he gave a loud groan and collapsed.

Outside a 'plane was overhead; one had passed already and three or four more were making for the ship.[31] They were

American-built "Mustangs" with Chinese Nationalist markings; *Glenearn* had been machine-gunned by one of them.*[462] First Mate Mr. F. G. C. Jones who had been on watch had been seriously wounded with a bullet in his chest,[463] another in his thigh, and shrapnel in his leg;[291] the Chinese steward had been hit in the neck,[463] and Mr. Cowan had a couple of slight scratches.[31] The Chief Officer was extremely ill.[12]

Glenearn's Medical Officer Dr. P. M. Bainbridge[77] had beds made up in the lounge recess for the two seriously injured men, and there he and the Chief Steward took care of them; Sydney Cowan sleeping close by until the ship could make port.[31] A cable arrived from Hong Kong directing Captain Russell to take his ship to Nagasaki, which was reached at 6.30 a.m. on the 17th.[289] An ambulance was waiting to take the two casualties to the train; Mr. Cowan went with them to the hospital at Kobe, then returned to the ship.[31]

17.7.50

Glenearn remained at Nagasaki while repairs were effected.[289] The bridge and steering gear had been damaged as well as the bulkhead round the Chief Steward's cabin. His port hole glass, and several others, had been shattered.[31] From the 19th the ship sheltered from a typhoon until sailing on the 22nd for Tsingtao.[289]

Meanwhile the British Consul in Formosa had received a verbal apology for the air attack. The Chinese Nationalist representative had promised compensation to those who had been injured and for the damage to *Glenearn*; he also gave an assurance that disciplinary action would be taken against the pilot.[463] General MacArthur, Supreme Commander of all United Nations forces in Korea – consisting of the over-run South Korean Army and an under-strength United States Division sent hurriedly from occupation duties in Japan – announced that naval air reconnaissance of the Formosan Straits was being set up to prevent any attack on Formosa, and any operations against the Communist mainland by the Nationalists.[460]

* 1045 GMT; 36° 38′ N. 121° 27′ E.[289]

Back home in Berwickshire, Thomas Hood, OBE, RNR (retd.), still retaining many unhappy memories of his two years in a wreck, hearing from the radio that a British cargo ship had been attacked off Formosa, said to his wife, "I bet it was *Glenearn*."[63]

CHAPTER 34

THE SURGEON'S LOG

Dr. W. G. M. Bell qualified in medicine at Queen's University of Belfast. While there he learned that a connection had been established between Queen's and the "Blue Funnel Line", and many of his friends and older acquaintances had been on voyages as ship's surgeons with this line, so it seemed the only one to approach. A few had joined the "P and O", but they were rather looked down upon.

He applied in the usual way, but heard nothing definite, so returning from London in the autumn of 1950 called in at Alfred Holt's office in Liverpool; the medical officer offered him a position in *Glenearn* – at that stage Bell had not heard of the Glen Line, but he was assured that it was all part of the one organisation, so he returned to Belfast to await notification. He bought tropical gear, but was excused buying blues; an ordinary blue suit of civilian clothes would be sufficient. He obtained his Seaman's Identity Card, received the necessary inoculations, and awaited events.

First intimation that the ship was due to sail was a telephone call from Liverpool wanting to know why he had not turned up at Head Office that morning. Apparently the letter had gone astray, so hurried arrangements were made to sail on the Liverpool ferry that night, and he reported next morning. Dr. Wilson gave a "pep-talk" on the duties and responsibilities on board, but after collecting travel vouchers and other documents the newly appointed Ship's Surgeon was recalled to talk rugby with one of the directors.

Glenearn was in King George V Dock, London, and due to sail in two days' time. The taxi left Dr. Bell and his trunk in 4.11.50 No. 11 Shed in the dark; all he could see was a huge black stern with golden "Glenearn" on it. There was no one about, so he climbed aboard and told the watchman who he was, and that he had a heavy trunk on the dock-side.

When the watchman reappeared with a Chinese quartermaster Bell was rather taken aback, as he was not sure how much English the other spoke. This worthy then searched out two seamen, but they all laughed when they saw how small the trunk was, and one of them carried it alone up the accommodation ladder. Then the watchman roused the 2nd Steward who in turn found a Chinese steward to show the newcomer to his cabin. He had seen many big ships being launched at Harland and Wolff's, Belfast, but had sailed only in Cross-Channel ferries; he was impressed by the size of *Glenearn*, and how far above the dock-side his cabin was, on the boat deck just below the bridge. He had tea with the 2nd Steward who told him that everyone else was ashore. Afterwards, a look at the *Chusan*, whose white hull and yellow funnel towered over *Glenearn*'s stern.

Next morning the new boy ate alone at a table intended for the Captain, Chief Engineer and the First Mate, but none put in an appearance. On the port side of the dining room were the engineer officers and electricians, whereas on the starboard side were the mates, radio operators and "middies". Later he found the First Mate who gave him the keys of the dispensary and poison locker.

Glenearn's dispensary was on the centrecastle deck, starboard side, between the engineers' cabins aft and the two stewards' cabin forward, with the galley and an engine room ladder inboard. It was in a great state of dirt and confusion, with half-opened boxes everywhere. Nevertheless he was surprised with the comprehensiveness of the equipment – everything from a curette to a trephine. At tea he met the Chief Engineer, who reckoned that doctors were only to square the Port Health Authorities and could do nothing a sailor could not do.

6.11.50   Next morning the Third Mate, the frig.-engineer and Dr. Bell were taken to the Local Office to sign on. The clerk consulted a Medical Register to see if the latter's name was included; the first time this had been done in his career.* Back on board, he checked the medical stores with the drug firm's representative and the victualling officer – particularly the

---

* And the only time.

dangerous drugs for which he had to sign. The Poisons Book had a long entry about an incident on the previous voyage when the doctor had been called from the dispensary to an emergency and when he had returned most of the morphia had vanished.

The passengers had come aboard. For dinner at 7 p.m. the Captain, Chief Engineer and Dr. Bell each sat at separate tables of passengers; the rest of the officers had dined earlier. After dinner, he found that the ship had sailed.

He had a long talk with the Mate about the duties of the Ship's Surgeon. It was explained that the Mate was also new to the ship as his predecessor had been seriously wounded when the ship had been attacked off Formosa. Filled bullet holes in the Chief Officer's cabin and outside the passengers' lounge on the deck below were pointed out; and it was carefully indicated that the numerous pieces of new panelling just above the Doctor's own bunk had also been bullet holes.

First day at sea was spent arranging for the Dispensary to be tidied up. On the second day the usual routine began. Breakfast at 8.30, then surgery at 9.00, followed by coffee in the cabin while the Confidential Log about illnesses seen was written up. At 10.45 the Mate, Chief Engineer, Chief Steward and the Doctor mustered outside the passengers' lounge to accompany the Captain on his inspection. The crew's quarters seemed crowded, but the Chief Steward said that they were much better than on the majority of ships. Certainly, their mess-rooms on the deck above were bright and airy. Nevertheless, there was a good deal of sickness among the crew; their quarters being at the stern, there was a considerable movement when the ship was pitching – like living in a lift. There was also an isolation hospital on the poop but it never had to be used, and it was only visited occasionally. Dr. Bell was surprised to note that the passengers' cabins, although nicely furnished and quite roomy, were smaller than his own.

Inspection took about three-quarters of an hour, then he was free until lunch. After lunch, although they had barely left the Channel, everybody retired for a sleep. A cup of tea before surgery at 4.00 p.m., then the log had to be written up. Then dinner at seven. Most of a surgeon's duty seemed to consist of being available just in case something happened.

11.11.50 On Saturday afternoon there was boat-drill. Bell was allocated to the Mate's boat, No. 2 on the port side, but immediately after mustering he had to make his way in his life jacket to stand on the poop ready to throw a lifebelt to any seaman who should fall overboard while the boats were being hoisted out.

After this, the bell on the fo'c'sle rang for fire drill, during which the Surgeon stood by at the Dispensary waiting for casualties, assisted by the two European stewards with several Chinese stretcher-bearers. The Chinese seamen working the hoses and handling the huge axes seemed to get much amusement out of this exercise; so much for the inscrutable Oriental. They always seemed to be laughing and treating their work as a great joke.

As he came to know the other officers better, he usually spent the evenings in their lounge playing endless board games – chess and draughts – as well as darts and cards. He played deck-quoits with the passengers, as the Surgeon was supposed to have some social duties to perform, but this only amused the other officers who preferred to have nothing to do with them; nevertheless, many of the passengers had been POWs and told extremely interesting stories of Changi, Repulse Bay and Borneo.

Passing through the Mediterranean Dr. Bell collected and sorted the health cards of the Chinese crew to make a list of those who would receive inoculations later. Approaching Port Said. No photos would be allowed in the Canal Zone and partly-exposed spools would be confiscated, so it was advisable to complete a roll of film and leave the camera empty.

15.11.50 At Port Said the electricians fitted the searchlight at the bows while the gully-gully men produced live chicks from your inside pockets and changed your half-crowns into pennies. The electricians finished the passage of the Canal with, as usual, conjunctivitis due to the glare of the light.

CARGO HANDLING

32. Colombo January, 1951.

33. Unloading at Penang November, 1950. No. 4 Hatch.

16.11.50 Leaning on the rail watching the people on the bank, the radio-operator remarked that it would not be long before the Egyptians would be shooting at them...

Glenearn refuelled at Aden and took on foul-tasting water for the voyage across the Indian Ocean to Penang and Port Swettenham. The Chinese had just entered the Korean War and there had been a fresh outburst of Communist activity in Malaya. A godown a few hundred yards from the wharf had been burned down, and a man shot, the night before 1.12.50 *Glenearn*'s arrival at Port Swettenham. News from Radio Malaya was full of shootings and train hold-ups. Most of the Europeans wore revolvers or carried rifles, and their advice was not to go to Kuala Lumpur because of the risk of raids. The passengers all turned out to say goodbye to a rubber-planter and his family who were leaving the ship; he had just received news that his manager had been killed, so when they set off it was in a convoy of lorries with an armed guard of six Malays.

At Port Swettenham's Seamen's Mission there was a football match against a team from the Blue Funnel *Cyclops*, a new ship of the *Anchises*-class. Their team all had beautiful blue and yellow jerseys, whereas only three of *Glenearn*'s even had boots; nevertheless, they won 3-0.

4.12.50 On 4th December *Glenearn* arrived at Singapore and most of the passengers left, except two families continuing to Hong Kong. The ship anchored a mile or so from the shore among forty or fifty other ocean-going liners outward-bound, all waiting to see how the Chinese Communist intervention in Korea would affect trade to North China. It was believed that *Glenearn* had been bound for Tsingtao and Taku Bar as on Voyage 19, but this had been cancelled because of the possibility of internment. As they were too far off-shore to make it worth while leaving the ship, a set of mahjong tiles was borrowed from the passengers' lounge and the game played almost continuously all day, much to the amusement of the Chinese crew.

Eventually *Glenearn* went alongside, was unloaded, and after the team had played a match against an Army side, which was lost 4-2, the ship left for Hong Kong. A keen 9.12.50 interest was taken in the radio news as United Nations troops were being evacuated in large numbers by sea from northern Korea, and there were many rumours that merchant ships would be called upon for this work. It was also heard that serious riots had occurred in Singapore just after they had left, over a Dutch girl who had been brought up as a Moslem and was being forced to become a Christian; eighteen people were said to have been killed and two hundred injured, with martial law declared and a curfew imposed.

Hong Kong was approached through the Lymun Pass as 14.12.50 the western entrance was covered by a Chinese Communist gun battery which occasionally fired on passing shipping. Dr. Bell went up the Peak and looked over Kowloon into the territory beyond, that only about a year before had passed into Communist hands. On leaving Hong Kong two large 17.12.50 Union Jacks were lashed across the hatches fore and aft for air identification.

Glenearn was bound for Keelung. The normal route was through the Formosa Straits, but since the previous voyage's air attack all the Company's ships had been routed to the east of Formosa. An appreciable feeling of tension built up as the ship approached the island, in expectation of another attack. Those who had been on board at the time indicated where they had sheltered, and there was quite a discussion about the best place to take cover if caught on deck again – close under the hatch-coamings was considered a good place. The Ship's Doctor took another look over his instrument box, just in case. There were many glances at the sky in the direction of Formosa during the day, but it was cloudy and blowing and 18.12.50 no aircraft were seen.

On arrival at Keelung Dr. Bell had considerable difficulty 19.12.50 with the Port Doctor as they had no common language; the radio-operator had even more trouble with his paperwork. There were hordes of officials, all in different uniforms and all covered in beautiful insignia. The entire crew had to file past to answer their names; this was because most of them came from Shanghai and were presumably regarded as possible

Communists. Nobody was allowed off the ship even on to the wharf, and harbour officials stayed on board at all times, even eating in the ship's saloon – although it was suspected that the restriction on shore leave was imposed by Captain Russell to avoid trouble involving his Chinese crew ashore.

Several men wearing arm bands with Chinese characters came on board to lecture the crew, and the European agent spent a night on board. He said the local inhabitants were Japanese sympathisers who disliked the recent huge influx of Chinese Nationalists. *Glenearn* was loading tea on the outward trip in case it proved impossible, in view of the delicate situation in Korea with rumours of American action against China, to call on the homeward run.

From Keelung the ship called at Kobe and then Yokohama, where an English-speaking Japanese from the agent's office was taken on board to conduct the ship's business at Otaru in Hokkaido. He told Dr. Bell that his brother had been killed as a suicide pilot, and he himself had been similarly trained but had not carried out his mission, when the atom bombs ended the war.

At Otaru one of the local stevedores fell into No. 2 Hold and fractured his skull. It was dark and snow was drifting into the hold. The Surgeon got him into a Neil-Robertson stretcher and he was hoisted on to a hatch cover – a launch was brought alongside but the cabin was only large enough for people standing, so the unfortunate man had to lie on the open deck in the snow, covered by a tarpaulin. Once ashore, when it was explained through the agent what had happened, a sledge was produced and, towed by four men, the patient was taken to hospital. *Glenearn* sailed on 1st January 1951.

Back at Hong Kong homeward-bound, some of the Chinese crew were paid off. As they were going on to Shanghai, they were not sure if they would be allowed back. Dr. Bell had a busy time examining members of the new crew and getting their inoculations in order, while trying to avoid getting unfit old crocks signed on. *Glenearn*'s 1st XI beat a team from a tanker under repair, 2-0, at the Merchant Navy Club.

26.12.50

1.1.51

At sea again, movement was somewhat limited by a huge deck cargo of cabbages and oranges, but at Singapore the ship 13.1.51 was met by a fleet of small boats which unloaded all this produce very rapidly. Another football match was played at Pasir Panjang against an Army team who won 6-0. The Bosun invited the Second Mate, the Second Engineer, the Chief Electrician and the Doctor to go aft one evening for Chinese chow to celebrate the New Year. It was a fabulous meal, of fifteen courses, eaten entirely with chop-sticks; after chewing continuously for two hours, the four guests were barely able to get back to their cabins.

On the voyage home calls were made at Port Swettenham, Penang, Colombo, Aden and then through the Canal again.

Returning to the Thames *Glenearn* re-entered a King 18.2.51 George V Dock already containing the Union-Castle *Durban Castle* and *Bloemfontein Castle*; also the P & O *Chitrol*. *Breconshire* and sister-ship *Glenartney* were tied up opposite each other. There was no vacant berth so *Glenearn* made fast alongside *Breconshire*; as the Glen ship was down to her marks the promenade deck was exactly level with the Shire vessel's upper deck.

Soon the Customs and Immigration people were on board, interviewing the passengers who then left for the shore. Dr. Bell went over the stocks of drugs, made up the medical abstracts of illness during the voyage, helped the radio-operator with the wireless accounts, packed his own gear and checked the dangerous drugs with the Victualling Superintendent.

The surgeon from *Glenartney* turned out, not too surprisingly, to be another doctor from Queen's University, Belfast, whom Bell knew very well so he lent him some gear. In the evening, farewells to the officers he had had such good times with, then sleep; to rise at 6.0 the following morning. The steward and the pantry boy got his trunk across 19.2.51 *Breconshire* to the dockside. There he took his leave of *Glenearn*, lying silent and untidy, waiting to be unloaded on a cold grey February morning; looking not at all like his favourite memory of her – spick and span on a blue sea under a tropic sun.[12]

CHAPTER 35

PEACETIME POTPOURRI

The postwar shipping boom, created by the loss of $2\frac{1}{2}$ million Allied merchant tons[R] and the virtual destruction of all the enemy-owned fleets, had been amplified by the damage to foreign shipyards and the inefficiency of port operating, and extended by the demands of the Korean War.[594] Throughout these years of plenty the *Glenearn*-class were hard-driven, high-earning ships of Alfred Holt's fleet, and as such many of the old reliable solid Masters, Mates and Chief Engineers were placed in them. But already a new generation was springing up: young men whose confidence had not been hammered by mass unemployment, and whose characters had not been steeled by the fire of war. To a young midshipman his seniors seemed unimaginative in their outlook, and motivated to an extraordinary extent by status and reputation.[10]

Be that as it may, these self-same deck officers and engineers kept the Company's ships on course and speed year in, year out; unremarkable voyages which when distilled to a residue of unroutine incidents may give the impression of a succession of disasters...[A]

* * *

16.6.54   In Empire Dock, Singapore in the course of Voyage 29,[290] *Glenearn* was struck by *Flintshire*, an ex-"Liberty" Ship, as the Shire boat was berthing alongside. *Glenearn*'s vertical stern plate and the adjacent plates were set in at poop deck level, the aftermost docking platform was completely smashed and the guard rails on each side of it buckled. Temporary repairs which were carried out included substantial cement boxes between frames at the underside of the poop deck.

Before permanent repairs could be effected at London,
1.8.54   *Glenearn* had a brush with the lock wall at Hull. On

examination however, no evidence of new damage was found, apart from paintwork slightly scraped.[297]

*　　*　　*

The amount of the claim arising from the air attack of 15th July, 1950, had come to £2,262. 8s. 10d. Of this £2,063. 9s. 9d. was recovered from the Chinese Nationalist Government, leaving a balance of £198. 19s. 1d; this the Committee of the Liverpool & London War Risks Insurance Association Ltd. agreed to pay.[291]

17.2.55

*　　*　　*

At the end of Voyage 31 *Glenearn* went into floating dock No. 5 at Howaldtswerke A.G.-Hamburg; whilst undocking she came into contact with it and damaged her side shell plating on the port side forward. A shell plate was indented and No. 3 Frame set in; scars which had to be carried about until the ship's return after the next voyage.[297]

7.5.55

*　　*　　*

Egyptian "nationalisation" of the Suez Canal at the end of July, 1956, did not immediately affect Alfred Holt's Far East ships as the Egyptians managed to keep the transits going more or less normally,[484] *Glenearn* herself passing through homeward bound on 8–9th October.[290] At the end of the month however, the war between Israel and Egypt, and the Franco-British expedition to Port Said, led to the Canal's being effectively blocked,[484] so when *Glenearn* sailed on her 36th Voyage her route was round the Cape by way of Dakar and Durban. Before the end of the next one the Canal had been reopened, in time for the homeward passage.[290]

8.10.56

19.11.56

15.7.57

*　　*　　*

Glenearn was at No. 14 King George V Dock, London, when a Chinese lamp-trimmer fell off a lighter into the dock. He could not swim. Assistant Marine Superintendent J. Marwood from the deck of *Glenearn* went down a rope into the water, while the Chinese Quartermaster Chen Ding King

25.4.58

also came to the rescue from a nearby lighter. Between them they got the now unconscious man, Lee Ping Koen, out. A Mr. Robert Henderson now arrived, having seen someone hurriedly removing a lifebuoy from the gangway, and he gave artificial respiration to the rescued man, whose life was thereby saved.

2.9.58   One voyage later, on board *Glenearn*, the Royal Humane Society's Special Resuscitation Certificate was presented to Mr. Henderson of J. Russell & Co., Ship Repairers, and testimonials on vellum to Captain Marwood and Chen Ding King.[473]

*   *   *

21.5.59   In the course of Voyage 42 *Glenearn* arrived at Suez Roads from Port Sudan.[290] Whilst waiting to join the morning convoy, smoke was recorded on the detector on the bridge. The fire was in No. 7 Hold and 'tween decks, and it was extinguished by filling up with gas from the carbon dioxide system. Once the cargo had been shifted and discharged, it was found that the trouble had started in a ground nut expeller, but no damage had been done to the materials carried nor to the structure of the ship.[297]

*   *   *

Since the signing of the Korean cease fire agreement in July, 1953, *Glenearn* had ceased to call at Keelung in Formosa and instead switched to the Communist ports on the mainland; usually Shanghai.[290] At first everyone was met with suspicion and hostility.[474] In December, 1954, John Swire and Sons Ltd., Alfred Holt's Agency in all the Chinese ports, was forced to close down by the People's Government;[485] thereafter the business dealings of the ships' officers and crews were almost the only contacts the Company had with China.[474]

*   *   *

Harald Brokenshire was Press Attaché at the Australian Commission at Singapore in July, 1961. At the end of the month he boarded *m.v. Glenearn* to greet a very old friend on passage from Hong Kong to England, and to invite him and his wife to stay ashore for the few days they would be in port. When he returned his guests Mr. Brokenshire was aboard again, but still could not be sure whether this was indeed the ship from which as a lance-corporal of the AIF he had done his amphibious training in Trinity Bay fifteen years before ...[18]

* * *

Back in 1946 Captain Conway, RN, had returned to the United Kingdom and to the command of *HMS Wildfire* at Sheerness. From there he had written to the Managing Director of the Glen Line to ask him if, sometime nearer his retirement, Captain and Mrs. Conway could have an assisted passage out East in *Glenearn* to revive old memories. In his delightful reply Mr. Wurtzburg recommended writing to the Company at the appropriate time, and there would be no difficulty.

The appropriate time came in the early 60's and Captain Conway, RN(retd.), wrote as bidden, referring to the previous correspondence.[29] Alas, Mr. Wurtzburg had died in 1952,[483] the new Managing Director was unable to accede to the request for many, many reasons; all of which added up to an uncompromising "No!"[29]

* * *

When Captain A. Millard took over as Master for Voyage 50[290] *Glenearn* joined the voluntary observing fleet of the Meteorological Office, and instruments were put aboard at London.[110] Weather reporting was a voluntary occupation on the part of the ship's officers, but the information sent out, to be of value had to be prompt and accurate; this part of the procedure depended on the enthusiasm of the Radio Officers, who had to transmit a coded message of five-figure groups every six hours.[59] Senior Radio Officer was Mr. Greville and the Principal Observing Officer Mr. A. E. J. Coates;[110] *Glenearn* sailed for the Far East on 24th February, 1962[290] and the first observations were made the following day.[110]

23.2.62

24.2.62

* * *

Another innovation of Captain Millard's was to bring his latest command under the British Ship Adoption Society again; the previous experience having been a brief period prior to the outbreak of war when *Glenearn* had been vaguely linked with the Training Ship *Exmouth* at Grays, Essex. Now the Glen Ship was to be adopted by Herne Bay Secondary 9.6.62 School,[43] with the result that on arrival at Genoa on the homeward run a bundle of mail from the school children was received. The letters were distributed among the officers and midshipmen who had to find the time and enthusiasm to reply, which they did; sending for good measure a track and distance chart of the round voyage, and a large plan of the ship showing details of the cargo spaces and the layout of the accommodation drawn by one of the midshipmen. Another midshipman sent an oil painting of *Glenearn*; a real free-hand effort using only the paints used on board ship.

Captain Millard's wife had flown out to Genoa to join her husband on the last leg of the voyage. This was her first time abroad and she thoroughly enjoyed the holiday, although succumbing to *mal de mer* off Portugal; brought on by *Glenearn*'s heavy pitching into a head swell in an otherwise smooth sea.[148]

*   *   *

2.12.62   In Baudouin Lock, Antwerp, *Glenearn* came into contact with *C. D. Kennedy*; damage on this occasion was confined to score marks on the port side, and no repairs were required.[297]

*   *   *

Four of the new *Glenlyon*-class commissioned in 1962–63; these were the first 20-knot ships of the Glen Line, and were a complete departure from the traditional three-island design, having six masts and two derrick posts. They were virtually all-welded flush-deck vessels with bulbous bows and open water stern frames.[526] Their speed would reduce the Far East trip by at least two weeks, and labour-saving devices such as hydraulically operated hatch-covers effected a saving in crew numbers of about a third.[130] Each of the 12,000-ton ships was believed to have cost about £2 million.[527]

*   *   *

With the delivery of the first of the new *Glenlyons*, four of the *Glenearn*-class were rescheduled on to the service to Thailand, Hong Kong, China and the Philippines which hitherto had been run with *Anchises*-class ships transferred from the "Blue Funnel Line".[70] *Glenearn*'s fifty-second voyage thus found her sailing from London bound for the first time for Bangkok.[290]

14.12.62

*   *   *

At Shanghai the Communist authorities were meticulous about searching the ship and about the correctness of dates of cholera injections and smallpox vaccinations. The ship's Second Cook was arrested and charged with having been involved in a shooting affray ten years before, during which a man had been killed. Despite the protests of the Master, the man was not freed, and the ship had to sail without him.

27.1.63

The severe winter weather in the north of the People's Republic froze up all the cold water pipes for two weeks, and the toilets had to be flushed with hot water. Dr. Adam P. Smith the Ship's Surgeon was making his second voyage for Alfred Holt & Co., having made his first back in 1923 in the old *Knight Companion*. He did not have much to do as the passengers were healthy and the crew pretty fit.

The Hong Kong Chinese were hard-working and efficient; neither the Chief Officer nor the Chief Engineer relished the idea of an exchange for a white British crew. The No. 1 was excellent, having good English, good looks and being prepared to converse – when spoken to. When the Chief Officer was questioned by a lady passenger Mr. Jones said something like, "If the Company had to choose between No. 1 and myself I would be worried. He needs no telling and things just get done. He's hard-working, experienced and efficient." The greasers too seemed equally up to standard in their work, and one got the impression that officers and crewmen were happy in the old ship, which they seemed to respect.[130]

* * *

4.2.64   Leaving Port Said *Glenearn*'s starboard propeller fouled a buoy chain. It was found that the four bronze blades had the tips torn. This propeller was removed ashore and re-conditioned while the exposed end of the screw shaft was visually examined and found to be in order.[297]

* * *

Captain Millard and his staff kept up the link with Herne Bay Secondary School, but when he had to give up his seagoing career early in 1964 because of ill health,[43] the new Master did not make contact and the children's letters got lost. There was a lack of real interest between the pupils and the ship...[148]

* * *

Glenearn's postwar conversion had been very much a case of putting her back the way she had been in 1939 – consequently the opportunity had not been taken to modernise very much, either mechanically or the living quarters.[10] Immediately after the war large numbers of Alfred Holt's agents, their families, freight shippers and other people of importance invariably travelled to and from the East by sea; consequently there had been commercial advantage in *Glenearn*'s ability to carry twelve first-class passengers, quite apart from considerations of finance.

Over the years however, the composition of the passenger lists had altered radically. More and more business people were flying, while the holiday passenger trade was uneven; the modest profits had to be weighed against the reduction in costs of running the Stewards' Department and the psychological benefits of providing better living quarters for crew members... The decision was made that all the older ships would be progressively "depassengerised".[479]

Glenearn's turn came in July, 1964, when she was taken in

hand by Harland & Wolff's London repair department for the
reconstruction of her accommodation. There was not a great
deal of work involved in the changes: the Chief Engineer
moved from the port side up one deck to the starboard
forward stateroom, the 2nd Engineer to the port forward
stateroom.[137] The Chief Officer was given a separate
dayroom, bedroom and office, together with private lavatory
facilities.[19] Junior officers, formerly based on the boat deck,
were relocated on the promenade deck in the staterooms
there;[137] the stewards moved to the engineers' former
cabins.[146]

And so on. Due to the reduction in the number of the crew,
together with the additional space made available, the
majority of the seamen had single-berth rooms in place of the
double formerly occupied.[479] The alterations were completed
in nine days.[290] An additional advantage was a reduction in
net tonnage of 421,[296] creating a small saving in port dues.[479]

*   *   *

During examination in dry dock at Hong Kong, it was
noted that the shell plating on the starboard side forward was
indented.[297]

*   *   *

At Hamburg in November, 1965, a fracture approximately
200 millimetres long was found on one of the starboard
propeller blades. A 10 mm diameter hole was drilled to stop
the crack extending, and in March, 1966, when the ship was
back in Hamburg the screwshaft was removed ashore and
checked for truth in a lathe. A sound propeller from
Breconshire was fitted and the damaged one sent away for
reconditioning.[297]

*   *   *

While manoeuvring at Singapore *Glenearn* was in contact
with *s.s. Asia Enterprises.* Damage was confined to the
starboard side of the poop, with the poop deck stringer and
about 15 feet of side railing buckled, but the forward bulkhead

of the firemen's washroom was broken away from the frame, and wood panelling in the adjacent cabin was splintered and broken.[297]

* * *

Glenearn's sister ship *Glenroy* was sold in October, 1966, and went to Kure in Japan for scrapping.[482]

* * *

29.5.67 On Voyage 62 *Glenearn* left Port Said for Genoa;[290] seven days later yet another Arab-Israeli war closed the Suez Canal again, trapping some Blue Funnel ships in the Bitter Lakes.[467] Another six days and the fighting stopped, but the Canal had become no-man's-land.[464] For Voyage 63

19.7.67 *Glenearn* called at Las Palmas before sailing non-stop to Penang; eventually reaching Tsingtao. On the return trip calls were made at Durban and East London before going into Las

12.11.67 Palmas again.[290]

Thereafter, by a combination of reducing the number of ports served on the home coast and leaving out some of the less important ones in the Far East, little or no time was added to the lengths of subsequent voyages round the Cape. Bunkering arrangements had to be changed, as Aden had been the main bunker port when Suez had been open. Dakar in West Africa was generally used now, but calls were made at Las Palmas or Durban in accordance with facilities available; when a call was made at Dakar outward-bound, topping-up took place at Singapore.[70] The Suez Canal remained closed.[465]

CHAPTER 36

ONE OF THE BEST

The engines of the *Glenearn*-class had been designed originally to burn marine diesel oil, but during wartime service the Royal Naval ships were, it seems, bunkered with gas oil. This very much lighter fuel would have helped the engines to operate more cleanly, and probably with less wear on fuel injectors and piston rings. Some of the benefit of these advantages would, however, have been reduced by the hard running frequently demanded by the Navy.

In 1950 Mr. John Lamb, superintendent engineer of the Shell Group advocated the burning of heavy fuel oil in marine diesels. Since so-called "boiler oil" was cheaper than marine diesel[70] – in November, 1949, the respective prices had been 109s. and 158s. per ton[538] – considerable savings were there to be made for a modest outlay on the conversion of engines for the heavier fuel. This meant that the oil was passed through steam preheaters to lower its viscosity before it reached the injection pumps. In turn the fuel pumps had to have slightly larger clearances in their barrels and the injectors slightly larger holes in the nozzles – which had to be cooled.[70] All this work was done on *Glenearn* at London between the 8th and 21st November, 1953;[290] she was the first of the class to be converted.[70] When the ship sailed on Voyage 28 she had 661 tons of fuel oil on board; also 151 tons of diesel oil[290] for use when manoeuvring and running at low speeds.[59] It was expected that there would be an annual saving in fuel bills of about £32,000.[291]

21.11.53

Everyone expected heavier wear and tear on piston rings and cylinder liners due to the higher ash content of the heavy fuel oil, and cylinder lubricating oils were developed to deal with this ash content, but these new lubricants were essentially mineral oils which did not provide the real answer. Liner wear rates soared and maintenance costs became substantial.

Eventually it was discovered in the laboratories of the Royal Dutch Shell Group that the real "bug" in the system was the corrosive effect of the products of combustion; principally sulphuric acid from the higher sulphur content. It was then possible to develop an emulsified cylinder oil which had high alkaline properties – this was the right answer; with the new cylinder oil, wear rates were dramatically reduced, almost back to what they had been when the engines had operated solely on marine diesel oil.

By 1957 a lot of experience had been gained of burning boiler oil, and it was decided to further reduce the need for maintenance by fitting new propellers.[70] The original screws consisted of two bosses, to each of which were bolted four separate blades; with the engines doing 110 r.p.m. these had driven the ship along at her maximum speed of 18 knots. Although about the same overall diameter, the new screws being integral units had smaller bosses and therefore larger blades, thus increasing the effective thrust. If the forward speed were to be kept the same, the engine speed could be reduced for the same horse power.[59]

9.12.57   *Glenearn*, on arrival at Hamburg, went into drydock in Howaldtswerke, and the old propellers were removed. The work, expected to take ten days actually took thirteen, but the result was an engine speed of 100 r.p.m., which further facilitated lubrication and cooling of the pistons and cylinder liners – and "breathing" of the engines; always a problem on two-cycle engines.[70] Fuel consumption at a service speed of 17 knots worked out at about 47 tons per day, compared with the earlier 52.[59]

All these measures helped to keep going engines which had been in an express service ship and hard-worked naval auxiliary for some twenty years. And they did run well; rarely giving trouble at sea and pounding along in all sorts of weather.[70] Development of the double-acting two-stroke Burmeister & Wain engine had brought surprisingly few teething troubles, and in every respect they had given excellent service.[538] Indeed, the design had been so satisfactory that it had formed[70] – with a number of improvements[538] – the basis of the "Blue Funnel Line's" post-war fleet replacement programme which had started with the 7,643 gross ton *Anchises* of 1947.[70]

But although Burmeister & Wain motors could work "as smoothly as steam engines",[108] and if the ship's staff knew the idiosyncrasies of their main engines and how to treat them they ran very well indeed, they required a high standard of watch-keeping for the maintenance of steady coolant temperatures and proper centrifuging of fuel and lubricating oils. Any double-acting engine means a lot of moving parts to keep maintained; a large number of joints and glands to be kept tight. Considering that each of twelve cylinders had two exhaust pistons, a main piston with two sets of rings in it, and a rigid stuffing box where the main piston-rod passed through the bottom exhaust piston, such engines presented the crew of ten engineers with a considerable amount of work, to say the least.[70]

At the time it had been accepted as a necessary evil that double-acting engines were complicated to overhaul. However, this attitude was bound to change in the long run; interest of designers shifted towards large single-acting two-stroke engines which could be more easily overhauled. With the introduction of turbocharging the era of the double-acting diesel had come to an end;[108] the *Glenlyon*-class of 1962–63 had Sulzer single-acting supercharged engines producing 16,600 brake horse power compared to *Glenearn*'s 12,000 b.h.p.[480] When the new *Glenalmond*-class commissioned in 1967 and 1968 the four *Glenlyons* had their engines uprated to give 18,000 b.h.p. and a service speed in excess of 21 knots to match that of the *Glenalmonds*. By this time the first of the *Glenearn*-class had been scrapped, although the name-ship was still going strong.[70]

The British Corporation Register of Shipping had amalgamated with Lloyd's in 1949[298] and since March, 1953, *Glenearn* had been fully classified with the latter Society. In February, 1968, the ship lay at Hong Kong in light condition for the advancement of Lloyd's Extended Special Survey (30 years). Extensive thickness gauging of shell, decks and tank top plating was carried out using a "Krautkramer" ultra sonic measurer to fulfil the requirements of the American cargo Underwriters and Owners. According to these results nine plates of the upper deck appeared to have worn down more than 30% and were required to be renewed.

Glenearn's owners subsequently requested further examination of these plates by drilling and gauging. This was put in hand at London and it proved that only three plates were reduced below renewal thickness. At Rotterdam the ship went into drydock at Schiedam to verify the thickness of her shell plates. While being towed in however, her sideshell was damaged on the starboard side, with the result that parts of three strakes of plating had to be renewed, as well as six frames; when these repairs were being carried out the nine controversial areas of deck were fitted with $\frac{1}{2}$-inch thick welded doubling plates.[297]

Back at King George V Dock, London, a little reunion had been arranged. As Marine Superintendent for the Royal Mail, Ken Cutler had often seen *Glenearn* when she was berthed nearby. With *Glenfalloch* and the other new ships operating, it seemed to him that it could not be long before the old ship would be scrapped. He asked permission to have a luncheon party on board[36] and the Glen Line's Marine Superintendent J. F. C. Dowie said it would be all right,[38] so Colin Arthur George was invited up from Southsea. In the absence of *Glenearn*'s Master on leave Captain Dowie acted as host. There were just four or five people altogether, including Glen Line's Superintendent Engineer[36] Mr. H. Cassidy, who as a Lieutenant (E) RNR had served in *HMS Glenroy*.[291] Captain Hutchison had recently applied for membership of the Magic Circle and claimed that the qualifying performance had been more frightening than any of his wartime experiences.[36]

Thus the Indian summer of a fine ship. Happy years with little to recall.[A] Her meteorological log books were frequently praised for their completeness and consistency, although unusual events had been rare. Waterspouts had been sighted five or six times in the early years, while in February, 1963, pancake ice in Japanese waters had been recorded; in April,

24.4.68

1.5.68

1968, a detailed account of moving bioluminescence had been provided.[6]

Each year the best hundred log books from all the Weather Reporting Ships received awards, usually in the form of books to the Master and Radio Officer; with, for those who had helped to produce the good log books but received nothing, the satisfaction – small consolation perhaps – of seeing their ship's name in print.[59] In 1963 and 1964 under Captain Millard awards were received, and again in 1969 for observations made the previous year under Captain G. I. Wright.[110]

The officers concerned did not always confine themselves to observing the weather, but noted such things as mirages and haloes round the sun and moon, unusual appearance or behavioural pattern of birds, sea animals; patterns, radar contacts at long range caused by refraction – in fact anything out of the ordinary. Some observers good at sketching drew birds and fish, insects and so on, with descriptions. This information was passed by the Met. Office to the curators of Museums of Natural History for their records and study; they in turn gave their explanations, and those of particular interest were printed in the quarterly Met. Office magazine, *The Marine Observer*.[59]

Captain C. H. F. Hill took over *Glenearn* in April, 1969, at the start of Voyage 68.[290] At this time business politics were much to the fore. The Communist-inspired Chinese crew were allowed to hold their political meetings and Chairman Mao, not the Queen, presided over their mess rooms. A Glen ship sailing from London was said to have been sent on her way by a mob of Chinese waving their little red books and shouting slogans, while grey uniforms of officials from their London Embassy mingled with the blue "comrade" outfits of the rest of the crowd. Such demonstrations, endless deputations to the Master with ill-founded complaints, outrageous demands and general surliness were tolerated by the Company as long as the ships were pursuing successful voyages – and the thought of three weeks in China cut off, with no representative or authority to turn to, tempered the actions of the ships' officers.

VOYAGE 13

34. Arriving at Sydney 4th March, 1948.

VOYAGE 68

35. At Cape Town 27th October, 1969.

Arriving back at London the situation reached a climax of 25.2.70 sorts with about six Glen ships congesting the Port. The Chinese were all on strike for more pay. At last they were told to accept the offer of $7\frac{1}{2}$% or go home. This first stand was the turning point and *Glenearn* was able to sail for Rotterdam, 11.3.70 but the difficulties remained and Captain Hill dealt with them well.[21]

A few days later news came that *Glenfalloch* had been held in Shanghai and her Master arrested.[466] Over the years Blue Funnel and Glen Line ships had been involved in several incidents – some less serious than others – despite extreme care and patience. This *Glenfalloch* affair had capped them all; it was decided to withdraw all calls to Communist China forthwith.[104] Thus when *Glenearn* next sailed she was bound 14.4.70 for Bangkok, Manila and Rejang; Shanghai had been dropped from the schedule.[290]

On 28th and 29th April a prolonged lightning display was staged as if for the benefit of those on board,[6] which included the wife of radio operator Albert Brown, "signed on" as Librarian at a nominal wage of 1s. per month. Mrs. Brown, who had coasted from Genoa to London for several years, still found the Chinese crew as cheerful, friendly and obliging as ever. It was a happy voyage, all the officers and men worked well together, there were no undercurrents of hostility or rivalry between the deck and the engine room. There was also a considerable social life with outward and homeward championships in darts, cribbage, scrabble, cards, dominoes, deck quoits and shuffleboard, table tennis and uckers – with no bad feeling and no betting. There was a kind of "family" life and birthdays were celebrated.[20]

The return route took in Trincomalee and Durban before the long haul to London, which was reached on the 15th 15.8.70 August.[290] Owing to a national dock strike during the second half of July[80] there was still a lot of congestion within the Royal group of docks, so *Glenearn* berthed at Sheerness;[59] the first Glen ship to use the deep water jetty there.[368] Here Captain Hill left and went on leave.[59] 21.8.70

As her two surviving sister-ships *Glengyle* and *Glengarry* had been transferred to the Blue Funnel Line,[298] *Glenearn*, the first of her class, had become the last to fly the Glen Line house flags.[70] She was still in very good condition, still able to carry on trading for a long time to come,[291] and valued for insurance purposes at £616,000; fractionally more than in 1939.[52] A ship still classed as first rate even after thirty-two years of rigorous service in a trade that demanded a high standard of performance and reliability, year in and year out – a tribute to her builders and to the design staff of Alfred Holt and Company. Methodically as they went about their duties on the gleaming white decks, even the Chinese crew seemed to have the same respect as her officers for one of the best fast cargo liners ever built.[70]

7.10.70   After coasting to Rotterdam and Hamburg – both twice – then Middlesbrough and Antwerp, *Glenearn* arrived back at London[290] where the recent industrial troubles had coincided with a chance reunion.[36]Since the war ex-Able Seaman John Earley had often worked on board *Glenearn*.[40] A real trouble-maker in ex-Lieutenant-Commander Cutler's opinion, when asked what he was doing now Earley had replied, "I'm a docker." With the dock strike much in mind Cutler's unspoken comment was, "That figures."[36]

15.10.70   After an exceptionally long leave Captain Hill was recalled, and very surprised to find that his ship had been sold to Japanese interests for breaking up at Kaohsiung in Taiwan.[59]

CHAPTER 37

VPS...DE...GPGC...$\overline{BT}$...$\overline{AR}$*

Early in 1970 Ocean Fleets Ltd., operated fifty-one ships under the Blue Funnel and Glen Line flags on the main Europe–Far East Trade. These gave a combined service of eleven sailings per month to the various ports of the Orient, including mainland China. In the Spring of that year, however, there was the decision to withdraw the service to China; the savings in voyage times enabled the number of sailings to be maintained with two fewer ships.

At about the same time cargo insurance interests put pressure on liner ship operators, by threatening to increase premiums on cargo carried in elderly vessels. For some time goods in ships over fifteen years old had been liable to an additional premium, except for liners on scheduled services; now the London underwriters put a limit on this liner-ship exemption by declaring that it would not apply to vessels over thirty years old.[291] Main targets of this ruling were the wartime-built *Liberty*, *Victory* and *Empire* classes, which through their casualty rates had become high risks,[59] but it was clear that it would become increasingly difficult to operate old vessels of any sort on competitive liner services.

Two ships had become surplus; over 30 year-olds were the obvious ones to sell. *Glenearn* at 32 was the eldest, *Glengarry* and *Glengyle* reached 30 within a few months; all of them were expensive to maintain, and their large reefer† capacity – the homeward trade from China had included large quantities of frozen cargo at good freight rates – was of no use except for the China service. Despite a heavy demand for tonnage, such old ships were virtually unsaleable for further trading; the decision to let *Glenearn* go for scrap was taken by the Managing Director of the Blue Funnel Line, Mr. R. H.

---

* Radio code: HONG KONG FROM GLENEARN – END OF WORKING.[19]
† Reefer: refrigerated.[104]

Hobhouse, with the agreement of H. O. Karsten, Chairman of the Glen Line.[104] Sad, but inevitable.

The Memorandum of Agreement between the Glen Line and Mitsui and Company of 83 Cannon Street, London, was drawn up on McGregor, Gow & Holland Ltd.'s paper and signed on 17th August;[291] the basis of the sale being U.S. $74 per light ton[368] – a good rate for demolition. On the strength of an inclining experiment carried out at North Shields back on the 10th November, 1947, the light displacement was taken as 8,518 tons, giving a purchase price of $630,332;* ten per cent of this amount had to be deposited as security.[291]

On the afternoon of Captain Hill's return he was handed a photostat copy of the contract of sale;[59] the price had been blacked over, but the figure could just be made out.[21] Some of the items seemed somewhat irrelevant, but presumably every contingency had to be taken into account; there must be more to getting rid of a ship than meets the inexperienced eye. One of the clauses said that everything which bore the name or crest of the Company could be retained by the Company, or by the Master at his discretion; Captain Hill therefore put in a request for the bronze plaque which listed *Glenearn's* wartime experiences. This request was granted.

The following day the ship was supposed to sail, but first her Master had to go to the Glen Line's city office at 16 St. Helen's Place for an interview, and whilst there it was decided that the loading of cargo could not be finished that day;† she would sail instead on Monday evening – Captain Hill could go straight home and return to the ship on Sunday, at noon. At the same time he promised *Glenearn's* bridge bell to one of the firm's Directors, who wanted a ship's bell for some Scout Troop.

Captain Hill duly returned – and was horrified to discover that in his absence, many things had been pilfered: the aneroid barometer from his own room, the photograph of Glen Earn which had hung in the lounge, and the signed

_17.8.70_

_15.10.70_

_16.10.70_

_18.10.70 ·_

---

* On 17th August, 1970, the rate of exchange was $2.3888 to the £.[465]
† Friday.

photographs of King George VI and Queen Elizabeth[59] – the personal property of Lord Louis Mountbatten[8] – had all disappeared. So, too, had the bridge bell.

No special instructions were given prior to departure, other than an explanation of some of the contract terms where these were not clearly understandable; the only thing that was impressed upon Captain Hill was that before he finally handed over his ship to the buyers, he must have confirmation direct from London that the letters of credit had been paid in to the owner's bank there.[59] *Glenearn* sailed on her 70th and last voyage at 1.06 p.m. on Monday 19th October, 1970,[290] 19.10.70 with a full complement of officers and seamen, and a full cargo for Penang, Port Swettenham, Singapore, Bangkok, Manila and Hong Kong. In her tanks were 1,119 tons of boiler oil and 300 tons of diesel; quantities sufficient to get as far as Singapore with a safe margin of reserve.

This departure was not heralded in any way; it was strictly a case of "business as usual".[59] There were, however, a few witnesses; employees of Harland & Wolff – men who had worked on her at the turn-round of each voyage. In one's opinion her shell and deck plates were as good as on the day she had been launched, but the places of *Glenearn* and her sisters had been taken by a new fleet, none of which carried on the name and none as solidly-built; soon the old ship would be no more. That's progress, and it's not to be stopped by an old man with a lump in his throat.[146]

Progress had indeed carried the world of shipping forward on a tidal wave of technology in recent years.[A] Even as far back as 1962 automatic helmsmen had been installed in most of the Company's vessels,[478] while the launching of the Japanese-built *Glenalmond* in 1966 had brought a substantial amount of automation on the scene;[291] with fully power-operated hatches and push-button control of topping winches for derricks.[478] Three of her main cargo holds had been designed to take "containerised" cargo – where offered,[291] for conditions at some Far East ports had hardly changed, with unloading into sampans, and so on.[64] Since the ubiquitous computer had gone to sea, a vessel's position could be found very accurately with the aid of an artificial satellite in a specially-chosen earth orbit. Using radar the same computer could track up to ten nearby ships at a time, calculate their courses, then make the necessary alterations to its own course to avoid collisions.[543]

In an associated company of the Ocean conglomerate – which Alfred Holt & Co., had become in recent years[291] – plans were being made for a scheme of shipboard management; each unit having its committee chaired by the "Ship Manager", the new name for the Master.[499] In a Swedish shipyard an oil tanker of 226,000 tons was being squeezed out "like toothpaste" for the Blue Funnel Line; a ship destined, it seemed, to shuttle endlessly between the Arabian Gulf and European oil terminal, with inward and outward passages all fused into one gargantuan voyage, the recurring highlight of which would be the arrival of the helicopter from Cape Town with relief crew members and a change of films for the recreational amenities.

Down below in his sound-proofed, air-conditioned,[498] pastel-coloured, softly-lit control room[291] the solitary console-minder sits, eyeing impassively the curved array of electronic displays.[498] In *Glenalmond* the same already applied, with the English Electric Logger recording signals from more than three hundred sensors located throughout the unseen, unheard machinery installation and the refrigerated and liquid cargoes. At pre-set time intervals one of the automatic typewriters prints out the current values of all these points, with those in an alarm state inked in red – but only for information;[528] the ship's computer has already switched off that faulty pump and over to the spare.[543] Control of the bunkering arrangements is out of human hands too; the tank-filling programme will see to that. Over it all broods the spectre of engine control from the bridge – already there is provision for stopping the vessel directly, in an emergency.[528]

As for skilled marine engineers, with only one man at a time operating the installation at sea, more routine maintenance is done at the base port and less during the voyage;[478] the sea-going engineer who worked, ate and even slept with one ear cocked for the slightest change in the regular rhythm of his beloved engines, is fast disappearing from the scene.[70] That there was still a place, at least for a little longer,[A] for this old-fashioned type was indicated when *Glenearn*'s starboard engine had to be stopped for repairs, followed some days later by the port one.[6] With insufficient water on board to cover the voyage to Penang, a call was made at Cape Town.[59] Next day the starboard engine was stopped for almost seven hours for more repairs;[6] it was almost as if the old ship were trying to delay the inevitable.[A]

24.10.70
30.10.70
4.11.70
5.11.70

An odd incident at 5° 45′ S, 78° 50′ E. A solitary white bird approached and then flew off; it brought attention to itself by its peculiar falls in the air of 15-20 feet – almost like an old biplane aircraft stunting, only much quicker. Although generally similar in shape to a frigate bird with the slender hooked wings, it was smaller and too far off to tell whether the tail was forked or not. To the First Mate,* its most distinguishing feature was a pair of black bands, one running forward from the body diagonally across each wing to terminate at the first joint. It was just a bird, but to the poetically-inclined it was like a departing spirit.

14.11.70

Glenearn's last Met. message was sent off in the first few minutes of 18th November,[6] and the vessel arrived at Penang in the afternoon of the same day. Then on to Port Swettenham. Singapore was reached on the 22nd;[290] there the meteorological instruments were withdrawn.†[6]

18.11.70
22.11.70

Thus far, the voyage had progressed much the same as any other, but now, instead of bunkering to capacity, careful calculations were made to determine the amount of oil required to get them to Kaohsiung where the ship was supposed to arrive with no fuel; 300 tons of boiler oil were taken on.

The grand piano, from what had been the passengers' lounge but had become the officers' smoke room on "de-passengerisation" was donated to Conneil House, the seamen's club of Singapore. The Singapore Agents had made

---

* Mr. P. A. Brown.
† Captain Hill received a Met. Office Award in 1970 and again in 1971.

arrangements for the Port of Singapore Authority Band to come and play on the wharf for *Glenearn*'s final departure, and for the press to be in attendance. The day before the ship was due to sail, however, the President of Singapore died, and the P.S.A. Band was cancelled. As the journalists had enough "hot" news to keep them happy, only one reporter and one photographer attended the evening departure. So to Bangkok.

They left Bangkok at 6.24 a.m. in nice fine weather, but by the time *Glenearn* had cleared the river entrance about three hours later, the sky had become very overcast and threatening. The wind was increasing and the barometer falling rapidly. There had been no warning of an impending storm, but none was needed; they were obviously in for quite a blow.

By noon it was blowing a gale and the rain was coming down in torrents; within the next hour there were three distress calls from different ships, and at 12.55 p.m. *Glenearn* was diverted from her course to go to the aid of *m.v. Empoh*, an Indonesian vessel which was drifting towards the Siamese coast in the vicinity of Prachuap Khiri Khan. The coast there, was on the whole, all rocks and cliffs in a lee shore, with the *Empoh* filling up with water and drifting towards it. She required portable pumps; *Glenearn* had no portable pumps, so the only thing Captain Hill could hope to do was to tow her away from the shore or take the crew off if they decided to abandon.

They found her at 4.24 p.m., when miraculously the rain cleared for about twenty minutes. She was then at anchor in the Bay of Prachuap Khiri Khan where she had drifted. Very fortunately; one mile either north or south would have meant being washed up at the base of very steep cliffs, whereas the shore of the bay was the only sandy beach for miles. There were many fishing boats within the bay, so as a last resort they could carry out any rescue operation that was needed. *Glenearn* could get no closer than 3 miles, for with her draught of 25'-7" the water was too shallow. Had it been calm the distance could have been reduced to 2 miles, but with the sea running the would-be rescuers were rising and falling about

23.11.70

24.11.70
26.11.70
30.11.70

10 feet; long before they could get anywhere near, they would have been bumping on the bottom.

No sooner had all this been sized up than the torrential rain started again, shutting out the whole view and reducing the effectiveness of the radar. When the Master of the *Empoh* realised that the British vessel could do nothing for him he released Captain Hill from his obligation to stand by, letting *Glenearn* proceed on her way to Manila. In the meantime, about 150 miles away, a German ship foundered. Not far from this one another ship was in distress, but the U.S. Navy and Air Force took charge of these rescue operations from their bases in Saigon and other parts of Vietnam. This small tropical depression had been very severe while it lasted, but from midnight it moderated very quickly and by the following morning had disappeared altogether.   1.12.70

On arrival at Hong Kong and concurrently with the   7.12.70
discharge of cargo a start was made on removing the items not required by the buyer. Under the terms of the contract the ship was to be handed over virtually as it was, except for certain specified items. These included such things as a spare armature from one of the forward generators, Nos. 1 and 2 fibre glass almost-new lifeboats and one Beaufort inflatable liferaft. There were other things which could not be removed at Hong Kong: for instance, the radio room equipment and the navigational instruments. For these, crates and boxes were made so that they could be packed up with the minimum of delay, and the buyers given the "notice of readiness" at the earliest possible moment after arrival at Kaohsiung.

Whilst at Hong Kong Captain Hill decided that instead of *Glenearn*'s normal complement of 64, he could manage to get the ship to her final destination with only 34; in any case, the numbers on board had to be reduced substantially if only to comply with the regulations, after the removal of so much safety equipment.[59]

Departing at 2.06 p.m. on 10th December[290] there was   10.12.70
rather more oil in the tanks than necessary to complete the intended one-way voyage. Because of certain things he had heard from private sources, Captain Hill had decided that he

would arrive with enough fuel to be able to get back to Hong Kong, albeit at reduced speed, should the deal fall through. Since the signing of the contract in August, the world prices for scrap had fallen drastically and the buyers were wanting to shed some of their commitments; the only way they could do this was if the vendor had committed some breach of contract. Apparently a couple of Greek ships had recently arrived for scrapping, but when it turned out that their Masters had been selling off bits of their ships along the way, the contracts had been repudiated – although in more prosperous circumstances this would have been overlooked. In *Glenearn*'s case there had been no such breach, but this Master was taking no chances ...

Owing to a lack of communication with *Glenearn*'s owners Captain Hill was now operating entirely on his own, as a vital letter which would have made life much easier for him at this particular moment had not been delivered to him. This letter should have contained all the necessary "gen" to carry out, in good time and in the prescribed way, the enormous amount of documentation resulting from the various clauses in the bill of sale; all sorts of Local Government, Customs and Harbour rules to be conformed to – the breach of which could lead to all sorts of penalties. Equipment to be retained had to be processed by Customs in a prescribed manner; radio equipment had to be dealt with in a special way. Crews paying off would not be allowed to enter and leave Taiwan willy-nilly, but had to proceed under police escort, to a reception centre at Taipeh until they could be flown out.

11.12.70   *Glenearn* arrived at the quarantine anchorage outside Kaohsiung at 11.54 next morning. There they waited until 3.48 p.m., when the pilot, the agent, quarantine, immigration and other officials boarded and the ship was able to proceed to the inner harbour. Kaohsiung was a very good natural harbour standing at the entrance to a lagoon. This lagoon had been dredged and exploited to such an extent that the harbour extended some five or six miles further south than was shown on the charts. On the east bank of the dredged fairway the ground was used for shipbreaking.

Although the contract specified that the ship was to arrive with no ballast, because of *Glenearn*'s draught of 12'-4" forward and 22'-2" aft Captain Hill was asked by radio if he could do anything to reduce the excessive stern trim. His answer was that he certainly could, by putting water ballast into Nos. 1 and 2 Double Bottom oil fuel tanks, but this would be in breach of contract. The agent replied, "Not to mind, this would be taken care of," so they ballasted accordingly.

Suddenly, or so it seemed, they were steaming through Kaohsiung Harbour towards an area for which there were no charts at what could be considered an excessive speed. The Master got the pilot to make a drastic reduction, although his answer was, "What for you worry, Captain? The ship is only scrap." When asked where they were going and what the manoeuvre would be – for by this time they were in a very narrow and shallow channel – the reply was that they were going to a certain berth and the pilot intended to ram the ship's head against one side of the channel then turn her round with the engines before mooring alongside. *Glenearn*'s Master was not particularly happy with these proposals, but decided he would let the pilot go ahead with his plan.

In the event the bow simply would not reach the bank, for there was so little water alongside that it grounded about 40 feet from the shore. It was now obvious that *Glenearn* could not go to the berth that had been intended for her. The pilot spent about fifteen minutes on his little walkie-talkie radio before another berth was allocated, not far from the previous one. The next manoeuvre should have been to back her into the middle of the channel, then set off at a dignified pace, but having apparently started on this the pilot suddenly telegraphed, "Half Ahead" on both engines. By the time this order had been countermanded *Glenearn* had hit the *Gibbes Lykes*, a ship in the process of being scrapped.

It transpired that the pilot had deliberately intended hitting *Glenearn*'s bow off the other ship and letting the force of the collision divert their heading in to the right direction. Captain Hill was horrified and nearly died on the spot. *Glenearn* with her strong build had hardly suffered in the encounter, but the other ship looked very sick indeed. Once *Glenearn* had stopped, the pilot was asked what his intentions were. His first reply was, "What for you worry, Captain? I do this job many times; the ship is only scrap." "Captain" then pointed out that the ship was not "only for scrap" until she had been delivered in a safe condition; the Chinaman pondered this for quite a while, then the penny seemed to drop and he became a different, not to say sane, individual.

However, a few minutes later when his actions had to be questioned again, still the phrase ran off his tongue, "What for you worry, Captain? Ship belong only for scrap." This was the moment before Captain Hill did take over, also threatening the pilot with physical violence if he opened his mouth again. Everything now went well until, as they were finally backing up to the berth, with the engines going half speed nothing was happening; even a touch of "Full Astern" and they brought up with the rudder only 5 feet from the dock wall. They had arrived. Obviously something was not quite right so immediately the officers sounded round the ship. It was now discovered that her stern was 12 feet in the mud; this decreased to a zero sounding amidships, and the bow, which was still freely floating, had 4 feet of water beneath it.

The time was now 5.06 p.m. and they were boarded by the buyers' representative – a Japanese who spoke very little English – his three assistants and four watchmen. They quickly went all over the ship to see that nothing had been removed other than excepted items; at the same time Captain Hill made out a note of readiness, stating that the ship could be handed over. Of course, the ship was not ready, in the sense that she was not "safely afloat", not empty of ballast, and there were still many items not included in the sale which had still to be packed; but, as it was Friday, it was hoped that if the buyer would accept the ship he could cable London and release his letter of credit – the time difference between Taiwan and Britain being 8 hours – so that Glen Line would get their cash before the week-end.

When the buyers' representatives had completed their

inspection and expressed their satisfaction, they accepted the notice of readiness, and it was agreed that the excepted items could be packed, the main engine crankshafts burned through and the water ballast pumped out. However, it turned out that they had no intention of releasing their letter of credit until a diver had gone down and examined the propellers to confirm that they were indeed "manganeze bronze working propellers" – which would not be until the following morning. Glen Line's representative for his part was not going to burn through the crankshafts until he knew that his employers had got their money, so that should the deal fall through he could still get the ship away, with the 34 tons of diesel and 4 tons of boiler oil left in the tanks.

As for the excepted items, there was no question of the buyers being able to take anything to which they were not entitled, and by the same token there was now no possibility of anyone removing more than was listed, for the Taiwanese Customs were so strict they made a note of everything, and should there be any discrepancy, duty would be charged. By the following afternoon everything had been packed up and the water ballast pumped out, so the rest of the week-end was spent watching the *Gibbes Lykes* gradually being broken up by the Tung Cheng Steel & Iron Works Co., Ltd. 12.12.70

On the Monday there was still no news from London, but nevertheless Captain Hill made arrangements with the agents to book passages for 31 of the ship's complement to fly to Hong Kong the following day. He had decided that the Chief and Third Engineers could, with him, stand by the ship, and if necessary they could manage on their own to get to an anchorage in the stream. 14.12.70

Taiwan was very much a Police State, with very little freedom of movement for foreigners. Also, there was only one international airport, which was at Taipeh; the method of getting ships' crews out of the country was to get them all together under Immigration and Customs escort, then travel up to Taipeh where they would all be kept together under house arrest in a transit hotel until such time as they could board an international flight out of the country.

By Tuesday noon word had been received that the Glen Line had been paid, and the Master gave the go-ahead to the Chief Engineer to burn through the crankshafts. After about 15 minutes Captain Hill wandered down to the engine room to see for himself how the job was going, and was amazed to find that already one $17\frac{3}{4}''$ crankshaft had been done, and they were half-way through the other.

It was now too late for the three "rear-guard" officers to get a flight up to Taipeh with the rest of the crew, so after lunch when all the others had departed they leisurely changed into their civilian clothes and finished their packing. When the launch arrived to take them ashore the Chief Engineer did his final thing. Putting on his engine room gloves Bill Wright went below and stopped the generator; then, returning on deck took off the gloves and tossed them over the side. How strange it was to walk out of one's room, leaving it with the bunk made up, towels hanging in the bathroom, papers on the desk and keys in the door of the safe! Even cans of beer still in the 'fridge – to walk down to the gangway in a deathly sort of silence, past the saloon with its tables all laid out again after lunch, ready for dinner. At the gangway they said, "Goodbye" to the four watchmen who would look after the ship until the work of demolition commenced. Walking down the gangway for this, the last time, left one with a very guilty feeling; a feeling that what they were doing was not really right – like leaving one's favourite dog at the vet's to be destroyed.

Accommodation had been booked at the Hotel Kingdom, Kaohsiung's best. For some reason the usual security arrangements were not imposed, and they were free to wander round the town at leisure. It was obvious that ship-breaking was Kaohsiung's biggest business; just about every other shop was selling cutlery, refrigerators, furniture, linen and all sorts of maritime stores. One wondered how long it would be before *Glenearn*'s equipment would start appearing in these shops.

That night Captain Hill slept like a log. For the previous six he had hardly slept at all, worrying about things – with the thought uppermost in his mind that he must get a signature from the buyers' representative, acknowledging that *Glenearn* had been delivered in good order and condition. When, next morning, he telephoned about this, he was told that there was no problem, and sure enough, within an hour he had a little piece of paper confirming receipt of the ship; with this were three airline tickets which would get them to Hong Kong.

At 3.00 p.m. they took 'plane at Kaohsiung Airport and arrived at Taipeh at 4.12. By 6.10 they were on a Cathay Pacific flight which got them to Hong Kong at 8.00 in the evening, and within an hour they had met up with the rest of the European crew at their hotel. The Chinese contingent had been paid off by the Hong Kong agents;[59] only one of them had come to say "Goodbye", and the First Mate was sure he was the commissar putting on an act[21] – in which case the others may have been forbidden to show any affection or courtesy.[A] The eleven Occidentals were all booked on a BOAC flight for the following evening.

Before they left, Bob Kee, the Chinese representative of the local agency – with whom they had become very friendly during their time in *Glenearn* – entertained the travellers to a Chinese dinner. From the restaurant he got them to the airport, and none of them was feeling any pain as they boarded flight BA 939.

Next thing they knew was disemplaning at London Airport at 11.50 in the forenoon, and from there on as they gradually dispersed on the route to the main London stations, the numbers got fewer and fewer. From Euston Captain Hill travelled to his home town of Northwich on his own. It was all a great anti-climax after what had been at stake only a few days before. Looking back he thought he had made a mess of things, but for the present he was simply grateful to be having Christmas at home.

However, the thing that amazed him most of all was that, having accomplished something which was unusual, without proper guidance from any of his principals, nobody was in the least interested in knowing how he had got on. And until now this story has never been told.[59]

SOLD FOR SCRAP

With sacred song and holy word
Both saint and sinner are interred:
the short, the tall, the fool, the sage,
Ermined Lord and buttoned page,
Premier, poet, pimp or peasant,
Under the Cross or under the Crescent,
When it's time for them to go
Are so carefully laid below.

Yet I, who all my life have worked
And never have duty shirked,
Who fought the winds and fought the seas,
Fought King George's enemies,
Brought cargoes home for such as you,
Kept safe my passengers and crew,
I know for me there'll be not heard
One sacred song, one holy word.

"God bless this ship!" the lady said.
And spilled champagne about my head;
The cheers were loud, the cheers were long,
And I was very young and strong,
And proudly slid I to the sea;
But now there's no champagne for me;
They'll make me into trains for boys,
And prams for girls, and such like toys.

For they will come with vicious tool,
Scarce waiting for my guts to cool;
And they will rip my plates apart,
And they will break my hull and heart:
When falls my stack then falls my pride,
No more I'll meet the morning tide;
So bid I farewell to the sea;
There's none will ever weep for me.

H.G

APPENDICES

APPENDIX A

SOURCES

Individuals

(Not all quoted)

[1] AIKEN,* Lieut.-Com. (E) A. C. L., MBE, RNR.
[2] AIKEN, Alexander.
[3] AIKEN,* James H., MBE.
[4] ALLISON, Kenneth J., late Sub-Lieut. RANR.
[5] ARNOLD, A. G., late Ocean Steamship Co. Ltd.
[6] AYRES, F. J., Meteorological Office.
[7] BARRACLOUGH, Captain E. M. C., CBE, RN.
[8] BARRATT, J. W., Romsey, Hampshire.
[9] BATEMAN, Reginald E., late Capt., Royal Marines.
[10] BELL, Andrew, late midshipman, *m.v. Glenearn.*
[11] BELL, F. G., late Lieutenant, Royal Marines.
[12] BELL, Dr. W. G. M., Newtownards, N. Ireland.
[13] BEST, Lieut.-Com. Julian W., DSO, RD, RNR (retd.).
[14] BIRTLES,* Jack M., MM, late 1st Bn. S. Lancs. Regt.
[15] BOWRING, R. A.
[16] BRADLEY, J., late 11th Scottish Commando.
[17] BRITTEN, S. E., late Ship Adoption Society.
[18] BROKENSHIRE, Harald, late 7 Australian Div., AIF.
[19] BROWN, Albert, Ocean Fleets Ltd.
[20] BROWN, Mrs. Albert, St. Helen's, Merseyside.
[21] BROWN, Peter A., Ocean Fleets Ltd.
[22] BUCHANAN, George, late Lloyd's Register of Shipping.
[23] BUXTON, J., Ocean Fleets Limited.
[24] CAPEY, R. F., late Grayson, Rollo & Clover Docks Ltd.
[25] CHURTON, J. K., late 24th Bn. NZ Infantry.
[26] CLARK, Lieut.-Col. C. R., GM, late Royal Engineers.
[27] COLWELL, F. J., late 7 Australian Div., AIF.
[28] COCKERELL,* J. A., late Royal Marines.
[29] CONWAY, Captain H. R., RN (retd.).
[30] COOK, Arthur, late Harland & Wolff Ltd.
[31] COWAN, Sydney M., MBE, late Glen Line Ltd.
[32] COX, Harold H., late *HMAS Westralia.*
[33] CRAUFORD, Major C. L., MC, late 2nd E. Yorks. Regt.
[34] CROWE,* J. W., late Harland & Wolff Ltd.
[35] CURLING, H. F., late Captain, Royal Marines.
[36] CUTLER, Commander K. M., RD, RNR (retd.).
[37] DAVIES, John, late 1st Bn. S. Lancashire Regt.
[38] DOWIE, Capt. J. F. C., late Glen Line Marine Supt.
[39] DUBOIS, James H., late Sub-Lieut. (E), RNVR.
[40] EARLEY, John D., late Able Seaman, Royal Navy.
[41] EDMISTON, Sir Archibald, Blanefield, Stirlingshire.
[42] ELSWORTH, Lieut.-Com. R. F. G., DSC, RN (retd.).
[43] EMSON, B. D., Secretary British Ship Adoption Society.
[44] EVANS, Major David E., OBE, GM, late Royal Tank Regt.

* Deceased.

415

[45] FELTON, Mrs. Christine, Old Heathfield, Sussex.
[46] FINKEL,* Commander G. I., RN (retd.).
[47] FLEMING,* Peter.
[48] FLETCHER, E. D., late Corporal, Royal Air Force.
[49] FORREST, J., Robb Caledon Shipbuilders Ltd.
[50] FREE,* George B., late *HMAS Hobart*.
[51] FULLJAMES, Commander G. J., RNVR.
[52] GARSIDE, R., Ocean Management Services Ltd.
[53] GARSON, David S., MBE, late Admiralty Pilot.
[54] GILHESPY, W. C. B., late cadet *m.v. Diloma*.
[55] GOW, Brigadier J. W. H.
[56] GRINDLE, Captain John A., CBE, RN (retd.), JP.
[57] HAMILTON, Admiral Sir John, GBE, CB.
[58] HART, A. M., late Lieutenant, RNR.
[59] HILL, Captain C. H. F., Ocean Fleets Ltd.
[60] HILL, Kenneth C., late Leading Stoker, RN.
[61] HILL,* Capt. Laurence B., DSO, CBE, RN (retd.).
[62] HOLLAND, G. R. D., late Lieutenant, RN.
[63] HOOD, Lieut.-Com. Thomas, OBE, RNR (retd.).
[64] HUNTER, Robert, late Glen Line Ltd.
[65] HUTCHINSON, Lieut.-Col. C. F., DSO, OBE, DL, 2nd E. Yorks.
[66] HUTCHISON, Capt. C. A. G., DSO and bar, OBE, RN (retd.).
[67] JOHNSON, Colonel E. F., OBE, MC, late 1st S. Lancs. Regt.
[68] JOHNSON, F., late 112 Fighter Squadron, RAF.
[69] JOHNSTON, Dr. H. C. A., late Surg.-Lieut., RNVR.
[70] KEITH-WILSON, J., late Ocean Steamship Co.
[71] KENNEDY, Duncan, late Sub-Lieut. (E), RNVR.
[72] KERR, William, late Caledon Shipyard, Dundee.
[73] KIRK,* Rev. George, Glasgow.
[74] LAMBLE, Kevin, late ship's butcher, *HMS Glenearn*.
[75] LEE, E. W., late Harland & Wolff Ltd.
[76] LEE-BARBER, Rear-Admiral J., CB, DSO and bar, RN (retd.).
[77] LINDSAY, Dr., Ocean Fleets Ltd.
[78] LODGE, Eric I., late Royal Australian Engineers.
[79] LOGAN, Robert A., late 7 Australian Div., AIF.
[79a] LUCKETT, D. W., late Royal Engineers.
[80] McARTHUR, J., External Affairs Dept., Port of London Authority.
[81] McBRIDE, Alex., late of Inveraray, Argyll.
[82] MacCALLUM, L. C., Head Forester, Culbin Forest.
[83] MACKECHNIE, J., late Schoolmaster, Inveraray.
[84] MACKENZIE, E. F., Burghead, Morayshire.
[85] McKENZIE,* William, MBE, late Lieutenant (E), RNVR.
[86] MACLEAN, A., late Lieut.-Com. (S), RNVR.
[87] MacLENNAN, Duncan, late Stoker, Royal Navy.
[88] MAIDMENT, Commander K. T., RD, RNR.
[89] MARRIOT, Frederick, Lamlash, Isle of Arran.
[90] MARSHALL, Walter, Lamlash, Isle of Arran.
[91] MARTIN, Stan. B., late Royal New Zealand Navy.
[92] MASON, Malcolm J., OBE, BA, late NZ Infantry.
[93] MATON, Oswald, late Lieutenant, Royal Marines.
[94] MAYHEW,* Lieut.-Com. M. F., CGM, VRD, RN (retd.).
[95] MEEK, M., BSc, Director, Ocean Fleets Ltd.
[96] MILVERTON, Leslie, late Stoker, Royal Navy.
[97] MIDWINTER, C. J., late Sub-Lieut. (E), RNVR.
[98] MIRRLEES,* William M., MM, Liverpool.
[99] MONEY, Col. R. A., late 2/6th Australian Gen. Hospital, AIF.

[100] MOORE, J., late 1st Bn. South Lancashire Regiment.
[101] MORRISON, Malcolm, late Seaman, Royal Navy.
[102] MORTON, Walter, late Able Seaman, Royal Navy.
[103] MURRISON, Arthur L., late Caledon Shipyard, Dundee.
[104] NAPIER, R. A., Ocean Fleets Ltd.
[105] NEARY, J., BEM, late 1st Bn. South Lancashire Regiment.
[106] PAYNE-JAMES, Dr. I., MB, ChB, late Surg.-Lieut., RNVR.
[107] PEACOCK, Commander R. M. T., RN (retd.).
[108] PETERSEN, Friis, Burmeister & Wain's Motor-Og Maskinfabrik.
[109] PICKEN, Lieut.-Col. Keith S., late 2/27th Bn., AIF.
[110] PHILPOTT, L. B., Meteorological Office.
[111] PHILPOTT, Mrs. Lena E., Bristol.
[112] PLUNKETT, H. M. O., late Lieutenant (S), RN.
[113] RAMSAY, William McK., late Lieut. (E), RNR and Ocean S. Co. Ltd.
[114] RAWLINGS, Peter L., late *HMS Glengyle*.
[115] RENISON, Col. J. D. W., DSO, TD, late 2nd Bn. E. Yorks. Regt.
[116] RICHARDS, Eric J., late Major, Royal Marines.
[117] RIGBY, Colonel G., OBE, GM, ERD, late Royal Engineers.
[118] RISHWORTH, John B., late 2nd Bn. Frontier Force Rifles.
[119] ROBERTSON, Captain Ian G., DSO, DSC and bar, RN (retd.).
[120] ROSE, John, Inveraray, Argyll.
[121] ROSEBERY, The Earl of.
[122] RUSHTON, G. W., late Royal Navy.
[123] RUSSELL, Mrs. J., late of Morayshire.
[124] SCOTT,* Peter W., late Lieutenant, RNR.
[125] SEYMOUR, Leslie A. T., late Able Seaman, Royal Navy.
[126] SHARP, George E., late Glen Line Ltd.
[127] SHAW, G. D., late Able Seaman, Royal Navy.
[128] SINCLAIR, George E., late Grayson, Rollo & Clover.
[129] SKINNER, John, Inver-Fearn, Ross-shire.
[130] SMITH,* Adam P., MB, ChB.
[131] STEEL, J. A. R., late *HMS Slinger*.
[132] STEEL, R. B., late Sub-Lieut. (E), RNVR. (Name changed.)
[133] STIRLING, Charles, Lamlash, Isle of Arran.
[134] SURRY, A., late Harland & Wolff Ltd.
[135] TAIT, John, late Stoker, Royal Navy.
[136] TAIT, Dr. W. M., late Surg.-Lieut., RCNVR.
[137] TAYLOR, Alastair R. L., late *m.v. Glenearn*.
[138] TAYLOR, David L., Robb Caledon Shipbuilders Ltd.
[139] TAYLOR, F. D., late Cook, *HMS Glenearn*.
[140] THOMAS, D. D., late X-Ray Technician, Royal Navy.
[141] THOMPSON, A. H., late Radar Mechanic, Royal Navy.
[142] TOOLE, Gerald, late Australian Imperial Force.
[143] TORBET, D. M., Corpn. of Dundee Public Libraries Dept.
[144] TRIMBLE, Lieut.-Com. Paul, RANR (retd.).
[145] TURNER, John, Lamlash, Isle of Arran.
[146] UTTERIDGE, C. R., late Harland & Wolff Ltd.
[147] WALKER, David S., late Leading Stoker, Royal Navy.
[148] WALLIS, R. S., MBE, BSc, Herne Bay County Secondary School.
[149] WAPPETT, Chris, late Smith's Dock Company Ltd.
[150] WARD, A. N., late 2/27th Bn., AIF.
[151] WARD, W. F., late Engineer Manager, Harland & Wolff Ltd.
[152] WATERS, Cyril, late Lieutenant, Royal Marines.
[153] WEARNE, Frederick, late 1st Bn. S. Lancashire Regiment.
[154] WEATHERS, V. G., late *HMS Glenearn*.
[155] WEBBER, Richard, FASI, late Lieutenant, Royal Marines.

[156] WEIR, John, Secretary, Hayston Golf Club, Kirkintilloch.
[157] WHEATLEY, Lawrence, late XI Squadron, RAF.
[158] WHEELER, H. P., late Gunner, Royal Navy.
[159] WILLIAMS, Alf., late 1st Bn. S. Lancashire Regiment.
[160] WILLIAMSON, John, late Able Seaman, Royal Navy.
[161] WILLING, D., Findhorn, Morayshire.
[162] WOOD, A. E., late Harland & Wolff Ltd.
[163] WURTZBURG, Mrs. Rhoda, Devon.

Public Record Office
(Crown copyright)

CENTRAL DIRECTION OF THE WAR
[164] CAB 82 23 840

ADMIRALTY – SHIPS' LOGS
[165] ADM 53/112 327   *HMS Glenroy*, October 1940
[166] ADM 53/112 328   *HMS Glenroy*, November 1940
[167] ADM 53/112 329   *HMS Glenroy*, December 1940
[168] ADM 53/113 766   *HMS Calcutta*, April 1941
[169] ADM 53/114 232   *HMS Glenroy*, January 1941
[170] ADM 53/114 310   *HMS Glasgow*, February 1941
[171] ADM 53/114 311   *HMS Glasgow*, March 1941
[172] ADM 53/114 323   *HMS Glengyle*, January 1941
[173] ADM 53/114 324   *HMS Glengyle*, February 1941
[174] ADM 53/114 325   *HMS Glengyle*, March 1941
[175] ADM 53/114 326   *HMS Glengyle*, April 1941
[176] ADM 53/114 327   *HMS Glengyle*, May 1941
[177] ADM 53/114 863   *HMS Phoebe*, April 1941
[178] ADM 53/114 899   *HMS Protector*, April 1941
[179] ADM 53/114 499   *HMS Glenearn*, December 1944
[180] ADM 53/120 730   *HMS Warspite*, June 1944
[181] ADM 53/121 432   *HMS Glenearn*, January 1945
[182] ADM 53/121 433   *HMS Glenearn*, February 1945
[183] ADM 53/121 434   *HMS Glenearn*, March 1945
[184] ADM 53/121 435   *HMS Glenearn*, April 1945
[185] ADM 53/121 436   *HMS Glenearn*, May 1945
[186] ADM 53/121 437   *HMS Glenearn*, June 1945
[187] ADM 53/121 438   *HMS Glenearn*, July 1945
[188] ADM 53/121 439   *HMS Glenearn*, August 1945
[189] ADM 53/121 440   *HMS Glenearn*, September 1945
[190] ADM 53/121 441   *HMS Glenearn*, October 1945
[191] ADM 53/121 442   *HMS Glenearn*, November 1945
[192] ADM 53/121 443   *HMS Glenearn*, December 1945
ADM 53/122 941*–   *HMS Glenearn*, January–
ADM 53/122 947*   *HMS Glenearn*, August 1946

ADMIRALTY – ADMIRALTY AND SECRETARIAT CASES
[193] ADM 116/4335   Conditions of Service for T.124 Personnel.
[194] ADM 116/5080   Combined Training Areas.

ADMIRALTY – WAR HISTORY CASES
[195] ADM 199/110   Enemy Air Raids on Naval Establishments.
[196] ADM 199/111   Enemy Air Raids on Naval Establishments.

* Not consulted.

[197] ADM 199/623   Japanese Air Attacks on Ceylon.
[198] ADM 199/666   Reports of Proceedings of HM Ships.
[199] ADM 199/806   1941 Naval Ops. in the Mediterranean.
[200] ADM 199/1177   1941 Enemy Air Attacks on HM Ships.
[201] ADM 199/1554   1943–1944   Rehearsals, etc.
[202] ADM 199/1561   1944   Force "S" Orders, etc.
[203] ADM 199/1628   1943–1944   Naval Forces – State of Readiness.
[204] ADM 199/1651   1944   Survivors' Interrogation Reports.
[205] ADM 199/1654   1944–1945   Operation "Neptune": Reports.
[206] ADM 199/1655   1944–1945   Operation "Neptune": Reports.
[207] ADM 199/1668   1944   Operation "Neptune": Signals, 14th–15th June.
[208] ADM 199/1669   1944   Operation "Neptune": Signals, 16th–18th June.
[209] ADM 199/1670   1944   Operation "Neptune": Signals, 19th–22nd June.
[210] ADM 199/1740   1945–1946   Fleet Train: Accommodation, etc.
[211] ADM 199/1743   1945–1946   Fleet Train: Ships of Force "X" etc.
[212] ADM 199/1749   1944–1945   Fleet Train: Manus Naval Base etc.
[213] ADM 199/1765   1945   Fleet Train: Operations after Collapse of Japan.
[214] ADM 199/2067   1941–1942   Damage to Ships: Reports.

ADMIRALTY – ROYAL MARINES
[215] ADM 202/327   Force "X" Landing Craft Flotillas.

ADMIRALTY – FIRST SEA LORD PAPERS
[216] ADM 205/4   Plan "Catherine".

COMBINED OPERATIONS HEADQUARTERS
[217] DEFE 2/1   Headquarters War Diary, June 1940–September 1941.
[218] DEFE 2/5   Headquarters War Diary, 1st–31st December 1942.
[219] DEFE 2/6   Headquarters War Diary, 1st–31st January 1943.
[220] DEFE 2/23   Headquarters War Diary, 23rd October–5th November 1943.
[221] DEFE 2/24   Headquarters War Diary, 6th–23rd November 1943.
[222] DEFE 2/52   War Diary No. 48 (RM) Commando.
[223] DEFE 2/66   Operation "Aconite".
[224] DEFE 2/116 Operation "Brisk" Part 1.
[225] DEFE 2/165 Operation "Coronet".
[226] DEFE 2/178 Dodecanese Islands.
[227] DEFE 2/431 Enemy Defences in the Invasion Area.
[228] DEFE 2/433 Report: Effect of Fire Support.
[229] DEFE 2/490 Opposition in Normandy on D-Day.
[230] DEFE 2/625–626   Operation "Workshop".
[231] DEFE 2/698 Early History of Directorate of Combined Ops.
[232] DEFE 2/764 1944   Details of Landing Ships.
[233] DEFE 2/790 1940–1941   Training for Ops. Overseas.
[234] DEFE 2/813 1940–1942   Inter-Services Training and Development Centre.
[235] DEFE 2/838 1940–1942   Glen Ships. Memo. on Experience Gained in the
                  Mediterranean.
[236] DEFE 2/890 1941   Report on Operations at Bardia.
[237] DEFE 2/1293 Evolution and Development of Amphibious Technique and
                  Materials, 1940–1945.
[238] DEFE 2/1327 Historical Notes on Landing Craft.
[239] DEFE 2/1333 Historical Notes on Combined Training Centres, Middle East.

HOME OFFICE
[240] HO 193/65   Bomb Census Maps: Liverpool, October 1940–January 1942.
[241] HO 198/197 Raid Summaries: NW Region, June 1940–January 1942.
[242] HO 198/207 Raid Summaries: Special Reports. Shipyards.
[243] HO 201/1 to 5   Daily Reports: 8th September 1939–December 1940.

WAR OFFICE – WAR DIARIES
[244] WO 166/4324   2nd Bn. Hampshire Regt., January 1941.
[245] WO 166/4558   2nd Bn. R. Norfolk Regt., January 1941.
[246] WO 169/1701   3rd Bn. Coldstream Gds., April 1941.
[247] WO 169/1702   1st Bn. Argyll & S'land H., April 1941.
[248] WO 169/1736   2nd Bn. Leicestershire Regt., April 1941.
[249] WO 171/1263   7th Bn. Argyll & S'land H., June 1944.
[250] WO 171/1265   1st Bn. The Black Watch, June 1944.
[251] WO 171/1332   1st Bn. S. Lancashire Regt., 1944.
[252] WO 171/1397   2nd Bn. E. Yorkshire Regt., 1944.

MINISTRY OF WAR TRANSPORT
[253] MT 9/3003   1938–1939   Conditions in the Shipbuilding Industry.
[254] MT 9/3122/M.12459   Merchant Shipping: Assumption of Control by Admiralty.
[255] MT 59/295   1940–1945   Rates of Hire.

BOARD OF TRADE
[256] BT 31/14356   Clyde Engineering and Iron Ship Building Company (Limited).

SCOTTISH RECORD OFFICE
[257] BT/454   State Line Steamship Co. Ltd.
[258] BT/797   Scotia Shipping Co. Ltd.

General Register Office, Edinburgh

OLD PARISH RECORDS
[259] County of Lanark, O.P.R. 644, Vol. 31, p. 248.
[260] County of Banff, Parish of Kirkmichael.
[261] County of Lanark, Parish of Glasgow.

REGISTER OF BIRTHS, BURGH OF GLASGOW
[262] District of Blythswood, Entry No. 762.
[263] District of Blythswood, Entry No. 833.

REGISTER OF MARRIAGES, BURGH OF GLASGOW
[264] District of Blythswood, Entry No. 504.

REGISTER OF DEATHS, COUNTY OF DUMBARTON
[265] Parish of Roseneath, Entry No. 1.

CENSUS OF SCOTLAND
[266] 31st March 1851. County of Lanark, Parish Glasgow N. Inner High 1851/555/20/49.
[267] 3rd April 1871. Burgh of Glasgow, District of Milton 644[7]/1871/99/84.

General Register Office, London

REGISTER OF DEATHS, COUNTY OF LONDON
[268] Sub-district of Hampstead, Entry No. 36.

High Court of Justice: Family Division

[269] Will of James McGregor. Registered 20th April 1896.

Companies House, London

TRADE & INDUSTRIES DEPTS. (LIMITED COMPANIES SECTION)
[270] For records of the London & Glasgow Engineering and Iron Ship Building
Company Limited and its predecessor, refer to Public Record Office reference
no. 943 (Company No. 1238C) and 14356 (Company No. 1207C).
[271] Company No. 111291 Glen Line Ltd.

Australian Department of Defence, Canberra

HISTORICAL STUDIES SECTION, NAVY SUB-SECTION
[272] Report of Proceedings – *HMAS Burdekin*, February–March 1945.
[273] Report of Proceedings – *HMAS Hobart*, 20th June–17th July 1941.
[274] Report of Proceedings – *HMAS Hobart*, January 1946.
[275] War Diary – *HMAS Hobart*, 1st–31st July 1941.
[276] Report of Proceedings – *HMAS Nizam*, April 1945.
[277] Report of Proceedings – *HMAS Norman*, April 1945.
[278] War Diary – *HMAS Stuart*, April 1941.
[279] Letter of Proceedings – *HMAS Voyager*, April 1941.
[280] War Diary – *HMAS Voyager*, April 1941..

New Zealand National Archives

WAR HISTORY COLLECTION (WAII) – WAR DIARIES
[281] DA 58/1/6–7 HQ 6NZ Inf Bde, 1st March–30th April 1941.
[282] DA 60/1/8–11 24 NZ Battalion, 1st March–30th June 1941.

Archives

[283] Australian War Memorial, Canberra City.
[284] Commonwealth War Graves Commission.
[285] Corporation of Lloyd's, London. Refer now to Guildhall Library, London, EC2P
2E3.

MINISTRY OF DEFENCE
[286] (Navy Department) Bath.
[287] Naval Historical Branch, London, SW6 1TR.

MITCHELL LIBRARY, GLASGOW
[288] Wotherspoon Collection, Vol. 10, p. 32.

OCEAN TRANSPORT & TRADING LTD., LIVERPOOL
[289] Ship's Log *m.v. Glenearn*.
[290] Journal *m.v. Glenearn*.
[291] Miscellaneous information.

[292] Riksarkivet, Oslo.
[293] Royal Marines' Museum, Southsea.

STRATHCLYDE REGIONAL ARCHIVES, GLASGOW
[294] Clyde Shipbuilding Lists, Vol. 2.

[295] University of St. Andrews.

Registers, Directories

LLOYD'S REGISTER OF SHIPPING
[296] Registers from 1868.
[297] Reports on *m.v. Glenearn*.
[298] Correspondence.

[299] Navy List.

POST OFFICE DIRECTORIES
[300] Glasgow.
[301] London.

[302] Who Was Who, 1961–70.

Newspapers

H.M. Customs and Excise
Clyde Bill of Entry
[303] 24th February 1848.
[304] 28th March 1848.
[305] 11th April 1848.
[306] 24th August 1848.
[307] 12th October 1867.
[308] 16th November 1867.
[309] 4th August 1868.
[310] 3rd December 1890.
[311] 23rd February 1892.

H.M. Customs and Excise
[312] *London "A" Bill*, 22nd July 1871.

Courier & Advertiser,
Dundee
[313] 29th December 1936.
[314] 23rd April 1937.
[315] 30th June 1938.

Courier Mail, Brisbane
[316] 15th January 1945, p. 3.

Daily News, Ceylon
[317] 3rd April 1942.
[318] 6th April 1942.

Dumbarton Herald
[319] 4th October 1867.
[319a] 12th November 1867.
[320] 25th June 1868.
[321] 9th July 1868.
[322] 26th November 1868.
[323] 24th December 1868.
[324] 22nd April 1869.
[325] 4th November 1869.

Evening Telegraph, Dundee
[326] 6th December 1888.
[327] 9th February 1937.
[328] 20th June 1938.
[329] 29th June 1938.

Glasgow Herald
[330] 28th February 1840, 2d.
[331] 20th September 1850, 2f.
[332] 1st July 1870, 8g.
[333] 3rd August 1870, 8h.
[334] 3rd October 1870, 8h.
[335] 5th October 1870, 8h.
[336] 10th October 1870, 8h.
[337] 11th October 1870, 8g.
[338] 13th October 1870, 7e.
[339] 3rd November 1870, 6f.

[340] 25th July 1871, 6e.
[341] 24th August 1871, 6f.
[342] 1st July 1875, 8f.
[343] 29th December 1875, 8g.
[344] 28th June 1877, 5g.
[345] 4th July 1877, 5h.
[346] 5th July 1877, 4g.
[347] 1st January 1880, 8g.
[348] 27th January 1897, 6g.
[349] 26th November 1910, 9c.
[350] 28th November 1910, 10a.
[351] 30th November 1910, 8f.
[352] 12th January 1911, 6f.
[353] 21st July 1931, 9, 10a–b.
[354] 22nd July 1931, 11c–d.
[355] 23rd July 1931, 7d–e.
[356] 24th July 1931, 12d–e.
[357] 25th July 1931, 9f–g, 10a–b.
[358] 31st July 1931, 11f–g, 12a–c.
[359] 4th March 1932, 16e.
[360] 22nd December 1934, 17d.
[361] 12th March 1936, 13c–d.
[362] 22nd December 1947, 5f.

Journal of Commerce and Shipping
Telegraph, Liverpool
[363] 6th October 1944.

Liverpool Daily Post
[364] 21st December 1940.

Liverpool Echo
[365] 8th May 1956.
[366] 9th May 1956.
[367] 10th May 1956.

Lloyd's List, London
[368] 5th September 1970.

London Gazette
[369] 18th November 1941, Supplement.
[370] 14th November 1944, Supplement.
[371] 14th June 1945, Supplement.
[372] 22nd January 1946, 4th Supplement.
[373] 2nd January 1947, 4th Supplement.
[374] 30th October, 1947, Supplement.
[375] 19th May 1948, Supplement.
[376] 2nd June 1948, Supplement.

Melbourne Herald
[377] 13th June 1945.

North British Daily Mail, Glasgow
[378] 9th September 1867, 3a.
[379] 24th September 1867, 4a.
[380] 29th August 1870, 4e.
[381] 30th September 1870, 4d.
[382] 1st October 1870, 4f.
[383] 3rd October 1870, 4d.
[384] 11th October 1870, 4c.
[385] 16th October 1871, 6g.
[386] 21st October 1872, 3f.
[387] 13th May 1873, 6e.
[388] 11th September 1873, 6g.
[389] 8th November 1873, 3f.
[390] 4th April 1874, 7b.
[391] 3rd July 1876, 6f, g.
[392] 3rd August 1876, 7d.
[393] 20th October 1876, 7b.
[394] 16th January 1877, 7c.
[395] 17th January 1877, 7b.
[396] 21st June 1877, 3g.
[397] 23rd June 1877, 3f.
[398] 23rd June 1877, 6f.
[399] 22nd November 1878, 7b.
[400] 28th November 1878, 7b.
[401] 8th May 1879, 6h.
[402] 22nd November 1880, 7c–d.
[403] 29th March 1882, 6e–f.
[404] 13th July 1882, 6g.
[405] 14th July 1882, 6g.

St. Andrew's Citizen
[406] 1st April 1905.

The Scotsman, Edinburgh
[407] 13th September 1939.
[408] 20th January 1945, 6f.

Shanghai Herald
[409] 1st October 1945.

South China Morning Post &
Hong Kong Telegraph
[410] 5th January 1939.
[411] 1st February 1939.
[412] 11th October 1945.
[413] 8th December 1945.
[414] 9th December 1945.
[415] 27th January 1946.

The Times, London
[416] 4th September 1868, 5a.
[417] 4th January 1869, 5b.
[418] 7th July 1875, 12a.
[419] 17th October 1876, 5f.
[420] 29th May 1879, 11a.
[421] 4th July 1879, 6b.

[422] 8th July 1879, 11d.
[423] 31st May 1882, 10c.
[423a] 1st June 1882, 10f.
[424] 23rd June 1882, 11e.
[425] 14th July 1882, 11f.
[426] 30th November 1882, 6e.
[427] 5th January 1883, 9b.
[428] 23rd May 1883, 8d.
[429] 24th May 1883, 7f.
[430] 22nd June 1883, 13c.
[431] 27th June 1883, 9c.
[432] 26th August 1884, 3f.
[433] 7th August 1885, 3b–c.
[434] 26th December 1885, 9c.
[435] 20th June 1886, 19d.
[436] 14th December 1887, 3f.
[437] 23rd August 1890, 9f.
[438] 11th July 1891, 12c.
[439] 12th June 1935, 17b.
[440] 22nd August 1939, 9b.
[441] 23rd August 1939, 11a–c.
[442] 25th August 1939, 12f.
[443] 26th August 1939, 3d.
[444] 28th August 1939, 11e–f.
[445] 2nd September 1939, 10d–e.
[446] 31st March 1941, 4a–b.
[447] 2nd April 1941, 4a–b.
[448] 4th April 1941, 4c.
[449] 5th April 1941, 5c.
[450] 7th April 1941, 4a, b, d.
[451] 15th July 1941, 3d.
[452] 19th January 1943, 4e.
[453] 21st January 1943, 4d.
[454] 26th August 1943, 4c.
[455] 16th May 1944, 4g.
[456] 17th May 1944, 4g.
[457] 24th May 1944, 4g.
[458] 2nd April 1945, 4g.
[459] 6th April 1945, 3c.
[460] 6th April 1945, 4a, b, d.
[461] 1st February 1946, 4e.
[462] 17th July 1950, 4e.
[463] 18th July 1950, 5d.
[464] 16th June 1967, 7d–e.
[465] 19th August 1970, 4g–h.
[466] 27th October 1970, 7a.
[467] 3rd June 1975, 6a.

Western Morning News, Taunton,
Somerset
[468] 9th July 1946.
[469] 10th July 1946.

Yorkshire Post, Leeds
[470] 24th May 1945.

Periodicals

"The Bailie"
[471] No. 557, 20th June 1883.
[472] No. 936, 24th September 1890.

Blue Funnel & Glen Line Bulletin
[473] January 1959, p. 117.
[474] January 1959, p. 111.
[475] July 1961, p. 6.
[476] January 1962, p. 57.
[477] January 1962, pp. 71–74.
[478] January 1962, p. 81.
[479] July 1963, pp. 253–257.
[480] July 1963, p. 272.
[481] January 1964, pp. 333–337.
[482] January 1967, p. 329.

Blue Funnel & Glen Line Staff Bulletin
[483] July 1952, p. 18.
[484] January 1957, p. 208.
[485] January 1957, p. 225.

Globe and Laurel
[486] 1946, *p.* 286.
[487] 1946, *p.* 339.

Illustrated London News
[488] 1st August 1874, p. 105.

"Iron"
[489] 17th November 1877, p. 621.
[490] 24th May 1879, p. 655.
[490a] 21st June 1879, p. 783.
[491] 24th March 1882, p. 229.

The Marine Engineer
[492] 1st March 1882, p. 270.
[493] 1st April 1882, p. 30.

The Motor Ship
[494] December 1935, p. 309.
[495] December 1935, p. 311.
[496] November 1938, p. 306.
[497] January 1939, pp. 356–358.

Ocean (The Journal of the Ocean Steam Ship Group)
[498] December 1971, pp. 2–4.
[499] December 1971, p. 10.

The Shipbuilder and Marine Engine-Builder
[500] December 1936, p. 616.
[501] March 1938, p. 151.

Shipbuilding and Shipping Record (Now *Marine Week*)
[502] 17th January 1935, p. 73.
[503] 28th March 1935, p. 356.
[504] 20th June 1935, p. 679.
[505] 12th December 1935, p. 651.
[506] 20th February 1936, p. 243.
[507] 9th July 1936, pp. 62–63.
[508] 30th July 1936, p. 133.
[509] 22nd October 1936, p. 499.
[510] 19th November 1936, p. 626.
[511] 26th November 1936, p. 666.
[512] 10th December 1936, p. 730.
[513] 30th December 1936, pp. 21–22.
[514] 25th March 1937, p. 392.
[515] 6th January 1938, p. 3.
[516] 24th February 1938, p. 247.
[517] 29th September, 1938, pp. 385–389.
[518] 19th January 1939, p. 67.
[519] 23rd May 1939, p. 379.
[520] 31st August 1939, p. 256.
[521] 5th December 1940, pp. 556–558.
[522] 13th March 1941, p. 242.
[523] 18th/25th December 1941, p. 576.
[524] 19th February 1948, p. 239.
[525] 10th May 1951, p. 572.
[526] 18th January 1962, p. 90.
[527] 10th May 1962, p. 626.
[528] 15th December 1966, pp. 797–804.

The Shipping World
[529] 1st February 1887, p. 285.
[530] 1st August 1889, p. 126.

The Shipping World and Herald of Commerce
[531] 1st October 1887, p. 105.
[532] 1st July 1888, p. 66.
[533] 12th December 1900, pp. 583–584.
[534] 1st February 1905, p. 143.
[535] 26th July 1905, p. 75.
[536] 20th December 1911, p. 535.
[537] 18th September 1918, p. 193.

Transactions, etc.

Institute of Marine Engineers
[538] 1950, Vol. LXII, No. 4, pp. 133–164.

Institution of Engineers and Shipbuilders in Scotland
[539] Session 1939–40, Vol. 83, pp. 1–21.

Institution of Naval Architects
[540] 1947, Vol. 88, pp. 50–71.

Liverpool Engineering Society
[541] 1938, Vol. LIX, pp. 144–175.

Clyde Steam and Sailing Shipowners' Associations
Lectures delivered during the Winter 1887–8.
[542] Introductory address by Leonard Gow, 29th November 1887.

Institute of Management & Control
[543] Lecture in Glasgow 10th December 1973 – "World's First Super-Automated Ship with Computer System".

Published Sources

[544] *History of Lloyd's and of Marine Insurance in Great Britain.* Frederick Martin. Macmillan & Co., 1876.
[545] *Lloyd's Code of Distinguishing Flags of the Steamship Owners of the United Kingdom.* Edited by the Committee of Lloyd's. Office of the Shipping & Mercantile Gazette, 1882.
Ordnance Gazetteer of Scotland. Edited by Francis N. Groome. Thomas C. Jack, Edinburgh.
[546] Vol. 3, 1883, p. 134b.
[547] Vol. 3, 1883, p. 187a–b.
[548] Vol. 5, 1885, p. 443a.
[549] *Kirkintilloch: Town & Parish.* Thomas Watson. John Smith & Son, Glasgow, 1894.
[550] *The Prophecies of the Brahan Seer.* Alexander Mackenzie, FSA (Scot.). Eneas MacKay, Stirling, 1899.
[551] *Cassell's Encyclopaedia.* Subscription Edition, c. 1903, Vol. 8, p. 225.
[552] *Who's Who in Glasgow in 1909.* Gowans & Gray Limited, Glasgow, 1909, p. 79.
[553] *Report of the Royal Commission on Shipping Rings.* HMSO, Vol. I, 1909, p. 10.
[554] *Glasgow Shipping.* Journal of Commerce, Glasgow. Fifth Edition, 1917.
[555] *The History of Govan.* T. C. F. Brotchie. The Old Govan Club, Glasgow, 1938, pp. 261–263.
[556] *Mediterranean Assignment.* Richard McMillan. Doubleday, Doran & Co. Inc., New York, 1943.
[557] *Before the Tide Turned.* Lieut.-Com. Hugh Hodgkinson, DSC, RN. George G. Harrap & Co. Ltd., 1944.
[558] *Six Years Hard Labour – Palmers Hebburn 1939–1945.* E. L. Champness. Printed by the Baynard Press, 1945, p. 21.
[559] *Port at War.* Mersey Docks and Harbour Board, 1946.
[560] *Workhorse of the Western Front: the story of the 30th Infantry Division.* Robert L. Hewitt. Infantry Journal Press, Washington D.C., 1946, p. 11.
[561] *British Merchant Vessels Lost or Damaged by Enemy Action during the Second World War.* Admiralty, HMSO, 1947.
Assault Division: A History of the 3rd Division. Norman Scarfe. Collins, 1947.
[562] p. 43.
[563] p. 49.
[564] pp. 53–55.
[565] pp. 58–59.
[566] pp. 69–70.

The Second World War. Winston S. Churchill. Cassell & Co. Ltd.
Vol. I, 1948.
[567] pp. 415–416.
[568] p. 495.
Vol. II, 1949.
[569] p. 539.
Vol. III, 1950.
[570] p. 60.
[571] p. 186.
[572] *The Clans, Septs and Regiments of the Scottish Highlands.* Frank Adam, FRGS, FSA (Scot.). W. & A. K. Johnston Limited, Edinburgh. Fourth Edition, 1952, p. 246.
[573] *Greece and Crete 1941.* C. Buckley. HMSO, 1952, pp. 117–118.
A History of the East Yorkshire Regiment (Duke of York's Own) In the War of 1939–45. Lt.-Col. P. R. Nightingale, OBE. William Sessions Limited, York, 1952.
[574] p. 149.
[575] p. 167.
[576] p. 170.
[577] pp. 173–174.
[578] p. 177.
[579] *Geoffrey Keyes.* Elizabeth Keyes. George Newnes Ltd., 1956.
[580] *History of the Argyll & Sutherland Highlanders. 1st Bn. 1939–1945.* Brig. R. C. B. Anderson, DSO, MC. Printed by T. & A. Constable Ltd., Edinburgh, 1956.
History of United States Naval Operations in World War II. Vol. XI. The Invasion of France and Germany, 1944–45. Samuel Eliot Morison. Little, Brown and Company, Boston, 1957, in association with the Atlantic Monthly Press.
[581] pp. 80–86.
[582] p. 163.
[583] p. 183.
History of the Second World War. HMSO.
[584] *The War Against Japan.* S. Woodburn Kirby. Vol. II, 1957, p. 116.
The War at Sea. S. W. Roskill. Vol. III, Part II, 1961.
[585] p. 38.
[586] p. 61.
[587] p. 69.
[588] Map 24.
[589] p. 430.
Victory in the West. Major L. F. Ellis. Vol. 1, 1962.
[590] p. 136.
[591] p. 142.
[592] p. 161.
[593] *Royal Australian Navy 1939–1942.* G. Hermon Gill. Australian War Memorial, Canberra, 1957, pp. 320–334.
British Shipping. R. H. Thornton. Cambridge University Press, 1959.
[594] pp. 94–95.
[595] pp. 160–161.
[596] pp. 164–165.
[597] pp. 168–171.
[598] p. 228.
[599] *Orders of Battle.* Lieut.-Col. H. F. Joslen. HMSO, Vol. I, 1960, p. 265.
[600] *Nicholl's Seamanship and Nautical Knowledge.* Charles H. Brown. Brown, Son & Ferguson Ltd., Glasgow. 21st Edition, 1961, p. 148.
A Merchant Fleet in War. S. W. Roskill. Collins, 1962.
[601] pp. 34–36.
[602] p. 188.

Royal Australian Navy, 1942–1945. G. Hermon Gill. Australian War Memorial, Canberra, 1968.
[603] pp. 11–13.
[604] pp. 18–21.
[605] *Norges Sjøkrig* (Norway's Sea War) *1940–1945*. E. A. Steen. Gyldendal Norsk, Forlag, Oslo, Vol. VI, 2, 1969, pp. 133–134.

Miscellaneous

BOOKLETS
[606] *Souvenir of the Panama Canal*. I. L. Maduro's Souvenir Store, Panama. Undated.
[607] *Services Guide to Alexandria*. Co-ordinating Committee for the Welfare of H.B.M. Forces in Alexandria. Undated.
[608] *Ceylon's Scenic Splendour*. St. Nihal Singh. Ceylon Government Railway. Undated, p. 42.
[609] *The Effects of the Atomic Bombs at Hiroshima and Nagasaki*. HMSO, 1946.
[610] *"The Story of H.M.S. Glengyle" 1940–1946*. Glen Line Ltd. Undated.
[611] *First Aid and Early Treatment of Burns in the Royal Air Force*. A.M. Pamphlet 168 (Second Edition), Air Ministry, 1956, pp. 26–27.

LEAFLETS
[612] *To All in Force "S"*. Rear-Admiral A. G. Talbot.
[613] *Soldiers, Sailors and Airmen of the Allied Expeditionary Force!* Dwight Eisenhower.
[614] *Life Blood*. D. MacG. Jackson, MD, FRCS. Scottish Home and Health Department, Nov. 1965.

PHOTOGRAPHS
[615] Coastal Silhouette from Franceville Plage (157793) to Lancrune-sur-Mer (033837) taken at zero feet and at right angles to the coast. I.S.T.D.50, March 1944.
[616] Imperial War Museum Negative No. B5093.
[617] Imperial War Museum Negative No. B5102.
[618] Australian War Memorial Photograph No. 83156.

DRAWINGS
[619] *T.S.M.V. Glenearn*. Arrangement of Promenade Deck. $\frac{1}{4}''$ to 1 foot. (Robb Caledon Shipbuilders Ltd., Dundee.)
[620] Ship No. J4179. General Arrangement. Scale $\frac{1}{16}''$ to 1 foot. Dated 17th April 1940. (Ocean Transport & Trading Ltd., Liverpool.)
[620a] *HMS Glengyle*. General Arrangement. Scale $\frac{1}{16}''$ to 1 foot. Dated 18th November 1940. (University of Glasgow Archives.)
[621] Drg. No. 10832, Sheets 1 and 2. General Arrangement. (As fitted.) Scale $\frac{1}{16}''$ to 1 foot. Dated 20th November 1943. (Ministry of Defence, Ship Dept. Section 191a, 'C' Block Annex, Foxhill, Bath.)

MONUMENTAL INSCRIPTION
[622] Gravestone Epsilon 52, the (Eastern) Necropolis, Glasgow.

LETTERED REFERENCES
R Information to be found in any standard reference work.
A The author's opinions, assumptions or conclusions.
X Origin unknown.

ACKNOWLEDGMENTS

Individual Assistance, Advice

BAKER, Sir Rowland, OBE, RCNC.
BIRRELL, J., Lloyd's Register of Shipping, Glasgow.
BEHARRELL,* L. V., MA, University of Glasgow.
CLARK, John, Central Press (Printers) Ltd.
DAGLISH, W. Alan, Hon. Sec. 51st (Highland) Division Dinner Club.
EASTAWAY, Derek E., Lloyd's Register of Shipping, Glasgow.
DONALD, Major A. J., RM, Royal Marines' Museum, Southsea.
DUNAN, James, Central Press (Printers) Ltd.
FERGUSSON, James, Lochearnhead, Perthshire.
GLAZIER,* M. B., Ocean Steam Ship Co. and Elder Dempster Lines.
GORDON, John P., Ocean Management Services Ltd.
GRAY, Nicol, late 45 Royal Marine Commando.
HANCOCK, Major J. T. (Retd.), RE Corps Library, Chatham.
HOWEL, John R., Ocean Fleets Ltd.
JONES, D. L., Bedwas, S. Wales.
KENNY, Major J., MBE, The Queen's Lancashire Regt.
LEGGETT, Mrs. E. A., Wolverstone Post Office, Ipswich, Suffolk.
LITTLEJOHN, David A., Lloyd's Register of Shipping, Glasgow.
McARTHUR, Mrs. Jean, Inveraray, Argyll.
MILLS-ROBERTS, Brig. D., CBE, DSO and bar, MC.
MULFORD, Mrs. E. A., Burnham-on-Crouch, Essex.
NESBITT, Adrian, Royal Australian Regiment.
NORTON, Gordon, Epping, Essex.
O'BRIEN, M. G., Easter Ross District Libraries, Dingwall.
PARNELL, John, Robb Caledon Shipbuilders Ltd.
ROLLO, T. Landale, OBE, MC, Cupar, Fife.
ROSS, Commander Donald, Lochgilphead, Argyll.
ROSS, Walter, Inver, Fearn, Ross-shire.
RYAN, Major P. J., The Queen's Lancashire Regt.
SHARPE, Mrs. K. E., Brixham, S. Devon.
SHEPHERD, George, Robb Caledon Shipbuilders Ltd.
SMYTH, H. N., Archivist, Ocean Transport & Trading Ltd.
STENNING, E. J., Crossways Post Office, Churt, Surrey.
WOOD, Lieut.-Col. G. P., MC, Argyll & Sutherland Highlanders.
WURTZBURG, Jenys, Edgeware, Middlesex.
WYLIE, Mrs. E. M. C., Castletown, Caithness.

Newspaper Editors

Canberra Times, Australia.
Evening News, London.
Evening Telegraph, Dundee.
Glasgow Herald.
Liverpool Daily Post.
Sunday Times, London.
Sydney Morning Herald, Australia.
Yorkshire Post, Leeds.

Librarians

British Library, London.
Devon County.
Dundee Public Libraries.
Eastwood District Libraries.
Liverpool Central Libraries.
Mitchell Library, Glasgow.
City of Sydney Public Library.
University of Glasgow.
University of Hong Kong.
University of Keele, Air Photo Library.
State Library of Victoria.

Institutions, Organisations

Army Records Centre, Hayes, Middlesex.
Australian Archives, Victoria.
The Boots Company Limited, Nottingham.
Department of the Chief of Naval Information.
Dept. of Health and Social Security, Newcastle-upon-Tyne.
2/4th Field Regiment Association, Melbourne.
H.M. Customs and Excise Library Services, London.
Imperial War Museum, London.
Dept. of Defence, Historical Studies Section, Canberra.
The Naval Club, London.
Navy Records Society, Surrey.
The Postmaster, Forres, Morayshire.

Copyrights

PHOTOGRAPHS
1. Norman Brown & Co. Ltd., Dundee.
3. D. C. Thomson & Co. Ltd., Dundee.
5. P. Rawlings, Leigh-on-Sea, Essex.
6. A. Aiken.
7. P. Rawlings.
10. Imperial War Museum E 2762.
11. Imperial War Museum E 2773.
13. Australian War Memorial.
18. A. Aiken.
19. Imperial War Museum H 38305.
21. Ministry of Defence. (University of Keele Air Photo Library No. 18972 Sortie No. 16/385 Print No. 4026.)
22. Imperial War Museum B 5111.
23. Imperial War Museum EA 26255.
24. Imperial War Museum B 5114.
28. Imperial War Museum H 38304.
30. The late W. McKenzie.
32. Dr. W. G. M. Bell, Newtownards, N. Ireland.
33. Dr. W. G. M. Bell.
35. J. K. de Vries, Jr., Cape Town, S. Africa.
36. Dr. W. G. M. Bell.

The poem below photograph No. 36 was originally published in the Blue Funnel & Glen Line Bulletins of January 1967, page 3, under the title, "Sold for Scrap *Glenroy* 1966"

The words quoted on page 75 are copyright 1939 by Max Eschig (France). Reproduced by permission of Keith Prowse Music Publishing Co. Ltd., 138–140 Charing Cross Road, London, WC2H 0LD.

Maps H, G and part of E are much simplified copies of originals in *The Times Atlas of the World* published in 1958 by Times Books, London.

Cartographers

John Bartholomew & Son Limited, Edinburgh.
Clarendon Press, Oxford.
Her Majesty's Stationery Office, Norwich.
George Philip & Son Limited, London.
Times Publishing Company Ltd., London.

Photographic Copies

ANNAN, T. & R. & Sons Ltd., Glasgow.
BOOTHER, John W., Thundersley, Essex.
STEVENSON'S STUDIO, Newtownards, N. Ireland.
TULLOCH, Newlands, Glasgow.

Translations

HØVIK, Mrs. Anne, Glasgow.
MacDONALD, K. D., Dept. of Celtic, University of Glasgow

Research

EVERSON, R. C., London.
MAHONEY, Patrick R. H., Romford, Essex.

Typescripts

ALEXANDER, Mrs. Alice, Fenwick, Ayrshire.
WYLLIE, Mrs. Dorothy, Newton Mearns, Glasgow

and

Encouragement and Support

AIKEN, Mrs. Janette P., the author's wife.